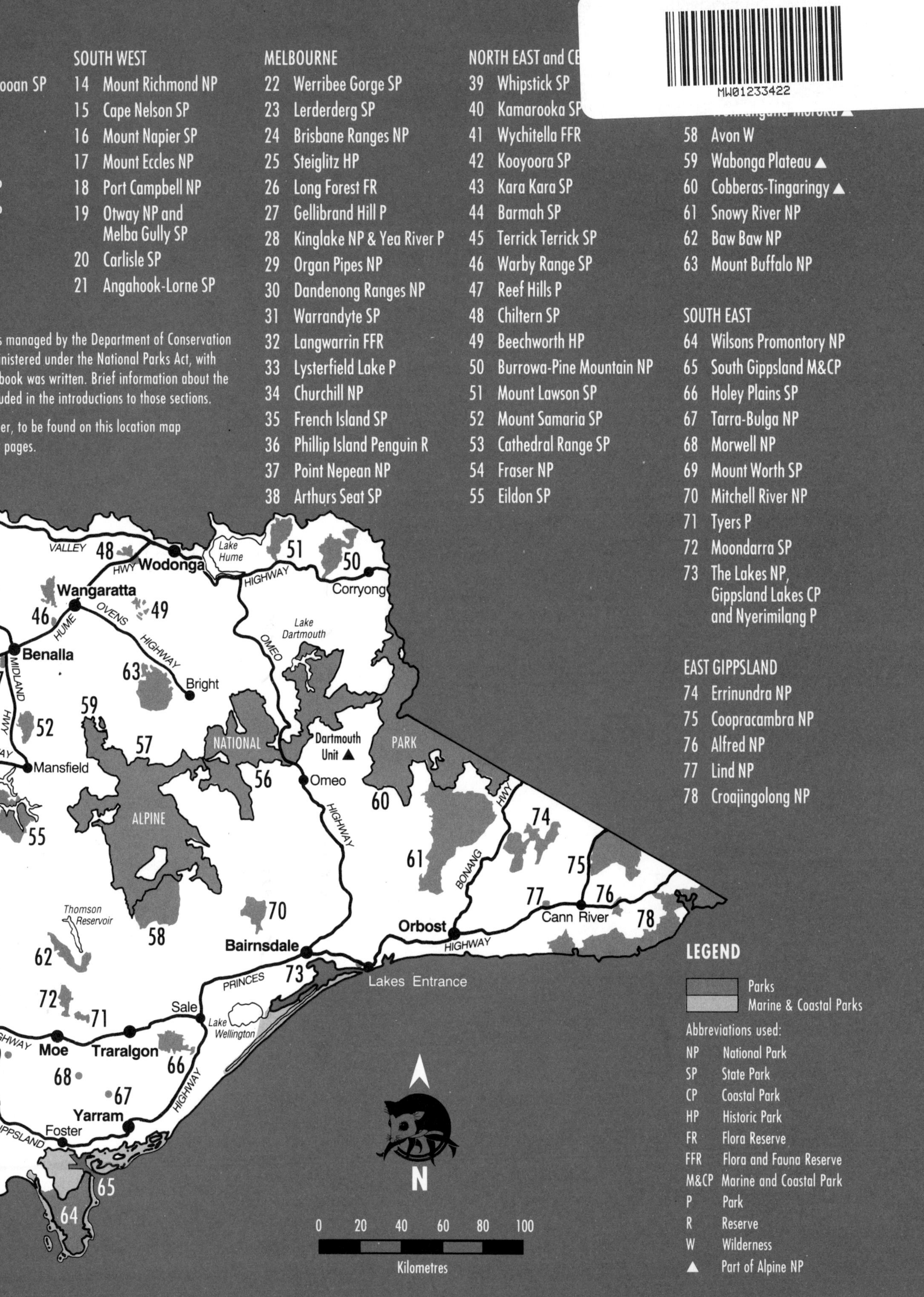

SOUTH WEST
ooan SP
14 Mount Richmond NP
15 Cape Nelson SP
16 Mount Napier SP
17 Mount Eccles NP
18 Port Campbell NP
19 Otway NP and Melba Gully SP
20 Carlisle SP
21 Angahook-Lorne SP
s managed by the Department of Conservation
inistered under the National Parks Act, with
book was written. Brief information about the
uded in the introductions to those sections.
ber, to be found on this location map
t pages.
MELBOURNE
22 Werribee Gorge SP
23 Lerderderg SP
24 Brisbane Ranges NP
25 Steiglitz HP
26 Long Forest FR
27 Gellibrand Hill P
28 Kinglake NP & Yea River P
29 Organ Pipes NP
30 Dandenong Ranges NP
31 Warrandyte SP
32 Langwarrin FFR
33 Lysterfield Lake P
34 Churchill NP
35 French Island SP
36 Phillip Island Penguin R
37 Point Nepean NP
38 Arthurs Seat SP
NORTH EAST and CE
39 Whipstick SP
40 Kamarooka SP
41 Wychitella FFR
42 Kooyoora SP
43 Kara Kara SP
44 Barmah SP
45 Terrick Terrick SP
46 Warby Range SP
47 Reef Hills P
48 Chiltern SP
49 Beechworth HP
50 Burrowa-Pine Mountain NP
51 Mount Lawson SP
52 Mount Samaria SP
53 Cathedral Range SP
54 Fraser NP
55 Eildon SP
MW01233422
58 Avon W
59 Wabonga Plateau ▲
60 Cobberas-Tingaringy ▲
61 Snowy River NP
62 Baw Baw NP
63 Mount Buffalo NP
SOUTH EAST
64 Wilsons Promontory NP
65 South Gippsland M&CP
66 Holey Plains SP
67 Tarra-Bulga NP
68 Morwell NP
69 Mount Worth SP
70 Mitchell River NP
71 Tyers P
72 Moondarra SP
73 The Lakes NP, Gippsland Lakes CP and Nyerimilang P
EAST GIPPSLAND
74 Errinundra NP
75 Coopracambra NP
76 Alfred NP
77 Lind NP
78 Croajingolong NP
Wodonga
Wangaratta
Benalla
Bright
Mansfield
Omeo
Corryong
Lake Hume
Lake Dartmouth
Dartmouth Unit ▲
Thomson Reservoir
Bairnsdale
Orbost
Cann River
Lakes Entrance
Sale
Lake Wellington
Moe
Traralgon
Yarram
Foster
NATIONAL
PARK
ALPINE
LEGEND
Parks
Marine & Coastal Parks
Abbreviations used:
NP National Park
SP State Park
CP Coastal Park
HP Historic Park
FR Flora Reserve
FFR Flora and Fauna Reserve
M&CP Marine and Coastal Park
P Park
R Reserve
W Wilderness
▲ Part of Alpine NP
N
0 20 40 60 80 100
Kilometres

DEAR DAD
+ PAPA,

WE KNOW YOU
REALLY ENJOYED
THIS BOOK WHEN
YOU WERE VISITING
US, SO NOW YOU
CAN ENJOY IT ALWAYS,

LOTS OF LOVE
WENDY, MIKE +

JANE CALDER

Port Campbell NP *JAC*

PARKS

VICTORIA'S NATIONAL AND STATE PARKS

Otway NP JP

VICTORIA'S NATIONAL AND STATE PARKS

Parks: Victoria's national and state parks.
First published in Australia in 1990 by the Victorian National Parks Association Inc., Box 785F GPO, Melbourne, Victoria 3001 and The Canterbury Press Pty Ltd, Unit 2, 71 Rushdale Street, Scoresby, Victoria 3179.

National Library of Australia Cataloguing in Publication Data
Calder, Jane, 1936–
Parks: Victoria's national and state parks

Includes bibliographies and index
ISBN 1 875100 02 4

1. National parks and reserves – Victoria.
2. National parks and reserves – Victoria – Guidebooks
3. Victoria – Description and travel – 1976 – –
Guide-books
I. Wojczuk, Ann, 1963–
II. Vaughan, Barbara, 1955–
III. Victorian National Parks Association
IV. Title

333.7809945

Designed by Ann Wojczuk
Typesetting by Printeam and Dezign
Colour separations by Scanagraphix
Printing by Impact Printing

Hattah-Kulkyne NP *JAC*

Cover: Waterloo Bay, Wilsons Promontory *JAC*

To all those people who have in the past and will in the future work towards the health of our natural environment, particularly our parks system. May these parks continue to delight and excite people at all levels, from pure enjoyment to scientific enquiry.

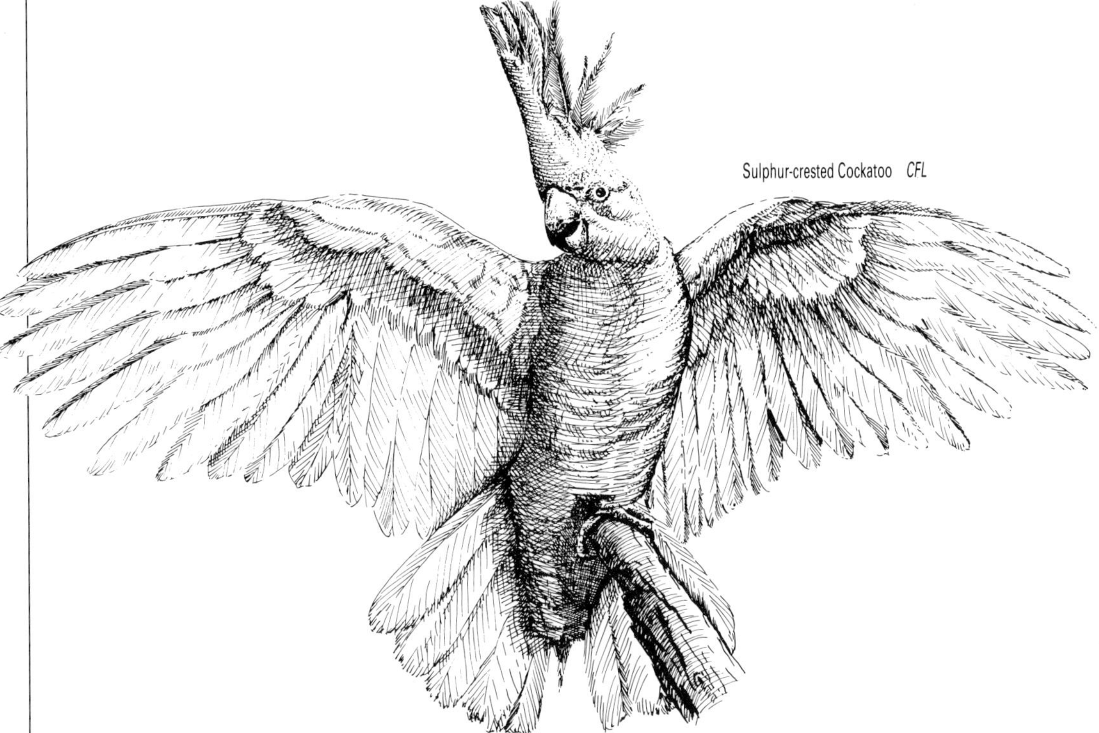

Sulphur-crested Cockatoo *CFL*

The affection that so many people show towards their parks, and their desire to help protect and promote them, was undoubtedly one of the most rewarding features of working on this project. I would like to express my sincere thanks to those who helped me throughout this undertaking, particularly:

- those people who allowed the Victorian National Parks Association to use their drawings and photographs, often free of charge;
- Conservation and Environment (abbreviated in the following pages as C&E) for help with the maps and a number of the illustrations;
- Conservation and Environment staff in Head Office, regional offices and parks who gave so willingly of their time and expertise, particularly Chris Ashe, Doug Hooley, Mike Howes, Phil Ingamells, Ken Mawdsley and Don Saunders;
- Peter Green from Community Technology for technical advice;
- Richard Archer and Rus Littleson from Dezign;
- VNPA staff and members, and friends who helped and encouraged, particularly Gwen McDowall for indexing, Colette Findlay and Juliette Le Feuvre for proof-reading, Denis Conway for proof-reading maps, Eileen McKee for help and support, Beverly Nuttall for researching information, Teresa Sfara for administrative help and Barbara Vaughan for editing and endless patience;
- Martin Powell for his magnificent efforts in preparing the maps, with assistance from Jill Poynton and John Nicholson;
- Ann Wojczuk for her guidance and skills in design and layout;
- family and friends who read drafts, discussed ideas and generally lightened my load, and especially my son James for the pleasure of shared photographic expeditions;
- Jean Wallis for permission to use the extract from Edna Walling's *On the Trail of Australian Wildflowers* in the Grampians section.

CREDITS

Photographers

Peter & Lex Abbey	P & LJA
Peter Adams	PBA
Arthur Rylah Institute	ARI
John Broomfield	JB
James Calder	JAC
Malcolm Calder	DMC
David Cheal	DC
Conservation, Forests & Lands (now C&E)	CFL
Robin Crocker	RC
Arthur Farnsworth	AF
Rudi Frankenberg	RKF
Friends of Organ Pipes	FOPNP
Friends of Whipstick	FWSP
Ken Hoppen	KH
Phil Ingamells	PI
Anne Kerr	AK
Russell Laidlaw	RL
Zillah Lee	ZL
Ian McCann	IMcC
David Munday	DM
John Piesse	JP
George Seddon	GS
Hal Skinner	HS
Graham Trigg	GT
Malcolm Turner	MT
Gretna Weste	GW
Erik Westrup	EW
Jim Willis	JW

Illustrators

Angela Brennan	AB
Barry Clugston	BC
Conservation, Forests & Lands (now C&E)	CFL
Leon Costermans	LC
A.J.Ewart	AJE
Robert Hollingworth	RH
A.W.Howitt	AH
Major Mitchell	MM
Mark Norman	MN
Royal Australasian Ornithological Union	RAOU
Margaret Sherwin	MS
Rosemary Swart	RS
John Turner	JST
Ferdinand von Mueller	FvM
Mark van Tatenhov	MvT
Rory Willis	RW
Ann Wojczuk	AW

CONTENTS

INTRODUCTION

'Victoria is the smallest of the mainland states, and yet it contains a great diversity of landforms, plants, and animals. It has everything from alps to rolling plains, from towering ash forests to desert mallee, from luxuriant fern gullies to open grasslands – and its national parks reflect this variety.'

Robert Raymond – *Discover Australia's National Parks* Ure Smith 1978

Victoria's national parks provide the foundation for the excellent system of conservation reserves in this State. National parks make up most of the land reserved under the National Parks Act, but there are also state parks, wilderness parks, coastal parks, marine parks and other special purpose parks reserved under the Act. In addition, Victoria has a variety of conservation reserves managed under other legislation, such as flora and fauna reserves, and wildlife reserves which are important elements of the State's total conservation program.

An outstanding feature of Victoria's national parks system is that the reserves have been selected on the basis of trying to ensure that all of the State's major habitat types are represented and protected in conservation reserves. This has largely been achieved through the procedures of the Land Conservation Council, which has, as part of its charter, the task of systematically studying the public land of Victoria and recommending its future use. The process, which includes extensive public participation, has been very successful and has led to a situation where we can justifiably claim that, based on representation, Victoria's national park system is one of the best in the world.

Another feature of Victoria's park system is its diversity. Although only a small state by Australian standards, Victoria's natural habitats range from alpine to semi-arid. We also have a magnificent variety of coastal features, cool temperate and warm temperate rainforests, the flood plains of the Murray River and extensive wetlands throughout the State.

Fortunately, the park system is backed up by good legislation and dedicated staff at all levels in the Department of Conservation and Environment. This has been achieved through the support given to Victoria's parks by successive Governments, reflecting the strong community interest and the work of groups such as the Victorian National Parks Association.

In browsing through this book, one is immediately impressed by Victoria's natural landscapes and its flora and fauna. However, for those looking for the spectacular, a word of advice. In 1957, the First Annual Report of the Victorian National Parks Authority of Victoria made the following comment, which is still relevant today:

> The National Parks of this State are reserved as samples of the Victorian countryside as Nature made it. They are the living and only true portrayal of the National character. It has been said, and justly, that Victoria has no Grand Canyon, no Yellowstone, no Jasper, no Kreuger to show the visitor to these shores. The inference intended is that Victoria's National Park System is of relatively small importance either to Victorians or to tourists from abroad.
>
> Those who argue in this way lose sight of the equally important complementary fact that no expenditure of money, energy, or intellect could give the United States, Canada, or South Africa a Wilsons Promontory, a Mount Buffalo, a Tarra Valley, or a Wyperfeld. Our parks and the unique living things they contain are the show-windows of the Australian bush, and as the years pass, with their advances in soil science and technology, the unspoilt bush will become confined more and more to the places which, in the words of the Act, we 'protect, preserve, and maintain'.

I hope that this book will inspire people of all ages and backgrounds to visit our parks and learn something of the beauty and fragility of our natural countryside and, in doing so, to help to protect it for others to explore in the future.

With that in mind, go and make the most of Victoria's magnificent parks – they are yours to enjoy.

Don Saunders
Director of National Parks and Wildlife

JAC

VICTORIA'S PARKS

Contrary to what is sometimes claimed, land that is set aside as a national or state park is not land that is 'locked away' but rather land that is carefully managed and protected for all people for all time. Certainly the level of funding required to manage a particular park may not always be as generous as the public, and especially as the National Parks and Wildlife Division, would wish, but too often the alternative is thinly disguised exploitation which leaves the land and environment generally in far poorer condition. National Parks have proved their worth time and time again, both as drawcards for people, often from all over the world, and as refuges for both plants and animals.

This approach of planned and co-ordinated caring for the land rather than exploiting its resources is of course comparatively new, especially in a 'frontier' country such as ours where bush was seen as a threat to be tamed and utilised and all too often removed in order to realise the land's wealth. It was not until the 1960's that the official attitude moved away from that in which national park status was appropriate only where land was not of economic importance.

The earliest Victorian national parks generally resulted from the efforts of dedicated individuals and clubs such as the Field Naturalists' Club of Victoria (FNCV) and in some cases local shire councils, who recognised the worth of a particular area. These early parks, such as Wilsons Promontory, Kinglake and Wyperfeld, were not seen by the government of the day as their responsibility. Instead, they were run by Committees of Management, made up of willing part-timers who were not necessarily skilled in park management. These parks were almost always so short of funds that the Committees had no option but to allow grazing and firewood licences as a means of raising revenue to run the park.

A watershed in the approach to national parks (as they then all were) came in the 1950's with the creation of the Victorian National Parks Association (VNPA) in 1952 and the passing of the first National Parks Act in 1956. The VNPA brought together public organisations concerned about national parks and their well-being into a single, representative body; the Act established the National Parks Authority and was the first such comprehensive legislation in Australia. Further important developments were the creation in 1970 of the Land Conservation Council (LCC) to develop a systematic approach, with public input, to the management of Crown Land in Victoria; and the passing of the National Parks Act in 1975 which established the National Parks Service.

Whereas in earlier years most parks came about through the representations of naturalists, now it is generally through the LCC and its recommendations to the government of the day which contributes most to the expansion of the parks system. Now too, we have a more diverse parks system – not only are large national parks with very high conservation values created, but also state parks where recreation is also of great importance, and flora and fauna reserves which may be quite small but which have a high level of protection for nature conservation. The apparent contradiction of 'national' parks being the responsibility of the state, in this case Victoria, rather than of the Commonwealth, is a direct result of Federation when control of Crown Land remained with the appropriate state. Some years ago an attempt was made to rationalise the status of some of the very small, early national parks by altering them to reserves, but many people saw the revoking of national park status as an extremely dangerous precedent and the issue was dropped.

The management of our present parks is a demanding and complex task and one which often causes considerable controversy. One of the most contentious issues is that of fire. The National Parks Act specifically states that there is a responsibility to protect life and property adjoining any park, and this may entail fuel reduction burning especially around the perimeter of the park. For the majority of our parks fire is an absolute necessity if ecological diversity is to be maintained, but these fires must not come too frequently or they destroy the very environment they are supposed to maintain. And of course the all-important question is 'How often is too often?', and the answer is that in almost all cases we simply don't know. For many years all fires were considered undesirable and therefore suppressed whenever possible, so the data on which to base an informed decision is simply not available.

Other contentious issues include vermin control, (and to farmers whose land adjoins a park vermin could well include native animals such as kangaroos) and feral or wandering domestic animals. Should people who live next to a park be allowed to keep cats and dogs? Should beekeepers be allowed to bring bees into or near a park and profit at the expense of native birds and insects? And what about tour operators, grazing, mining, harvesting of water and timber, firewood collection? The list goes on.

Then there are the immediate day to day concerns of people management, people who flock to our parks in ever-increasing numbers. For a 'one-entrance' park such as Wilsons Promontory, it's comparatively easy – develop facilities to the level the park can withstand and then restrict further entry. But another very popular park, the Grampians, has so many entry points that that approach is quite unworkable. So, should facilities be developed outside rather than inside the park? Should dispersed bush-camping and its attendant risk of stream pollution and other impacts be allowed? How many tracks should be maintained and to what standard – 4WD, 2WD? What recreational uses are compatible with park values – boating and of what type, skiing, swimming, horseriding with its risk of introduced weeds in the dung? And over-riding all of these concerns is the paramount one of the conservation of natural values, closely followed by that of allowing people a sense of renewal and release from everyday worries rather than a feeling of restriction and red tape.

The present approach to this maze of issues is to develop a draft management plan for each park and then submit this plan for public comment before a final management plan is prepared. For small, non-contentious parks the process is usually quite simple, but for the larger and more popular parks it is often long and difficult. Certainly we, the public have cause to be grateful for the care and effort that is put into the management of our magnificent parks, both large and small.

The need to escape to natural areas, whether for a Sunday barbecue with family and friends or for a wilderness bushwalk, is an obvious expression of a deep inner need for contact with a wider, non-urbanised environment. As our society becomes steadily more urbanised the necessity for meeting this need becomes greater, as does the pressure on these same natural areas. If our children and their children, as well as we ourselves, are to continue to enjoy the healing and peace of the natural world, our parks must have our support, the best management, and protection from exploitation.

Jane Calder
Victorian National Parks Association

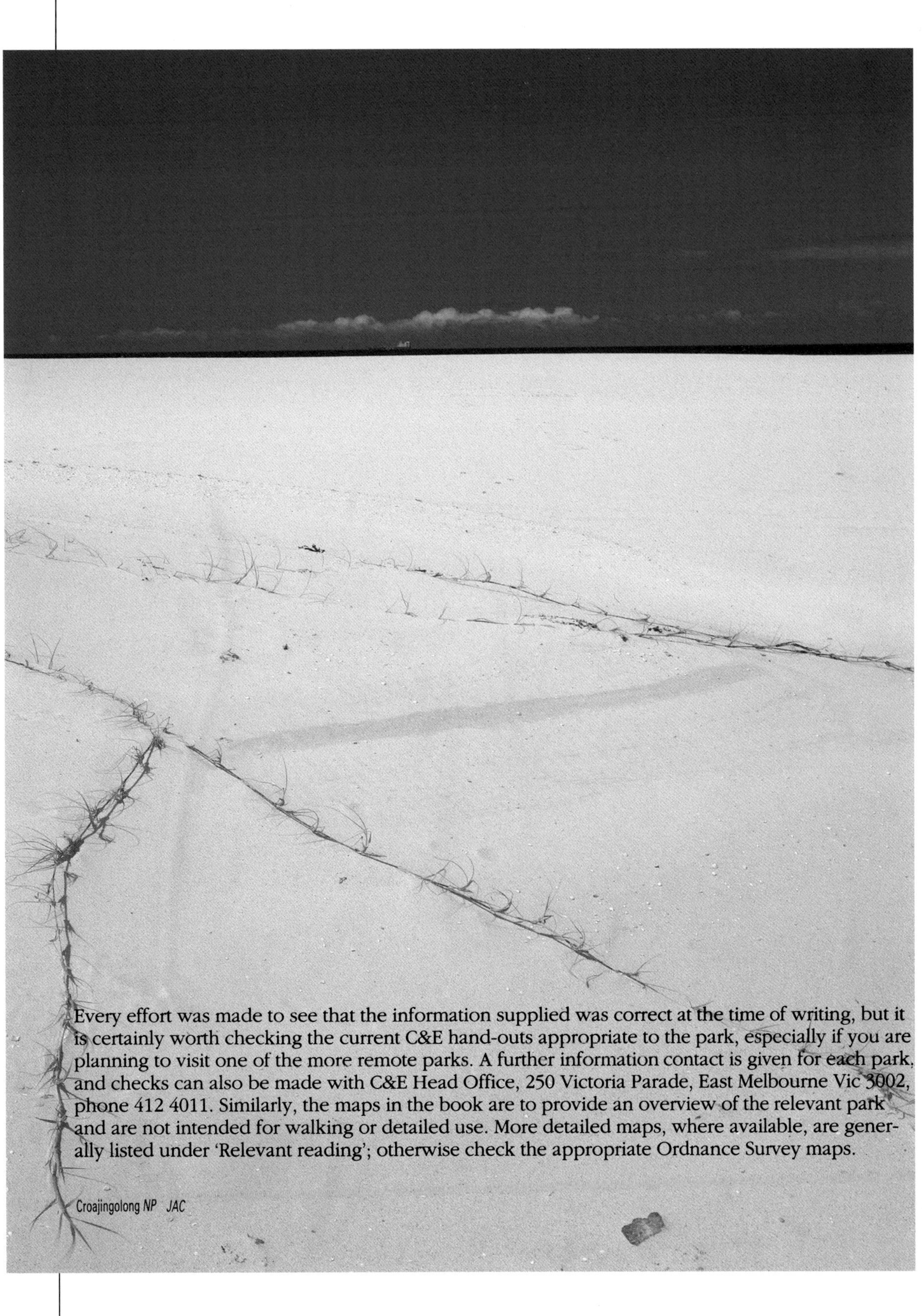

Every effort was made to see that the information supplied was correct at the time of writing, but it is certainly worth checking the current C&E hand-outs appropriate to the park, especially if you are planning to visit one of the more remote parks. A further information contact is given for each park, and checks can also be made with C&E Head Office, 250 Victoria Parade, East Melbourne Vic 3002, phone 412 4011. Similarly, the maps in the book are to provide an overview of the relevant park and are not intended for walking or detailed use. More detailed maps, where available, are generally listed under 'Relevant reading'; otherwise check the appropriate Ordnance Survey maps.

Croajingolong *NP JAC*

▲ Hoary Sunray *EW*
◀ Pink Lakes SP *JAC*

▲ Echidna *DC*
▼ Effects of erosion in the Mallee *ZL*

▲ Mallee Eucalypts, Wyperfeld NP *P&LJA*
◀ Murray Cod, 1950 *ARI*

NORTH WEST PARKS

The parks included here are loosely grouped as Mallee parks. They lie in the semi-arid part of Victoria known as the Mallee, which lies between the rich coastal lands and the truly arid interior of Australia. The name Mallee derives from the characteristic multi-stemmed mallee eucalypts which grow there. The Little Desert, further south than the defining 36° S, is not strictly within the Mallee, but because it is similar in so many ways it is included here. In this north-west parks section, different aspects of the mallee environment have been dealt with under different parks, so that much of what is described for one park applies equally well to others in the area.

Presently, (Autumn 1990), Land Conservation Council proposals to protect a magnificent total of 1 131 610 ha of mallee country have all but been realised. Included in this are the proposed Murray-Sunset NP (incorporating the Pink Lakes SP) and Leaghur SP on the Loddon River in the South-east Mallee, as well as additions to Wyperfeld NP, Murray-Kulkyne Park and Lake Albacutya Park.

The Mallee has been exploited in a number of ways, including harvesting of broom-bush (Broom Honey-myrtle), and bee-keeping, both of which create tracks through this fragile environment, but the most notable, and controversial, activity is undoubtedly grazing. It is only recently that the damage caused by grazing has been duly recognised. Grazing prevents the regeneration of native species, spreads weeds and, by destroying the crust of lichens on the soil surface, increases the likelihood of wind erosion. For many years the question of whether the present grazing licensees should give up their cheap access to public land and so preserve it for all Victorians has been debated. If the Mallee vegetation were more robust there might not be a problem, but it's not. It is highly specialised to cope with an extremely demanding environment, and it is at the very time of greatest vulnerability – seedling establishment – that grazing takes its toll, leaving a landscape of old trees, dead and dying, with none to replace them.

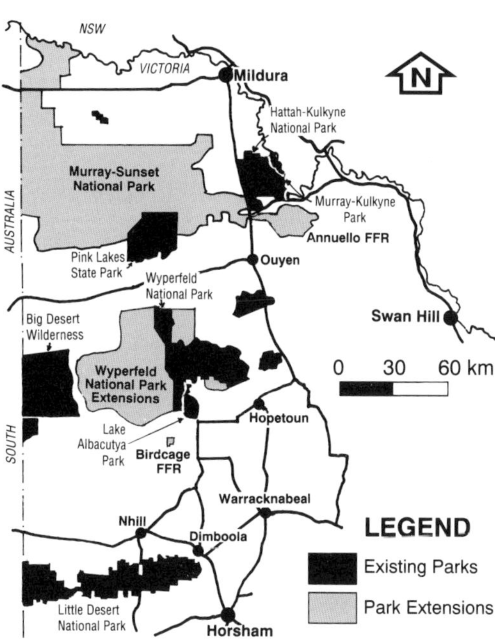

	Page No.	Entrance Fee	Information Centre	Multilingual Information	Picnic Areas	Fireplaces	Toilets	Disabled Access	Walking Tracks	Nature Walk or Drive	Swimming	Climbing	Horseriding	Fishing	Boating	Camping	Caravans	Km from Melbourne	Date Declared
Big Desert **x**	11																	400	1979
Hattah-Kulkyne	2		■		■	■	■		■	■	■		■	■	■	■	■	495	1980
Lake Albacutya★	12		■			■	■				■		■	■	■	■	■	400	1980
Little Desert	19		■			■	■		■	■						■	■	375	1968
Murray-Kulkyne	7										■			■	■	■	■	490	1980
Pink Lakes	8					■	■		■	■						■	■	530	1979
Wyperfeld	15		■		■	■	■		■	■						■	■	450	1921

x = No facilities or water ★ = Aquatic activities when Lake is filled with water.

1 Hattah-Kulkyne National Park

Physical features: 48 000 ha. This Park has two quite different faces: the dry, sandy country with multi-stemmed mallee eucalypts and open, pine woodlands; and the meandering waterways of lakes, creeks, billabongs and floodplains. Not that these waterways are always filled, that depends very much on the season, but when the water level in the Murray River, which borders the Park for 32 km, rises high enough, a natural rockbar diverts water westwards into Chalka Creek, an anabranch of the Murray. From there it flows into Lake Lockie, then on into the other lakes, and finally northwards back to the Murray. A River Red Gum at Lake Hattah, with a mark at 6.6 m, shows the height of the record 1956 floods. If the floodwaters are sufficiently high, the lakes overflow and new swamps and marshes form, attracting a great variety of waterbirds. Because water is drawn from Lake Hattah to supply the tiny township of Hattah and some nearby farming areas, a channel has been cut between Lakes Lockie and Hattah and a small weir has also been built to retain the water.

The land is low-lying and is crossed by ridges of both Parilla sand and aeolian (windblown) deposits. The north-west to south-east Parilla sands were formed as sand dunes along successive coasts, as the sea receded from and then re-invaded the Murray Basin many times in the Pliocene Epoch, beginning about 4 million years ago. This dune surface has weathered into a hard, resistant layer, suggesting that this weathering occurred under monsoonal conditions. Today, there are two main soil types in the Mallee: the yellowish sand of the 'deserts' and the more fertile reddish clayey loams which have now largely been cleared for agriculture. Saltpans, often with powdery white gypsum known as copi, also occur.

Some two million years ago, the climate became much colder and drier as available water was locked into ice sheets over much of the world. During these arid periods, aeolian deposits accumulated and now form a large sandy mass in South Australia with three tongues – the Sunset Country, the Big Desert and the Little Desert – extending eastwards into Victoria. Hattah-Kulkyne NP is at the easternmost tip of the Sunset tongue. These aeolian dunes are oriented more or less east to west, following the initial depressions between the underlying Parilla dunes and the prevailing westerly winds. Sixteen thousand years ago the climate was again wet enough for plants to colonise and stabilise the dunes. The Mallee had begun to form.

Typically, summers are long, hot and dry, though sudden downpours do occur. Nights, especially in winter, are often very cold. Rainfall is generally less than 300 mm per year, soils very porous, and evaporation high. The only permanent 'stream' is the mighty Murray River.

Plants and animals: Again what there is to see varies considerably with the season. After a wet winter the sandhills are carpeted with ephemeral plants which germinate, grow, flower, set seed and die, all within the space of a few weeks; after a dry winter there are few if any of these flowers and the landscape appears almost barren. But there is still plenty of life; mallee vegetation is superbly adapted to cope with drought as well as fire. Fire, drought, floods and frosts will all radically alter what is growing and in flower. Plant growth often reflects past weather patterns, as in the fringes of young River Red Gums and Black Box around the lake edges – in the more arid parts of Victoria these trees germinate only after a flood.

A combination of various soil types and climatic conditions has led to 25 different, identifiable plant communities in the Mallee, with nearly 1 000 plant species listed. Of these, six are extinct and almost 200 are regarded as rare or threatened, and are not found within a protected area such as a park or reserve.

Most of Hattah-Kulkyne NP is covered with mallee eucalypts which vary according to soil type. On the deep, yellowish sands Yellow Mallee is dominant, with Scrub Cypress-pine, Mallee Tea-tree and wattles such as Nealie and Small Cooba also found here. Beneath these are showy shrubs, many of them pea-flowered, and small ephemerals also. On the more fertile and stable reddish loamy sands, White Mallee is dominant, with scattered smaller trees such as Hop-bush, Desert Cassia and the highly palatable Cattle-bush, which often has an obvious browse line. Towards the lakes, the sandhills are more fertile and support deeper-rooting trees such as Buloke and Slender Cypress-pine. Many of these trees were cut for buildings, fence posts, and stock feed in pre-Park days. Others were burnt and the seedlings that regenerated were soon grazed out, leaving a badly degraded environment.

Around the lakes are riverine woodlands with River Red Gum near the water, Black Box further away on the ridges, and some shrubs such as Prickly Bottlebrush and the long-leaved wattle, Eumong. In the more permanent lakes aquatic vegetation flourishes and forms an important habitat for waterbirds, while in the saltpan areas the salt-tolerant glassworts are found. Overall, though, the saltpan environment is very species-poor and it is not until further up the slopes, away from the extreme salt, that other plants such as Rounded Noonflower, Saltbush and a variety of ephemeral daisies start to appear. Where there is gypsum as well as salt, there are further limitations on what plants will grow. Gypsum-tolerant plants include the Sea-heaths and Nitre-bush.

Mallee animals are also of great interest. Among the more important species in Hattah-Kulkyne NP are the Long-thumbed Frog, Carpet Python, Regent Parrot, White-bellied Sea-eagle, Yellow Rosella, Red Kangaroo and two rare species of bat. More than 200 birds have been recorded for Hattah-Kulkyne, including the Ground Cuckoo-shrike and Black Honeyeater, both of which are more characteristic of areas further north. Because of the more or less permanent water available, Hattah-Kulkyne NP is regarded as one of the most important waterfowl habitats in Victoria. The many hollow trees for nesting are also significant. An interesting historical account of the Park, particularly its birds, including the Spotted Bowerbird which is no longer found here, is given in the Victorian Naturalist article mentioned below.

Both the plants and animals of this area have evolved strategies for avoiding heat and dryness or else for tolerating these stresses. Many of course do both. All living things lose water more or less continuously – plants through their leaves, animals through evaporation and through droppings and urine. One of the simplest avoiding strategies is to stay deep within a burrow, or perhaps under a clump of Porcupine Grass where the temperature is very much lower than it is in the open. One such animal, the Blind Snake, often shares a subterranean ant nest with its rightful inhabitants, but unfortunately for the snake, the ants don't like its droppings and carry them to the suface. This was a sure sign of a tasty meal to the Aborigines.

A number of burrowing animals, such as Mitchell's Hopping-mouse, are active on the surface at night when it is cooler. Others, including the Burrowing Frog, Grunter Fish and freshwater mussels, remain within their burrows and emerge only when there is enough water to breed. Brine-shrimps, on the other hand, survive the drought as highly resistant eggs, which hatch when there is sufficient water to go through a breeding cycle again as far as the egg stage.

Many desert animals avoid much of the heat by feeding and drinking early and late in the day, and then resting in the shade, so conserving water. Kangaroos have also been shown to have a remarkable cooling mechanism in the form of a network of tiny bloodvessels just under the skin of the forepaws. When this skin is wetted by licking, evaporation helps to keep the animal cool. Feathers and fur are good insulators against the heat, feathers particularly so, and many larger birds are able to avoid the heat still further by soaring on thermals up to cooler altitudes. Both birds and reptiles also conserve water by not urinating, but instead producing a concentrated white paste of uric acid.

As to drinking water, strategies again vary – the Mitchell's Hopping-mouse virtually doesn't drink, but instead relies on retaining the water that is released within the body as food is broken down, the same water that we less efficient water-conservers lose as steamy breath. Also, its urine is concentrated and its droppings almost dry. Birds, on the other hand, need to drink which makes a waterhole a good place to see them, especially in the early morning. Reptiles also need water, and one, the Mountain Devil, gets this in a novel way which has given rise to the expression 'flat out like a lizard drinking'. The animal flattens itself into the dew, allowing water to flow along fine skin channels to its mouth. Many carnivorous birds and mammals, especially the insect feeders such as bats and Antechinus, obtain most of their water from their food.

The availability of water has a marked effect on the breeding behaviour of birds in particular – dry conditions mean less food, and this delays or even prevents breeding until conditions improve. Both Malleefowl and Emu lay fewer eggs in harsh seasons than in good ones, while a wet year brings waterbirds in their thousands.

When Hattah-Kulkyne NP was recommended by the Land Conservation Council in 1976, it was described as the worst rabbit-infested area in Victoria, and soon after the Park's declaration, vigorous efforts were made to reduce rabbit numbers. The Mournpall Block of 6 000 ha was fenced off and eradication began. But as rabbit numbers dropped, Western Grey Kangaroo numbers rose until it was clear that it was now the kangaroos that were responsible for the continuing land degradation. In 1984 plans were made to cull all but 200 kangaroos – a viable number for that area – leaving about 10 000 elsewhere in the Park. Public reaction was such, however, that instead of culling an attempt was made to drive the kangaroos out of the fenced block into the rest of the Park. The results were horrific – kangaroos are wild animals and cannot be led or driven. Many animals were stressed or injured and had to be destroyed, while those that did manage to get out suffered further as they tried to re-enter their home range. In August 1984, 787 kangaroos were shot by professional marksmen under CFL orders, but public protest stopped any further culls. And so the management dilemma continues – culling and a chance for the Park to regenerate or, because the issue is so politically sensitive, uncontrolled kangaroo numbers? Many of the animals in Mournpall Block will almost certainly die of starvation anyway, as soon as there is a lack of food in a dry summer.

Human history: When the Europeans first saw this country they found it wild and inhospitable and therefore assumed that it must have also been like that for the Aborigines. However, recent evidence does not support this view, but suggests rather that the Mallee was well used by the Aborigines and that for much of the time populations were settled and not nomadic. Over the last decade, the Victoria Archaeological Survey's research in the Mallee shows that Aborigines have used areas near the Murray for the last 5 000 years, and sites further away from the river for about 16 000 years. During this time there have been considerable climatic and other physical changes; for instance, lakes that were once fresh are now saline. The sites recorded for the general area include many surface campsites, scarred trees, burial sites and shell middens.

The first known Europeans to see the Mallee were Captain Charles Sturt in 1830 and Major Thomas Mitchell in 1836, who explored the northern and southern borders respectively. By the 1840's settlers were beginning to move into the Mallee, and from then on the numbers and living standards of the Aborigines declined. At one time an Aboriginal station was set up to try to improve the lot of the survivors near the southern junction of Chalka Creek and the Murray, a site that is now within Hattah-Kulkyne NP. The Kulkyne run, originally *Gayfield*, was taken up in 1847, and the homestead, which was unfortunately burnt down in 1982, was built about 20 years later. Many relics of Hattah's individual history remain, including the camel tracks used for taking salt from Pink Lakes to barges on the Murray, and the pump house used to refill railway locomotive boilers.

Before World War II, moves were made by field naturalist and bird groups, and then after the war by the newly formed Victorian National Parks Association, to have some mallee-lakes area set aside and protected. This ultimately led to Hattah Lakes NP in 1960. The Land Conservation Council then recommended that the Kulkyne Forest be added, resulting in the present day Hattah-Kulkyne NP. In 1982, Hattah-Kulkyne was listed, along with Murray-Kulkyne, by UNESCO as a World Biosphere Reserve. As such, it is one of 12 Biosphere Reserves in Australia and one of more than 260 worldwide. It represents one of the world's principal ecological systems – the semi-arid environment – which in many parts of the world has been drastically altered by settlement and agriculture.

Things to do: Kangaroo watching; camping; walking; cycling; enjoying the nature drive and the Visitor Centre; canoeing; swimming; fishing, but please, don't leave pieces of line, especially when it has hooks on it – many unfortunate birds, particularly the delightful, inquisitive choughs, become entangled and die slowly and painfully. Hattah-Kulkyne is a wonderful place to cycle – there's a good network of tracks (some along old camel tracks) and you'll probably have them to yourself. You do need wide, deep-treaded or puncture-proof tyres though – the Three-cornered Jacks pierce ordinary tyres easily. Remember too, take a hat, compass and water bottle for most activities here.

Best season to visit: Winter, or spring, especially after good rains.

Special features: Flowers and birds; summer thunderstorms; expansive skies; stars; tranquillity.

Relevant reading:

Blakers M. and Macmillan L. (1980) *Mallee Conservation in Victoria.*
Chandler M.J. (1988) *Tribal Lands to National Park.*
Conservation, Forests and Lands (1984) *Hattah-Kulkyne NP Management Plan.*
Conservation, Forests and Lands (1988) *Victoria's Desert Country.*
Land Conservation Council (1987) *Mallee Area Review.*
McCann I.R. (1989) *The Mallee in Flower.*
O'Donohue J.G. 'Wanderings on the Murray Floodplain', *Victorian Naturalist* (1915) Vol XXXII, No. 1, pp. 7–20 and No. 2, pp. 26–35.

Further information:

Senior Ranger, Hattah-Kulkyne NP, RSD, Hattah, Vic 3501. Phone (050) 29 3253.
Friends' Group: Phone (050) 25 2771.

Red Kangaroo *AW*

Hattah-Kulkyne and Murray-Kulkyne

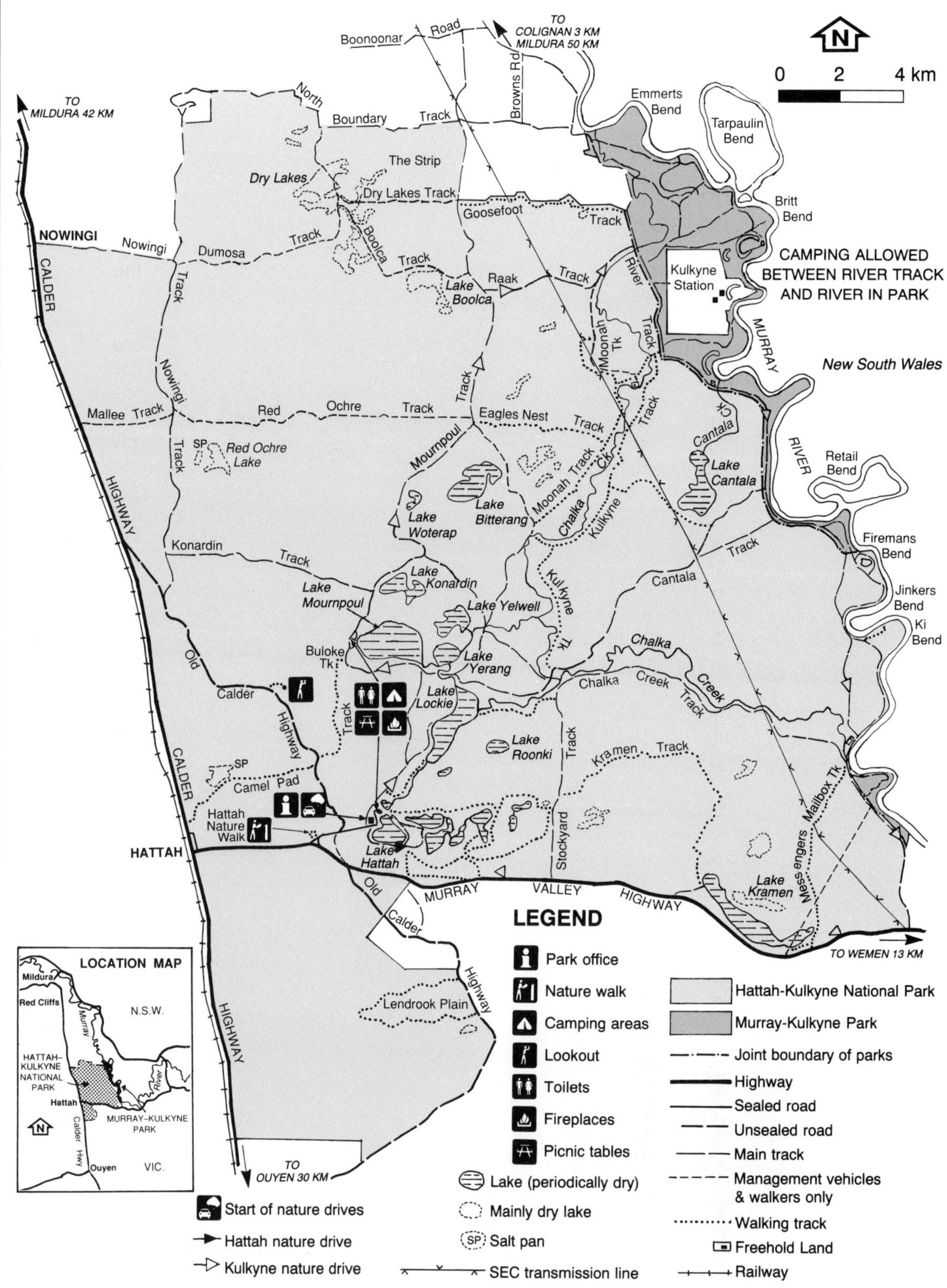

2 Murray-Kulkyne Park

Physical features: 1 550 ha. This long, narrow Park has an eastern frontage of 32 km on to the Murray River, some of it as cliffs up to 5 m high. On its western edge the Park borders Hattah-Kulkyne NP. Essentially the two are part of the same riverine woodlands system and are managed as a single unit, although the emphasis in Murray-Kulkyne is that of recreation and conservation. For this reason some of the regulations differ between Hattah-Kulkyne NP and Murray-Kulkyne Park.

Plants and animals: The birds and other animals in Murray-Kulkyne are similar to those riverine species of Hattah-Kulkyne and include Platypus and Yellow-footed Antechinus (although both of these are rare here). The River Red Gums and Black Box eucalypts often have hollows where branches have fallen and are important for many small mammals and nesting birds, especially the lovely Smoker or Regent Parrot. Murray-Kulkyne is also a significant habitat area for the Carpet Python, a beautiful, non-venomous snake.

Human history: Murray-Kulkyne has important Aboriginal relics, particularly middens and canoe trees. Since European settlement it has been a popular recreational area with both local people and others. Unfortunately, some parts have suffered from many years of uncontrolled access, and the creation of the Murray-Kulkyne Park was recommended in order to halt this degradation, by providing reasonable controls and supervision. Certainly the mighty but sadly misused Murray could do with some care and attention along much of its fascinatingly tortuous course.

Things to do: Fishing (perhaps a Murray Cod!); boating; birdwatching; camping (but Red Gums may drop branches without warning); exploring shipping relics – sunken barges, old jetties.

Best season to visit: Summer for water-based activities, although access roads may be difficult after rain and could be impassable when the Murray is in flood. Because of its normally low rainfall, this is often an excellent place for winter camping. Waterbirds are likely to be particularly plentiful when Hattah Lakes are full and conditions are very dry elsewhere.

Special features: The Murray easing its way past the pleasant sandy beaches; the river vistas, many of which can be easily seen from the road. Try sometime to fly over this country just to realise how the Murray twists and turns and how many of its old beds are still visible.

Relevant reading: See Hattah-Kulkyne NP.

Further information:
Ranger-in-Charge, Murray-Kulkyne Park, PO Colignan, Vic 3494. Phone (050) 29 1404.

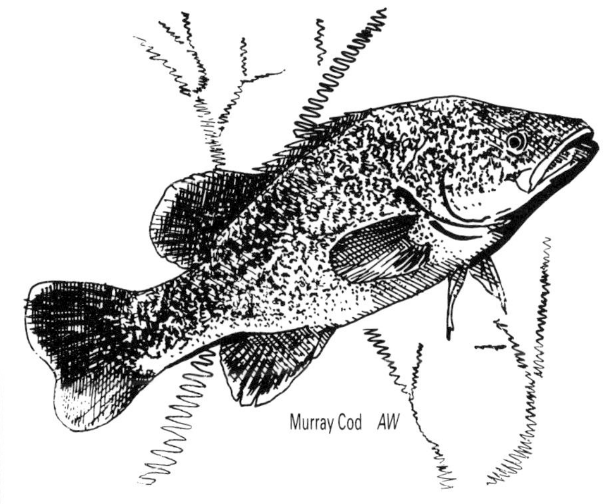
Murray Cod *AW*

3 Pink Lakes State Park

Physical features: 50 700 ha. Dominating the Pink Lakes SP, soon to be incorporated into the new Murray-Sunset NP, is the feature from which the Park takes its name – the pink lakes. The pink colour, at its most intense early or late in the day and especially when it is cloudy, is due to millions of microscopic, single-celled plants which concentrate the orange pigment, carotene, in their bodies. The Pink Lakes area is described as a boinka, a picturesque name for an area which forms where the soil surface dips below the level of the groundwater. So saline is the groundwater here that, when the lakes dry out, a salt crust is left to glitter brilliantly in the sun. Beyond these salinas, or salt lakes, the ground slopes abrubtly upwards and many of these rises are rich in gypsum, known as copi rises. The northern part of the Park, beyond the lakes, presents a satisfying contrast with its jumble of irregular, white sand dunes.

Plants and animals: On the edge of the Lakes are salt-tolerant plants such as Samphire, with Bladder Saltbush, paperbarks, grasses and eucalypts occuring in rapid succession as the saltiness diminishes. On the northern sand dunes is typical mallee scrub, with cypress pines and Porcupine Grass.

This is an excellent area for Red Kangaroos and for dry country birds, including the Crested Bell-bird, and occasionally the Scarlet-chested Parrot. This Park has a great deal of dead wood, both standing and on the ground, forming an important habitat for birds and reptiles such as the rare Yellow-faced Whip Snake and the Earless Dragon.

Human history: The most noteworthy activity was salt harvesting which began in 1916 with shovel and wheelbarrow, later replaced by horse and dray. A tramline, built in the early 1920's, was of little use because of problems with sand on the tracks and rusting equipment. Camels were used to carry the salt to barges on the Murray and stockpiles of salt remain on the shores of Lake Crosbie.

Pink Lakes has been grazed for many years and where stock grazing has ceased the effect on the re-generation of vegetation is already noticeable. Over the years watering points have been put in for stock, and these are now creating problems by maintaining artificially high kangaroo and rabbit populations. It is, however, encouraging to see the success of carefully protected, small-scale replantings.

Things to do: Walking, especially around the Lakes; birdwatching; studying the wildflowers; photography – the Lakes, the vegetation, and often the skies too, are all photogenic.

Best season to visit: Winter and spring for wildflowers and the chance to see nesting birds. Pink Lakes can be very hot in summer, and special care is needed.

Special features: Changes of light and weather altering the colour of the Lakes; remains of salt-harvesting; a lone Sugar Gum where the Pink Lakes School, closed in 1941, stood.

Relevant reading: See Hattah-Kulkyne NP.

Further information:
Work Centre, c/o Underbool Post Office, Vic 3509. Phone (050) 94 6267.

Crested Bellbird *RAOU*

Pink Lakes

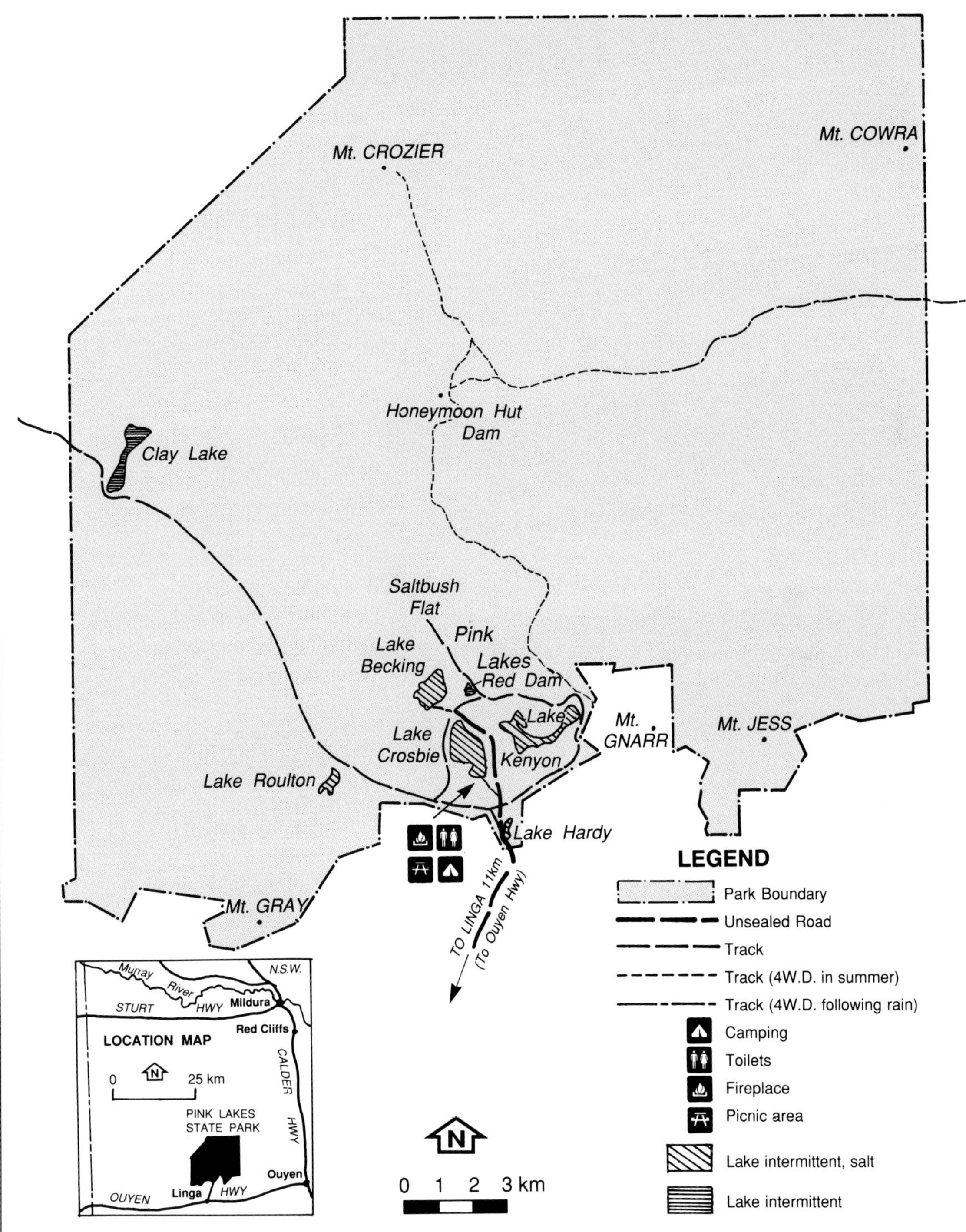
Mt. CROZIER
Mt. COWRA
Honeymoon Hut
Dam
Clay Lake
Saltbush
Flat
Lake
Becking
Pink
Lakes
Red Dam
Lake
Crosbie
Lake
Kenyon
Mt.
GNARR
Mt. JESS
Lake Roulton
Lake Hardy
Mt. GRAY
TO LINGA 11km
(To Ouyen Hwy)
LEGEND
Park Boundary
Unsealed Road
Track
Track (4W.D. in summer)
Track (4W.D. following rain)
Camping
Toilets
Fireplace
Picnic area
Lake intermittent, salt
Lake intermittent
N
0 1 2 3 km
Murray
River
N.S.W.
STURT
HWY
Mildura
Red Cliffs
LOCATION MAP
N
0
25 km
CALDER
HWY
PINK LAKES
STATE PARK
Ouyen
OUYEN
Linga
HWY

Big Desert

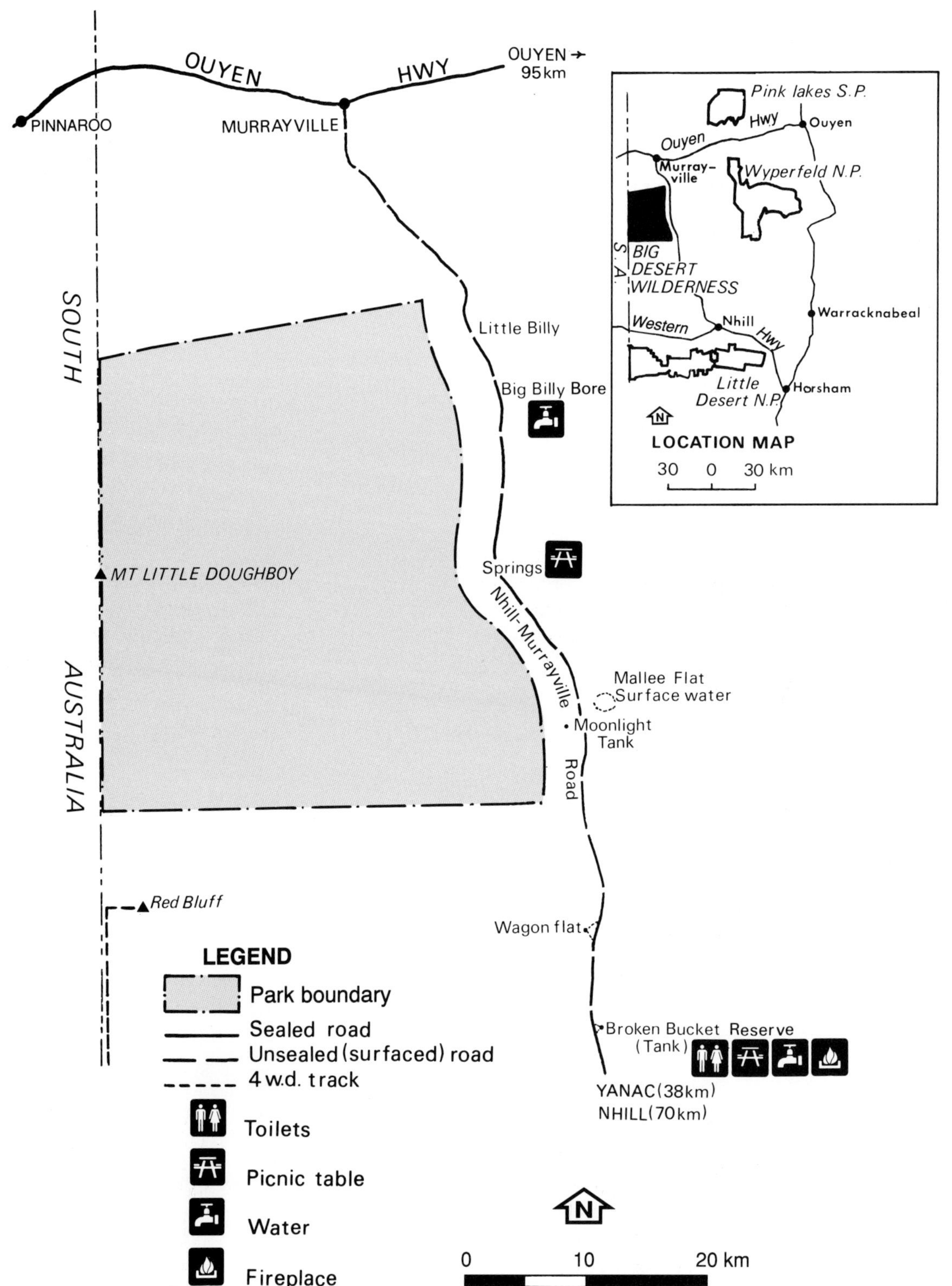
OUYEN HWY
OUYEN →
95km
PINNAROO
MURRAYVILLE
SOUTH AUSTRALIA
Little Billy
Big Billy Bore
Springs
MT LITTLE DOUGHBOY
Nhill-Murrayville Road
Mallee Flat
Surface water
Moonlight
Tank
Red Bluff
Wagon flat
Broken Bucket Reserve
(Tank)
YANAC(38km)
NHILL(70km)
LEGEND
Park boundary
Sealed road
Unsealed (surfaced) road
4 w.d. track
Toilets
Picnic table
Water
Fireplace
N
0
10
20 km
Pink lakes S.P.
Hwy
Ouyen
Ouyen
Murray-
ville
Wyperfeld N.P.
S.A.
BIG
DESERT
WILDERNESS
Western
Nhill
Hwy
Warracknabeal
Little
Desert N.P.
Horsham
LOCATION MAP
30 0 30 km

4 Big Desert Wilderness

Physical features: 113 500 ha. At first sight there is a sameness about this vast landscape, but the diversity and complexity of the sand dunes and red sandstone ridges soon become apparent. (See also Hattah-Kulkyne NP.)

Plants and animals: Like the other Mallee parks, this is a rewarding place for natural history. Its sheer size alone ensures suitable habitats for the many Mallee animals. The Big Desert is especially known for its small mammals such as Mitchell's Hopping-mouse, the Western Pygmy-possum, and the Silky Mouse. Of particular interest is the Mallee Ningaui, a minute, nocturnal, carnivorous marsupial which has only been described in recent years. In addition, the Big Desert is a very rich reptile area, with more than 50 species present. Among these are a number of snakes, many of them venomous, but they are only dangerous if disturbed. Snakes, like all other native animals, are fully protected.

Human history: The Aborigines were familiar with this area and its rich resources, as they were with the Mallee generally. The Europeans, on the other hand, were inclined to keep well out of such an apparently inhospitable area. Major Mitchell, in 1836, saw it as 'one of the most barren regions in the world'. The name alone, Big Desert, tells much about the early settlers' reactions and it has been left to walkers and naturalists to come to terms with its beauty and subtlety. Much of the Big Desert has been exploited in various ways, (see North West Introduction) and the Wilderness area was created to protect at least some of this special region.

Things to do: Walking; studying natural history; photography. Mallee skies alone are worth a visit – often with magnificent cloud effects – and of course, sunrises and sunsets, not to mention night skies with stars of unparalleled brilliance. Then there are the birds, the flowers and the many subtle wonders that come with increasing familiarity with the Big Desert. There are no facilities provided in the Wilderness, so you must be self-sufficient; take in all your supplies, including water, and take out all your rubbish. You also must to be able to use a map and compass. There are no vehicular tracks; the best approach is to walk in from the Nhill-Murrayville Road (dry weather access only).

Best season to visit: Late autumn, winter and early spring; not summer, when it is too hot for safe, much less comfortable, walking.

Special features: The sense of remoteness and timelessness, and of human insignificance.

Relevant reading: See Hattah-Kulkyne NP.

Further information:
C&E Office, Pool St, Murrayville, Vic 3512. Phone (050) 95 2161.

Mitchell's Hopping-mouse *AB*

5 Lake Albacutya Park

Physical features: 10 700 ha. The Park consists of the lake and some surrounding land, and adjoins Wyperfeld NP. Like Wyperfeld, it is part of the Big Desert sand tongue. On the edge of the lake is a characteristic land form known as a lunette, formed when particles of clay and salt-rich debris are swept up off a dry lake bed by the prevailing westerly winds and then deposited as a crescent. Lunettes are easily eroded, and over recent years Albacutya's regenerating cypress-pines – which are effective soil binders – have had guards placed around them by the Friends of Wyperfeld. When the Lake is dry its bed is used for grazing, but after a succession of wet years the Wimmera River flows north through Lake Hindmarsh and out via Outlet Creek into Lake Albacutya. At the time of writing, Lake Albacutya has effectively been dry since the severe drought in 1982–3, when the last of the water from the 1975 floods dried up.

Plants and animals: The dunes of the Big Desert, Wyperfeld and Lake Albacutya are all part of the same system and are all covered with similar vegetation. The Lake is fringed with River Red Gums, often with an understorey of wattles, including the Three-nerve Wattle which only occurs in very restricted localities. The lake bed, when dry, readily becomes infested with weeds, but it is a good place to see emus and kangaroos, here Western Greys rather than the more familiar Eastern Greys further south.

Provided there is sufficient water, Albacutya is a wonderful haven for waterbirds, both as the Lake is filling and then again when it is drying out, leaving rich feeding grounds exposed – picture 15 000 Banded Stilts feeding on the exposed mud. Freckled Duck and Blue-billed Duck, both rare birds all too often shot by careless duck hunters, can be found here. Perhaps the new regulations requiring shooters to pass a wildfowl identification test will better serve these and other protected species. Beyond the Lake there are many other birds well worth looking for, including two tiny but colourful wrens, the Splendid and the Variegated, as well as many parrots, especially the Regent Parrot, which nests in the Park, and that superbly camouflaged bird, the Bush-curlew.

Human history: This Park was created primarily to cater for the recreational needs of the district, with conservation as a secondary aim. As a result of the recent Land Conservation Council Recommendations, nearly 3 000 ha of Albacutya, which have high conservation values and are not widely used for recreation, have been added to Wyperfeld NP and so receive greater protection. Albacutya SP is one of ten wetlands in Victoria declared to be of international significance.

Things to do: When there is water in the Lake it is a popular spot both with the locals and tourists for water-based sports – swimming; boating; yabbying; fishing; and in season, hunting. But even without water it's a good spot for picnicking, walking and camping.

Best season to visit: This depends on whether there is water in the Lake. As with other Mallee parks, summers are hot and winters pleasant.

Special features: The Three-nerve Wattle; when there is water, the abundance of waterfowl.

Relevant reading: See Hattah-Kulkyne NP.

Further information:
Park Office, RMB 1479, Rainbow, Vic 3424. Phone (053) 95 7246.

Red-lored Whistler *RAOU*

Lake Albacutya

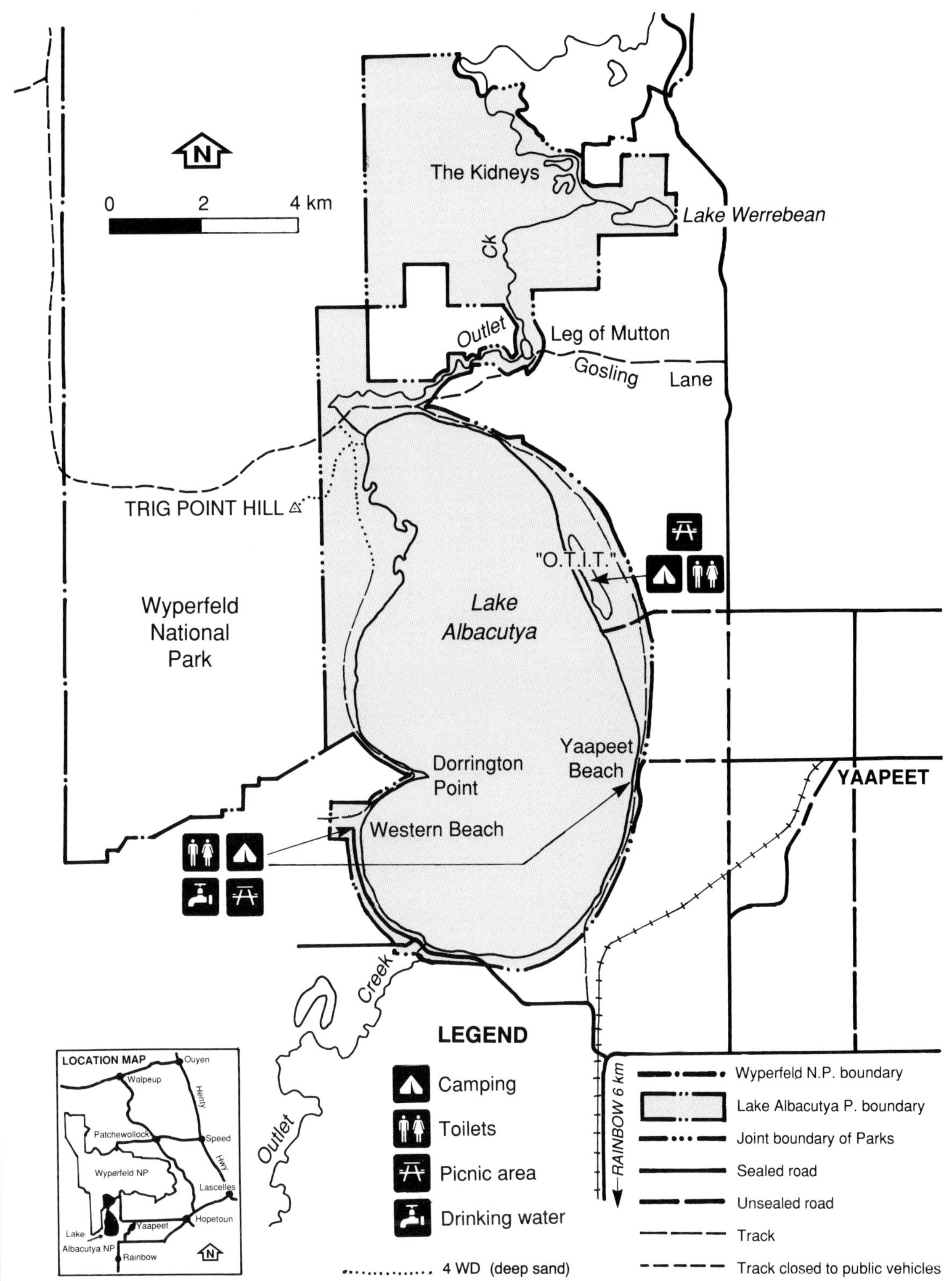

Wyperfeld

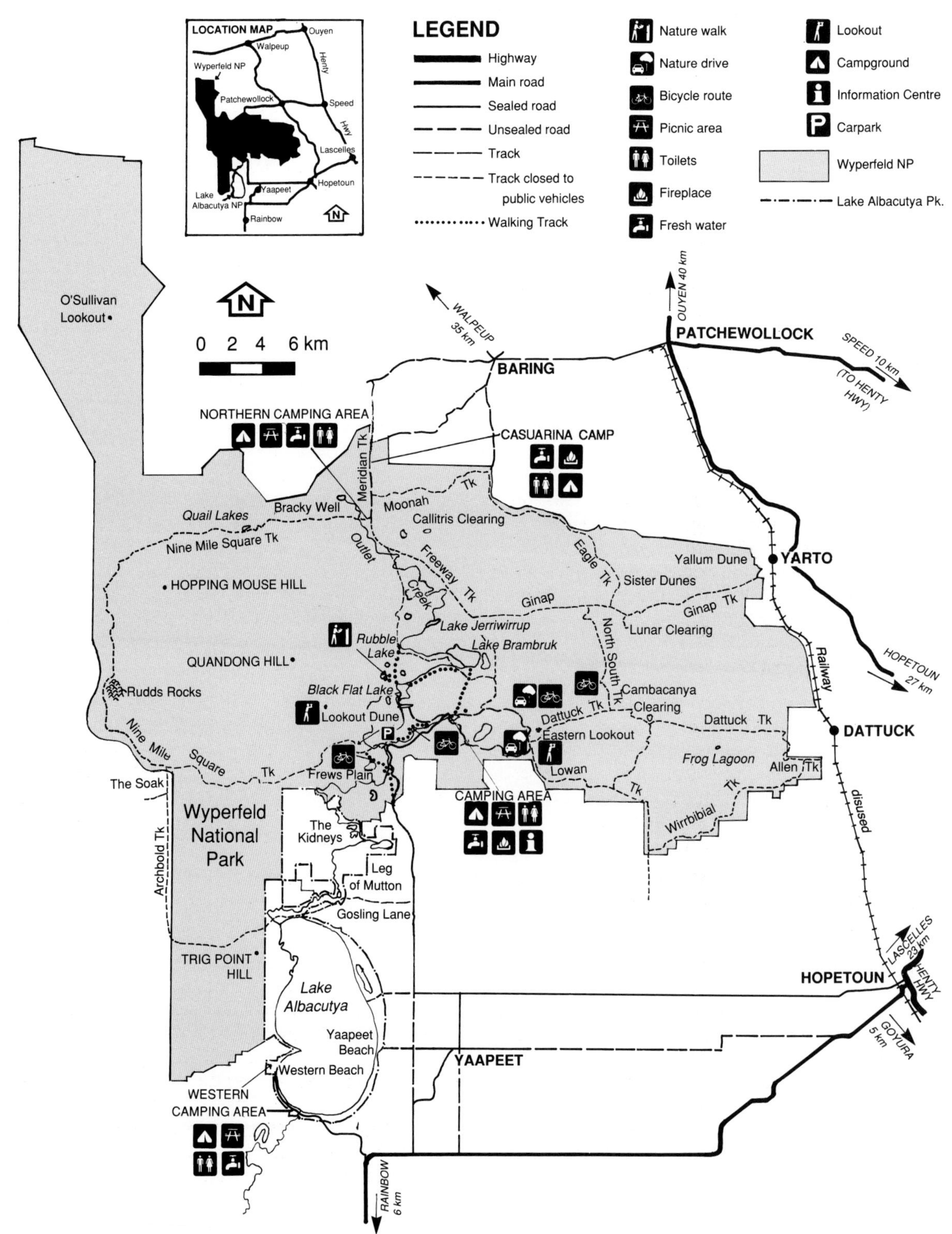

LOCATION MAP
Ouyen
Walpeup
Wyperfeld NP
Henty
Patchewollock
Speed
Hwy
Lascelles
Hopetoun
Yaapeet
Lake Albacutya NP
Rainbow
N
LEGEND
Highway
Main road
Sealed road
Unsealed road
Track
Track closed to public vehicles
Walking Track
Nature walk
Nature drive
Bicycle route
Picnic area
Toilets
Fireplace
Fresh water
Lookout
Campground
Information Centre
Carpark
Wyperfeld NP
Lake Albacutya Pk.
0 2 4 6 km
O'Sullivan Lookout
WALPEUP 35 km
OUYEN 40 km
PATCHEWOLLOCK
SPEED 10 km (TO HENTY HWY)
BARING
NORTHERN CAMPING AREA
CASUARINA CAMP
Meridian Tk
Bracky Well
Quail Lakes
Nine Mile Square Tk
Moonah
Callitris Clearing
Outlet
Freeway Tk
Creek
Eagle Tk
Yallum Dune
YARTO
Sister Dunes
HOPPING MOUSE HILL
Ginap
Ginap Tk
Lunar Clearing
Lake Jerriwirrup
Lake Brambruk
North South Tk
Rubble Lake
QUANDONG HILL
Railway
HOPETOUN 27 km
Rudds Rocks
Black Flat Lake
Cambacanya Clearing
Lookout Dune
Dattuck Tk
Dattuck Tk
DATTUCK
Eastern Lookout
Nine Mile Square Tk
Frews Plain
Lowan
Frog Lagoon
Allen Tk
The Soak
CAMPING AREA
Tk
Wirrbibial Tk
disused
Wyperfeld National Park
The Kidneys
Archbold Tk
Leg of Mutton
Gosling Lane
LASCELLES 23 km
TRIG POINT HILL
HOPETOUN
HENTY HWY
Lake Albacutya
Yaapeet Beach
GOYURA 5 km
YAAPEET
Western Beach
WESTERN CAMPING AREA
RAINBOW 6 km

6 Wyperfeld National Park

Physical features: 100 000 ha. Like the other Mallee parks, Wyperfeld was once part of the Murray Basin and has the characteristic Parilla and aeolian sand dunes (see Hattah-Kulkyne NP). Wyperfeld's sand dunes are a fascinating jumble of shapes and sizes, but generally are quite low and undulating with an east to west trend. Sometimes on a cool morning, when the dune crests stand clear above ethereal, mist-filled hollows, this can be seen quite clearly from Mt Mattingley near the campground.

Wyperfeld today has a chain of lake beds linked by a meandering creek bed, which, although almost always dry, can easily be traced by the River Red Gums and Black Box along its course. When the Wimmera River carries sufficient water it fills Lake Hindmarsh, then Lake Albacutya, and finally Wyperfeld's Black Flat and Lake Brambruk. Back in 1918, water reached Wirrengren Plain. Now, however, much of the Wimmera's flow is diverted to towns and farms. Because seventy-five per cent of this water is lost from open channels by seepage and evaporation, pipelining, as recommended by the Land Conservation Council, could mean that sufficient water remained to reach Wyperfeld more often and so revitalise its dying River Red Gum and Black Box woodlands. This Park, which is so often very dry, has a novel way of providing water for campers – a 'roof on the ground' – a large expanse of corrugated iron which collects rain and condensation.

Plants and animals: While much of Wyperfeld's vegetation is similar to that of Hattah-Kulkyne NP with riverine woodlands, pine ridges, and areas of mallee and heath, there is also vegetation like that of the Big Desert. Six mallee eucalypts are found in Wyperfeld and all have marked lignotubers (mallee roots) where the trunk and roots meet. It is this lignotuber that is the key to the mallee's ability to survive drought and fire. Each lignotuber consists of dense storage tissue with many dormant buds. When the crown of the tree is lost, for instance after fire, these buds sprout – up to 70 shoots per plant. Some trees have shown that they can be defoliated 26 times before the tree is killed! Many mallees rely almost entirely on regeneration from lignotubers, partly because little seed survives the foraging of ants in these areas, and partly because, after a fire, there is often inadequate moisture for germination. The true roots of many mallees store water, a fact that was well known to the Aborigines who used to cut lengths of root and drain the water from them.

Another characteristic and important mallee plant is Porcupine Grass, often incorrectly called Spinifex. Many small mammals, birds and reptiles shelter underneath clumps of Porcupine Grass, which, with its vicious, spine-tipped leaves, provides excellent protection. These clumps are so dense that the temperature is far less variable inside than outside, and to small animals, which have special problems with temperature regulation, the difference between 50° C and 35° C can literally be life-saving. Often, too, the only significant regeneration of cypress-pine seedlings is within a ring of Porcupine Grass, where the rabbits cannot reach what is obviously a favourite delicacy.

A tree dear to many Wyperfeld visitors is Old Be-al, a National Trust 'significant tree'. This enormous River Red Gum suffered badly in the 1985 fires and there is still some doubt whether it will survive.

For many people, though, Wyperfeld's birds are the special attraction, especially the parrots for which this Park has a worldwide reputation. Certainly, they are a constant and noisy delight. More than 200 bird species have been recorded, and at first sight the list comes as a suprise because of the many waterbirds. These, however, are only present during the rare periods of flooding, when an amazing variety of birds appears within a very short time, in some cases breeding almost immediately. For many people who missed the chance to visit Wyperfeld during the last floods in 1975–6, it will be a case of 'drop everything' rather than miss out again. Some of the birds, such as the Chestnut Quail-thrush, Mallee-fowl, Pink Cockatoo and Regent and Mulga Parrots, are near their southern limit in Wyperfeld. Spotting a Redthroat would be a real bonus. It would be rare, though, not to see Emus or Western Grey Kangaroos – many of both graze in the campground.

One interesting display in the excellent Visitors' Centre brings home, in a novel way, the importance of food chains in the arid environment by displaying rolls of termite-chewed toilet paper (almost pure cellulose). The message behind this is 'please keep your campfire as small as possible' – termites feed on dead wood (also largely cellulose) and many animals and birds in turn feed on these termites.

Human history: To Europeans this area may appear inhospitable, but for the Aborigines with their skills this was a more kindly country, especially in times of flood and when the lerps were plentiful. Lerps are small, white, sweet coverings exuded by some sap-sucking insects and they were greatly relished by the Aborigines. Wirrengren Plain, north of Wyperfeld, was a site for trading with Murray River tribes, and some fascinating trade routes have been deduced from Aboriginal artefacts of Portland flint, Grampians sandstone, New South Wales chert and Western District lava.

Major Mitchell was the first European to reach the Wimmera in 1836, followed two years later by John Eyre. The first settler was James Clow who, in 1847, selected Pine Plains. Other licensees followed, including the Camerons, whose baby's grave is near Wonga Flat. Legacies of Wyperfeld's pastoral history remain in the dog-leg fence and the replica of a water-drawing whim near the camping ground, and of course in the many weeds. One of these, Horehound, has been the focus of regular working bees by the Friends of Wyperfeld who have now cleared it from the area near the camping ground, and who even went so far, one year, as to brew some of it into the traditional bitter horehound beer.

Protection of Wyperfeld began with the temporary reservation of nearly 4 000 ha in 1909, followed by full national park status in 1921. Since then, many additions have been made, recently including the very important Pine Plains to the north.

Things to do: Camping (bring a stove if you can and help the termites!); walking; cycling (see Hattah-Kulkyne NP); enjoying the nature drive; investigating the visitor centre; birdwatching; photography; stargazing. But remember, this is a 'desert' park and you do need to carry water and to be sun-wise.

Best season to visit: Winter and spring for flowers; autumn for lovely weather; all of these for walking and cycling; summer if you don't mind the heat.

Special features: Peace; spaciousness; wonderful birdlife; wildflowers in a good year.

Relevant reading:

Allen T. (1975) *Wyperfeld: the history of station and settlement and the flora and fauna of Wyperfeld NP.*
Campbell A. 'Field Notes from the Lower Wimmera', *Victorian Naturalist* (1899) Vol. XVI, No. 8, pp. 121–130.
Garnet J.R. (1965) *Vegetation of Wyperfeld.*
Everard G. (1892) *Pioneering Days in the Wimmera and Mallee.*
Mattingley A.H.E. 'In the Heart of the Mallee', *Victorian Naturalist* (1909) Vol. XXVI, No. 6, pp. 64–77.
Morton W.L. (196–) 'An Old Bushman', *Notes on a Tour in the Wimmera District 1861.*
(See also Hattah-Kulkyne NP.)

Further information:
Park Office, Wyperfeld NP, RMB 1465, Yapeet, Vic 3424. Phone (053) 95 7221.
Friends' Group: Phone (03) 859 3738.

Malleefowl *CFL*

◀ Mitchell's Hopping-mouse *ARI*
▼ Feathertail Glider in captivity *ARI*

◀ Big Desert Wilderness *CFL*

▲ River Red Gums *JAC*

7 Little Desert National Park

Physical features: 132 000 ha. This Park falls within a large tongue of wind-blown sand similar to those that make up Wyperfeld and Big Desert (for more detail see Wyperfeld NP). The surrounding Wimmera country has fertile clay soils which were settled and developed for agriculture from the middle of the 19th century. In the Little Desert the land is generally low-lying, with lateritic, iron-rich sandstone ridges, some swampy low-lying areas and also some salt pans. Water – some of it fresh, some of it saline – lies about 50 m below the surface. In some of the salty surface pools sea grasses, more commonly found as marine plants, grow. The Wimmera River, on its way north from the Grampians, forms the eastern boundary of the Park. The rainfall at about 450 mm per year is similar to that of the surrounding land; it is the soil type that creates the 'desert'. Most of the rain falls in winter, and a dry winter often means a drought to follow. Summers are hot.

Plants and animals: The Little Desert is best known for its spectacular displays of wildflowers in spring, when, as in so many other infertile heathland areas of Australia, the whole scene is transformed into a mass of colour, from bold yellows, purples, reds and blues to more subtle pinks and whites, greens and browns. More than 600 species of flowering plants are found here, including more than 40 ground orchids. The plant communities vary greatly with soil type and to some extent with fire history. Where the sand overlies clay and is not very deep, the dominant plants are the mallee eucalypts – Green, Yellow and Slender-leaf Mallee – with their multi-stemmed trunks and sparsely-leaved crowns (fewer leaves mean less water loss). On the deeper sands the trees are Brown Stringybark and Silky Tea-tree; on the clay soils there are tall Yellow Gum; and along the river, on the alluvial soils, are fine specimens of River Red Gum and Black Box. All these trees, plus the rich diversity of the heathlands on the deep sands, means that this very special Park is certainly no desert. As in Wyperfeld, many of the plants have become well-adapted to this harsh environment with its extremes of temperature and unreliable water supplies. One plant, the Desert Phebalium, has evolved a remarkable method of luring pollinating insects into its flowers – a shimmer of light-reflecting scales, looking like a rich pool of nectar, lie in the heart of each flower. Result – one pollinated flower with no loss of precious water in the form of nectar.

The animal life is also extremely interesting, perhaps the best known example being that remarkable bird the Malleefowl or Lowan. Of the world's 19 mound-building birds the Malleefowl is the only one to inhabit arid regions. The mound, which may be as much as 5 m in diameter and 1.5 m high, is built by the male while the female searches for the food necessary to maintain her massive egg output – usually about 25 large eggs in an average season. The mound is built in autumn from dry plant material which the male bird scrapes in from up to 25 m away. When the litter is well-wetted from the rain, he covers the mound with sand and leaves it to ferment and heat. In spring, when the female is ready to lay, the male digs out an egg chamber, tests the temperature of the mound with his sensitive bill, and if the temperature is suitable, the female lays her egg. The male then covers up the mound. This whole process is repeated with every egg, and may well involve the moving of 3–4 cubic metres of sand and leaf litter each time, quite an undertaking for a bird the size of a small turkey. The temperature testing goes on continually. If the fermenting mound with its precious eggs is too hot, the male opens it in the cool of the early morning to release heat, then re-covers it with a thicker layer of insulating sand. If it is too cool, he opens it to the sun's rays then scoops back the warmed sand.

The chicks, which hatch in about 49 days, dig their way up from deep within the mound, quite unassisted by either parent. They are well developed and must fend for themselves, but too often the exhausted chick, instead of finding a quiet spot to recover, becomes an easy meal for a fox or a feral cat. Those hazards, plus fire regimes which do not allow the growth of suitable food plants, grazing which removes potential mound-building material and land-clearing which totally removes habitat, have drastically reduced Malleefowl numbers in Victoria. One of the best ways to see and learn more about this gentle, industrious bird is to visit the Little Desert Lodge Malleefowl Aviary, just beyond the Park boundary. Here, Whimpey Reichelt, who is one of Victoria's living treasures, maintains a few Malleefowl in a natural, but easily seen, environment.

Little Desert

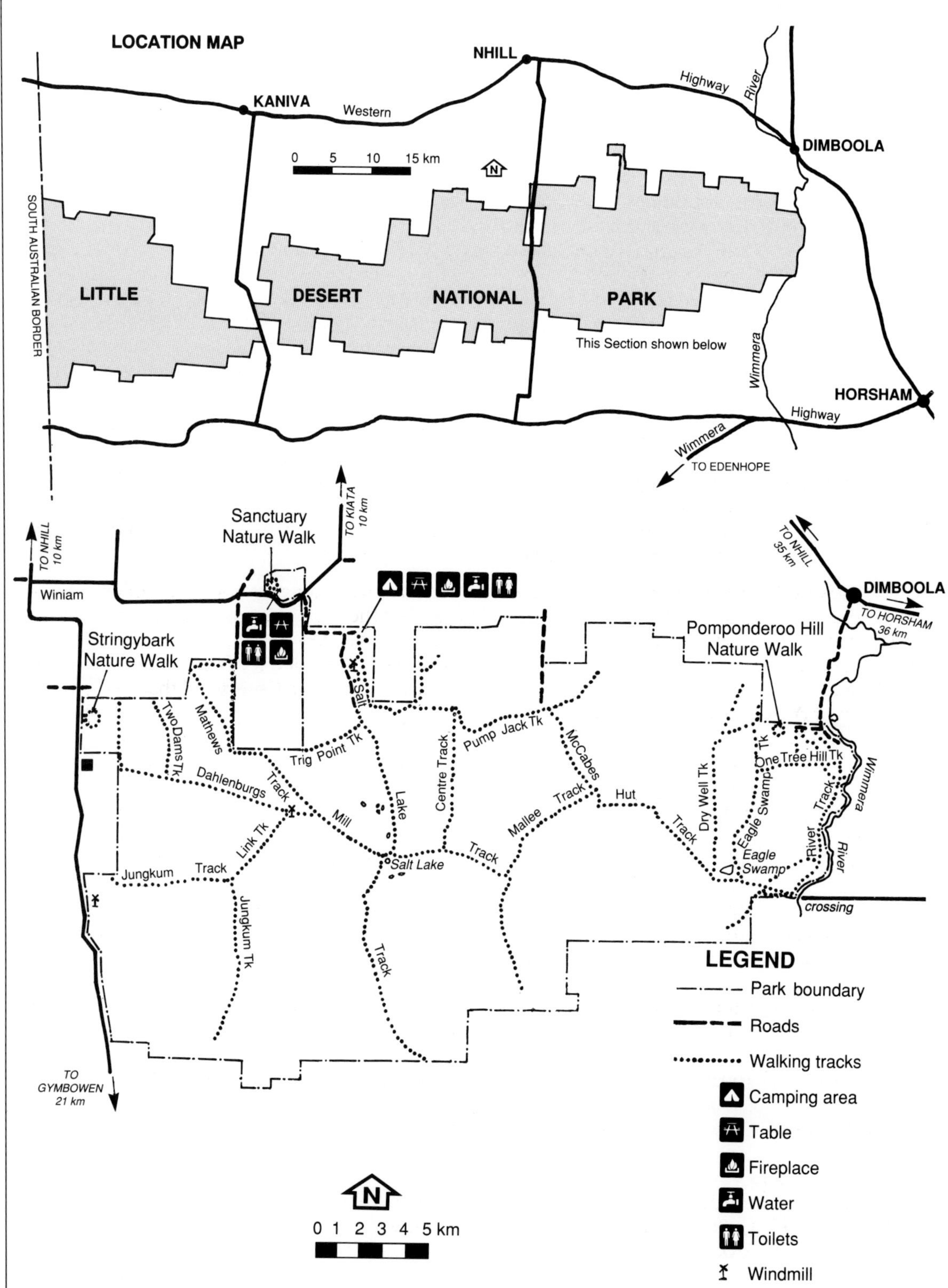

There are many other birds in the Little Desert besides Malleefowl, 218 species in all, 19 of which are classified as rare, and three, the Australian Bustard, Samphire Thornbill and Pied Honeyeater, as very rare. The flowering trees and shrubs are a rich source of nectar for many birds, and for insects which in turn attract other birds. Mammals and reptiles are also well-represented though probably less easily seen than most of the birds. Two of the most charming of the small furries are the superficially similar Western Pygmy-possum and Mitchell's Hopping-mouse. The former is a marsupial; the latter a true placental mammal. Both animals are nocturnal The pygmy-possum shelters during the day in a leaf-lined nest; the hopping-mouse spends its day underground in a deep burrow which is constructed to seal off the telltale pile of excavated earth from the burrow system proper.

Human history: The Aborigines were well aware of the rich resources of the Wimmera and knew it as Tatyara, the good country, but they were also aware of its difficulties, particularly the lack of water. This they obtained from lakes and streams, freshwater soaks which were carefully covered and maintained to prevent contamination, and mallee roots which, when cut and drained, give good clean drinking water. Both plant and animal foods were abundant – the roots of Yam-daisy, rushes, sedges and orchids; the fruits of Pig-face, Sweet Quandong and Kangaroo Apple; the seeds of wattles and native grasses; birds and game of all sizes; mussels and yabbies from the swamps; and fish from the lakes – certainly a land of plenty. Scarred trees along the Wimmera River show where bark was taken for canoes used by the Aborigines to fish and hunt.

When the Europeans came they were quick to take up the fertile clay land but the Little Desert they saw as 'a mere wilderness ... a dreary wretched desert, scorched in summer, and barely wet by winter rains'. Perhaps the only people to willingly enter this empty terrain were Chinese gold-seekers who walked across from Robe in South Australia to the Victorian goldfields, hoping to avoid the ten pound landing tax levied on them by the Victorian Government. The gold escort from the Victorian fields to Adelaide also passed close to the Little Desert.

Settlers took up land around the Desert and used it for grazing, frequently firing it in order to promote the growth of young, palatable grasses and herbs, but the real challenge did not come until the late 1960's. Then, at the same time as declaring a small Little Desert National Park, the Victorian Government announced that more than 80 000 ha would be subdivided for farming. Suddenly the Little Desert was a major issue – naturalists, conservationists and scientists argued that it would be little short of criminal to 'develop' such a natural asset, while economists argued that the only way that such a scheme would be economic was as a tax haven for the wealthy. Public meetings were held, and very well attended, newspapers ran editorials, and people everywhere rallied to 'Save the Little Desert'. Meanwhile the politicians involved maintained that the subdivision would go ahead regardless. Or rather they did so until the Government lost a 'safe' seat in a by-election. Suddenly the development was shelved and the spectacle of a 'dusty monument to a politician's obsession' was averted. Not long after, the National Park was greatly enlarged and the Land Conservation Council was set up to 'carry out investigations and make recommendations to the government with respect to the use of public land in order to provide for balanced land use in Victoria.' As a result of the Little Desert controversy, public awareness of conservation issues was greatly heightened – now people realised they had a voice to which the decision makers must listen.

Things to do: Enjoying the wildflowers and nature walks; birdwatching; walking; camping (BYO water). There are 4WD tracks, but remember, this is a fragile and easily damaged environment.

Best season to visit: Late winter; spring and early summer for the wildflowers.

Special features: The wonderful contradiction between the name and the reality of this Park.

Relevant reading:

Blake L.J. (1977) *Gold Escorts in Australia* and (1976) *Land of the Lowan.*
Hamilton J.C. (1981) *Pioneering Days in Western Victoria.*
Land Conservation Council (1985) *Report of the Wimmera Area.*
Thiele C. (1975) *The Little Desert.*

Further information:
C&E Office, McPherson St, Nhill, Vic 3418. Phone (053) 91 1273.
Friends' Group: Phone (03) 874 2641.

Spring calls to tourists –
in rugged four-wheel drives,
which, if the beaten track is barred by water or a fallen tree,
force their way through lesser obstacles,
to leave behind:
  a trail of bruised and broken shrubs and saplings,
  a withering canopy for colonies of orchids,
  now crushed, or buried in the ground.
In vain pretence of love for desert lands and nature,
people such as these destroy
forever
without discrimination, the desert's richest flowers.

Jean Wallis

Wheel-fruit *FvM*

CENTRAL WEST PARKS

These parks are all rocky and rugged, which gives them a distinctive appearance and character. Two of them are familiar to most Victorians. Certainly the long, jagged outline of the Grampians and the squat, steep-sided bulk of Mt Arapiles are welcome landmarks to anyone who travels the Western Highway. The other two parks, Langi Ghiran and Black Range, are much less well-known and somewhat less accessible, but are also well worth a visit. Langi Ghiran has the unmistakable rounded outline of a well-weathered granite mass, and is comparable in age to the granites of the Grampians, but is visually overshadowed by the latter's jagged, jointed sandstones.

Two other state parks have very recently been declared in this region but too late be be dealt with as separate entries in this edition. Paddy's Ranges (1 670 ha) is about 10 km S of Maryborough and has beautiful wildflowers and many birds. Mount Buangor (2 400 ha) is 25 km NW of Beaufort and was declared to safeguard this popular picnic and recreational area. Other parks near here, but not under the National Parks Act, are also worth visiting.

This part of Victoria has particularly interesting historical associations. Major Thomas Mitchell passed through this country in 1836 on his way south to the coast. Originally he and his party set out from Sydney to follow the course of the Darling River, but when, on climbing Mt Hope near Kerang, he saw 'land too inviting to be left unexplored', the party altered course and headed into the rich fertile country that he called *Australia Felix*, the blessed south land. After climbing and naming the Grampians and various landmarks within this range, they travelled north again and attempted to follow the Wimmera River, encountering and climbing Mt Arapiles en route. From there they turned south, in hope of finding a worthwhile harbour at the mouth of the Glenelg River, only to be met by a wide, sandy estuary. Major Mitchell's route is now being developed as a cultural trail for walkers, cyclists, horseriders, canoeists and motorists. A booklet of notes to accompany the Trail, including extracts from the Major's diaries, is shortly to be published.

Relevant reading:
Conservation and Environment (in preparation) *The Major Mitchell Trail.*
Douglas M.H. & O'Brien L. (eds) (1974) *The Natural History of Western Victoria.*
Mitchell T.L. (1966 facsimile edition) *Three Expeditions into the Interior of Eastern Australia Vol II.*

	Page No.	Entrance Fee	Information Centre	Multilingual Information	Picnic Areas	Fireplaces	Toilets	Disabled Access	Walking Tracks	Nature Walk or Drive	Swimming	Climbing	Horseriding	Fishing	Boating	Camping	Caravans	Km from Melbourne	Date Declared
Mount Arapiles-Tooan	24				■	■	■		■			■				■		340	1987
Black Range	27				■	■	■		■							■		300	1988
Grampians	28		■		■	■	■	■	■	■	■	■	■	■	■	■	■	260	1984
Langi Ghiran	33				■	■	■	P								■		185	1987

P = Proposed

8 Mount Arapiles-Tooan State Park

Physical features: This park is in two main parts which are quite separate in both locality and character. Mt Arapiles (1 500 ha) is a rugged outlier of the Grampians and was formed from the deposition of similar sediments; Tooan (3 550 ha), is made up of sand dunes on Parilla sand ridges deposited by retreating Pliocene seas and so is more like the Little Desert. Mitre Rock, to the north of Mt Arapiles, covers an additional ten hectares. Mt Arapiles (370 m) is surrounded by scree and outwash deposits, many of which are now becoming quite badly eroded. Rainfall is around 500 mm per year, falling mostly in the winter, when the clayey soils readily become boggy and impassable.

At present there is no map available for the Tooan section of this Park. It is 343 km NW of Melbourne, 40 km W of Horsham. Turn right off the Edenhope Road, about 7 km beyond Mt Arapiles, but because access is still poorly defined you may need to ask locally.

Plants and animals: The vegetation at Mt Arapiles is similar to that of the Grampians, and both the animals and plants include a number of species, such as the Southern Scrub-robin and Gilbert's Whistler, which are at or near their southern range. In Tooan there are a number of mallee eucalypts. Because of the variety of microclimates that exist in this small area, Mt Arapiles has more than 500 native plants, over one-seventh of the State's total flora. Among the more important plants are the Rock Wattle, abundant in the Park but rare elsewhere in Victoria, and the Skeleton Fork-fern, an odd looking plant not far removed from the earliest known land plants of 400 million years ago. Most of the trees on Arapiles are Long-leaved Box, with a few White Cypress-pine. Around the base of the mountain are Yellow Gums, the trees that once covered much of the Wimmera and made up the open woodlands that so impressed Major Mitchell as he journeyed through *Australia Felix*. Tooan, on the other hand, has a variety of woodland species, particularly Brown Stringybark, along with Black and Yellow Box, Yellow Gum, River Red Gum and Buloke on the alluvial flats. These woodlands are important habitat for that majestic bird, the Red-tailed Black-Cockatoo, whose name *Calyptorhynchus* (covering beak) *magnificus* is almost as spectacular as the bird itself.

The Peregrine Falcon nests on the cliffs of Mt Arapiles, on the western side at Campbells Kingdom. It is proposed to close this area to rock climbers during the nesting season, as has been done in other parks. This magnificent bird has been greatly threatened by the widespread use of pesticides in the environment, which has led to the thinning of its eggshells and therefore the loss of the chicks before they hatch.

Human history: Although there are few signs of Aboriginal occupation of this area, they are thought to have used the resources of the many lakes, both fresh and salt, around the base of Mt Arapiles. The first European known to have explored the area was the energetic Major Thomas Mitchell, who climbed and named Mt Arapiles in July 1836 while trying to determine the course of the Wimmera River. He and Stapylton, his second-in-command, were fascinated by the many small lakes that they saw from the summit. Most of the area was settled in the 1870's and from then on Mt Arapiles became a popular picnic spot. Local people have always had a strong affection for The Mount, with its striking contours and changing colours. In 1913 they installed a plaque at the Bluff, and in 1970 erected a cairn to the north of Mt Arapiles, both of which commemorate the Major. Centenary Park was named and the pines planted in 1936. These pines, being alien to the environment, will not be replaced as they die.

Things to do: Superb rockclimbing; just watching the climbers and listening to the gentle chinking of their equipment as they ease their way up a face is fascinating in itself, but there are many other interesting things to do. The spring wildflowers are a delight, and it is worth spending time observing the variety of plants in the different habitats, especially on the wet, mossy slopes which are rich with small lilies and orchids. Two short walks from the camping ground to the summit can be linked into a round trip. You can also walk around the base of the plateau, visiting both the Major Mitchell plaque and cairn en route, and drive almost to the summit for superb views, particularly across to the Grampians. The Tooan part of the Park is as yet undeveloped, and the tracks are sandy and largely unsuitable for 2WD. The interest here is that of natural history.

Mount Arapiles

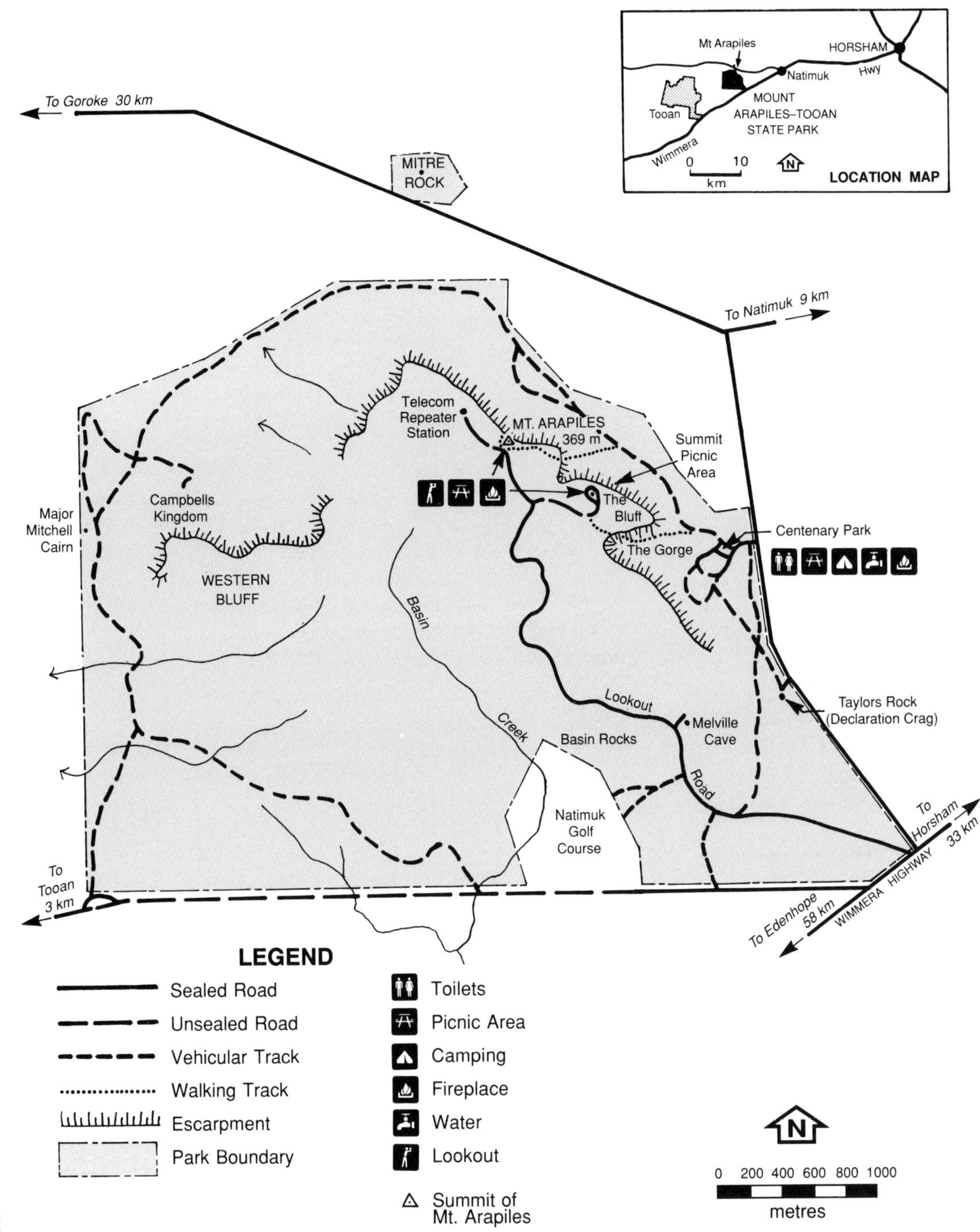

Best season to visit: Spring for wildflowers; otherwise any season, although some roads may well be closed in wet weather.

Special features: Panoramic views; the sense of being on an island in a sea of farmland; watching rock climbers on the precipitous face of Mt Arapiles.

Relevant reading:
Conservation, Forests and Lands (1987) *Mt Arapiles-Tooan SP Inventory of Resources and Uses* and (1987) *Proposed Management Plan for Arapiles-Tooan.*
Land Conservation Council (1979) *Study Report South-west 2.*

Further information:
C&E Office, Elmes St, Natimuk, Vic 3409. Phone (053) 87 1260.

Western extremity of Mt Arapiles *MM*

9 Black Range State Park

Physical features: 11 700 ha. The Black Range (often known as the western Black Range to distinguish it from the other Black Range, south of Stawell) is a small outlier of the Grampians, but although formed in the same way it is less rugged and the scenery is less spectacular. Besides the typical Grampians quartoze sandstones, there are small areas of Cambrian greenstone, but none of the Devonian granite that is found in the Grampians. The highest point is Mt Byron (520 m) in the north of the Park, barely half the height of Mt William in the Grampians. The rainfall is correspondingly less, around 600 mm per year, most of which falls in the winter and spring. The soils are shallow, with leached sands on the outwash slopes.

Plants and animals: Most of this Park is dry and rocky and has open forest of Brown Stringybark, some Long-leaved Box and Oyster Bay Pine. Messmate, Scent-bark and Manna and Swamp Gums grow in the moister areas. Where the soil is sandy there is often a colourful understorey of heathy shrubs which give a springtime display to rival that of the Grampians. There is an endemic species, the Mt Byron Bush-pea, and also the only known Victorian occurrence of the Lemon Star-bush. Essentially the Black Range is similar to the Grampians. The two together, however, increase the total wildlife habitat available making it more likely that plant and animal populations will remain viable.

Human history: There are a number of Aboriginal rock art sites in this Park, one of which is easily reached from the picnic ground at the end of the main access road. Better known for its Aboriginal rock art, however, is the other Black Range, 10 km south of Stawell off the Stawell-Pomonal Road. Here, at Bunjil's Cave, there is an excellent site with a viewing area and interpretation material.

Black Range has been mined for gold, and the remains of a poppet head can still be seen. Some gemstones such as topaz and garnet have been found near Rocklands Reservoir. Timber has also been taken from the Black Range, and cattle and sheep grazed in the Park. Black Range SP was declared largely because of its high value for flora conservation.

Things to do: Walking, though this would be on rough gravelled roads rather than bush tracks; 4WD touring; picnicking; viewing the Aboriginal rock art; wildflower and bird photography.

Best season to visit: Spring.

Special features: A spring wildflower display comparable with that of the Grampians, but without all the people.

Relevant reading:
Land Conservation Council (1979) *Study Report South-west 2.*

Further information:
Ranger, 4 Cadden St, Cavendish, Vic 3381. Phone (055) 74 2308.

Sugar Glider *CFL*

10 Grampians National Park

Physical features: 167 000 ha. This rugged and imposing sandstone range stands out clearly from its surroundings, both by virtue of its isolation from other similar terrain, and by the colour contrast between its unchanging Australian eucalypt-blueness and the seasonal European grass-greens and yellows. Its sandstones are ancient, having been laid down nearly 500 million years ago in estuarine waters from sediments eroded from nearby higher land. These sediments were laid down in four series, from the oldest, the Mt William series in the east, to the youngest, those of the Victoria Range in the west. About 50 million years later there was an upwelling of igneous material from the earth's interior. This molten mass lay blanketed by overlying rock and so cooled slowly to form granite. Subsequent earth movements led to uneven uplift of the land, forming the characteristic cuesta landscape with a steep scarp on one side and a gentle dip slope on the other. It is the effect of subsequent weathering and erosion along the cracks and joints of these exposed sedimentary layers that has given us the Grampians that we know today. Each of the four sedimentary series now has its own character according to the composition and the erosion of the sediments. Mt William is now a lofty plateau; Silverband has almost eroded away, leaving instead the valley in which Lake Bellfield and Halls Gap lie; the Serra Range is spectacularly jagged; and finally there is the solid, reddish Victoria Range. Quite recently, only about 14 million years ago, the Grampians were all but isolated by the sea transgressing from the south into the Murray and Otway Basins. It is largely this isolation that has been so important in the development of a distinctive Grampians flora.

Plants and animals: This isolation has led to the evolution of 20 known endemic plants, including five bush-peas and the beautiful Grampians Thryptomene with its mass of tiny white flowers. There are also a number of interesting disjunct distributions such as the Incense Plant found here and in eastern Victoria, and the Pincushion Lily otherwise only found in Western Australia. There is no need though to know anything at all about plants to enjoy the sheer exuberance of a Grampians spring when many of the 1 000 or so plants are in flower, from the subtleties of a tiny rush or sedge, to the brilliance of guinea-flowers, parrot-peas, Purple Hardenbergia and many, many more. Because there are so many different environments within the Grampians, from the sub-alpine, rocky heathlands of Mt William, down to the tall forests of the wetter gullies, there is a great richness of bird and other animal life. However, since animals are more mobile than plants, none are actually endemic to the area. The heathlands, with their many nectar-producing plants, are excellent for birds, especially honeyeaters and insect-feeders, while the wetlands and lakes are good places for waterbirds. There are a number of animals of particular interest, such as the tiny Smoky Mouse, which requires both tall open forest and sub-alpine heathlands in order to survive; the Heath Rat, confined to the Grampians and coastal heathlands in the south-west of Victoria; and the Brush-tailed Rock-wallaby. This little wallaby, which was once common throughout the Grampians, was feared to be extinct here, but a small colony is now known from the Victoria Range.

Human history: Although Europeans by land clearing and agriculture have made the Grampians stand out prominently from their surroundings, they would still have been a distinctive and important landmark to the Aborigines. This is borne out by the many rock art sites – it is the most significant Aboriginal rock art site in southern Australia – and by the many artefacts that have been found here. One site, Glenisla No. 1 in the Victoria Range, has now been protected and interpretation boards erected.

The European settlers, while quickly recognising the hills as being 'too steep to graze, too rocky to plough', soon realised that they were a source of excellent timber for mines, railway sleepers, charcoal burning and general building; not to mention wattle bark for tanning; stone for building; and to a small extent, gold. In many cases there is now little or no evidence, other than place and road names, of these and other activities. For instance, Homestead Road in the Victoria Valley, now just another rough bush road, marks the site of an ambitious Village Settlement scheme. This settlement, which lasted less than two years, was developed to create work for and to rehouse the poor and unemployed of Melbourne in the 1890's. None of these early activities, however, brought

Grampians splendour *JAC*

Grampians

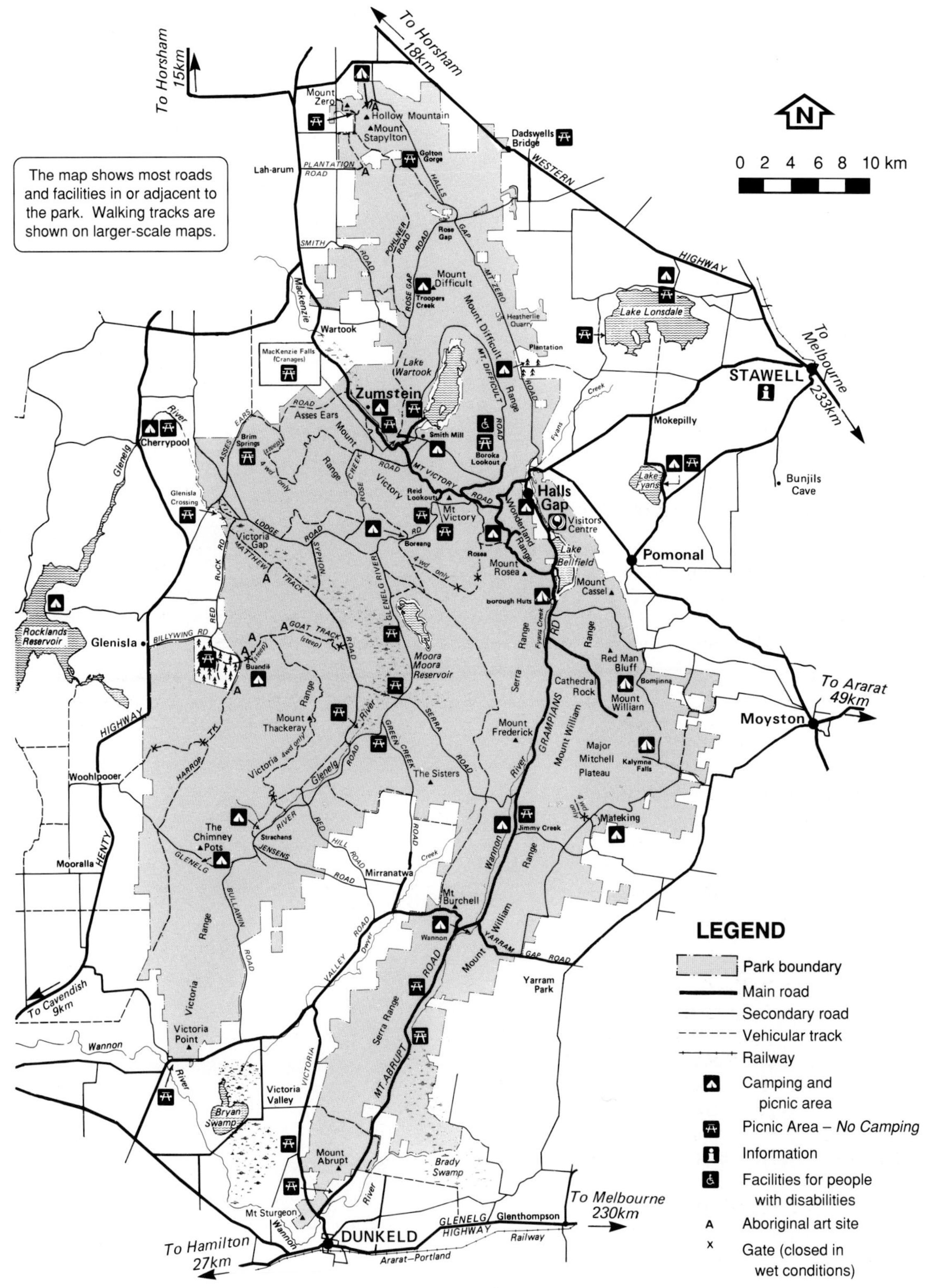

The map shows most roads and facilities in or adjacent to the park. Walking tracks are shown on larger-scale maps.
To Horsham 15km
To Horsham 18km
0 2 4 6 8 10 km
N
Mount Zero
Hollow Mountain
Mount Stapylton
Golton Gorge
Dadswells Bridge
WESTERN HIGHWAY
Lah-arum
PLANTATION ROAD
SMITH ROAD
POHLNER ROAD
HALLS GAP ROAD
Rose Gap
ROSE GAP ROAD
Mount Difficult
Troopers Creek
Mt ZERO
Mount Difficult Range
MT DIFFICULT ROAD
Heatherlie Quarry
Lake Lonsdale
To Melbourne 233km
STAWELL
Plantation
Mackenzie
Wartook
MacKenzie Falls (Cranages)
Lake Wartook
Zumstein
Asses Ears
ASSES EARS ROAD
Mount Victory Range
Brim Springs
4 wd only
Smith Mill
Boroka Lookout
Mokepilly
Lake Fyans
Bunjils Cave
River
Cherrypool
Glenelg
Glenisla Crossing
ROSE CREEK
ROAD
MT VICTORY ROAD
Reid Lookout
Mt Victory
Halls Gap
Visitors Centre
Wonderland Range
Pomonal
LODGE
Victoria Gap
MATTHEW TRACK
SYPHON ROAD
Boreang
Rosea
Mount Rosea
Lake Bellfield
RUCK RD
GLENELG RIVER ROAD
Mount Cassel
borough Huts
Fyans Creek
RD
Serra Range
Range
Rocklands Reservoir
Glenisla
BILLYWING RD
RED
GOAT TRACK
(steep)
Buandik
Moora Moora Reservoir
Red Man Bluff
Cathedral Rock
Bomjinna
Mount William
To Ararat 49km
Moyston
HIGHWAY
Mount Thackeray
Victoria Range
4 wd only
Mount Frederick
GRAMPIANS
Mount William
Major Mitchell Plateau
Kalymna Falls
HARROP TK
Woohlpooer
Glenelg
River
GREEN CREEK
SERRA ROAD
The Sisters
4 wd only
Mateking
The Chimney Pots
Strachans
RIVER
RED HILL ROAD
JENSENS ROAD
Jimmy Creek
Wannon
Range
Mooralla
HENTY
GLENELG
BULLAWIN ROAD
Mirranatwa
Creek
ROAD
Mt Burchell
Wannon
William
YARRAM GAP ROAD
VALLEY ROAD
Dwyer
Mount
ROAD
Yarram Park
Victoria Range
To Cavendish 9km
Victoria Point
Wannon
Serra Range
MT ABRUPT
River
Bryan Swamp
VICTORIA
Victoria Valley
Mount Abrupt
Brady Swamp
River
Mt Sturgeon
Wannon
To Melbourne 230km
GLENELG HIGHWAY
Glenthompson
Railway
DUNKELD
To Hamilton 27km
Ararat—Portland
LEGEND
Park boundary
Main road
Secondary road
Vehicular track
Railway
Camping and picnic area
Picnic Area – No Camping
Information
Facilities for people with disabilities
A Aboriginal art site
x Gate (closed in wet conditions)

in anywhere near the number of people who are now coming to the Grampians as tourists, especially since the National Park was declared in 1984. Now the challenge is to promote this precious and sensitive area, one of Victoria's seven officially recognised tourist zones, without damaging or down-grading the very things that people come to see and enjoy. The new Information Centre, just south of Halls Gap, provides a fascinating array of exhibits, displays, books and an audio-visual display on the formation and history of the Grampians, and of the many attractions that are found in today's Grampians. One of the most attractive features is a large mural in the theatrette, painted by local people and visitors, including schoolchildren, which shows a Grampians day through the four seasons, even including the infamous 'Grampians puma' and a Coke can! An Aboriginal Interpretation Centre is currently being built alongside the Visitor Centre.

Many visitors find it hard to believe that this exciting and rewarding area has not always been a national park, but until 1984 only small areas received any protection. The rest was state forest, and there was considerable local opposition when the Land Conservation Council proposed the relevant change in management. Once again, though, the words 'national park' have proved their power to draw people from far and near.

Things to do: The Grampians are undoubtedly best seen on foot, and there are many interesting and enjoyable walks, from easy well marked ones such as the ever popular Wonderland Track and the road up Mt William, to more challenging walks such as those along the crest of the Serra Range and across the Major Mitchell Plateau. There are many enjoyable scenic drives also, often to a good lookout, or perhaps to see the kangaroos at Zumstein, but please resist the temptation to feed these animals. It is not good for them – soft, refined food does even worse things to wild animals' jaws and teeth than it does to ours; nor is it good for future visitors who may well be molested by impatient animals in search of a handout.

For the more adventurous, there are some excellent cliffs for rockclimbing, many of which offer almost as much challenge as those at nearby Mt Arapiles, and considerably more solitude. Camping is also popular, as are swimming, fishing, photography, painting and sketching, and of course enjoying the wonderful array of wildflowers. To quote Edna Walling, who in her book, *On the Trail of Australian Wildflowers*, in the chapter entitled 'Off to the Grampians' writes:

> For all the ruggedness and for all the sheer drops into space this mountain range seems to have such a friendly atmosphere about it, both from the distance and when you are actually walking there amongst the flowers. One always leaves it with regret and we immediately start to arrange life so that we will be back there again next Spring SOMEHOW.

Best season to visit: Spring for the peak of wildflowers, though there are at least some flowers out all year; otherwise any time of year, though winters can be wet and cold, and the height of summer may be too hot for pleasurable walking.

Special features: Dramatic landscapes, especially when seen at different times of day and in different lights; Aboriginal rock art; wildflowers; historical sites.

Relevant reading:

Calder J. (1987) *The Grampians – a noble range.*
Conservation, Forests and Lands (1985) *Grampians NP Management Plan.*
Day J.C. et al (1984) *Grampians National Park – Inventory of Resources and Uses.*
Elliot R. (1984) *A Field Guide to the Grampians Flora.*
Land Conservation Council (1979) *Study Report South-west 2.*
McCann I.R. (1982) *Grampians Birds* and (1984) *Grampians Wildflowers.*
Stanton I. (1988) *Bridging the Gap: the History of Halls Gap from 1840.*
Thomas T. (1977) *50 Walks in the Grampians.*

Further information:

C&E Park Office, Grampians Rd, Halls Gap, Vic 3381. Phone (053) 56 4381.
Friends' Group: Phone (053) 56 4218.

Langi Ghiran

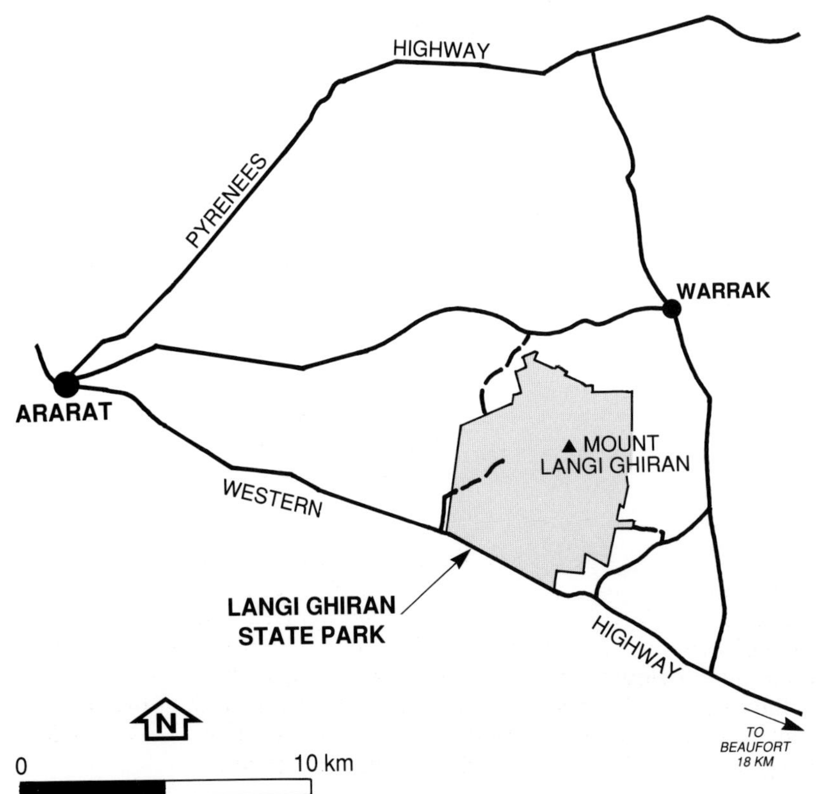

11 Langi Ghiran State Park

Physical features: 2 695 ha. Almost the entire Park is of granite about 400 million years old. Around the granite is a ring of metamorphic rock at the contact area with the older sedimentary rocks. The highest point is Mt Langi Ghiran, 922 m, with a rainfall of over 800 mm per year. The headwaters of many streams, some flowing north into the Wimmera, others south into the Hopkins Rivers, arise in this Park.

Plants and animals: There are two main types of vegetation in Langi Ghiran. On the lowlands there is open woodland of River Red Gum and Yellow Box with an understorey of Wedge-leaf Hop-bush, various wattles and Silver Banksia. On the slopes are open forests of Red Stringybark and Long-leaved Box with again an understorey of wattles and Silver Banksia. Many of the massive granite boulders are clothed with a most attractive assortment of lichens, mosses and ferns and are starred with small plants such as Early Nancy. Of particular interest are Veined Beard-heath and Shiny Tea-tree, which occur here and at the nearby Grampians and nowhere else in Victoria. Birds are numerous. Some of them, such as cockatoos – including the magnificent Yellow-tailed Black-Cockatoo after which Langi Ghiran is named – cuckoos and corellas, are conspicuous not only to the eye but also to the ear. Others, like the many robins, thornbills, honeyeaters and finches, are plentiful but less obvious.

Human history: This was, and is, an important Aboriginal area. Aborigines are believed to have used the lagoon on the saddle between Mt Langi Ghiran and nearby Mt Gorrin, and there are also red ochre paintings such as those in the Cave of the Serpent. Like Aboriginal art elsewhere, the paintings here are at the mercy of weathering. Flaking away of pieces of granite has led to the two conspicuous 'eyes' in the round motif below the human figure in the drawing shown. Driplines to deflect water trickling down the rock have been installed at other rock art sites such as that at Glenisla in the Grampians, but these may well have unexpected and adverse effects, for example, creating a moist area for algal growth or a dry spot just right for a mud-wasp nest.

The most obvious sign of European use of the area (apart from the shameful picnic ground) is an elegant old reservoir further upstream which was built late last century of locally quarried stone. Little timber has been taken from here and the Park is largely untracked and unaltered.

Things to do: Walking, both longer tracked and untracked walks and shorter walks. The longer walks include a fascinating climb to the very rugged summit of Mt Langi Ghiran. This can be done in one day but it is better to camp overnight, perhaps at the lagoon on the saddle. A pleasant short walk is up to the reservoir and possibly on to the lagoon or to the summit of Mt Gorrin (don't be deterred by the picnic ground, the rest of the valley, with the track running beside the stream, is lovely). This is also a pleasant area for birdwatching, especially in spring when there is a good flow of nectar.

Best season to visit: Any for walking (except midsummer); spring for wildflowers.

Special features: Mossy granite boulders and tors; magnificent views from the higher ground, especially of the Grampians.

Relevant reading:
Land Conservation Council (1980) *Study Report Ballarat Area*.
Victorian Archaeological Survey (1983) *Langi Ghiran*.

Further information:
C&E Regional Office, Cnr Doveton & Mair Sts, Ballarat, Vic 3350. Phone (053) 370 0783.

One hundred year old granite wall at Langi Ghiran reservoir *JAC*

▲ Sheet of water, Victoria Valley, Grampians NP *JAC*
◀ Streamside, Langi Ghiran SP *JAC*
▼ Scented Sundew *DC*

▲ Freckled Duck *ARI*

▼ Rock-climbing at Mt Rosea, Grampians NP *EW*

▲ Wonderland Track, Grampians NP *RC*

◀ Morning mists, Grampians NP *JAC*

◀ Regrowth after 1983 fires, Angahook-Lorne SP *JAC*

▼ Common Correa *AK*

▲ Johanna Beach, Otway NP *JAC*

▲ Early morning, Port Campbell NP *JAC*

SOUTH WEST PARKS

Whilst many people are familiar with the spectacular scenery of Port Campbell NP, and perhaps some with the lush forests of Otway NP and Melba Gully, very few know the other parks in this fascinatingly diverse region of Victoria.

Most of the South-west parks are geologically very young and are unlikely to remain as we know them for long – sun, wind and particularly water will all continue to sculpt and alter what we see today. Discovery Bay's impressive sand dunes will drift and be moulded and remoulded with every wind change; the lava-strewn landscape of Mt Eccles and Mt Napier will gradually lose its raw newness; the stalactites and stalagmites of Lower Glenelg's caves will continue their slow and stealthy growth; while the stacks and arches of Port Campbell will tumble, only to be replaced by new forms as the sea continues its relentless work. Only the towering trees of the Otways and Melba Gully give a feeling of primeval strength and solidity, until here too, one crashes to the ground, creating a precious clearing of light and nutrients in which its successors may grow.

	Page No.	*Entrance Fee*	*Information Centre*	*Multilingual Information*	*Picnic Areas*	*Fireplaces*	*Toilets*	*Disabled Access*	*Walking Tracks*	*Nature Walk or Drive*	*Swimming*	*Climbing*	*Horseriding*	*Fishing*	*Boating*	*Camping*	*Caravans*	*Km from Melbourne*	*Date Declared*
Angahook-Lorne	65				■	■	■	■	■	■	■		■	■		■		100	1987
Cape Nelson	46				■	■	■		■					■				363	1978
Carlisle	62																	150	1988
Discovery Bay	43					■	■		■		■		■	■	■			400	1979
Lower Glenelg	40		■			■	■		■	■	■			■	■	■	■	425	1969
Melba Gully	59				■	■	■		■									200	1978
Mount Eccles	49					■	■	■	■	■	■					■	■	330	1960
Mount Napier	48																	310	1987
Mount Richmond	45					■	■		■	■								390	1960
Otway	59		■		■	■	■	■	■		■		■	■	■	■	■	200	1981
Port Campbell	53		■			■	■	■	■	■	■			■		■	■	240	1964

12 Lower Glenelg National Park

Physical features: 27 300 ha. The dominant feature of this Park is Victoria's most westerly river, the magnificent Glenelg, which, with its beautiful tributary, Moleside Creek, flows through much of the Park. The Glenelg rises in the Grampians, only about 150 km away by 'crow' but nearly 400 km by river, and in spite of its capture by the Rocklands Reservoir early in its course, it is still a very impressive river as it flows through this park that bears its name. Because its mouth is only a few kilometres south of the Park (at the picturesque town of Nelson), the Glenelg is salty for a considerable distance upstream into the Park, with the heavier salt water running beneath the lighter fresh water. For the last 40 km of its course, the Glenelg runs through an impressive gorge, which it has cut through Miocene limestone laid down about 25–40 million years ago. Through changes in sea level, and some land uplift, the Glenelg has carved out cliffs nearly 50 m high. Sometimes these cliffs are on one side only, with the other side having a gentler ascent. In these places, silt has been deposited on the outside of the bends as the water slows and is forced to drop some of its load. Much of this silt represents good farmland from erosion along the course of the Glenelg and its tributary, the Wannon, above the reaches of the Park.

As often happens in limestone areas, there are many caves, but only one of the 60 known is open to the public, the Princess Margaret Rose Cave. This cave did run right out to the wall of the gorge, but is now blocked by an earth fall. This means that its stalactites and stalagmites and other delicate formations have kept their colour and 'life', unlike those in other caves which have been dulled by prolonged exposure to the outside air. Another limestone formation is the Inkpot, an infilled circular sinkhole, about 10 m deep, with a layer of dark organic matter lying on the bottom.

Plants and animals: Biologically this is one of the richest areas in Victoria, both because of the wide diversity of habitat and because east and west overlap here. There are some species such as Snow Gum and Porcupine Grass which are more typical of the Alps and the Mallee respectively. Altogether there are more than 700 plants, including the liverworts, mosses and ferns. Most of the Park is covered with eucalypt woodlands, from Brown Stringybark on the dry river terraces to Manna Gum along the Glenelg. The eastern end of the Park, Kentbruck Heath, consists of largely infertile and often swampy heathland. Once again it is this harsh environment which gives us some of our most brilliant wildflower displays, including many orchids. Also here, along Moleside Creek, are Australia's westernmost treefern gullies, along with a bewildering variety of other non-flowering plants such as ferns, mosses, liverworts, lichens and fungi. One of these non-flowering plants, the Long Fork-fern, is a plant with an impressive lineage which goes back almost unchanged to the very first land plants, 400 million years ago. At the western end of the Park, along the gorge, are a number of lime-loving plants such as the Oval-leaf Logania, which is found here and in similar formations in South and Western Australia. For the Park as a whole there are about 60 species of plants at their westernmost limit, including Hop Bitter-pea and Rosemary Everlasting.

The massive clearing of land in the south-west for farming and pine plantations has made Lower Glenelg, with its wide variety of habitats, an extremely important area for many animals, such as the rare and localised Rufous Bristle-bird and the Heath Rat. There are 30 species of mammals here, including three Antechinus species, two gliders and at least four bats. Until recently, wombats were rare in the Park, but gradually they seem to be moving back in from adjacent wooded areas in South Australia. The birdlife is also rich, with a diversity of waterbirds along the river, and bush birds in the wet gullies and open woodlands. Discovery Bay Coastal Park, which all but joins Lower Glenelg NP, provides different birds again, but even without the Coastal Park, nearly 170 birds have been recorded, including Yellow-tailed Black-Cockatoos which feed in the nearby pine plantations.

One of the most fascinating aspects of the fauna of Lower Glenelg is the rich array of bones found in many of the caves, from animals which tumbled down the narrow entrances and then were trapped many feet underground. A sad testimony to their desperation is seen in the scratch marks on the cave walls below the faint light of the solution tube down which they fell. Some of the bones have been shown to date back tens of thousands of years, and include such long-gone creatures as the Marsupial Lion, Giant Kangaroo and Diprotodon. Others are from animals such as the Thylacine and Tasmanian Devil which had already disappeared from mainland Australia at the time of white settlement. These caves are important places for scientific study of the animals themselves and of the climatic changes that are reflected by the animals. Had the land been cleared and settled, these caves could well have been seen as a risk and filled in.

Human history: The first European to see the Glenelg was Major Thomas Mitchell, who named it in 1836. Impressed by the beauty of the gorge, he was disappointed soon after by the mouth of the river, having hoped to find a good deep-water port, and not a sandy bar across a wide estuary.

Moves to have the area protected as a park came largely from the Portland Field Naturalists' Club (FNC), who, in 1947, organised an excursion to survey the Glenelg area, particularly Moleside Creek. At this time, native vegetation was being cleared for pine plantations and settlement, threatening the botanically-rich but economically-marginal Kentbruck Heath. Naturalists intensified their efforts to protect this area of great scenic beauty and conservation value. The Forests Commission of Victoria was prepared to recognise the former claim by leaving three chains (about 60 m) along the riverbanks still under native vegetation. The Portland FNC and others, including the Victorian National Parks Association, knew this to be totally inadequate in terms of habitat, and pressed for a mile (1.6 km). Finally, in 1968, Sir William McDonald introduced legislation into the Victorian Parliament to establish a park of just over 9 000 ha, and incidentally, a small Little Desert NP at the same time. As a result of the political impact of these two conservation-based controversies (see Little Desert NP also) it was felt that a better way of deciding land use should be found, and in 1973 the Land Conservation Council was set up. The Council began looking at public land in Victoria region by region, the first to be considered being South-west I which included Lower Glenelg NP. Consequently, the Park was enlarged in 1975 to its present size, covering almost exactly the area proposed by the Portland FNC. Nearly thirty years of careful work was finally rewarded.

When the Park was declared, the problem of the riverside shacks arose. The initial grounds for allowing these to be built had been that they were boatsheds in the days before boat-trailers, but beds, stoves and all the appurtenances of a comfortable week 'away from it all' soon crept in. Not surprisingly, the owners of these shacks were reluctant to give up their occupancies and what they saw as their land to its rightful owners, the people of Victoria. The last of these 'boatsheds' has now been demolished and the exotic vegetation that had been planted around many of them is gradually being cleared. Jetties and launching ramps have also been built to provide access to the river.

Undoubtedly the most popular tourist attraction in the Park is the Princess Margaret Rose Cave, discovered in 1936 when a local man, Keith McEachern, noticed a large depression in the ground. Before the cave could be opened to the public, a new stepped entrance had to be cut through the tough limestone, a long hard job. Electric lighting, then run by a generator (not always reliable!) was installed, and in 1941 the cave was officially opened.

Things to do: Visiting the Princess Margaret Rose Cave; camping; picnicking; boating (the Glenelg River is zoned to allow both canoeing and power boating); waterskiing; fishing; walking (part of the Great South West Walk runs through the Park); studying natural history; enjoying the nature drive. The Glenelg RiverCanoe Trail, part of the new Major Mitchell Trail, runs from Dartmoor to the sea.

Best season to visit: Spring for wildflowers, particularly in the east of the Park; otherwise any.

Special features: The limestone gorge; the tranquillity of the River, especially at night with the Nankeen Night Herons fishing along the banks; the Ink Pot; Moleside Creek.

Relevant reading:
Conservation, Forests and Lands (1988) *Lower Glenelg NP Proposed Management Plan.*
Land Conservation Council (1972) *Report of the South-west Area 1.*

Further information:
Park Office, Forest Rd, Nelson, Vic 3292. Phone (087) 38 4051.
Friends' Group: (of the Great South West Walk) Phone (055) 29 5228.

Lower Glenelg

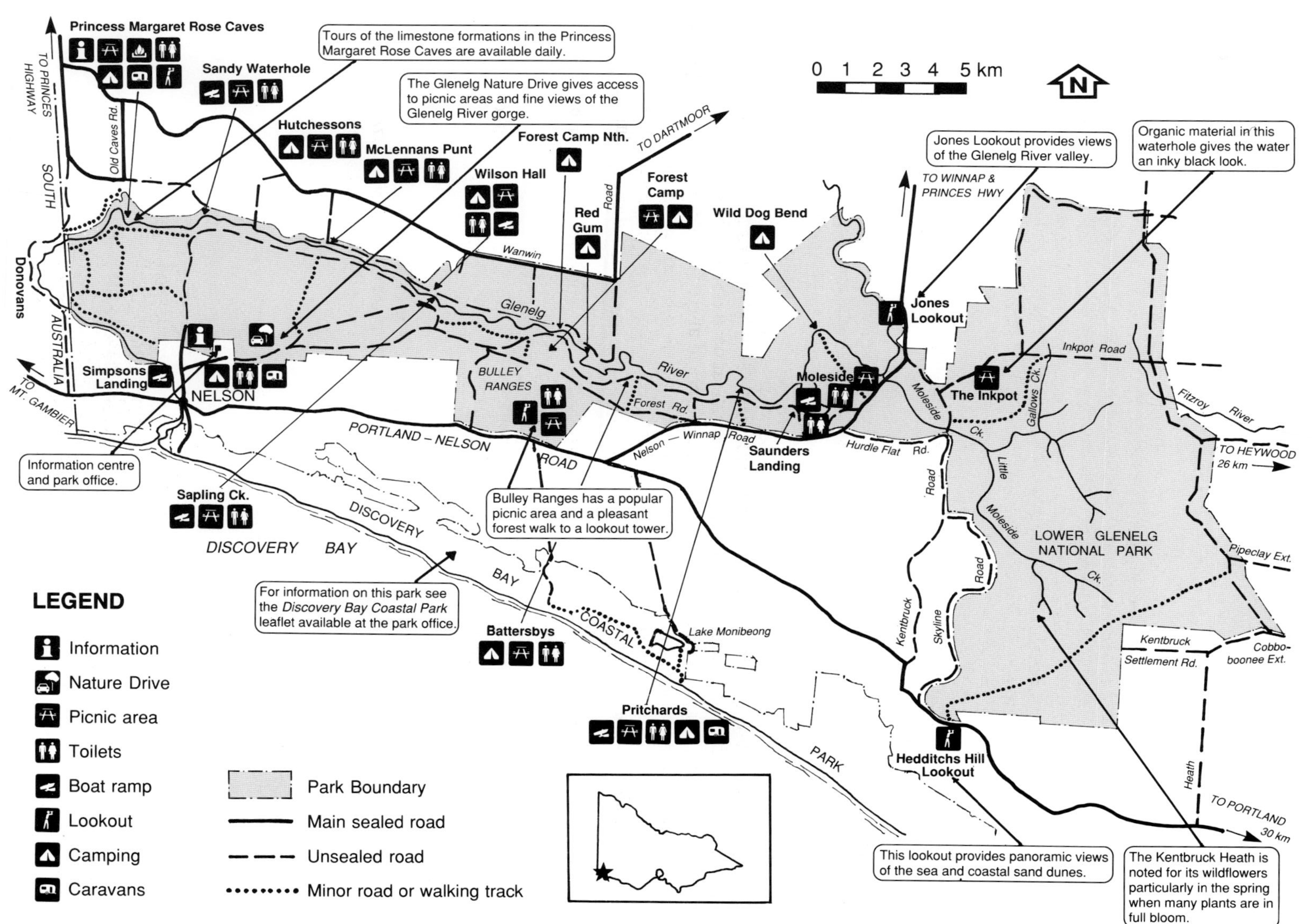

13 Discovery Bay Coastal Park

Physical features: 8 590 ha. This Park consists of a long narrow coastal strip of ocean beach, with large sand dunes, often quite mobile, up to 60 m high. (For more detail see Cape Nelson SP.) Behind these there used to be a shallow lake which was navigable from Nelson to Bridgewater Lakes, but now is mostly swampy with only a few, though very attractive, small lakes. The climate is mild with winter rain and warm, dry summers, but watch for southerlies coming in off the ocean.

Plants and animals: The more specialised environment and therefore fewer different types of habitat are reflected in fewer types of plants here (215) than in nearby Lower Glenelg NP (more than 700). Along the beach are typical sand-binding plants, then shrubs, often pruned on the windward side by the strong salt-laden winds. Behind the dunes are swamps and lakes with a variety of reeds, sedges and rushes around their edges, then thickets of small trees and shrubs further from the water. Both the swamp vegetation and the thickets are excellent habitat areas for small mammals and birds, including some rarities such as the Swamp Antechinus, the Heath Rat and the Rufous Bristle-bird. Generally the open beaches are poor for birds but occasionally small plovers (dotterels) can be seen twinkling their way ahead of you. A number of birds and animals are at their westernmost limit here, and it is an important refuge and breeding area for several species of ducks.

Human history: European settlement has led to the removal of much of the native vegetation, allowing mobile sand dunes to develop. The country the Aborigines knew as they feasted on shellfish from the rocks, leaving behind considerable middens, would have been what Lieutenant Grant saw in 1800 from the brig *Lady Nelson* – 'land covered with bushes and large woods inland'.

Things to do: Nearly half of the 200 km long Great South West Walk runs through this Park and provides wonderful opportunities for savouring a remote and wild coastline. A pamphlet of track notes is available, but appropriate topographical maps should also be carried. Camping and swimming are good at the lakes, but the ocean beaches have treacherous rips and currents and are not suitable for swimming. Waterskiing is allowed on some lakes and fishing is popular at both the beaches and lakes. Dune buggies are allowed in certain areas under controlled conditions.

Best season to visit: Oct–early Dec and late Mar–early June for the Great South West Walk; summer for camping and swimming at the Lakes; otherwise any season.

Special features: Enormous sand dunes; remoteness; turbulent beaches and gentle lakes; the mercurial flight of swifts feeding on insects at the edge of an approaching cold front.

Relevant reading:

Bardwell S. 'The Great South West Walking Track', *Wild* (Autumn 1983).
Conservation, Forests and Lands (1978) *Discovery Bay Coastal Park Management Plan.*
Great South West Walk Committee (1983) *Great South West Walk* (map and brochure).
Land Conservation Council (1972) *Report of the South-west Area 1.*

Further information:

C&E Regional Office, 8–12 Julia St, Portland, Vic 3305. Phone (055) 23 3232.
Friends' Group: See Lower Glenelg NP.

Chestnut Teal *CFL*

Mount Richmond

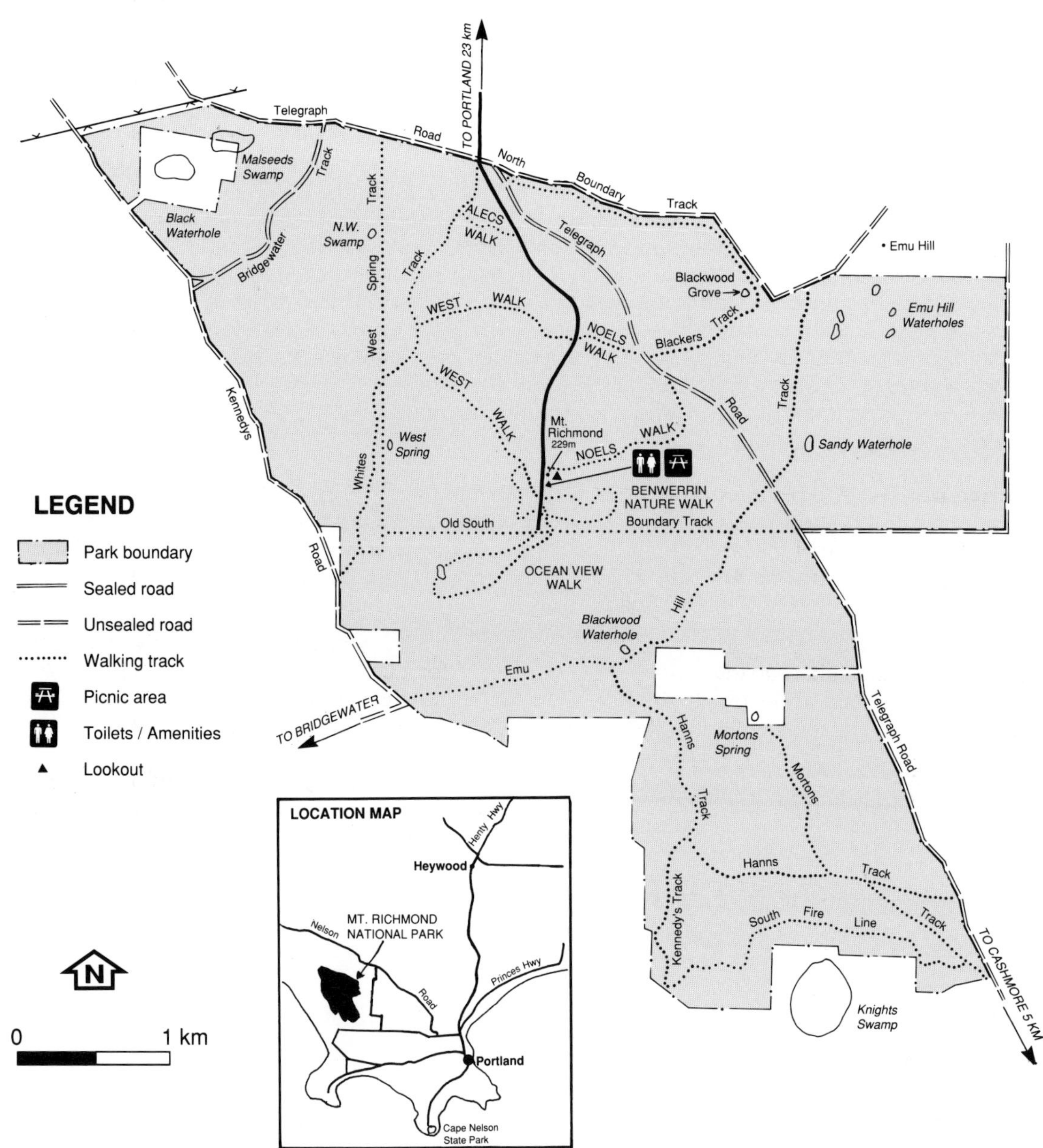

14 Mount Richmond National Park

Physical features: 1 733 ha. Mt Richmond, 229 m high, is one of many volcanic cones dotting the landscape in Western Victoria. There is little surface evidence of this today, however, since the tuff and scoria ejected by the volcano are now covered by a thick layer of windblown siliceous sand from Discovery Bay (see Cape Nelson SP). There are no creeks here. Instead, rain seeps down through the porous soils and forms swamps and wetlands at the lower levels. Although the Park is some distance from the coast, the low-lying land means that many of the onshore winds are still very salty.

Plants and animals: This Park is a botanical treasure trove with its sheer exuberance of spring colour and its unusual plants. These include Leafless Beard-orchid, which relies on a specialised fungus processing compost in the soil for its food; the Tiny Duckweed, which, at 1 mm, is our smallest flowering plant; and the Gippsland Mallee, more usually found where its name suggests. A wealth of plants usually means the same of birds and animals generally, and that is certainly so here – at least 100 species of birds including the magnificent Powerful Owl and the rare King Quail, as well as many small mammals, such as the Heath Rat. A good place to see a variety of plants and birds is along Noel's Walk, named after Noel Learmonth, one of the most active campaigners for the creation of the Park.

Human history: The first Europeans through here were the Henty brothers in 1835, who named the hill after one of their children. Fortunately the very sandy nature of the country generally discouraged clearing of the land, and the little that was cleared was soon abandoned. In 1857 the first telegraph line between Adelaide and Melbourne was constructed along what is now Telegraph Road, from which the Mt Richmond Road turns off.

Mt Richmond's botanical significance had long been recognised when, in the 1950's, the Portland Field Naturalists' Club, (already campaigning vigorously for a Lower Glenelg NP and increasingly alarmed by the scale of clearing in the Portland area) turned their attentions to Mt Richmond. This time their efforts were much more quickly rewarded and the Park was proclaimed in 1960.

Things to do: Climbing the lookout tower for magnificent views along the coast, and on a good day, as far as the Grampians; walking, including part of the Great South West Walk (see Lower Glenelg NP).

Best season to visit: Spring for a magnificent wildflower display; otherwise any.

Special features: The wealth of wildflowers and birds; the views.

Relevant reading:
Land Conservation Council (1972) *Report of the South-west Area 1.*
Learmonth N.F. 'Mount Richmond NP', *Victoria's Resources* (Sept–Nov 1968).

Further information:
C&E Regional Office, 8–12 Julia St, Portland, Vic 3305. Phone (055) 23 3232.
Friends' Group: See Lower Glenelg NP.

Heath Rat *AW*

15 Cape Nelson State Park

Physical features: 210 ha. This Park is at the tip of the prominent headland which separates Nelson and Bridgewater Bays, and which was formed in Recent times from dunes along an old coastline, stranded as the sea retreated. Over many thousands of years, the limestone from the shells in the sand was dissolved out by water seeping downwards, and then redeposited as hard secondary dune limestone, leaving a surface layer of silica-rich sand. This siliceous sand has since blown inland and is now found as sheets behind the dunes and in other sheltered areas. In the dune limestone at Cape Nelson, cross-bedding, indicating gently flowing water, can readily be seen. There is also some basalt underlying the dune limestone, from a small volcano that once erupted on Cape Nelson.

Plants and animals: The most notable plant here is the Soap Mallee which, though quite common in South Australia, occurs nowhere else in Victoria. It is a small tree, usually of mallee habitat, with large, flat-topped fruit, and is found growing away from the exposed cliff tops on dry, sandy rises. In the hollows between these rises are heathlands with many typical coastal plants such as Boobialla, White Correa and Coast Pomaderris, as well as the more fragile Morning-flag and the rare Maroon Leek-orchid. Where the shrubs are exposed to the strong salty winds they are severely pruned into elongated shapes which closely reflect the contours of the slope.

A number of the heathland shrubs yield good nectar and so attract many insect-feeding birds such as woodswallows, Grey Fantails and Southern Emu-wrens as well as the nectar-feeding honeyeaters and wattle-birds. Not far from the Park, at Lawrence Rocks off Point Danger, is one of Australia's few known breeding colonies of Australian Gannets and, as you walk along the cliff tops, these magnificent birds can often be seen diving into the sea below. Considering the speed at which they hit the water, it is not surprising that they need specially reinforced and cushioned skulls.

Human history: Much of the heathland in the western section of the Park is growing on land that was cleared in 1968, and windrows of dead vegetation can still be seen. The Park was declared largely to protect the stands of Soap Mallee, and to meet recreational needs.

Things to do: Enjoying the Sea Cliff Nature Walk, constructed by the National Parks Service and local students; sightseeing; walking, including the part of the Great South West Walk that goes through the Park (see Discovery Bay CP); visiting nearby Cape Bridgewater and viewing its blowholes and petrified forests.

Best season to visit: Any, although the exposed cliff tops are hot in summer.

Special features: The Soap Mallee; coastal scenery.

Relevant reading:
Land Conservation Council (1972) *Report of the South-west Area 1.*

Further information:
Ranger-in-Charge, 8–12 Julia St, Portland, Vic 3305. Phone (055) 23 3232.
Friends' Group: See Lower Glenelg NP.

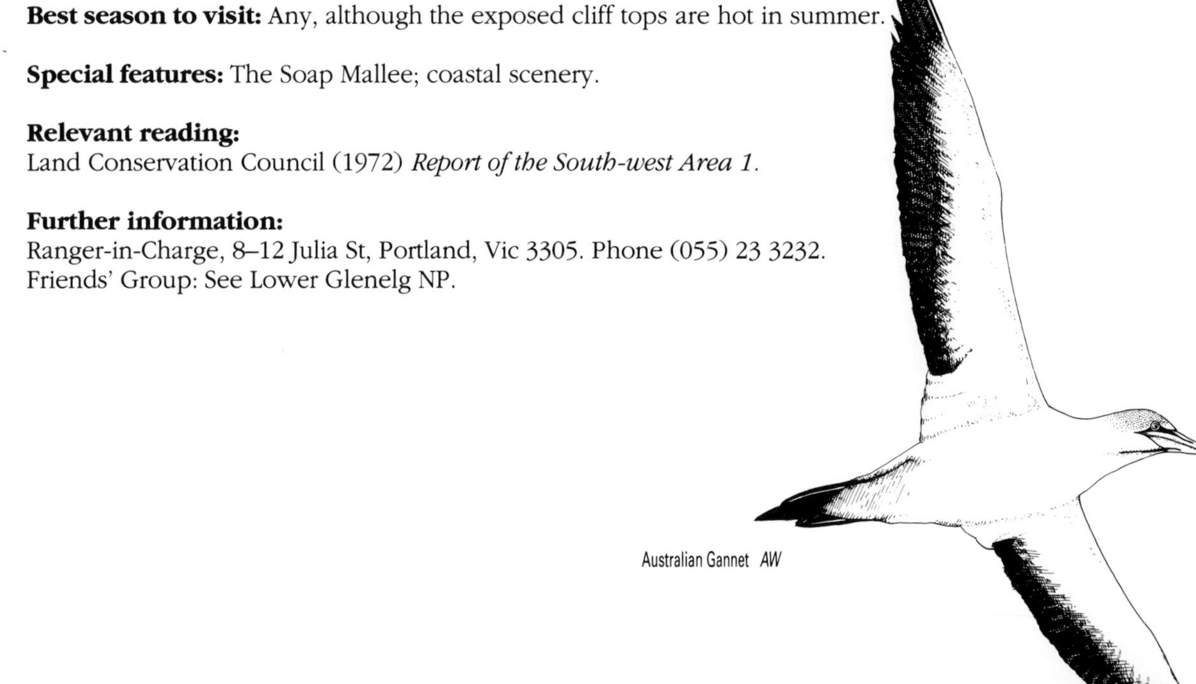

Australian Gannet *AW*

Cape Nelson

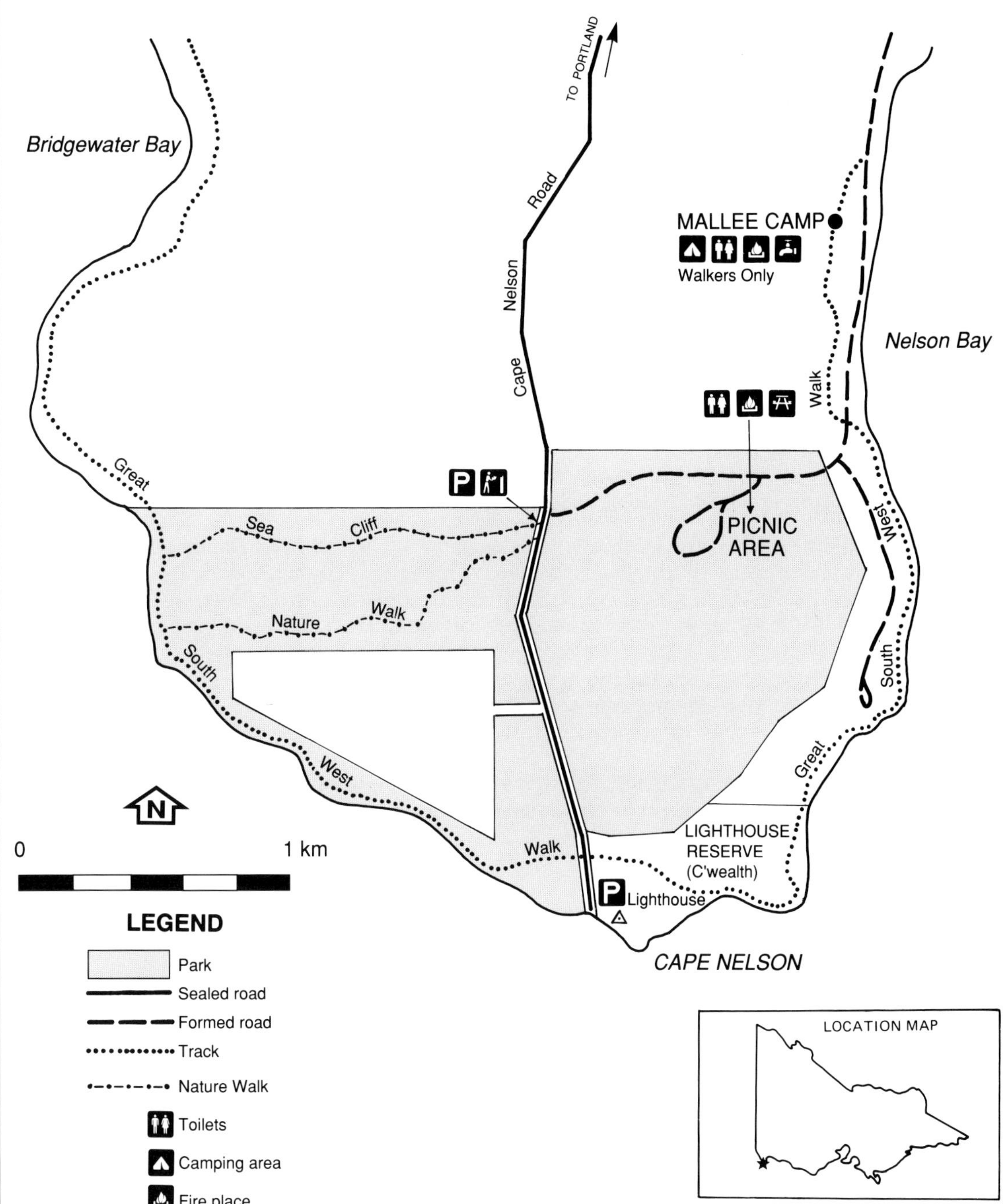

TO PORTLAND
Bridgewater Bay
Cape Nelson Road
MALLEE CAMP
Walkers Only
Nelson Bay
Walk
Great
Sea Cliff
Nature Walk
PICNIC AREA
West
South
South West
Great
LIGHTHOUSE RESERVE (C'wealth)
Walk
Lighthouse
CAPE NELSON
0
1 km
LEGEND
Park
Sealed road
Formed road
Track
Nature Walk
Toilets
Camping area
Fire place
LOCATION MAP

16 Mount Napier State Park

Physical features: 2 800 ha. This Park lies 15 km S of Hamilton, off the Hamilton to Macarthur Road. Like Mt Eccles NP, this Park has a number of fascinating volcanic features, including Mt Napier itself, a classically-shaped volcanic cone rising from a much older basalt plain; the Stony Rises, an eroded lava flow with rocks, blisters and hummocks; and the Byaduk Caves, lava caves which formed below the present ground level in very liquid lava. Mt Napier is 447 m high, with a crater 137 m across and 25 m deep. The almost perpendicular rim is breached on the NW side. Below this breach is a lava tunnel with stalactites of lava hanging from its roof. At a probable age of less than 7 000 years Mt Napier is almost certainly Victoria's youngest volcano. Nearly 40 eruption points have been mapped on the cone, but many of these would be hard to distinguish.

Plants and animals: When Major Thomas Mitchell climbed Mt Napier in 1836 he had to clear away luxuriant vegetation before he could set up his surveying instruments. Since then, however, the summit has been repeatedly burnt and grazed, and now is bare of all but grass and small plants for about the last 100 m. Below this are Manna Gums, tall and white-barked higher up, low and rough-barked near the base of the cone. Generally the flora and the birdlife is poor, although there are a number of interesting mosses and ferns (including the rare Willow Spleenwort) in the caves, particularly the Byaduk Caves. It is fascinating to see how the ferns gradually disappear as you go deeper into the caves away from the light. Deeper still, you may well pick up fungi in the beam of your torch. Of course, the caves provide good roosting areas for both owls and bats.

Many sub-fossil bones have been found in the Byaduk Caves, presumably left there by predators. In all, the remains of 25 species of mammals have been identified from the Caves, including the White-footed Rabbit-rat, and five others now extinct in Victoria. Surveys of living mammals have shown ten species now in the Mt Napier area, including many Dusky Antechinus and Bush Rats.

Human history: In spite of the very stony nature of the ground, the fertile volcanic soils provided good feed for stock and the area has been grazed and burnt for many years. Evidence of settlers attempting to clear the land of stones remains in the dry stone walls around the district.

Things to do: Exploring the caves and lava tunnel, but you do need a good torch; walking to the summit; visiting Devil's Hole, an explosion crater, and also the nearby quarry to see the layers of black cinders topped by red scoria; trying to visualise how this landscape must once have looked.

Best season to visit: Any time.

Special features: The caves with their distinctive atmosphere; the Willow Spleenwort.

Relevant reading:
Land Conservation Council (1972) *Report of the South-west Area 2.*
Victorian Naturalist Vol. 80, pp. 279–290, and Vol. 89, pp. 77–83.

Further information:
C&E Office, Thompson St, Hamilton, Vic 3300. Phone (055) 72 3033.

Tiger Quoll *AW*

17 Mount Eccles National Park

Physical features: 6 120 ha. In an area of basically low relief, rounded Mt Eccles and conical Mt Napier stand out very clearly and it is fascinating to try to visualise how the landscape that we see today came about. Twenty million years ago shallow seas began flooding in over the mudstones and other sedimentary rocks that now make up the bedrock of this area. By about six million years ago, a thick deep bed of marine limestone had been laid down. A long period of erosion then followed until 20 000 years ago when the area was rocked by massive earthquakes, and clouds of red hot ash and pumice shot high into the sky followed by molten magma flowing from fissures and weaknesses in the earth's crust.

The lava flow at Eccles was very fluid, and as it poured from the vent of the volcano it moved in wide, glowing rivers across the land along existing drainage lines, which then became blocked. It ultimately formed a plain to the southwest of nearly 100 square kilometres, which in turn is part of the 15 000 square kilometres of lava that makes up the world's third largest lava plain. A narrower tongue, the Tyrendarra Flow, extended down to the coast 30 km away, and then a further 19 km out to sea, a scenario not unlike the present-day Hawaiian eruptions.

The summit of Mt Eccles, 180 m above sea-level, consists of scoria, a frothy material that was light enough to be blown by the prevailing westerly winds as it issued from the crater and piled up into a 'pimple' on the edge of the main crater. Spurts of heavier basaltic material often followed, and depending on the force with which they were ejected, either ended some distance from the crater or just rolled down its sides, in still-molten form. Sometimes though, the molten spurts solidified on the outer walls of the crater and then pulled away pieces of crater wall as they too rolled down and joined the general debris. An early observer remarked how 'the stones and swamps of Mt Eccles and Mt Napier turn the traveller many miles out of his way, as no road can pass through such a desolate and rough district'.

As the lava rolled out and over the crater lip and along various channels, or canals, some of it spilled over on to the surrounding countryside, adding further layers to the lava plain. Within the channels, the upper surface sometimes skinned over, forming a roof, while the still molten interior flowed on and left a hollow tunnel behind it, the roof of which may or may not have remained intact. In the Canal, the molten interior retracted back into the crater as the flow lessened. In other places, side-flows developed, skinned over and then retracted, leaving caves such as Tunnel Cave. This cave is well worth visiting, with its black basalt walls, sometimes with benches marking different lava levels, and its stalactites of solidified lava. These formed when the heat of the lava flow in the tunnel melted the tunnel roof and the molten rock dripped down. Today, Tunnel Cave is cool and moist inside, an ideal microclimate for many ferns and for the strange curtain of Manna Gum roots that have grown down in search of water. In Gothic Cave, the layering of the lava walls is very contorted, indicating that the walls must have been intensely stressed before solidification was completed, though interestingly, the roof is not so.

There are many small cones, vents and craters around the main area of activity. These are more or less in a line, raising the question of whether this was a fissure eruption, a rare type that takes place at a number of points along a line of weakness in the earth's crust, or whether all the vents are just subsidiaries of the main magma chamber. Altogether, Mt Eccles is a most complicated and interesting volcano.

The most visually impressive feature of Mt Eccles NP today is the last formed – the beautiful and tranquil Lake Surprise that lies within three blocked crater vents 30 m below the crater rim. No streams flow in or out of the lake, and since its level varies only slightly throughout the year, it is presumably fed by an underground source.

Altogether the period of volcanic activity lasted until only about 6 000 years ago, and there are many vulcanologists who maintain that until a volcanic area has been inactive for at least 10 000 years there is still a possibility of further activity!

Mount Eccles

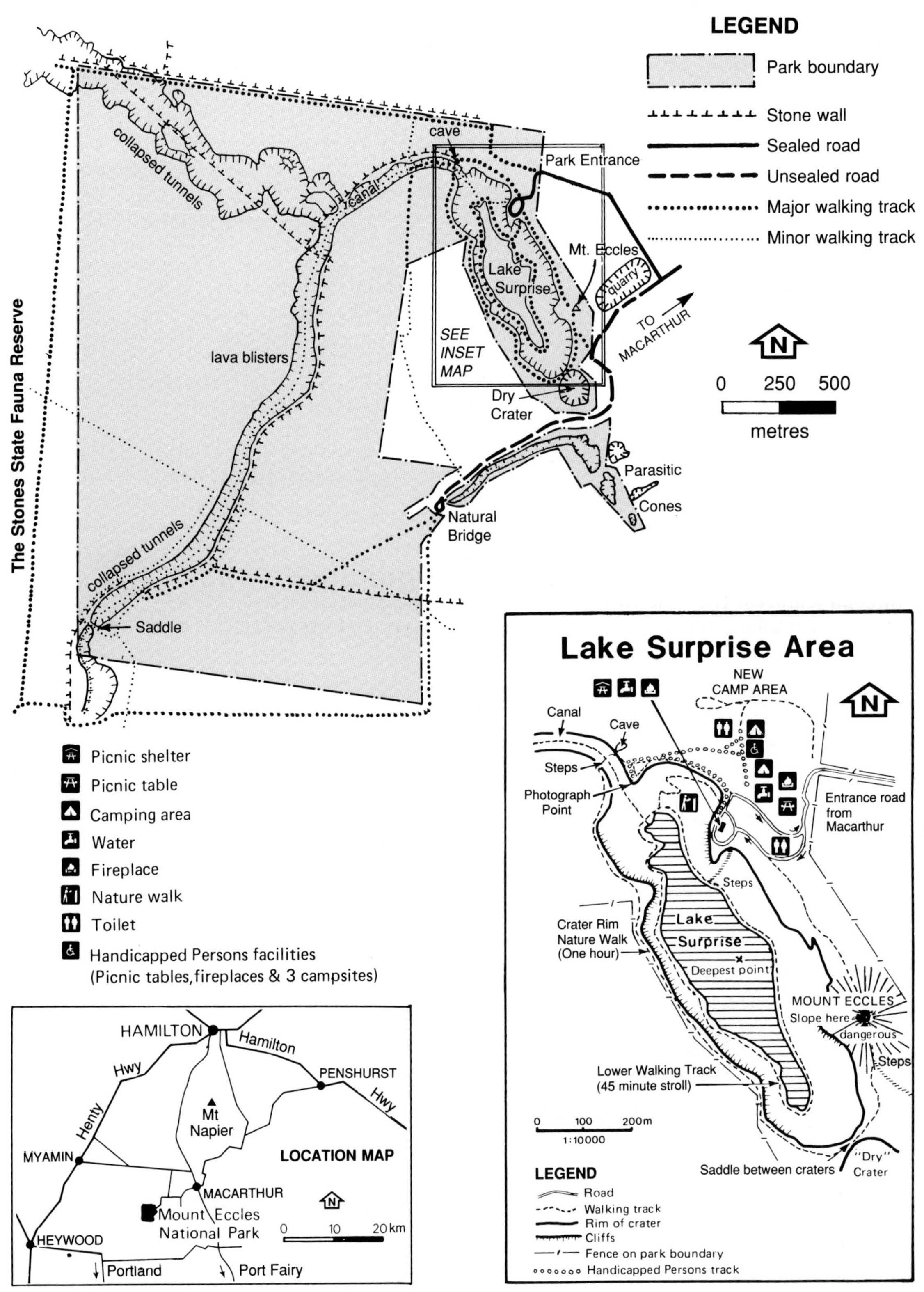

Plants and animals: The sides of Mt Eccles are still tree-covered with Manna Gums, Blackwood and Black Wattle, some Cherry Ballart and a variety of small understorey plants. Overall, there is not a great variety of plants, and many of them are introduced weeds. Perhaps the most interesting plant community is that found within the caves, where ferns are abundant. A delicate filmy fern, the Veined Bristle-fern, is of particular interest. Animal life is also rather sparse, though Tiger Quolls are reported from here. There are a number of bush birds and, down at Lake Surprise, some water birds also.

Human history: Aboriginal myths from Western Victoria tell of happenings that could well be explained by volcanic eruptions. Certainly the anthropological evidence points to Aborigines having been in Western Victoria well before 7 000 years ago. At nearby Lake Condah (formed by lava flows from Mt Eccles damming creeks and streams in the area) the remains of permanent houses have been found – a hunter-gatherer people can settle in any one area only when it offers permanent food. The first recorded sighting of Mt Eeles, as it was known until 1855 when a mis-spelling rendered it 'Eccles', was probably by Matthew Flinders in 1802 who noted but did not name, 'a round hill' in the locality of Mt Eccles. The area was settled in the mid-1840's with the seemingly inevitable conflict between the resident Aborigines and the settlers. In one particularly tragic series of events, a family group of about 30 Aborigines was all but wiped out in reprisal for the death of a shepherd.

Things to do: Walking around the crater edge, and to Trig Point on Mt Eccles, for a view of the surrounding countryside as far as Port Fairy and Lady Julia Percy Island (itself a flat lava flow); exploring Tunnel Cave and the Canal; camping; caving; swimming in Lake Surprise. Mt Eccles NP is not a park to hurry through; it really does take time to absorb all that is here.

Best season to visit: Any.

Special features: The wide range of well-preserved volcanic formations, including the appropriately named Lake Surprise; being able to enter the magma chamber of an extinct volcano.

Relevant reading:

Bonwick J. (reprint 1970) *Western Victoria: its Geography, Geology and Social Condition.*
Land Conservation Council (1972) *Report of the South-west Area 1.*
National Parks Service *Mt Eccles NP Information Booklet.*
Victorian Naturalist (1968) Vol. 85, No. 12, pp. 350–356.

Further information:

Ranger-in-Charge, 21 Huntly St, Macarthur, Vic 3286. Phone (055) 76 1042.

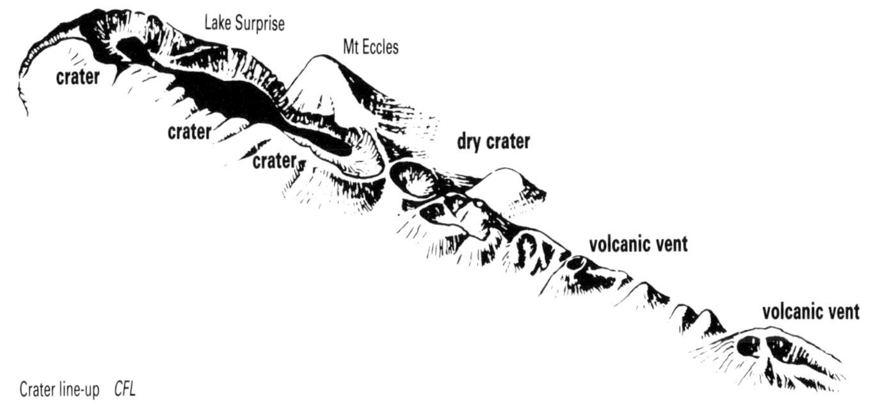

Crater line-up *CFL*

Port Campbell

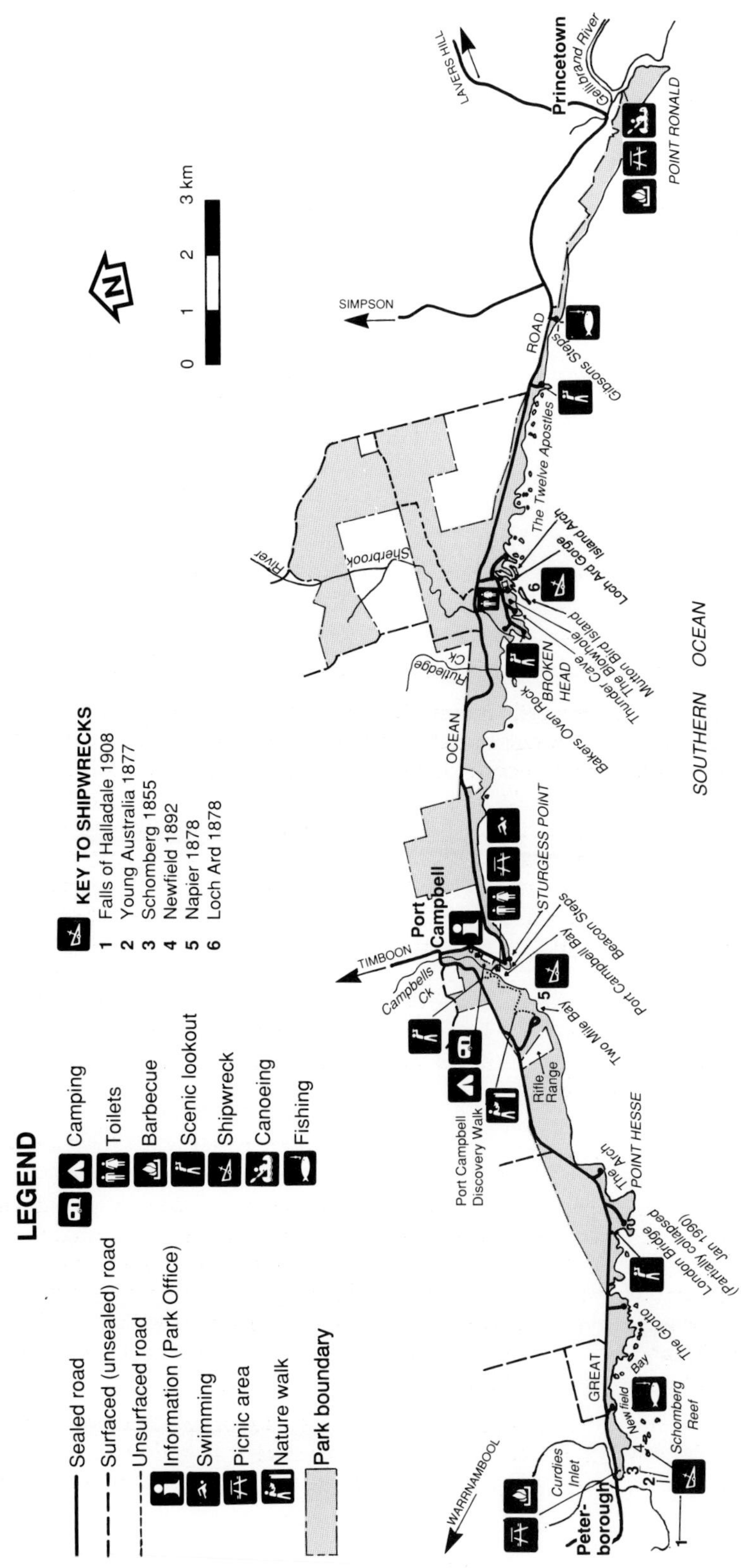

18 Port Campbell National Park

Physical features: 1 750 ha. This Park is very much a linear one, running 27 km along the southern coast of Victoria and only a bare 4 km at its widest. Driving along the Great Ocean Road, on a near level plain clothed in windswept vegetation, there is little to see until you follow one of the signposts and go down a side road to the cliff edge. And then there they are – massive limestone cliffs rising out of the sea to a height of nearly 70 m, with huge isolated stacks of rock and fragile-looking arches stretching out into an always turbulent ocean.

The limestone, including some important fossils, was laid down in flat beds from about 26 million years ago, into a massive layer over 250 m thick. It is only in the last 5 000–7 000 years that the erosion that we see today has been taking place. Before that the sea-level was 100 m or so lower. The limestone has weaknesses along the flat bedding planes and also along vertical joints, and it is on these weaknesses that the power of the sea works, compressing air in the cracks and cavities with the force of a mighty jack-hammer. Added to this is chemical weathering – sea water is some ten times more erosive than fresh water. The softer areas of rock and those most exposed to the force of the waves gradually crumble away, until formations which are now joined to the land become isolated stacks and islands, as was the case with London Bridge early in 1990.

Plants and animals: Although it is undoubtedly the spectacular coastal scenery that has earned this Park its reputation as one of Victoria's most popular tourist destinations, there is also plenty of natural history interest. There are a number of different plant communities, from the most obvious, the heathland at the top of the cliffs, to the wetlands of Lower Sherbrooke River and Campbells Creek. There are 24 plant species of conservation significance, though many of these are small and somewhat insignificant to look at. In the eastern part of the Park there is one of the few remnant areas of the once widespread Heytesbury Forest, and also the vegetation of the basalt plains.

As in other parks, most of the mammals are generally inconspicuous, except for the Eastern Grey Kangaroo and Swamp Wallaby. Because of the range of habitats, from open sea to inland scrub, this is a good place for birds, almost 100 having been recorded, including the Beautiful Firetail, Fairy Penguin and Rufous Bristle-bird. It is an excellent place to see birds of prey including that prince of raptors, the Peregrine Falcon. Mutton-bird Island took its name from the colony of Short-tailed Shearwaters (Mutton-birds) that nest here after returning from the North Pacific, where they spend our winter. The return takes place in late September. In 1798 Matthew Flinders reported an uninterrupted black 'cloud' of Mutton-birds flying east which took more than five hours to pass an observation point on the Victorian coast – an estimated 151 500 000 birds! The Mutton-birds may be in an emaciated condition after their long journey, and if there is a food shortage when they arrive, large numbers die. Little Fairy Penguins also nest in the Park, but because of damage from trampled burrows and dogs (which should not have been brought into the Park) the nesting area has been closed off to the public. There are a number of reptiles and amphibians too, including the rare Mourning Skink which is restricted to heathy swamps.

Human history: The large number of shell middens along this coast show that it was popular with the Aboriginal people, and in some places they cut steps down the cliffs to reach the rich wave-platforms below. No doubt the whalers and sealers at the end of the 18th century were also familiar with this coast, but there are no records until those of Matthew Flinders, who named Moonlight Head in 1802. Land was taken up from the middle of the 1840's, actual settlement beginning in about the 1870's. From then on the tiny township of Port Campbell slowly grew, but it was very isolated, all supplies having to be brought in by sea. For many years, fishing was Port Campbell's mainstay, until in 1932 the Great Ocean Road was opened and tourists were able to reach what is now one of Australia's best known stretches of coastline.

It is not just the scenery, though, for which this coastline is famous, but also for its tragic but fascinating shipwrecks, the most notable of which is undoubtedly the *Loch Ard,* wrecked in 1878. The fastest sea route to Melbourne involved a massive leg from the Cape of Good Hope at the southern tip of Africa across to Cape Otway, with no landfalls in between with which to check navigational accuracy. It was easy to be slightly off-course, or to mistake one lighthouse for another, or even not to see the light at all because of heavy fog, as was the case on that fateful night of 1 June 1878. When the *Loch Ard* hit the island just west of today's Loch Ard Gorge, she was soon overwhelmed by the massive seas, and all but two of the 54 aboard were drowned. The dramatic story of Tom Pearce's rescue of Eva Carmichael is told on the sign above the Gorge, and soon captures the imagination of all who read it. Only four bodies were ever recovered; they are buried in the nearby cemetery on the windswept cliff top. The wrecks of both the *Loch Ard* and the *Schomberg*, lost on her maiden voyage in 1855, have been located and are now classified under the Commonwealth Historic Shipwrecks Act 1976.

A nearby homestead, *Glenample*, where Eva Carmichael spent time recovering from her ordeal, is now being restored by Conservation and Environment as a Shipwreck Information Centre.

This coastline was first given protection as a reserve at the end of last century, but it was not until it attained national park status in 1964 that the emphasis shifted from just scenic values to a recognition of its important conservation potential. The majority of its 300 000 visitors, though, are far more interested in the scenery than in the natural history, and catering for their needs while still protecting the flora and fauna is not an easy task. The Port Campbell coast is one of the seven Victorian tourism 'resort zones' and will doubtless attract ever-increasing numbers of visitors. These conflicts have recently been addressed in a Proposed Management Plan for the Park.

Things to do: Visiting both the Port Campbell NP Information Centre, where there are many interesting displays and relics, including an anchor from the *Loch Ard,* and also the many scenic and historic sites, especially Loch Ard Gorge. Generally, walking is somewhat limited in this Park, but there is the Discovery Walk, and there are proposals to construct a track of about 8 km between Port Campbell and Lower Sherbrooke River. Photography; fishing; diving and swimming (but from only a few beaches, and then only when the weather is calm).

Best season to visit: Any; winter, though it can be cold and windy, is an ideal time to see the coast as it was when many of the ships were wrecked. During onshore gales, waves all but reach the clifftops – a truly spectacular sight.

Special features: The magnificent coastal scenery, which changes character dramatically as the light and weather conditions alter. The sense of isolation, best if you're there when few others are!

Relevant reading:

Charlwood D. (1978) *Settlers Under Sail.*
Conservation, Forests and Lands (1988) *Port Campbell NP Proposed Management Plan.*
Land Conservation Council (1976) *Report of the Corangamite Area.*
Loney J. (1967) *Shipwrecks along the Great Ocean Road* and (1970) *The Loch Ard Disaster.*

Further information:
Port Campbell NP, Tregea St, Port Campbell, Vic 3269. Phone (055) 98 6382.

▲ Surf-fishing, Port Campbell NP *P&LJA*

▲ Ground Parrot *ARI*

▼ Stony Rises near Lake Condah, Mt Eccles NP *RKF*

▲ Lake Surprise, Mt Eccles NP *MT*

◀ Evening at Loch Ard, Port Campbell NP *JAC*
▼ Pink Heath *DC*

◀ Glenelg River, Lower Glenelg NP *P&LJA*

▼ Lerderderg SP *P&LJA*

▲ Ghost Fungus *DMC*

19 Otway National Park and Melba Gully State Park

Physical features: 12 750 ha (Otway NP) and 65 ha (Melba Gully SP). Otway NP and the adjacent Otway State Forest are rather like an island, isolated to the north by the basalt plain and to the south by Bass Strait. There is no comparable country closer than 400 km away. Access to this part of Victoria is still very limited, which adds to the feeling of remoteness, although the Great Ocean Road has now been upgraded to accommodate tourist buses and to give faster access to the attractions of the Port Campbell coast.

The Otway Range runs 80 km in a SW direction, with two branches, one running down to Cape Otway and the other to Lavers Hill near Melba Gully. The slopes are significantly steeper to the south, where the streams are shorter and swifter, often with attractive waterfalls (many of them outside the Park). The streams to the north are slower and gentler and many of them have been harvested to provide water to cities such as Geelong and Colac.

The geology here is generally older than that of the Port Campbell area, and its Lower Cretaceous sediments are harder and less prone to erosion, with the result that the coastline, although very spectacular, does not have the arches and stacks of further west. The sandstones and shales of the Otway Group were laid down in the Otway Basin, a vast downwarped area that formed as the Gondwana landmass began to pull apart 150 million years ago. The sea periodically transgressed over, and regressed from, the nearby land, which was ultimately uplifted into a complex domal structure, reflected today in the radial nature of the streams draining the Range. The sediments along the coast are proving a rich source of both animal and plant fossils, with valuable evidence coming to light on the evolutionary history of dinosaurs and flowering plants. The earliest known fossils of those important Australian plants, the acacias, have also been found here.

The climate is temperate, though changeable, rain falling mostly in winter. North of the Park is Victoria's wettest settlement, Weeaproinah, which averages nearly 2 000 mm and sometimes receives as much as 2 700 mm of rain in a year.

Plants and animals: The Otways are best known for their towering Mountain Ash forests and lush tree fern gullies, often with Myrtle Beech (some estimated to be 2 000 years old). This cool temperate rainforest only occurs where there are sheltered conditions and a sufficiently high rainfall. Though we may well marvel at the forest that we see there today, this is little more than a shadow of what was there before fire, clearing and timber-getting took their toll of the forest giants.

As well as the tall wet forests, there are also drier open forests, with shorter trees and a heathy understorey, on the more exposed slopes and on the sands flanking the Ranges. Along the coast are typical low coastal shrubs and grasslands, similar to those further west. Many of the Otways plants show affinities with those of Tasmania, with which this area was once joined, and with the tall wet forests of Gippsland. Plants at their westernmost limit include the Forest Boronia and the Skirted Treefern, while the beautiful Satinwood, a feature of an Otways spring, is otherwise only found in Tasmania. Interestingly though, Southern Sassafras does not occur here.

With the animals there is as much interest in what is absent as in what is here – there are no wombats or Superb Lyrebirds and their associated Pilot-birds, for instance, and it would seem that only those species capable of bridging the ecological gap from other similar areas have been able to colonise the Otways. In all there are nearly 250 bird species, of which over half breed here. A number of others are migrants: from the Arctic, the Knot; from the Antarctic, the Wandering Albatross; from New Zealand, the Fluttering Shearwater; and from Eurasia, the Japanese Snipe. The 45 native mammals include the Tiger Cat and ten species of bat. There are 20 reptiles, some of which are characteristic of southern Australia, others of more arid areas, and there are 15 amphibians and 50 fish. Among the invertebrates are a rare carnivorous snail, the Otways Black-snail, which is quite often seen in the wet forests, and the beautiful and somewhat mysterious glowworms (larvae of the Fungus Gnat) at Melba Gully dangling their sticky 'fishing lines' to capture their prey.

Otway and Melba Gully

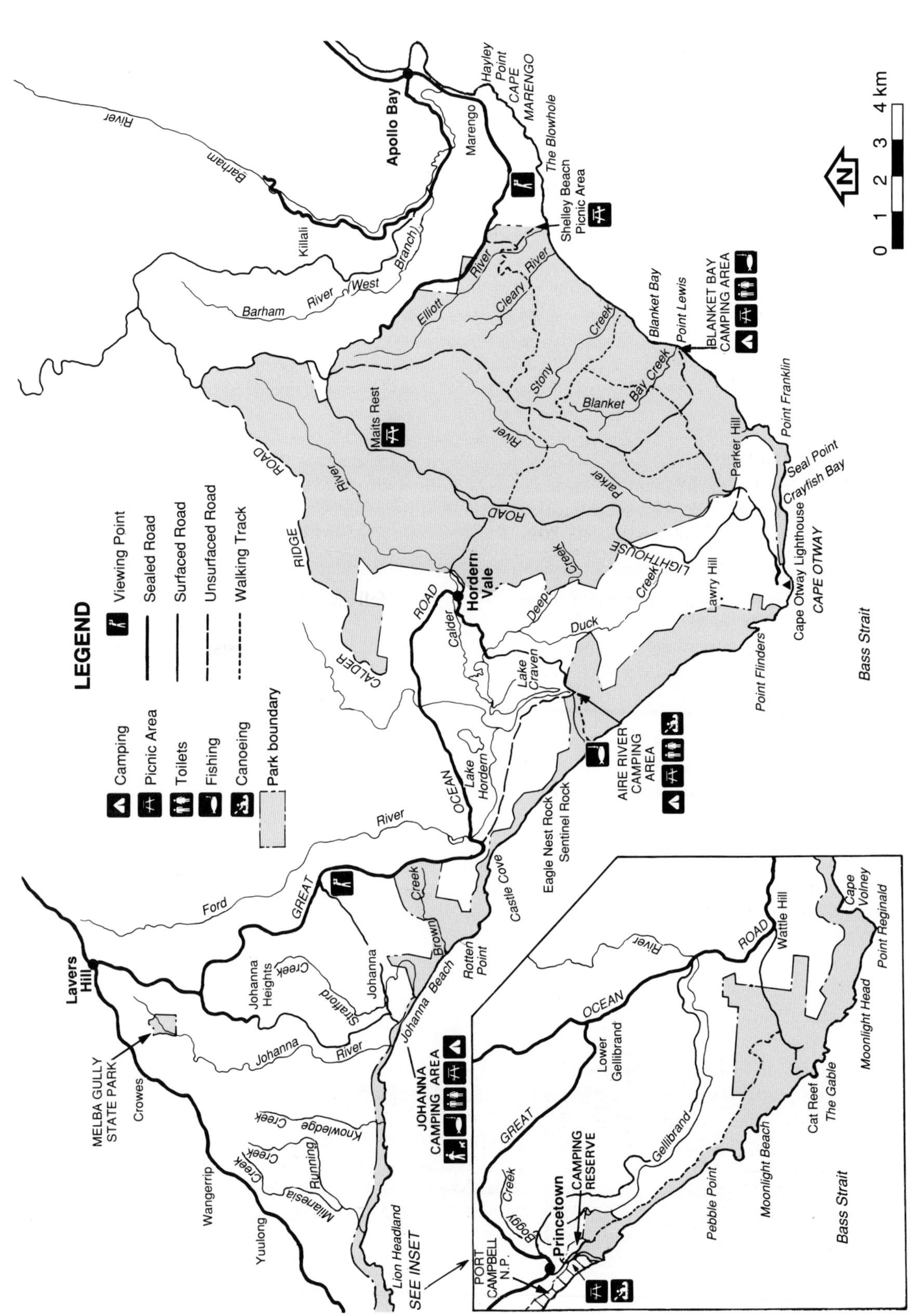

Human history: The first Europeans to see the Otways were probably seafarers such as sealers and whalers, followed by Matthew Flinders, who named the Cape in 1802. The coastline soon made its treacherous nature apparent, but in 1846 Charles La Trobe finally succeeded in reaching the Cape and selecting a site for a lighthouse. By 1848, after a number of trials, including the wrecking of one of the supply boats, the lighthouse began operating.

By now the magnificent timber of the Otways was also becoming known, and mills were gradually established, the first at Apollo Bay in 1852. For three years before that, timber had been pitsawn on site, then dragged to the sea by bullocks and finally floated out to the waiting ships. One of the mills sited in what is now the Otway NP was at Elliot River, from where logs were sent to Apollo Bay, 6 km away, on horse-drawn tramway. Part of this tramway can still be seen, as can sleepers from the tramway in Melba Gully that took Blackwood timber out to the Victorian Railways narrow-gauge line for making staves for tallow barrels.

The establishment of Otway NP resulted from the Government's acceptance of Land Conservation Council recommendations for this area, which in turn recognised its high biological, historical and landscape values. Although the creation of the Park was welcomed, there were also some doubts expressed as to whether its boundaries were dictated more by timber than by ecological values, the omission of stream waters being a case in point, and there is certainly a strong case that the West Barham Valley, with its tall and ancient trees, should be included in the Park.

Things to do: Sightseeing; visiting the lighthouse, but phone ahead first; camping; surfing, particularly at Johanna Beach and Castle Cove; fishing; walking. A number of walks such as the one down from Cape Horn, and the Nature Walk through Melba Gully, pass through a variety of environments. Join a guided walk to see the glow worms at Melba Gully but remember they are very sensitive to noise and light. For those who like the sea there are exhilarating beach walks, though you do need to keep an eye on the tide.

Best season to visit: Any, but this is an area of high rainfall and changeable weather.

Special features: The magnificence and sheer wealth of green in the forests; the spectacular coastal scenery; the tranquillity of the Parker estuary.

Relevant reading:
Land Conservation Council (1976) *Report of the Corangamite Area.*
Pescott T. (1976) *The Otways.*
Houghton N. (1975) *Sawdust and Steam.*

Further information:
C&E Office, Cartwright St, Apollo Bay (for Otway NP and Melba Gully SP), Vic 3233.
Phone (052) 37 6889.
Friends' Group: Phone (052) 37 6230.

Coastal rocks *AB*

20 Carlisle State Park

Physical features: 5 600 ha. This Park lies on the north-western flank of the Otway Ranges, Gellibrand and Carlisle River. Its rocks are mainly Tertiary sediments, and are therefore younger than those making up the bulk of the Otway NP. It includes isolated areas of high-level plateau country; these have a layer of hard weathered material under the surface which causes the land to be poorly drained and swampy, and 'hanging swamps' are a feature of Carlisle SP. Rainfall and temperature are adequate for year-round growth, but the soils are infertile and therefore the land was not cleared for agriculture.

Plants and animals: The trees, generally Shining Peppermint and Brown Stringybark, with some Red Ironbark, are mostly short and widely spaced over a shrubby understorey. There are also large areas of wet heathland and Button-grass swamps. Birds are numerous, especially honeyeaters, which find the shrubs useful as sheltered nesting sites, as well as providing a rich source of nectar and insects. An important bird here is the Ground Parrot, which feeds largely on Button-grass. It is a small, yellow-green parrot with suprisingly long legs, which allow it to run through the undergrowth rather than to waddle as most parrots do, although it will fly when flushed out. It is largely nocturnal and can often be found by listening for its clear, spaced, bell-like call at dawn and dusk. Small mammals such as the Bush Rat and Antechinus, as well as a number of reptiles, are also found here.

Human history: This Park, and a Flora and Fauna Reserve further south near Carlisle River, escaped clearing in the 1880's when pressure for land led the Government to release large areas for selection in the Otway district. The Park was recommended both on the grounds of its conservation values (particularly for the rare Ground Parrot) and for its recreational potential.

Things to do: Walking; birdwatching. There are no facilities available yet in this Park.

Best season to visit: Spring for wildflowers; otherwise any season.

Special features: The chance of seeing a Ground Parrot, especially in the Button-grass swamps.

Relevant reading:
Land Conservation Council (1976) *Report of the Corangamite Area.*

Further information:
C&E Office, Charlie's Creek Rd, Gellibrand, Vic 3250. Phone (052) 358 301.

Dusky Wood Swallow *RAOU*

Carlisle

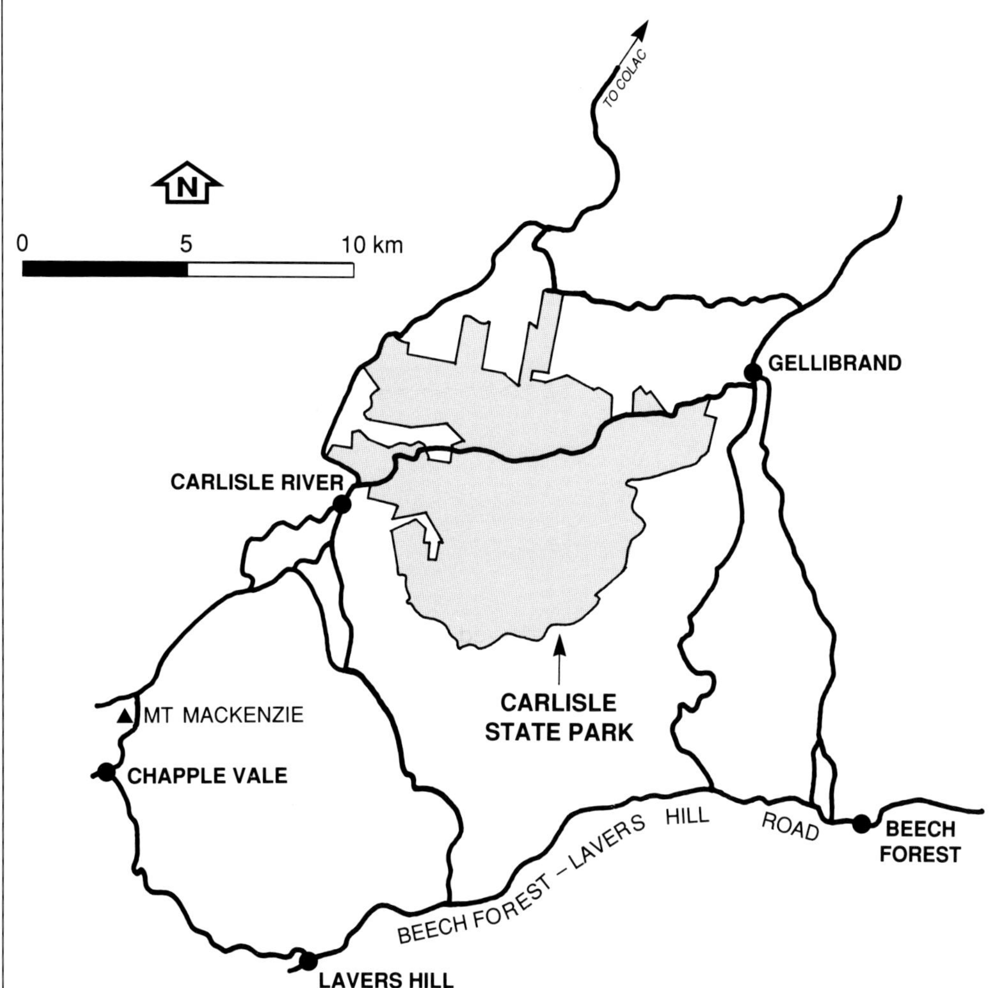
TO COLAC
N
0
5
10 km
GELLIBRAND
CARLISLE RIVER
CARLISLE
STATE PARK
MT MACKENZIE
CHAPPLE VALE
BEECH FOREST – LAVERS HILL ROAD
BEECH
FOREST
LAVERS HILL

Angahook-Lorne

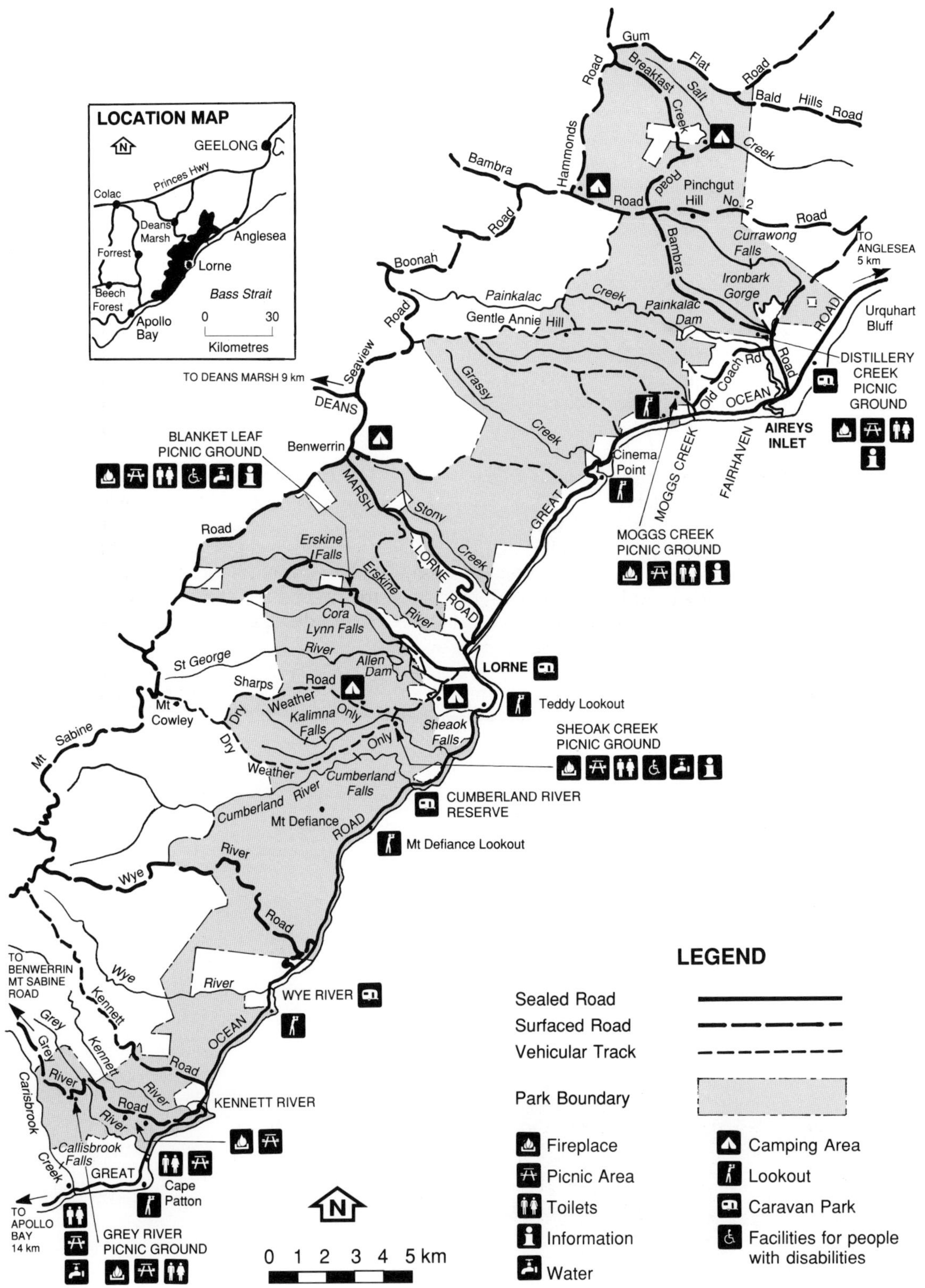

21 Angahook-Lorne State Park

Physical features: 21 000 ha. This Park was created by joining Angahook and Lorne Forest Parks, and since much of it is effectively a coastal extension eastwards of the Otway NP, there are many physical features in common with the Otways. In Angahook-Lorne the sediments outcrop along the coast and are exposed by marine erosion. They are non-marine and are made up of alternating bands of evenly-bedded mudstones and sandstones, the youngest outcrops in the east. Active coastal erosion and comparatively recent uplift of the land means that the rivers have not formed terraces; instead, many enter the sea as waterfalls. Some of the slopes into the sea are unstable, so landslips can occur along the Great Ocean Road. On the beaches there are fine rock platforms. The climate is temperate, and some of the eastern Park falls within the Otway rainshadow.

Plants and animals: Both the vegetation and fauna are very diverse here, ranging from wet mountain forests to dry open heathlands. Overall, this Park has one of the richest floras in Victoria, including heathland orchids that are of international significance. In the east there are biological links with the Grampians, and in the west with Tasmania. A local naturalist group, Angair, has surveyed the area extensively since the 1983 Ash Wednesday fires and found that no plant species have been lost, and that at least one plant – Wrinkled Buttons – previously thought extinct here has reappeared. The mammals and birds have also have made a remarkable post-fire recovery. Moggs Creek, struck by a fire tornado, and Ironbark Gully show good examples of post-fire regeneration.

Human history: Much of this is similar to that of Otway NP, early development being based around timber. By 1900 the Lorne area had become popular for holidays, especially with Western District people. Guesthouses and hotels were soon scattered along the coast, and when the Great Ocean Road was opened in 1932, Melburnians began to arrive in greater numbers. At first the Road had toll gates, and two sites can still be seen at Grassy Creek and Castries Point, as can a freshwater tank near Cathedral Rock, and an explosives store at Castries Point. Walking tracks to the waterfalls and scenic attractions were constructed. Some of these fell into disrepair when Lorne declined in the late 1950's but they have since been restored and improved.

Things to do: Driving; walking; picnicking; horseriding; swimming; surfing and fishing.

Best season to visit: Spring for wildflowers in the eastern section; otherwise any time.

Special features: Coastal scenery; waterfalls; ferns at Grey River; post-fire regeneration.

Relevant reading:
Conservation, Forests and Lands (1987) *Angahook-Lorne State Park Resource Inventory.*
Land Conservation Council (1976) *Report of the Corangamite Area.*

Further information:
C&E Regional Office, cnr Fenwick & Lt Malop Sts, Geelong, Vic 3220. Phone (052) 26 4667.
Angair: Phone (052) 63 1975.

White headed Petrel *RAOU*

MELBOURNE PARKS

Being close to Melbourne, nearly all these parks suffer from people-pressure. As a result, they need very sensitive management, as well as great care from their visitors. Since it is abundantly clear that people care most for what they have grown to love and feel a special affinity for, a significant amount of time and effort is put into ranger-guided walks and interpretation programs that build on children's love of the outdoors. It's always worth checking, therefore, to see what activities might be planned for the time you intend visiting a particular park (and of course that does not apply only to 'Melbourne' parks).

	Page No.	*Entrance Fee*	*Information Centre*	*Multilingual Information*	*Picnic Areas*	*Fireplaces*	*Toilets*	*Disabled Access*	*Walking Tracks*	*Nature Walk or Drive*	*Swimming*	*Climbing*	*Horseriding*	*Fishing*	*Boating*	*Camping*	*Caravans*	*Km from Melbourne*	*Date Declared*
Arthurs Seat	117	■			■	■	■	■	■	■						■		70	1988
Brisbane Ranges	72				■	■	■		■							■		80	1973
Churchill	104				■	■	■		■									32	1941
Dandenong Ranges	91	■			■	■	■	■	■	■			■					26	1987
French Island	106				■	■	■		■					■				65	1988
Gellibrand Hill	82		■		■	B	■	■	■	■			■					20	1981
Kinglake	85	■	■		■	■	■	■	■	■						■		65	1928
Yea River	85				■	■				■				■				65	1979
Langwarrin	100				■				■				■					42	1985
Lerderderg	71				■	■	■		■		■	■				■		75	1988
Long Forest	81								■									50	1985
Lysterfield	102	■	■		■	■	■	■	■		■	■	■		■			35	1981
Point Nepean	111	■	■		■	■	■	■	■	■	■		■	■	■			100	1988
Phillip Island	108	■	■		■	■	■	■										140	1985
Organ Pipes	88			★	■	B	■	■	■	■								20	1971
Steiglitz	79				■		■											88	1979
Warrandyte	94				■		■				■		■	■	■			24	1985
Werribee Gorge	67				■	■	■	P	■		■	■						65	1975

★ = in preparation **B** = barbeque (gas) **P** = Proposed

22 Werribee Gorge State Park

Physical features: 375 ha. Four of the parks in the Melbourne area – Brisbane Ranges NP, Steiglitz HP, Werribee Gorge SP and Lerderderg Gorge SP – share a similar geological history and so the physical features of all four are included here.

The country around Bacchus Marsh became world famous about the middle of last century as one of the places where ancient glacial deposits could be readily studied, but this is only one of many fascinating aspects of the geology of this part of Victoria. Werribee Gorge, which is almost 300 m deep, shows a profile of over 500 million years of geological history within its walls.

The deepest, oldest rocks exposed are Ordovician marine slates and sandstones which are now tightly folded and steeply inclined. Looking rather like piles of crumpled ribbon, they are easily seen in the bed of the Werribee river as you walk up the main track through the Park. About 100 million years after the deposition of these rocks there was a period of strong earth movements which caused a weakening in the earth's crust and allowed molten magma to intrude into the upper crust. This material did not reach the surface, but cooled slowly into a coarse-grained granite, buried deep beneath insulating layers of rock. Where this hot magma came into contact with the surrounding bedrock, it metamorphosed or 'cooked' the existing rock into a contact zone of hornfels, a medium to fine-grained granular rock. In some cases the molten rock squeezed along cracks in the bedrock forming vertical dykes of hard, dense, pale grey rock with relatively large crystals of smoky grey quartz. This igneous rock, which is known as quartz porphyry and which weathers to an orange colour, can easily be seen as a large dyke either side of the river about two kilometres upstream from the Werribee Gorge picnic ground. It was this period of weakening of the earth's crust and penetration of molten magma into the sedimentary rocks that led to the gold mineralisation that is so much a part of the history of nearby Steiglitz.

A long period of erosion followed, and then the climate cooled. Ice gradually built up to a great thickness over the land. Rocks embedded in the ice scraped over underlying rocks, and both became polished and scratched with lines that now tell us which way the ice was moving. Finally, the glaciers melted and deposited their load – a mixture of boulders, pebbles and rock flour. This later consolidated into the multi-coloured rock known as tillite which can be seen in the quarry on the right of Myers Road on the way down to the Werribee Gorge picnic ground.

Following this glaciation, erosion continued for many millions of years until practically the whole of Victoria was reduced to a vast, featureless plain. This was followed by the laying down of non-marine sandstones to a depth of about 100 m. Some of these sediments contain plant fossils which enabled the great age of the underlying glacial deposits to be calculated. Above these sandstones is a further 100 metres of various sediments, followed in some parts by a capping of basaltic lava from outpourings which began about 70 million years ago and continued until only about one million years ago. The more recent of these flows came from cones such as Mt Darriwell, 8 km north-east, and Mt Blackwood, 12 km north of Werribee Gorge, and are comparable to the flows that led to the formation of the columns of the Organ Pipes. Most of these basaltic flows have now eroded away, but some small cappings can be seen on the south side, high above Werribee Gorge.

Last in this long sequence of geological events comes the one that enables us to see and interpret all that has been going on – the uplift of the land within the last million years. This gave the rivers and streams new impetus to carve deep down through the layers of surrounding rock. There are five distinct earthblocks which were brought about by this process. The Rowsley Fault is easily seen as you approach and drive up into the Brisbane Ranges. Fortunately for us today, the soils derived from the rocks in the region are generally very poor and infertile, and so the land has not been cleared for farming.

Plants and animals: Much of the vegetation of Werribee Gorge and therefore its animals and birds are similar to the Brisbane Ranges, but there is one special bird 'treat' to be found high up on the cliffs of this spectacular Park – the nesting sites of the Peregrine Falcon. This magnificent falcon has

Werribee Gorge

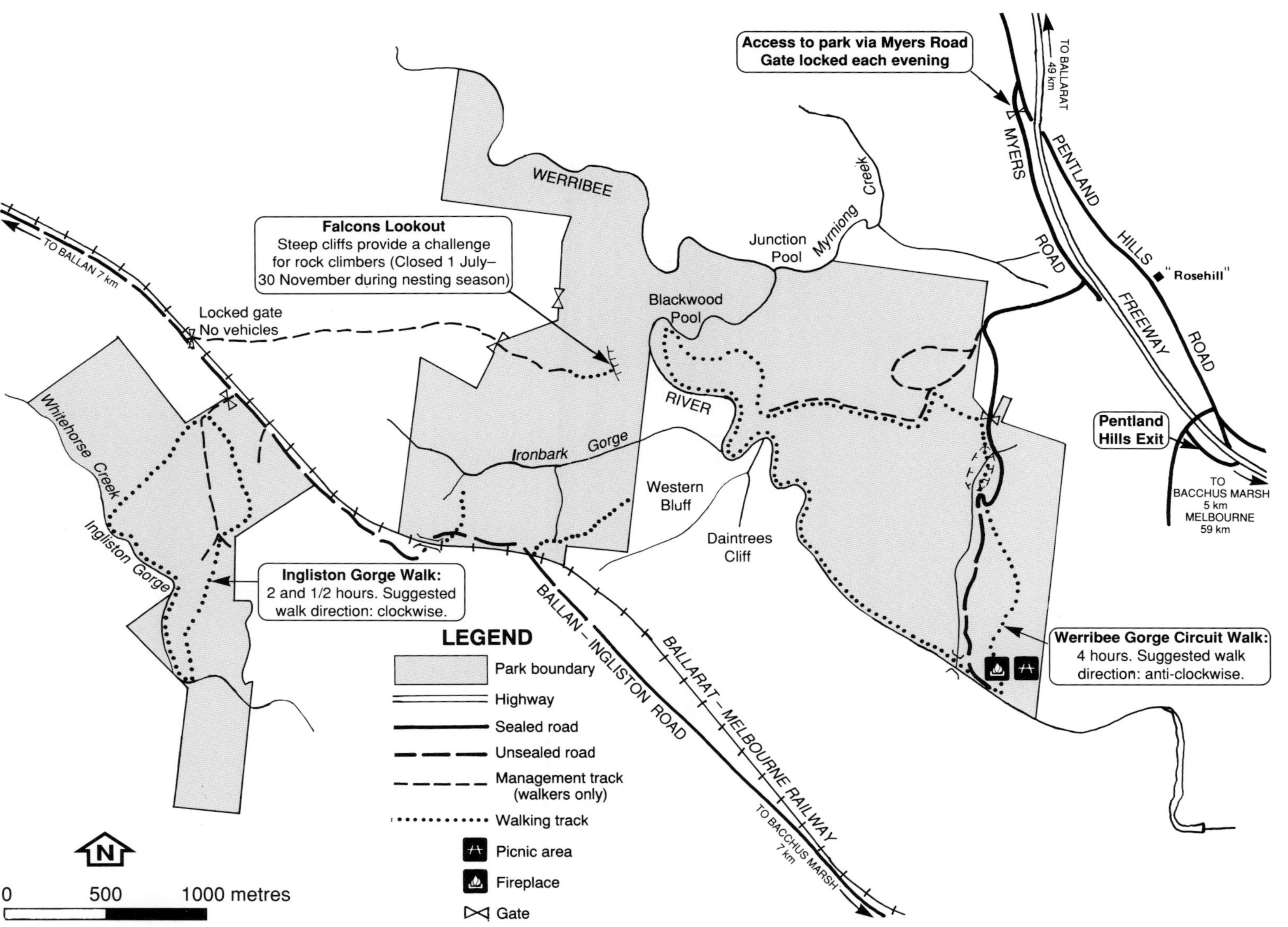

been receiving special attention over recent years because of the drastic effects of the pesticide residues in its diet on the thickness of its eggshells, and the effects in turn on its ability to raise young. To improve the Peregrine's chances of nesting successfully the cliffs are closed to rock climbers during the breeding season each year.

Human history: Aboriginal scrapers, spear points and small knives have been found in the Park, and early settlers mentioned 'natives camped on a flat'. The country around Werribee Gorge was opened up to grazing in the 1840's but because of its poor soils and precipitous walls the Gorge itself was largely untouched. Goldminers searched the area at various times and the remains of their activities can be seen today. In 1870 the railway line from Bacchus Marsh to Ballan was opened, and it became much easier for groups to visit the area and appreciate its importance. In 1906, a local resident by the name of McFarlane dynamited a water channel along the western side of the river down to his residence. This act of vandalism led to the formation of a committee to protect and preserve the area, and a year later the Gorge was reserved as a public park. The committee also built walking tracks and shelter sheds. One of these, high above the north side of the river, is being restored by the very active Friends of Werribee Gorge and Long Forest.

During the Depression, the water channel that the present track follows for much of its way was constructed to take water to Bacchus Marsh. About the same time gold prospectors moved back into the area, but with only limited success. The oft-repeated call for the area to be given proper park status and protection was finally realised in 1975 when Werribee Gorge State Park was created and placed under National Parks management.

Things to do: Rockclimbing, except from July to November when the Peregrines are nesting; walking; studying the geology.

Best season to visit: Early spring, when the Peregrines are performing their spectacular courting flights, and late summer when the parents pursue the young to drive them off to new territories; any season for walking and geology, though the river can be high in winter and early spring.

Special features: The sense of wonder that comes with looking at 500 million years of history laid bare for us to see; the Peregrines; the Wedge-tailed Eagles that course through the Gorge.

Relevant reading:
Clark I. & Cook B. (eds) (1988) *Victorian Geology Excursion Guide.*
Hills E.S. (1975) *Physiography of Victoria.*

Further information:
C&E Office, 176 Main St, Bacchus Marsh, Vic 3340. Phone (053) 67 2922.
Friends' Group: Phone (053) 67 2672, 67 2462.

Lerderderg

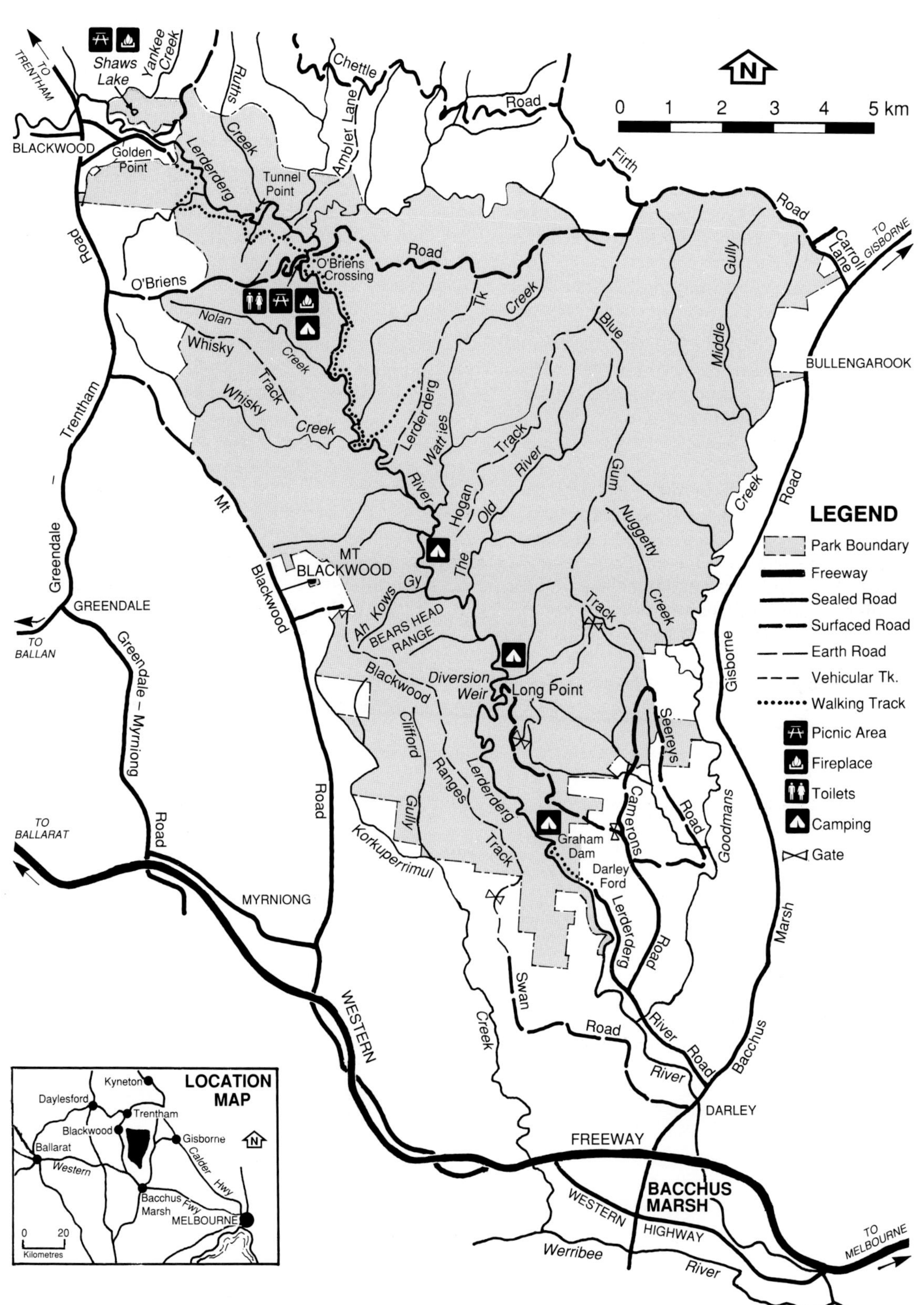

TO TRENTHAM
Shaws Lake
Yankee Creek
Ruths Creek
Chettle Road
Ambler Lane
Firth Road
N
0 1 2 3 4 5 km
BLACKWOOD
Golden Point
Lerderderg
Tunnel Point
Road
O'Briens
O'Briens Crossing
Road
Carroll Lane
TO GISBORNE
Nolan Creek
Whisky Track
Whisky Creek
Tk
Creek
Blue
Middle Gully
BULLENGAROOK
Trentham
Lerderderg River
Watties
Track
Old River
Hogan
The
Gum
Nuggetty Creek
Creek
Road
Mt
Greendale
MT BLACKWOOD
Blackwood
Ah Kows Gy
BEARS HEAD RANGE
Track
GREENDALE
TO BALLAN
Greendale – Myrniong
Blackwood Ranges Track
Diversion Weir
Long Point
Clifford Gully
Lerderderg
Seereys
Gisborne
Camerons Road
Goodmans
TO BALLARAT
Road
Road
Korkuperrimul
Graham Dam
Darley Ford
Lerderderg Road
Marsh
MYRNIONG
Swan
Creek
Road
River Road
Bacchus
WESTERN
River
DARLEY
FREEWAY
BACCHUS MARSH
WESTERN HIGHWAY
Werribee River
TO MELBOURNE
LEGEND
Park Boundary
Freeway
Sealed Road
Surfaced Road
Earth Road
Vehicular Tk.
Walking Track
Picnic Area
Fireplace
Toilets
Camping
Gate
LOCATION MAP
Kyneton
Daylesford
Trentham
Blackwood
Gisborne
Ballarat
Western
Calder Hwy
Bacchus Marsh
Fwy
MELBOURNE
0 20
Kilometres

23 Lerderderg State Park

Physical features: 13 340 ha. This Park, with its surprisingly remote atmosphere, is surrounded by farmland and state forest and is dominated by the Lerderderg River and its spectacular gorge which almost bisects the Park. The river is winding, with rapids, shallow rocky stretches and deep pools. Because of the steep, narrow gorge, the river may flood very rapidly, and walkers should be aware that they could easily become trapped. The soils are shallow and prone to sheet erosion, tunnelling and gullying, especially where vegetation has been cleared. For more detail see Werribee Gorge SP.

Plants and animals: A number of vegetation communities here are poorly represented in conservation reserves elsewhere in this region. These include river and gorge communities, freshwater wetlands and Yellow Gum woodlands. Some 24 significant plants are recorded for the Park; among them are the Violet Westringia and the Fragrant Saltbush. Blackwood wattles are common throughout the Park, and in summer, fallen seeds, each with its bright pink seedstalk coiled around it, are thick underfoot. The seedstalk contains an oily material which is attractive to ants; they carry the tough-coated seeds back to their nests where they ultimately germinate.

There is a wide diversity of animals, many of which are at or close to their western limit here. Regionally significant mammals are the Greater Glider, Bobuck (or Mountain Possum), Feathertail Glider, Eastern Pygmy-possum and Tuan. It is also an important area for birds of prey such as the Peregrine Falcon, Wedge-tailed Eagle and that magnificent night hunter, the Powerful Owl.

Human history: As in much of the surrounding countryside, gold was mined here. The remains of some of the water races built to carry water for washing the gold can still be seen upstream from O'Briens Crossing, as can the tunnel that was used to divert the river thereby exposing its bed. Many of the names of landmarks betray the river's history: Ah Kow Gully, Nugget Creek, Broken Back Mine, and a fascinating collection of tracks in the north-west of the Park – Champagne, Whisky, Rum, Vodka and a little further off, Square Bottle Track. Timber has also been harvested from the Lerderderg and some old machinery and a sawmill site can still be seen.

Things to do: Bushwalking in a remote area (some of which is very demanding); camping; swimming; horseriding; and scenic driving, though tracks may be closed in winter and early spring.

Best season to visit: Spring for wildflowers; any for walking and driving, but see above.

Special features: Spectacular scenery, particularly along the Gorge, with most of it having little obvious sign of human modification.

Relevant reading:

Conservation Forests and Lands (1987) *Lerderderg Gorge* (map and information).
Land Conservation Council (1973) *Study Report Melbourne Area* and (1985) *Melbourne Area District 1 Review.*
(See also Werribee Gorge.)

Further information:

C&E Office, Main St, Bacchus Marsh, Vic 3340. Phone (053) 67 2922.

24 Brisbane Ranges National Park

Physical features: 7 517 ha. The Brisbane Ranges are low-lying, with a high point of only 400 m above sea level. The rainfall, 680 mm per annum, is less than expected for this elevation because of the rain-shadow effect of the Otway Ranges to the south-west. Since the geological features of this Park and of four other nearby parks – Werribee and Lerderderg State Parks, Steiglitz Historic Park, and Long Forest Flora and Fauna Reserve – are similar, the geology is covered under Werribee Gorge SP.

Plants and animals: The soils of the Brisbane Ranges are infertile, which is fortunate for us today since otherwise they would have been cleared for agriculture long ago. Such clearing has been the fate of more fertile lands to the east of the Ranges and of the Kinglake Ranges, north of Melbourne. In the Brisbane Ranges, as elsewhere, it is the infertile soils that have given us some of our loveliest wildflower displays. Differences in slope, aspect, exposure to sun and wind, drainage and fire history mean that these dry-looking hills offer a wide range of environments. The major vegetation associations reflecting these different environments are:

- open forest dominated by Red and Brown Stringybark eucalypts on those soils derived from older rocks. The understorey is usually light, and in spring the Golden Wattle makes a brilliant display. There are many ground orchids here also. If this open forest is on a southerly slope, the greater protection from sun and hot winds and the increased moisture will allow plants like Long-leaved Box, Pale Wallaby-grass, mosses and ferns to grow, but if it is on a northerly slope hardier plants such as Red Ironbark (well-named – you can easily skin your knuckles on this tree's bark), lichens, Diggers' Speedwell and Grey Everlasting will dominate. In the gullies the understorey is much thicker, with shrubs such as Dense Mint-bush and Sticky Boronia.
- heathy woodland, found on the leached sands of the higher level areas. This is where most of the colourful and botanically interesting wildflowers are to be found. The canopy trees are Brown Stringybark, along with White Sallee and some peppermints. Below these are many of the Park's twenty species of Acacia, Austral Grass-trees, the endemic Brisbane Ranges Grevillea, and a number of plants with unexpected, disjunct distributions such as Rusty Pomaderris and Golden Grevillea, otherwise found in Gippsland; and the Velvet Daisy-bush and Scented Bush-pea, more typically found in western Victoria. Again, there are a number of ground orchids here, and sometimes in the most unlikely places – a drift of tiny Blue Caladenias growing and flowering in apparently rock-hard red soil is a memorable sight. The low nutrient level of many of the soils, particularly that of nitrogen, is reflected in the number of insectivorous plants – six sundews and two bladderworts. One of these, the Scented Sundew, has a particularly lovely pure white flower, and like the grass-trees and many of the orchids is stimulated to flower by fire.
- streamsides, where the eucalypts are mostly Manna and Swamp Gums, both possible host trees for Koalas. Below these are Blackwoods, Swamp Bottlebrush and Woolly Tea-tree.

Along with this wide variety of plants – almost a quarter of Victoria's plants occur here – there is a corresponding richness of birdlife. More than 180 different birds have been recorded, and while most are resident throughout the year, others like the Rainbow Bee-eater are seasonal visitors only. One particularly interesting honeyeater is the brightly-coloured Yellow-tufted Honeyeater, very closely related to the almost extinct Helmeted Honeyeater – Victoria's bird emblem. The high, inaccessible cliffs of this Park, and of nearby Werribee Gorge State Park, are ideal nesting places for the magnificent Peregrine Falcon and the majestic, and often maligned, Wedge-tailed Eagle. Apparently Malleefowl also occurred here once, but such a large and succulent bird was too tempting to the early settlers, and none has been seen for many years now.

Mammal surveys in the Brisbane Ranges have revealed a surprisingly low number of smaller mammals, perhaps because of a lack of dense ground cover or possibly because of illegal shooting. One mammal that has been, and still is, particularly well-studied here is the Koala. For a number of years now there has been increasing concern over a sexually-transmitted disease among Koalas that is caused by a bacteria-like organism called *Chlamydia*. This disease may lead to serious infertility and therefore a drop in numbers. To more easily track the animals being studied, they have each

Brisbane Ranges

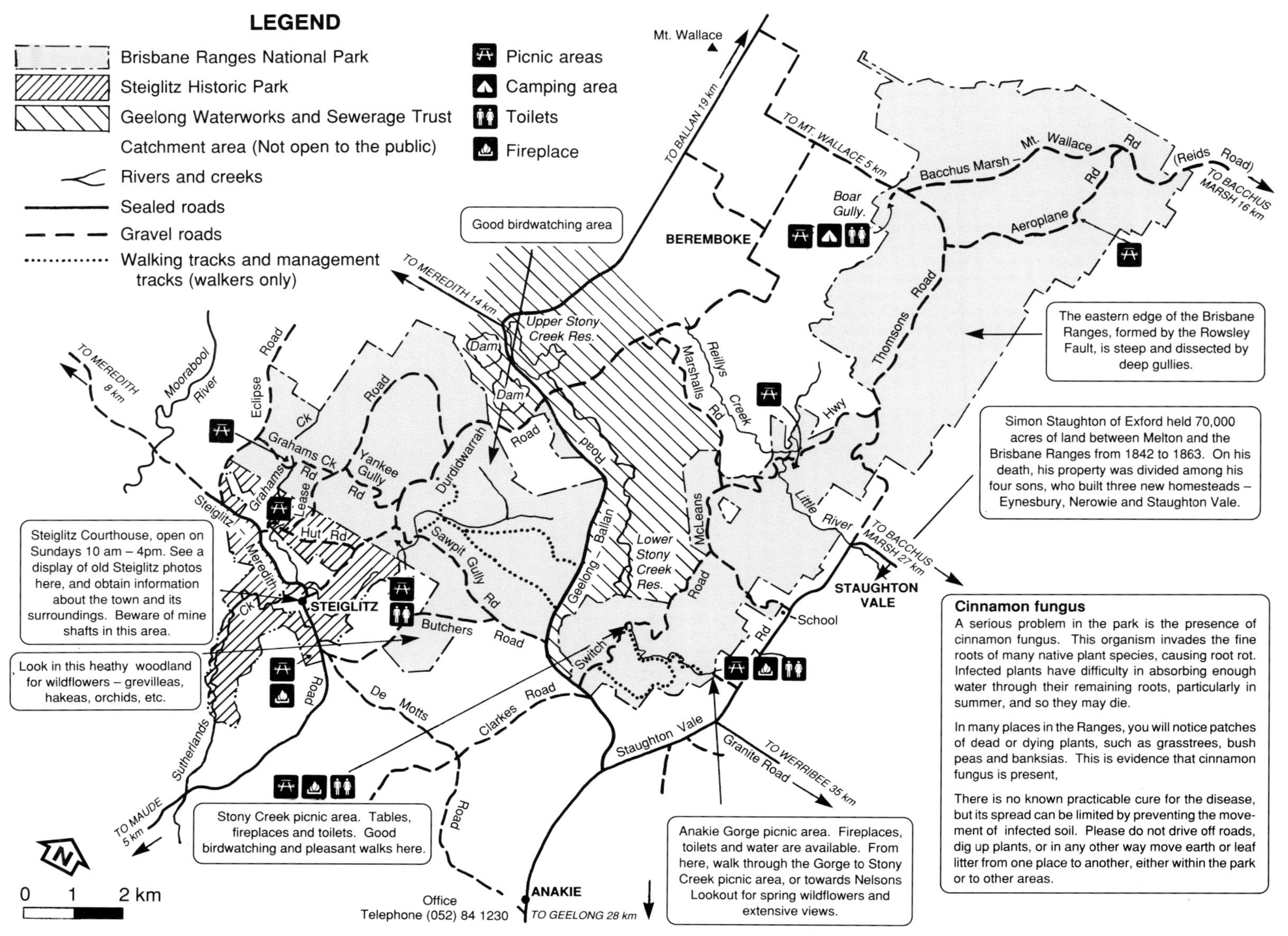

been fitted with a tiny radio transmitter which gives off a signal easily picked up by an appropriate receiver. Although the disease is present in the Brisbane Ranges – about 80% of Koalas here have been found to be infected with *Chlamydia* – few of the animals show outward signs of the diseases such as 'pink eye', 'dirty tail' or 'wet bottom'. Their fertility is certainly reduced – only 40% of the Brisbane Ranges' female Koalas breed each year, as compared with 70–80% of the French Island population, from where most of these animals originally came.

The effect of the disease varies considerably from one animal to another. Some females become infertile soon after they first mate at about two years of age; others become infected at this time but continue to produce one young each year. In spite of this overall reduction in fertility, the Brisbane Ranges' population is continuing to grow and is in fact one of the most substantial in Victoria. Even without a radio receiver you have an excellent chance of spotting one or two sleeping Koalas in the trees above you, generally in their preferred food trees of Manna Gum or perhaps Swamp Gum, or even occasionally a Red Stringybark. This habit of sleeping for much of the time is an essential part of a Koala's survival technique since its diet of eucalypt leaves is so low in energy that it simply cannot afford to be more active.

A plant disease, Cinnamon Fungus, has also been studied here. This fungus destroys the tiny root hairs on susceptible plants and so prevents them taking up water and nutrients, ultimately killing the whole plant. The infective spores are carried in wet soil and the effects of the disease can often be seen downhill from tracks along which contaminated vehicles have driven. One of the most susceptible of our native plants is the graceful Austral Grass-tree which is common in this Park. Dead and dying grass-trees are an indicator that this pathogen is present and that appropriate precautions need to be taken to prevent the spread of infected soil.

Human history: There is evidence that the Aborigines used both the Brisbane Ranges and the banks of the nearby Moorabool River. By 1837, grazing leases had been let in the fertile lowlands, but this had little effect on the Ranges and it was not until the discovery of gold in 1851 that major changes began. Probably the whole of the Brisbane Ranges was worked over for gold, the main concentration being in what is now Steiglitz Historic Park. Many trees, especially Yellow Gum, were felled, and much of what we see now is coppice regrowth from the stumps of felled trees.

In 1870, the Brisbane Ranges became the main water catchment area for Geelong, and dams and reservoirs were built along Stony Creek. These are not in the Park, but form an effective link between its two parts. Slate and gravel have also been mined over the years from what is now Park.

Things to do: Picnicking; walking; rockclimbing (except during the Peregrine Falcons' nesting season when the cliffs are closed to allow the birds to nest); driving; studying natural history; and koala spotting, an activity that is nearly always successful!

Best season to visit: Spring for wildflowers; otherwise any time, but it can be hot in summer.

Special features: Spring wildflowers; Koalas; a picnic among the Brown Tree-creepers and the Olive-backed Orioles with their constant call of 'orry-orry-ole'.

Relevant reading: Lee A. and Martin R. (1988) *The Koala*.
(See also Werribee Gorge SP.)

Further information:
C&E Office, Ballan Rd, Anakie 3221. Phone (052) 84 1230.
Friends' Group: Phone (052) 96388.

Grass-tree *BC*

▲ Windsurfer, Lysterfield Park *JAC*

▼ One Tree Hill track, Dandenong Ranges NP *JAC*

▲ Powerful Owl *IMcC*

▼ Brisbane Ranges NP *JAC*

▲ Little River scene, Brisbane Ranges NP *JAC*

◀ Peregrine Falcon *ARI*

▼ Courthouse at Steiglitz HP *JAC*

▲ Brisbane Ranges Grevillea *JAC*

25 Steiglitz Historic Park

Physical features: 670 ha. See Werribee Gorge State Park.

Plants and animals: The description of the plants and animals of the Brisbane Ranges is relevant here although much of Steiglitz Historic Park is highly modified by man, indicated by the coppiced Yellow Gums above the Courthouse and the many exotic trees around the town.

Human history: Like other old mining towns, the Steiglitz of today needs a generous helping of imagination as you walk around its streets and along the creek that once supported a thriving town of 1 000 people. The first gold was discovered in the area in 1853, but it was not until 1855, when a rich quartz reef was found, that the first Steiglitz goldrush really began. Six years later, the lack of any more surface gold and the high charges for crushing the gold-bearing quartz led to a marked population decline, but by the mid 1860's quartz mining operations began in earnest. For nearly ten years Steiglitz flourished, only to decline again until new technology in 1893 led to the reopening of the mines and consequently to another brief period of prosperity for the town. In 1913, a member of the Field Naturalists' Club of Victoria observed:

> Its deserted streets and dilapidated habitations plainly evidenced how Fortune has finally dealt with this one-time flourishing mining centre. In the heyday of its existence it was the hub, as it were of ... diggings spread over an area of 70 square miles of country. Today its habitable houses might be numbered on one's fingers.

The elegant Steiglitz Courthouse that we see today was opened in 1875 to cope with the usual rough and tumble and lawlessness of goldfields, and was used until 1879. It was then closed until 1895 when it was once again reopened, only to close in 1899 as people moved away from the town. Since then it has served as a church and a private house, followed by twenty years of disuse. It now has a future as an appropriate setting for the Steiglitz Historic Park Information Centre.

Things to do: Picnicking; fossicking; exploring the town and the old cemetery; and walking along Sutherlands Creek, but check for current opening times of the Information Centre in the Courthouse so you have a copy of the excellent notes and map available. Allow time to enjoy the display of historic photographs in the Courthouse.

Best season to visit: Any, but as your time in Steiglitz is probably combined with a visit to the Brisbane Ranges, see the Brisbane Ranges NP section also.

Special features: The Courthouse; the remains of mines and buildings (including the old covered wells) in the town and along the course of Sutherlands Creek.

Relevant reading:

K.R. von Stieglitz (ed) (1964 reprint) *Emma von Stieglitz: her Port Phillip and Victorian Album.*
National Parks Service (1973) *Steiglitz Historic Park Management Plan.*
National Parks Service (1982) *Steiglitz: Memories of Gold.*
(See also Werribee Gorge SP.)

Further information:

C&E Office, Ballan Rd, Anakie 3221. Phone (052) 84 1230.
Friends' Group: see Friends of Brisbane Ranges.

Long Forest

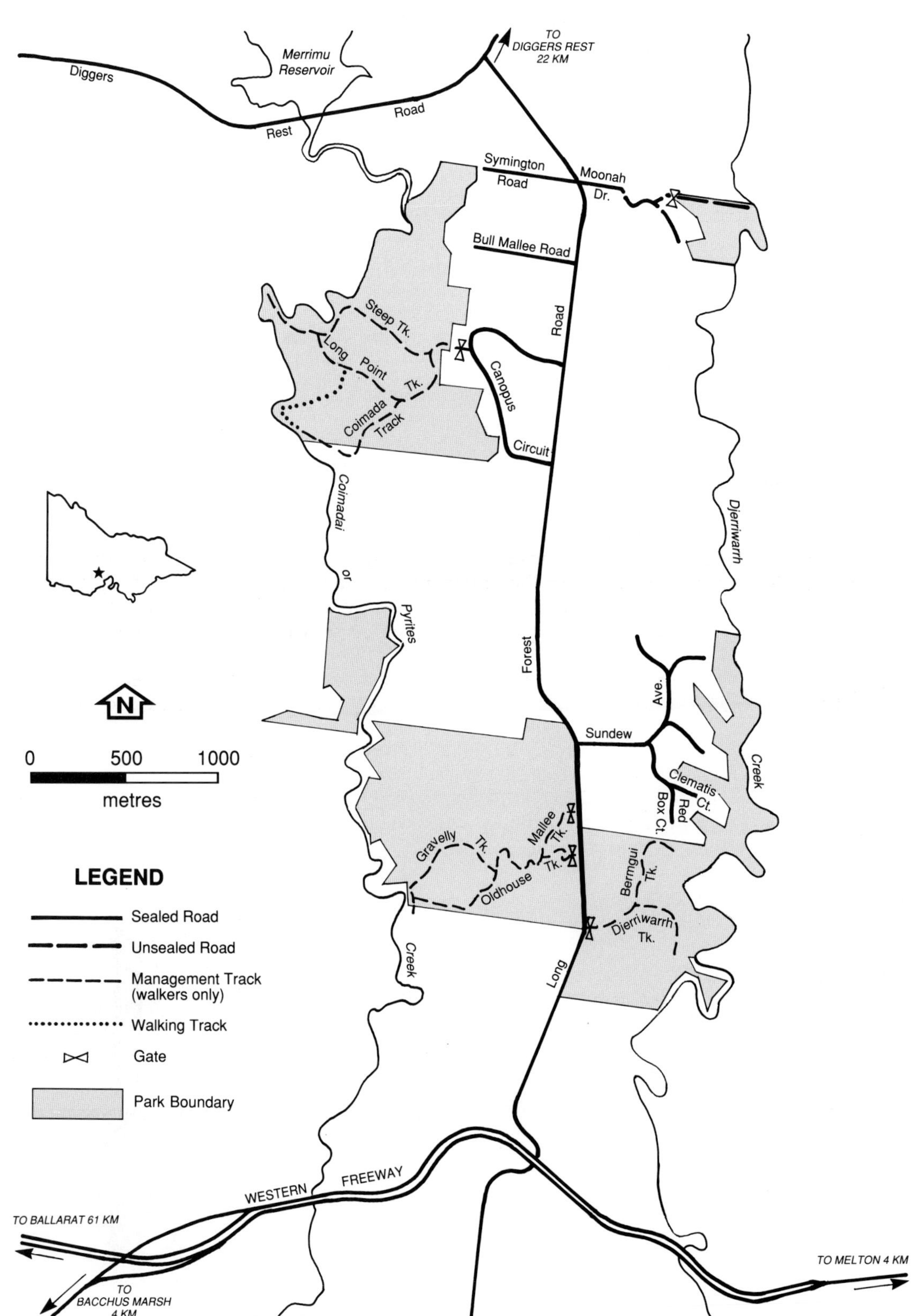

TO DIGGERS REST 22 KM
Merrimu Reservoir
Diggers Rest Road
Symington Road
Moonah Dr.
Bull Mallee Road
Road
Steep Tk.
Long Point Tk.
Coimada Track
Canopus Circuit
Coimadai or Pyrites Creek
Djerriwarrh Creek
Forest
Ave.
Sundew
Clematis Ct.
Box Ct.
Red
Mallee Tk.
Gravelly Tk.
Oldhouse Tk.
Bermgui Tk.
Djerriwarrh Tk.
Long
N
0
500
1000
metres
LEGEND
Sealed Road
Unsealed Road
Management Track (walkers only)
Walking Track
Gate
Park Boundary
WESTERN FREEWAY
TO BALLARAT 61 KM
TO BACCHUS MARSH 4 KM
TO MELTON 4 KM

26 Long Forest Flora Reserve

Physical features: 283 ha. Long Forest lies at the foot of the Rowsley Scarp (see Werribee Gorge) and its 450 million years old slates and sandstones are bordered on the west by a lava flow. The land is dissected by the valleys of Djerriwarrh and Coimadai Creeks; the latter has had its flow altered by damming to form Merrimu Reservoir further upstream. The nearby Pentland Hills create a marked rainshadow, and the soils are generally porous, so the environment is typically arid.

Plants and animals: Mallee vegetation is still common in Victoria's north-west and in other states, but years ago, when the climate was drier than at present, mallee came much further south. Long Forest, with its particular combination of soil type and low rainfall, is now the only mallee south of the Great Divide. Some of these trees are believed to be hundreds of years old, despite their small size. Only one mallee species, Bull Mallee, grows here, which is unusual in that generally at least three mallee eucalypts grow together. There are also a number of other plants that are typically found in arid areas. There is very little permanent understorey, apart from mosses and lichens, although in late winter and early spring many delicate ground orchids appear, then die down again after flowering. Along the creeks there is a very different scene, with cool shade and trees of Blue Box (more typically found in eastern Gippsland). Long Forest is also rich in birdlife with about 140 species, including some 'island' populations of birds such as the Crested Bellbird that are typical of arid country. There are many insects too, including 12 different types of bullants, two of which have not been found elsewhere. Kangaroos and wallabies, Koalas, Echidnas, possums, Tuans and gliders are also found here.

Human history: Long Forest remained largely untouched, except for wood-gathering for the Bacchus Marsh milk factories and some unsuccessful grazing, until the 1960's, when the first of a number of subdivisions took place. From then on there was a rapid increase both in the human population and its attendant domestic pets, and in the pressure from scientists, conservationists and many others to have this unique area adequately protected. At present about a third is reserved.

Things to do: Studying natural history, especially the opportunity to observe arid species; walking. This is a fragile and sensitive environment best suited to those who like to go quietly and gently.

Best season to visit: Any season for walking; late winter and spring for wildflowers and birds.

Special features: Arid vegetation on Melbourne's doorstep; a visit in the rain, when the Forest puts on quite another greener, mossier face; rainbow birds darting out across the creek bed.

Relevant reading:
Baker M. in *Parkwatch* No. 139.
(See also Werribee Gorge.)

Further information:
C&E Office, Main St, Bacchus Marsh, Vic 3340. Phone (053) 67 2922.
Friends' Group: Phone (053) 67 2672, 67 2462.

Bull Mallee *MS*

27 Gellibrand Hill Park

Physical features: 658 ha. Gellibrand Hill (240 m), a low hill just north of Melbourne Airport, is an island of 380 million year old granite standing in a sea of much younger basalt. This basalt, only about one million years old, makes up the nearby Keilor Plains and much of Victoria as far west as Portland. Moonee Ponds Creek flows along the south-western edge of the Park, and where it has cut through the basalt, the underlying sedimentary rocks can easily be seen.

Plants and animals: Much of the Park has been altered by grazing over the last 140 years, but the original landscape of creek banks and open grassland interspersed with Grey Box and impressive River Red Gums is still apparent. There is also rocky scrub below the granite tors of Gellibrand Hill, and some quarry holes with permanent water. Cattle have been excluded from the Nature Reserve – about half the Park – so that trees are regenerating, and plants that once clothed the basalt plains are starting to reappear. Although most native mammals have long since disappeared from the area, there are now more than 70 species of birds. There are plans to reintroduce appropriate mammals as suitable habitat becomes available. One of the most exciting reintroductions is that of an endangered species, the Eastern Barred Bandicoot – a small but thriving population was discovered living in the Hamilton tip a few years ago. Six of these animals have now been released into the Nature Reserve, where it is hoped they will colonise what was almost certainly once part of their range. This reintroduction is part of the new Flora and Fauna Guarantee scheme which recognises the vital importance of the preservation and maintenance of habitat for the survival of plant and animal species. Where the Gellibrand Hill grasslands are of native Kangaroo Grass, this will be encouraged at the expense of introduced grasses by careful burning.

Human history: Scar trees and tools show that the area was used by the Aborigines before Europeans took up pastoral runs here. When Hume and Hovell, the explorers, went through here in 1824, they observed that the area was 'equal to the best of any land and the grass and herbage denotes it'. The first settlers at Gellibrand Hill were William and Anne Greene who brought out a prefabricated cottage from England, and parts of this can still be seen in the *Woodlands* homestead. The Greenes and many of the later owners kept stables for racing and hunting. Two other houses at Gellibrand Hill, *Dundonald* and *Cumberland*, have now been demolished.

By the mid-1970's the property was reserved under the National Parks Act, and in the 1980's extensive work on the conservation and restoration of *Woodlands* homestead began. Details of early construction and decorating techniques are part of a fascinating display of architectural details, many of them original features from the 1840's, now on show at *Woodlands*.

Things to do: Picnicking; walking; horseriding; bicycling; visiting *Woodlands*; birdwatching.

Best season to visit: Any, although a hot summer's day is usually less popular.

Special features: Closeness to Melbourne; the views; *Woodlands* homestead and garden.

Relevant reading:
Conservation, Forests and Lands (1982) *Gellibrand Hill Park Management Plan*.
Stawell M. (1911) *Recollections* (out of print but excerpts available for reading at *Woodlands*).
Land Conservation Council (1973) *Study Report Melbourne Area* and (1985) *Melbourne Area District 1 Review*.
Presland G. (1985) *Land of the Kulin*.
(Reports on the restoration of *Woodlands* are available for on-site reading at the homestead.)

Further information:
Park Office, Somerton Rd, Vic 3047. Phone (03) 307 1164.
Friends' Group: Phone (03) 306 8180.

Gellibrand Hill

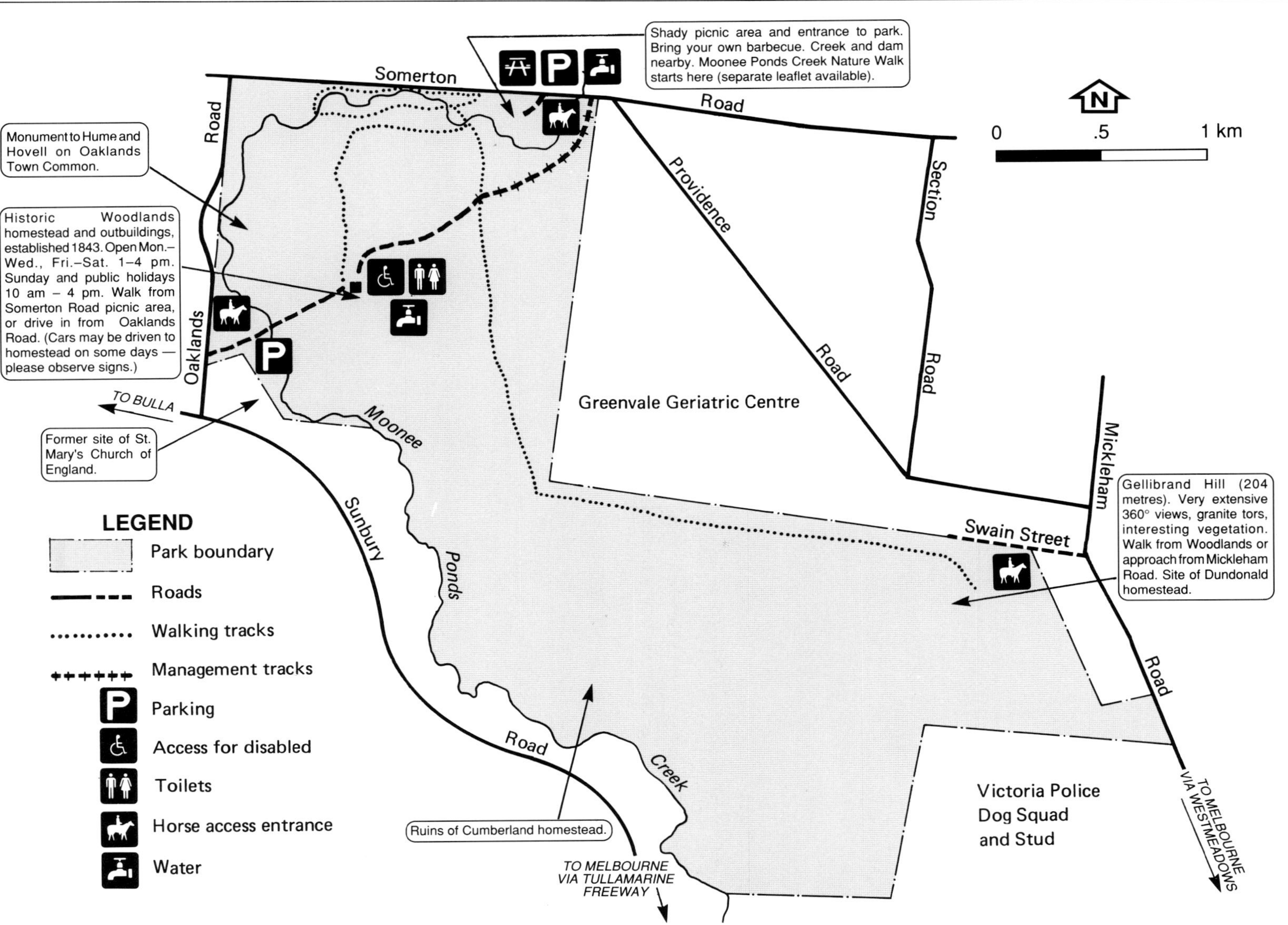

Kinglake and Yea River

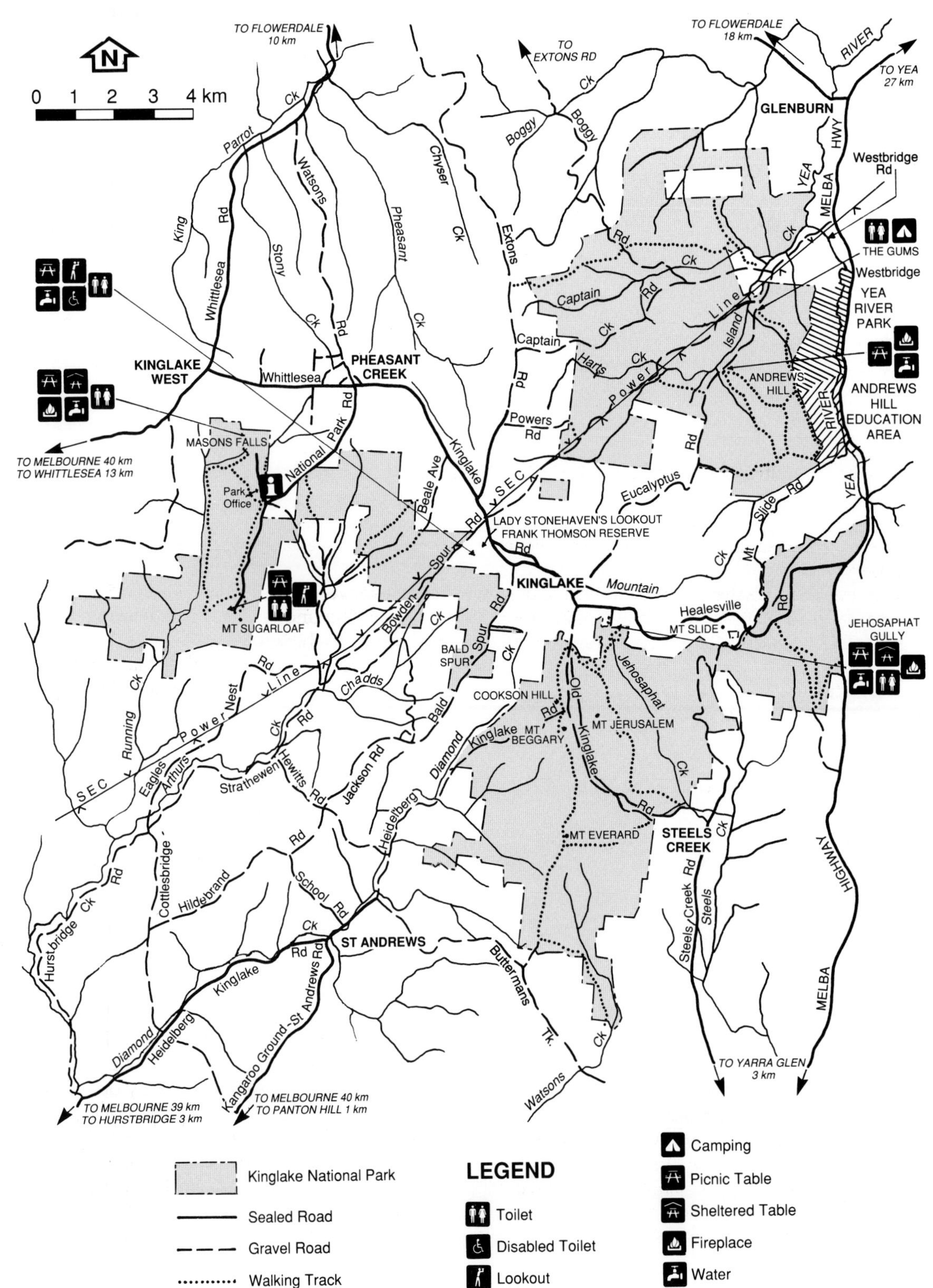

28 Kinglake National Park and Yea River Park

Physical features: 11 430 ha (Kinglake) and 220 ha (Yea River). Kinglake National Park is in the low range of hills about 50 km north of Melbourne, easily seen from the city. Because of its piecemeal establishment over the years, the Park is in three sections; one on the northern and two on the southern slopes of the Great Dividing Range. The road from Toolangi in the east to Kinglake West in the west runs along the Kinglake Plateau, where the elevation varies from 450–550 m. The highest point in the Park is Andrews Hill, 661 m, in the northern section. On the plateau, the rainfall is about 1 200 mm per year. The rain that falls on the southern slopes finds its way into the River Yarra, while that from the northern slopes enters the Murray via the Goulburn River. The moist air can often be seen from the plains below as a line of cloud along the skyline, even on an otherwise clear day. Yea River Park lies in a valley just north of Kinglake NP and is essentially part of the same system, but with a greater emphasis on recreation.

Much of the Kinglake plateau is strongly dissected and drops away steeply on the southern side. The underlying rocks are of sandstones and mudstones laid down about 350 million years ago. These rocks, which are often folded, can be seen at Masons Falls and in road cuttings along the Kinglake to St Andrews Road. A number of interesting and remarkably well-preserved marine fossils, including trilobites, have been found in these rocks.

In the higher parts of the Park, the greater rainfall has led to more weathering of the rocks and therefore more soil formation particularly of the rich, red, fertile soils that have now largely been cleared for cultivation. Elsewhere, including in much of the Park, the soils are grey, more leached and less fertile.

Plants and animals: There are three distinct vegetation types in the Park, largely dictated by aspect:

- on the drier northern slopes, Broad-leaved and Narrow-leaved Peppermint with Red Stringybark, and Red and Long-leaved Box form an open canopy layer. The understorey is made up of Austral Grass-tree, Hairpin Banksia and many smaller shrubs, most of which have hard dry (sclerophyllous) leaves – an adaptation to the low supplies of nutrients and perhaps of water also. Many of these plants belong to the pea, myrtle, heath or protea families, and contribute to a colourful spring display. Orchids are also quite common in this type of vegetation.
- on the plateau country the vegetation is dominated by Broad-leaved Peppermint and Messmate Stringybark, with an understorey which, while including some wet gully plants such as Hazel Pomaderris, Wonga-vine and Forest Clematis, is largely made up of open sclerophyllous shrubs such as Common Heath and many different types of peas.
- in the wet gullies in the sheltered southern valleys, there are small trees such as Austral Mulberry, Blanket-leaf, and Musk Daisy-bush with a dense understorey of treeferns – Soft Treefern in the gullies and Rough Treefern a little higher up. Everywhere there is an abundance of small ferns and mosses. Slightly higher up on these southern slopes, out of the actual gullies, Mountain Grey Gums and Messmate dominate, with some Mountain Ash. A walk along the Jehosaphat Gully track from the carpark to the Mt Jerusalem track takes you through a good selection of all three of these vegetation types.

That same walk will also show you many of the 100 or so bird species found in this Park. One of the most obvious to the ear, though less so to the eye, is the Superb Lyrebird, whose calls echo up and down the gully. Often though, if you are quiet, you can be rewarded with at least a glimpse of this bird at the Jehosaphat Gully picnic ground, sometimes even when you are barely out of the car. This walk is definitely one which is enriched by being able to recognise a few of the commoner bird calls (the Bird Observers Club has some excellent tapes). Tree-creepers, with their strong persistent one-note call, are usually heard well before they are seen, as are Gang-gangs and Yellow-tailed Black-cockatoos, each with their distinctive version of a squeaky door; while the strong melodious call of the Golden Whistler is quite enough to make most people stop and look for the songster. Sometimes though, it is not an actual call that betrays the presence of a particular bird –

the first indication of the Eastern Shrike-tit is seldom its striking colouration but rather the sound of tearing bark as the bird searches for hidden insects.

Most other animals are harder to see – apart from Koalas, introduced from French Island – because they are either nocturnal, like the various possums, bandicoots, marsupial mice and native rats, or because they are very timid, like the snakes and lizards. The reptiles in the Park were surveyed a few years ago by the Montmorency Field Naturalists' Club, which found many species previously unknown to the area, a situation that probably holds good for many of our parks.

Human history: The area that is now Kinglake NP was worked over by the goldminers of the 1850's, some of whom are commemorated in names around the Park – Cooksons Hill, for instance, is named after a miner who was murdered for his gold. Reminders of the mining days can still be seen in some parts of the Park, such as the old shafts near the Steels Creek picnic ground. The miners cut some timber for their own use, but it was not until Melbourne expanded and timber was needed for building and firewood that the demand really increased. Tommy's Hut, now Kinglake West, was one of the main milling centres until it was burned down in the bushfires of 1926. A tramline of 300 or so ladder-like steps led down to the mill which was sited just above Masons Falls. These steps were a popular but demanding way for visitors to reach the Falls. The remains of Carman's mill site, the tramway tracks and an old log ford can be seen as you go around the walking track from the Masons Falls picnic area.

Kinglake NP was declared in 1928 largely as a result of the efforts of three men: Sir James Barrett, a tireless worker for Victoria's national parks; William Everard, a local politician; and Professor William Laver, who donated his land at the head of Jehosaphat Gully and who, soon after, was instrumental in having the northern Wombelano Falls area added to the new Park.

Kinglake Range soon became a popular tourist destination, with a number of guesthouses and tea rooms catering for the visitors' needs. As with other parks at this time the Park was administered by a Committee of Management who were always short of money to run the Park. For many years the ranger had to make his income up to a livable wage by cutting and selling timber and firewood from the Park!

In 1980, the area of the Park was almost doubled as a result of the Land Conservation Council's recommendation that the area north of the Divide be extended.

Kinglake NP, in common with other parks close to a large city, has a number of problems associated with very high usage, often by people who, for various reasons, have little understanding of park values. For instance, the 'please take your rubbish home' campaign tried a while ago in the popular picnic grounds was definitely not successful. Also, because of an enormously long and fragmented boundary, and a large number of access points, Kinglake is a difficult Park in which to maintain an obvious ranger presence. Like the Dandenongs, this is a Park that desperately requires a buffer zone around it and also some type of restrictions to prevent domestic pets being allowed on properties adjoining the Park. Parks are for people but are decidedly not for their cats and dogs.

Things to do: Visiting the Information Centre on the Masons Falls entrance road; picnicking; camping at The Gums in the northern section, (this is a very popular site, and you do need to book); horseriding in some parts; walking on the many tracks of varying lengths and degrees of challenge. There is a very pleasant track with wheelchair access and information signs leading out from the Masons Falls picnic area. Keeping tracks free of wet, slippery leaves is always a problem, but here it has been solved by the children from Janefield Centre who take a special pride in seeing that the area is clean and safe.

Best season to visit: Spring for wildflowers; winter for the chance of seeing a Superb Lyrebird displaying on his mound; any season for walking and riding.

Special features: The waterfalls, especially after rain; the extensive views from the Frank Thomson Reserve and from many of the walking tracks; Spine-tailed Swifts doing high speed flypasts at the Sugarloaf vantage point on a summer's evening; Jehosaphat Gully.

Relevant reading:
Land Conservation Council (1973) *Study Report Melbourne Area.*
Light Railway Research Society of Australia (1980–82) *Wooden Rails to Kinglake and Flowerdale.*

Further information:
Kinglake NP Office, National Park Rd, Pheasant Creek, Vic 3757. Phone (057) 86 5351.
Friends' Group: Phone (057) 86 1395.

Picnic at Kinglake, 1900 *CFL*

29 Organ Pipes National Park

Physical features: 85 ha. This Park is very much at two levels – the flat ground of the Keilor Plains where you enter the Park, and then a lower level where Jacksons Creek has carved a course through this plain. The most distinctive feature, the group of basalt columns known as the Organ Pipes, is along the bank of the creek. It was formed about one million years ago, when lava flowed from Mount Macedon and other nearby volcanic outlets. The lava poured over the land, and where it was shallow and therefore able to cool quickly, it formed a vast basalt plain. In the river and creek valleys, however, it formed a much thicker layer which cooled more slowly. First, a crust formed on the surface which would have protected and insulated the deeper lava against both movement and rapid cooling. As the interior of the mass slowly cooled it shrank, setting up tensions which led to cracking, typically into hexagonal blocks. This cracking happened at about 550° C and gradually extended down through the basalt as it cooled further. In this way long columns formed, some of which then also cracked across, leading to the 'stack of cheeses' effect that we see today. The creek then wore its way down through the basalt and revealed the strange columnar formation of the Organ Pipes and that of the Tessellated Pavement and Rosette Rock further upstream. Just downstream from the Organ Pipes, the 400 million year old sedimentary bedrock is exposed and forms an interesting geological contrast in both colour and form.

The climate of the Keilor Plains is harsh, with frequent strong winds, often as hot northerlies in summer. Because of the rainshadow effect of the Otway Range to the south-west, the annual rainfall is only about 500 mm.

Plants and animals: The Organ Pipes NP shows a dramatic contrast with the surrounding land where much of the ground is bare or else infested with noxious weeds – a similar picture to what the land of today's Park was like less than twenty years ago. Now, almost all the plants at Organ Pipes NP are native to the area. There are pleasant open grasslands, slopes covered with trees and shrubs such as Yellow Gum, wattles, she-oaks, White Cypress-pine and Desert Cassia, and dense vegetation of River Red Gum, River Bottlebrush and Woolly Tea-tree along Jacksons Creek.

Both water birds and bush birds are plentiful in the Park and are obviously responding to the greatly improved quality of environment. This situation will improve still further if, or (we hope) when, land is acquired to link Organ Pipes NP to Maribyrnong Valley Metropolitan Park (Brimbank) on the banks of the Maribyrnong downstream towards Melbourne. This would create a magnificent wildlife corridor along which birds and other animals could move freely.

Human history: By 1971, when this land was donated to the National Parks Service, it had seen 130 years of agricultural use, including grazing and the growing of vegetables. There was severe land erosion and rabbit infestation, and almost the whole area was covered by a formidable assortment of particularly noxious weeds such as Boxthorn and Artichoke Thistle. In short, it was an ecological disaster.

Now the area is a delight to visit, thanks to careful planning and direction, plus a lot of hard work on the part of the Parks Service, and a massive and well-coordinated effort by the Friends of the Organ Pipes. One important part of the project was to try to find out what the Organ Pipes area had originally been like. For this the newly-formed Friends went back to articles in early issues of the *Victorian Naturalist* and *The Emu* in which naturalist outings early this century were described. Once this was established, maps of soils, aspects and slopes, and of the appropriate vegetation, were drawn up and the business of seed collection and propagation began. All material was collected locally, either from residual pockets in the Park or from nearby land, and seedlings were mulched and protected from rabbits by wire netting guards to give plants a chance to become established. All of this was carefully recorded and documented, so that now there is an accurate and valuable record of the work that was carried out. The project was one that not only the Friends' Group but also local people took to their hearts, and this community involvement has been one of the many rewarding features of the whole undertaking. Official recognition was given to the

Organ Pipes

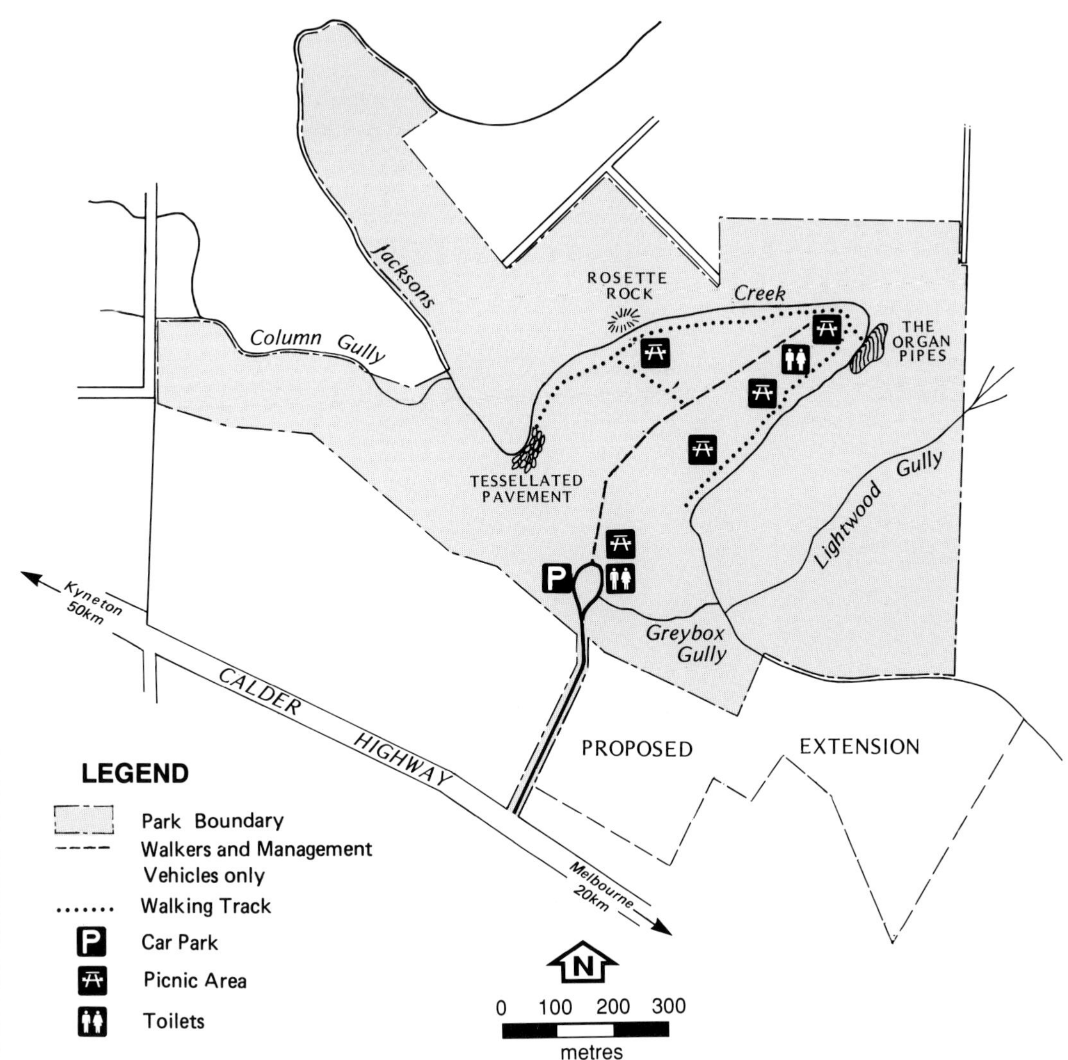

Jacksons
Creek
ROSETTE ROCK
Column Gully
THE ORGAN PIPES
TESSELLATED PAVEMENT
Lightwood Gully
Greybox Gully
Kyneton 50km
CALDER HIGHWAY
Melbourne 20km
PROPOSED
EXTENSION
LEGEND
Park Boundary
Walkers and Management Vehicles only
Walking Track
Car Park
Picnic Area
Toilets
N
0 100 200 300
metres

Friends when, in 1982, the Victorian Government presented them with the Premier's Innovative Award for landscape enhancement and a cheque for $500, an impressive beginning for the very first group of the Friends of National Parks, of which there are now nearly forty. A recent development is the Information Centre with its display and interpretation of Organ Pipes NP.

Things to do: Picnicking; walking; sketching; photography.

Special features: Geological formations; the contrast of the Park with its surroundings.

Relevant reading:
Land Conservation Council (1973) *Study Report Melbourne Area* and (1985) *Melbourne Area District 1 Review*.
Victoria's Resources (Mar–May 1974) pp. 21–25.
Victorian Naturalist (1911) Vol. XXVIII, No. 3, pp. 51–56.
National Parks Service (1973) *Organ Pipes NP Teachers' Guide*.

Further information:
Park Office, Calder Hwy, Diggers Rest, Vic 3427. Phone (03) 390 1082.
Friends' Group: Phone (03) 49 2413.

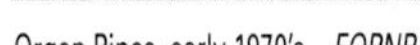

Organ Pipes, early 1970's *FOPNP*

Organ Pipes, ten years on *FOPNP*

30 Dandenong Ranges National Park

Physical features: 1 920 ha. This Park is in three separate parts: Ferntree Gully, Sherbrooke and Doongalla. The Dandenong Ranges, or the Dandenongs as they are known, form a conspicuous and attractive backdrop to Melbourne and its eastern suburbs. The Ranges are a dissected plateau of acid volcanics with a general elevation of 500–600 m, up to Mt Dandenong, 622 m. Rainfall is about 1 200 mm per year, and the climate is generally mild, although occasionally there are falls of snow in winter.

The story of the Ranges began about 350 million years ago when earth movements caused a general weakening of the earth's crust. A roughly triangular volcanic cauldron (centred somewhere near present-day Olinda) erupted through the older rock and began pouring lava into an underground depression. Four successive flows of lava eventuated, sometimes punctuated by light ashy tuff. By the time of the final lava flow, the cauldron walls were so thin and weak that when the lava contracted back down its vent, the whole mass collapsed inwards, plugging the cauldron. Similar events took place elsewhere, including at Mt Disappointment and Mt Macedon, to the west and north of Melbourne respectively. The lava eruption took place quite near the earth's surface, so the molten rock cooled comparatively quickly to form the fine-grained rock dacite, rather than coarser grained granite which requires slower cooling. In the intervening 300 or so million years since these eruptions, the overlying blanket of sedimentary rock has worn away, and the softer ash-rich rocks have weathered to deep fertile soils, whereas the hard dacite has weathered comparatively little to give us the contours of the Dandenongs as we know them today.

Plants and animals: Most people who know this area would immediately think of velvety treeferns growing under lofty Mountain Ash (*Eucalyptus regnans* must be one of our best named eucalypts). This picture is only one face of the Dandenongs – that of the cool moist gullies on the upper southern and eastern slopes. On the lower slopes and on the exposed northern and western faces there are extensive areas of open forest of Messmate and Red Stringybarks, Long-leaved Box and Narrow-leaved Peppermint, with some Mountain Grey Gum and Blue Gum in the less dry areas. Down on the flats and streamsides of the lower slopes, Manna Gums send up tall white trunks reminiscent of the Mountain Ash. The understorey varies with the moisture and light available. Below the treeferns there is little other than smaller ferns and mosses, but in the slightly more open areas there is a wealth of typical wet gully shrubs such as Victorian Christmas-bush, Blanketleaf, Banyalla and Austral Mulberry. One tree, the delicately scented Sassafras, was once common and gave its name to a settlement in the Dandenongs, but its suitability for saddle-making meant it was rapidly cut out. On the dry slopes the understorey is typically showy, often pea-flowered, shrubs and small herbs such as lily-like plants, and perhaps still a few orchids. Fire is a significant feature on these slopes and bad fires have occurred there over the years.

As would be expected where there is a variety of habitats, the birdlife is rich, more than 70 resident and 60 migrant/vagrant native birds having been recorded. The most famous is undoubtedly the Superb Lyrebird, with its fascinating ability to mimic a wide variety of natural and mechanical sounds, all in a rich strong voice and often in bewildering succession. Not many years ago, you could all but guarantee to show visitors one of these birds as it scratched for food among the leaf litter, or perhaps even spot a male in full display. Now, although they can generally still be heard, they are seldom seen. Because of the predation of foxes, and domestic cats and dogs, numbers have dropped alarmingly over recent years and a special effort now must be made to ensure a higher level of protection, and, it is hoped, a more secure future for these delightful birds.

Other native animals include 31 mammals, mostly nocturnal and therefore not easily seen; 21 reptiles such as snakes and lizards; nine amphibians; six species of fish; and of course a variety of small animals, including an endemic snail and a number of rare and interesting insects.

Human history: The first inhabitants, the Aborigines, left behind them stone implements and other artefacts, but it was, of course, the Europeans who had a far greater impact as they settled the land and cleared much of its timber. As early as 1907, less than 20% of the Dandenong State Forest, declared in 1869, remained. The Ferntree Gully component of the Park was set aside in 1882 and as such can claim to be Victoria's oldest national park. Sherbrooke Forest Park was declared in 1958, and the Doongalla estate was purchased by the Government as a Reserve in 1950. Many people over the years have fought long and hard against the despoliation of the Dandenongs and accounts of their efforts make fascinating reading (see 'Relevant reading' below). The fight is by no means over, although now there is generally greater public awareness and perhaps more sympathy towards the controls that must be imposed if we are to retain the charm of this much-loved forest playground right on Melbourne's doorstep.

Things to do: The Dandenong Ranges are enormously popular and well-loved by Melbourne people – they attract more than two million visitors each year and at least half of these spend time in the National Park. This of course places the Ranges under continuing and increasing pressure, although the usage is unevenly distributed in that far more people visit the southern rather than the northern end. People come for a variety of reasons and, to judge by the roads on any fine day, scenic driving is the main attraction. Picnicking is almost as popular, the smell of barbecues dominating the many picnic grounds throughout the Ranges. Many come to walk or perhaps jog on the excellent bush tracks. Others are there on horseback or in wheelchairs – there is a marked nature trail with wheel chair access near Grants Picnic Ground. The higher points provide excellent views across Melbourne and beyond, to Mt Macedon in the west and Donna Buang in the east. Beyond the Park boundaries there is a plethora of 'olde worlde' craft and afternoon tea shops.

Best season to visit: Although it is a pleasure to visit this Park in any season, it's more a matter of trying to choose a time or a place that is likely to be a little less popular! A hot day attracts visitors seeking the cool of the fern gullies, but winter has a special charm with misty landscapes, especially when dominated by the tall white trunks of Mountain Ash and the vigorous calls of Lyrebirds. Spring is the best time for wildflowers in the drier areas, but in the dense bush there is little change throughout the year, although in spring the Wonga Vine displays an abundance of small creamy flowers.

Special features: The sheer majesty of Mountain Ash towering up and up (and these are only the youngsters that the loggers left); the walk from Ferntree Gully to One Tree Hill up the reputedly 1 000 steps. Sadly, there is a negative side too, with weeds and garden escapes prevalent in many parts, although the Friends' Groups are doing a wonderful job in this respect.

Relevant reading:

Conservation, Forests and Lands (1987) *Dandenong Ranges NP Draft Management Plan.*
Land Conservation Council (1973) *Study Report Melbourne Area.*
Coulson H. (1959) *Story of the Dandenongs.*
Larkins J. (1978) *The Book of the Dandenongs.*
Palmer N. (1952) *The Dandenongs.*
Public Interest Research Group (1974) *The Dandenong Ranges Report.*
Bardwell S. (1982) *Fern Tree Gully National Park: a centenary history 1882–1982.*

Further information:

C&E Office, Kallista-Emerald Road, Kallista, Vic 3791. Phone (03) 755 2726.
Friends of the Dandenong Ranges: Phone (03) 758 6935.
Friends of Sherbrooke Forest: Phone (03) 754 3093.

Soft Treefern *MS*

Dandenong Ranges

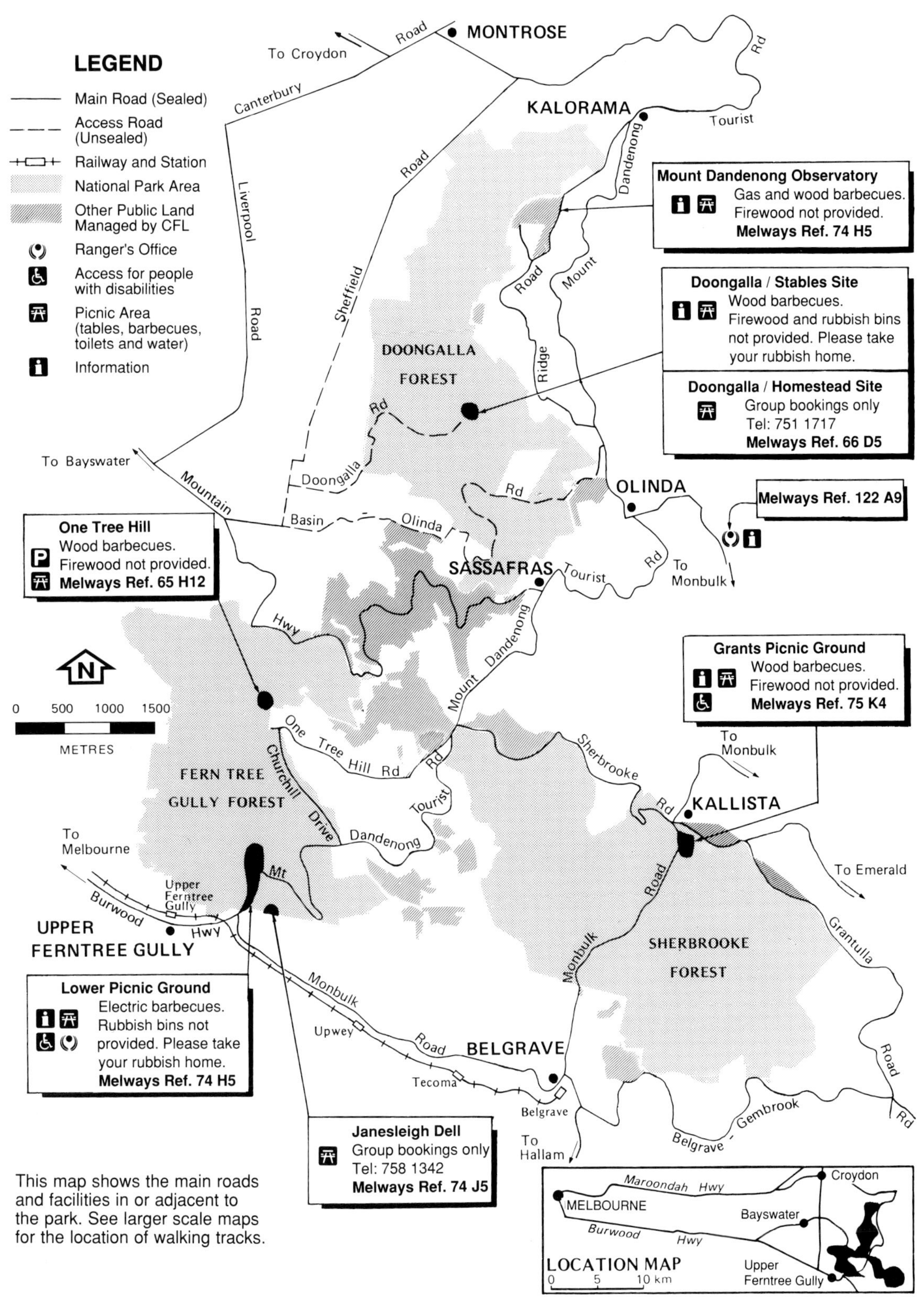

This map shows the main roads and facilities in or adjacent to the park. See larger scale maps for the location of walking tracks.

31 Warrandyte State Park

Physical features: 586 ha. This Park consists of a number of small reserves which have been united into an essentially linear park along the Yarra River. The Yarra and Warrandyte Gorge through which it flows are the dominant landscape features. Although the general topography, other than the Gorge, is almost level, and the highest point is only 138 m, folding and faulting in the 420 million year old rock beds show clear evidence of earlier earth movements. These Silurian sediments are of marine origin, often in quite thick beds, with some conglomerate but few fossils. Gold-bearing quartz reefs are also found in Warrandyte. Soils are generally clayey and unstable, prone to erosion and to setting hard in summer. The climate is similar to Melbourne's, but with more rain – 780 mm as compared with 655 mm.

Plants and animals: Much of the Park is regrowth after mining activity over 100 years ago, and most of this is of indigenous vegetation since there were then fewer pest plants around to re-colonise the disturbed land. Fires have also been important, and there is clear regrowth after major fires in 1939 and 1962. The riparian, or river, vegetation is a particularly important remnant of a type that has almost all been cleared elsewhere. Here it is largely intact, thanks to the steepness of the terrain. Likewise, Warrandyte is a haven for animals, although there are few ideal old trees with nesting sites. Because of this perhaps, some of the bats have colonised old mines. In many ways, Warrandyte is an extension of the dry country habitat of the northern goldfields, and this is reflected in birds such as the Dollar Bird which is here at its southern limit. The survival of the birds and of the other animals recorded here depends very much on the retention of their habitat and the control of introduced predators, often from nearby houses.

Human history: Warrandyte is known to have been a corroboree ground for the Wurundjeri Aborigines, and stone artefacts have been found here. The first settler, James Anderson, overlanded cattle from Sydney in 1839, but it was the discovery of gold in 1851 that was more significant for Warrandyte. Evidence of goldmining can be seen in the tunnel at Pound Bend and in the man-made Island, both of which were the result of diverting the Yarra to expose its bed.

Things to do: Picnicking; walking; horseriding; birdwatching; canoeing; swimming; studying history; simply savouring this peaceful refuge on the edge of the city.

Best season to visit: Spring for wildflowers, especially the wattles along the river; summer for swimming; otherwise any season.

Special features: The imposing presence of the Yarra River; Pound Bend tunnel.

Relevant reading:
Conservation, Forests and Lands (1988) *Warrandyte State Park Draft Management Plan.*
Land Conservation Council (1973) *Study Report Melbourne Area.*

Further information:
Park Office, Pound Bend Road, Warrandyte, Vic 3113. Phone (038) 44 2659.
Friends' Group: Phone (03) 844 1060.

Shingle-back Lizard *CFL*

▲ Organ Pipes NP *JAC*

▼ Janefield group clearing the wheelchair-access track, Kinglake NP *DM*

▲ Kinglake NP *JAC*

◀ Hyacinth Orchid *JAC*

▲ Bull Mallee Long Forest Flora Reserve *JAC*

▲ Cape Schanck headland, now protected by a boardwalk, Point Nepean NP *JB*

▼ Point Nepean NP *JB*

◀ White Correa *AF*

Warrandyte

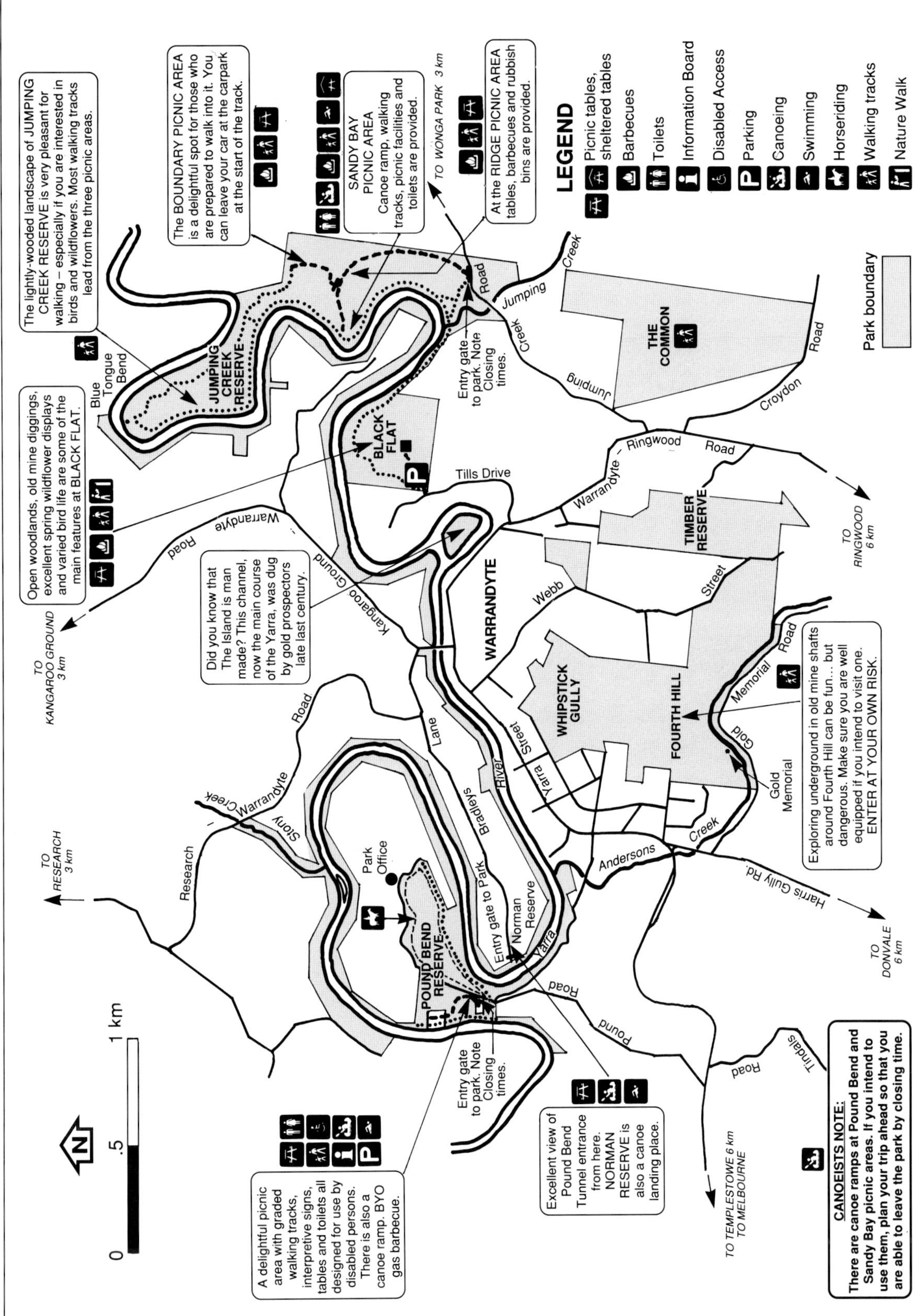

The lightly-wooded landscape of JUMPING CREEK RESERVE is very pleasant for walking – especially if you are interested in birds and wildflowers. Most walking tracks lead from the three picnic areas.
The BOUNDARY PICNIC AREA is a delightful spot for those who are prepared to walk into it. You can leave your car at the carpark at the start of the track.
SANDY BAY PICNIC AREA
Canoe ramp, walking tracks, picnic facilities and toilets are provided.
TO WONGA PARK 3 km
At the RIDGE PICNIC AREA tables, barbecues and rubbish bins are provided.
LEGEND
Picnic tables, sheltered tables
Barbecues
Toilets
Information Board
Disabled Access
Parking
Canoeing
Swimming
Horseriding
Walking tracks
Nature Walk
Park boundary
Open woodlands, old mine diggings, excellent spring wildflower displays and varied bird life are some of the main features at BLACK FLAT.
Blue Tongue Bend
JUMPING CREEK RESERVE
BLACK FLAT
Entry gate to park. Note Closing times.
Jumping Creek Road
Jumping Creek
THE COMMON
Croydon Road
Warrandyte – Ringwood Road
Tills Drive
TIMBER RESERVE
TO RINGWOOD 6 km
TO KANGAROO GROUND 3 km
Warrandyte Road
Kangaroo Ground
Did you know that The Island is man made? This channel, now the main course of the Yarra, was dug by gold prospectors late last century.
WARRANDYTE
Webb Street
WHIPSTICK GULLY
FOURTH HILL
Memorial Road
Gold Memorial
Exploring underground in old mine shafts around Fourth Hill can be fun... but dangerous. Make sure you are well equipped if you intend to visit one. ENTER AT YOUR OWN RISK.
TO RESEARCH 3 km
Research – Warrandyte Road
Stony Creek
Lane
Bradleys
River Street
Yarra Street
Andersons Creek
Harris Gully Rd.
TO DONVALE 6 km
Park Office
POUND BEND RESERVE
Entry gate to Park
Norman Reserve
Yarra
Pound Road
Tindals Road
Entry gate to park. Note Closing times.
Excellent view of Pound Bend Tunnel entrance from here. NORMAN RESERVE is also a canoe landing place.
TO TEMPLESTOWE 6 km TO MELBOURNE
0 .5 1 km
N
A delightful picnic area with graded walking tracks, interpretive signs, tables and toilets all designed for use by disabled persons. There is also a canoe ramp. BYO gas barbecue.
CANOEISTS NOTE:
There are canoe ramps at Pound Bend and Sandy Bay picnic areas. If you intend to use them, plan your trip ahead so that you are able to leave the park by closing time.

32 Langwarrin Flora and Fauna Reserve

Physical features: 214 ha. Langwarrin Reserve is in sandy heathland that slopes gently from north to south, with a high point of 107 m. Although most of the land is well-drained, clay subsoil on the lower land means low-lying areas are quite swampy. Aquifers below ground were once an important source of freshwater in the area.

Plants and animals: This Reserve is important for flora and fauna conservation, not only because it contains nearly half of all the indigenous plants and animals of the Mornington Peninsula, but also because it is one of the last remaining areas of almost undisturbed natural bushland on the southern fringe of Melbourne. More than 50 species of native ground orchids have been recorded, as have eight of Victoria's nine species of sundew. One of the important plant communities here, Silver-leaf Stringybark open forest, is now rare elsewhere having been cleared for settlement. The New Holland Mouse, a tiny native rodent, classified as rare and inadequately protected in Victoria, and the beautiful little Southern Emu-wren, have both been recorded from here and are particularly interesting. Correct habitat management, particularly the appropriate burning regime, for species such as these poses a major problem, especially difficult in areas such as Langwarrin that are both small and close to human settlement. Another major plant community, that of the sandy heathland, is still well-represented elsewhere, and has some interesting plants such as the dainty Tufted Blue-lily and the elegant Wedding Bush with its clusters of rich creamy flowers in spring.

Weeds are a considerable problem in the Reserve, particularly where the land was once cleared or grazed, and of course the sandy soil is ideal for rabbits, so they too are a problem. Another concern is that of domestic animals, particularly cats and dogs, which come into the Reserve from surrounding residential developments. Cats are one of the most efficient of all predators and can soon kill large numbers of native birds and small animals, whereas dogs are probably more of a threat from their mere presence in an area – the smell of dog disturbs small animals and scares them away.

Human history: From 1886 to 1980, most of the Flora and Fauna Reserve was part of Langwarrin Military Reserve. Langwarrin, along with the fortifications at Port Phillip Heads (see western end of Point Nepean NP), was established as the focus for Victoria's defences against possible invasion. Both permanent and reserve soldiers were trained at the Reserve. One Easter encampment, nearly 4 000 men and 900 horses were stationed there, a massive undertaking which from all accounts was somewhat reminiscent of Dad's Army. Later, 2 500 men were trained at Langwarrin for the Boer War. The site was later used for German prisoners-of-war, and as a venereal diseases hospital in World War I. Very little evidence now remains of the encampment, the rifle range, the buildings for men and horses, or the well-developed drainage and water systems that were once at Langwarrin.

Things to do: Walking; studying natural history; photography. Public facilities are not provided.

Best season to visit: Late winter and spring for wildflowers; any season for walking.

Special features: The large number of birds and of native orchids to be seen.

Relevant reading:

Calder W. (1987) *Australian Aldershot.*
Conservation, Forests and Lands (1986) *Langwarrin Flora and Fauna Reserve Draft Management Plan.*
Land Conservation Council (1973) *Study Report Melbourne Area.*

Further information:
C&E Regional Office, 205 Thomas St, Dandenong, Vic 3175. Phone (03) 706 7000.
Friends' Group: Phone (03) 783 5015.

New Holland Mouse *CFL*

Langwarrin

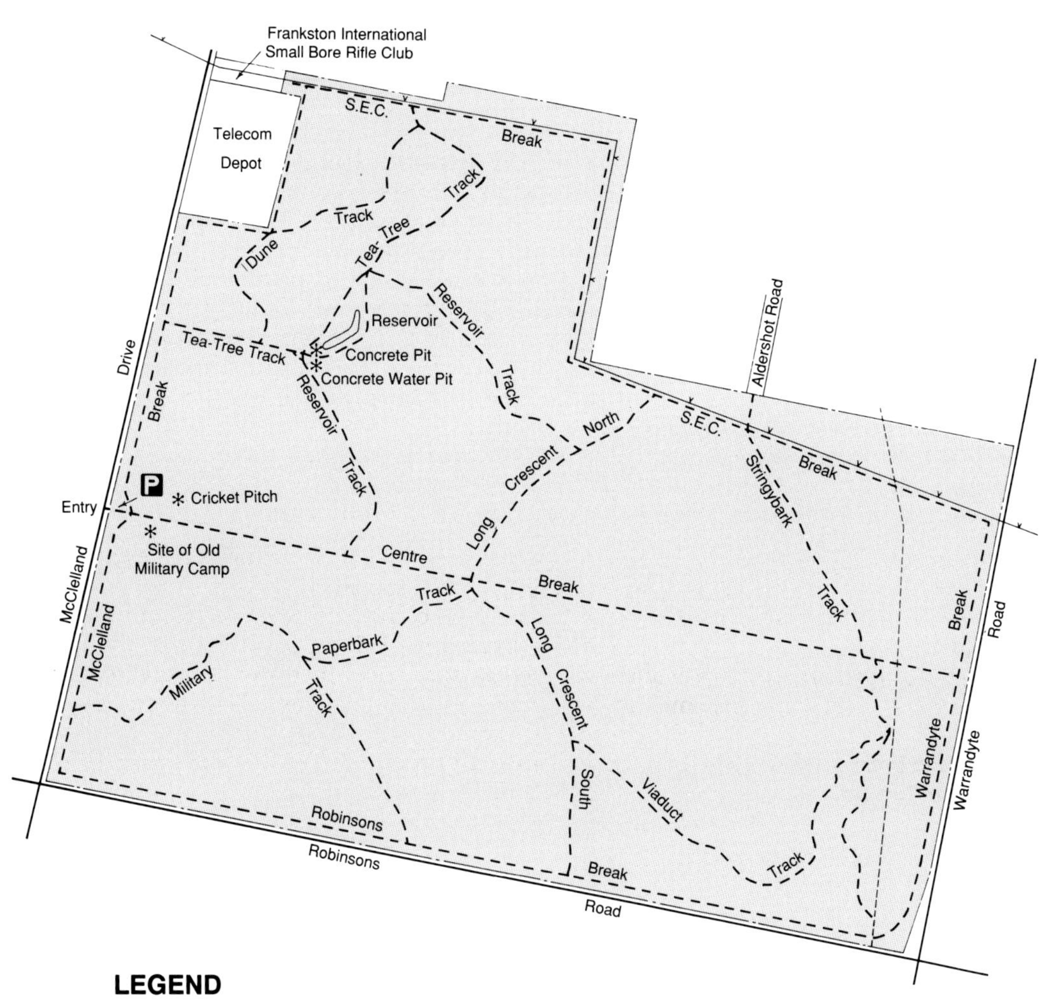

LEGEND

Major Road

Track

Open drain

Reserve boundary

S.E.C. transmission line

Car park

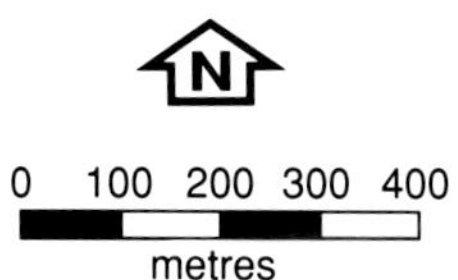

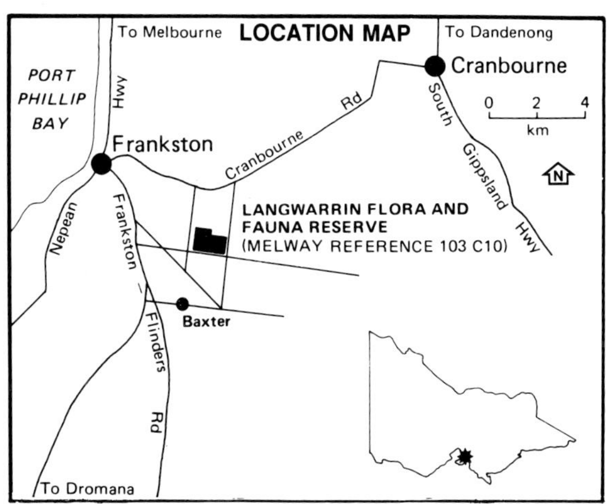

33 Lysterfield Lake Park

Physical features: 1 151 ha. This Park, with its man-made lake, lies in a single catchment area in the Lysterfield hills. The main ridge is of hornfels, a resistant metamorphic rock formed at the edge of the molten mass that cooled to give the granodiorite of Churchill NP. Large areas of Lysterfield were cleared for agriculture in the 1920's and '30's, and there is an extensive track network throughout the Park. The soils are prone to erosion and compaction, and their stability is poor when wet.

Plants and animals: This Park contains both a valuable remnant of native bush and also extensive eucalypt plantations, particularly Spotted Gum, Messmate and River Red Gum, which were planted in the 1950's to stabilise the cleared catchment areas. Lysterfield has been largely undisturbed for many years and waterbirds favour the excellent shallow feeding waters and breeding cover at the northern end of the Lake. Nearly 30 waterbirds, including migratory species such as Japanese Snipe which spend the northern winter in Australasia, have been recorded from here. Recently, land has been purchased to link Churchill NP and Lysterfield, which will enhance the conservation value of both Parks.

Human history: Construction of the dam to form Lysterfield Lake began in 1930, using stone that was quarried on site. From its completion in 1936 to 1975 (when Cardinia Reservoir became available) the Lake was used to supply water to the Mornington Peninsula. When the land passed to the National Parks Service it was decided that because of the marked shortage of inland waters for recreation close to Melbourne, this would be an important focus of the new Park. A major task in the creation of the new facilities has been to bring in thousands of tonnes of sand for beaches.

Things to do: Walking; abseiling; cycling; picnicking; horseriding; water-based sport provided it does not involve power boating (this includes motorised model boats). Restrictions have been placed on the location of various activities, both because of conservation values and the unstable soil. Unrestricted access for swimming and boat launching would soon muddy the lake water and destroy the delicate natural balance upon which the birds and other aquatic life depend.

Best season to visit: Spring for wildflowers; summer for swimming; otherwise any season.

Special features: The safe waters for training in water sports such as sailboarding and yachting; there is a visitor information centre.

Relevant reading:
Conservation Forests and Lands (1982) *Lysterfield Lake Park Recreation Use Plan.*
Land Conservation Council (1973) *Study Report Melbourne Area.*

Further information:
Park Office, Reservoir Rd, Lysterfield, Vic 3804. Phone (03) 796 8763
Friends' Group: (Lysterfield and Churchill) Phone (03) 873 2635.

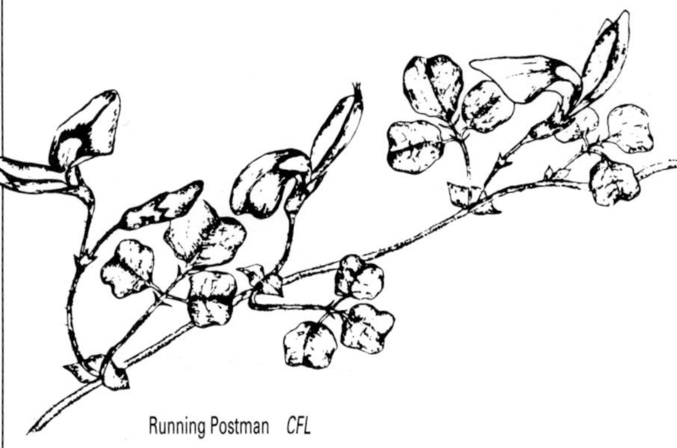

Running Postman *CFL*

Lysterfield

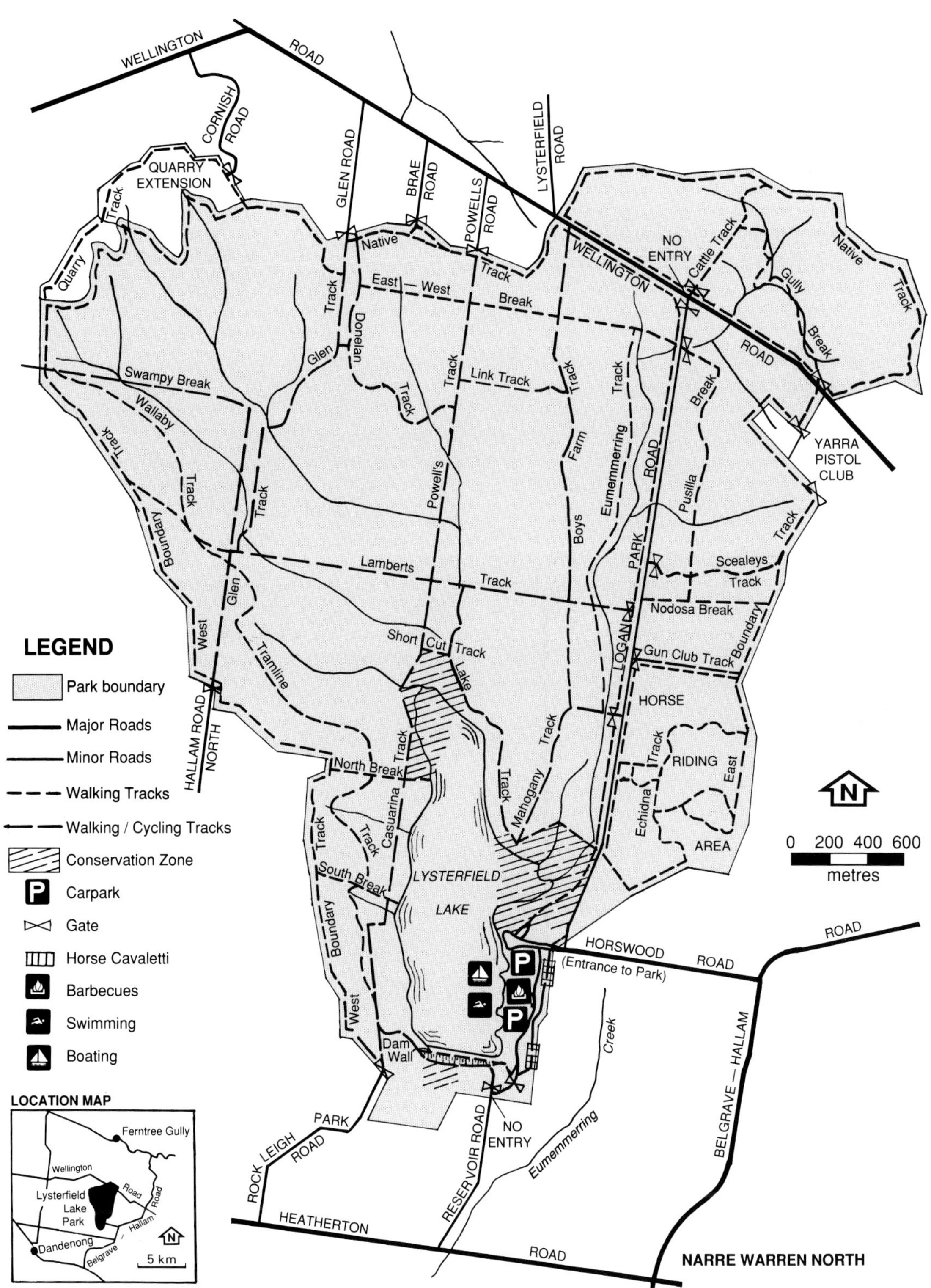

34 Churchill National Park

Physical features: 193 ha. The things that first strike you about Churchill NP are the high cyclone wire fence around its perimeter, and the SEC transmission lines looping their way intrusively above the Park. The fence was erected in the 1960's to protect the Park, while the powerlines date from the early 1950's, through an easement which was granted in the 1920's. The Park lies on the southern slopes of the Lysterfield Hills, a granodiorite range which was formed at about the same time as the Dandenong Ranges, but from less deeply buried igneous activity. (See also Dandenong NP and Lysterfield SP.) As the sedimentary rocks overlying the granodiorite mass eroded away, the alluvial deposits accumulated, and these now form the low-lying country of Churchill NP.

Plants and animals: Although none of the plants or animals found in this Park is considered rare, or even uncommon, it is the total community that is important since so much of any similar country has now been lost to clearing and settlement. There are a number of different types of vegetation in the small area of Churchill NP, although much of it is regrowth after fires and firewood collecting. At least 12 orchids and 14 wattles have been recorded here. Open woodland is common, especially in the west of the Park, and also between the SEC easement and the aqueduct. Here there is wavy-leaved Swamp Gum, Yellow Box and Black She-oak. The sound of wind moving through the she-oaks and the powerlines is a characteristic impression of this Park. Swampy vegetation provides habitat for the native Swamp Rat and Green and Golden Bell Frog along the creek and aqueduct. Kangaroos and wallabies are common, but the Park's other animals, such as possums, gliders and bandicoots, are seldom seen. Birds are plentiful and usually easy to see or hear, especially the Bell Miner with its clear one-note call.

Human history: Churchill NP escaped early settlement because it was once part of the Police Paddocks, set aside soon after colonisation. By the 1920's the Paddocks were no longer used, and with the threat of clearing and subdivision, moves were made to protect the land. This was finally realised in 1941. The disused aqueduct, built in 1921, supplied water to Dandenong.

Things to do: Picnicking; walking; jogging and cycling; birdwatching and studying natural history.

Best season to visit: Spring for wildflowers and birdlife; otherwise any time of year.

Special features: The views; a greater understanding of the impact of people on parks.

Relevant reading:
Land Conservation Council (1973) *Study Report Melbourne Area.*
National Parks Service (1978) *Churchill NP Proposed Management Plan.*
National Parks Service (1984) *Churchill NP Activity Trail.*

Further information:
Park Office, Park Drive, Rowville, Vic 3178. Phone (03) 707 4280.
Friends' Group: (Lysterfield and Churchill) Phone (03) 873 2635.

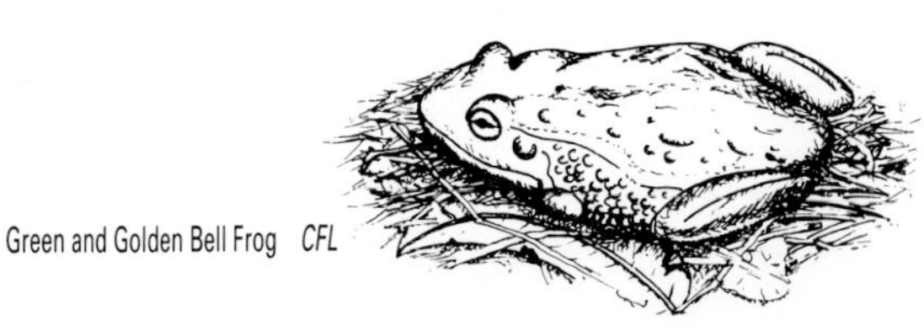
Green and Golden Bell Frog *CFL*

Churchill

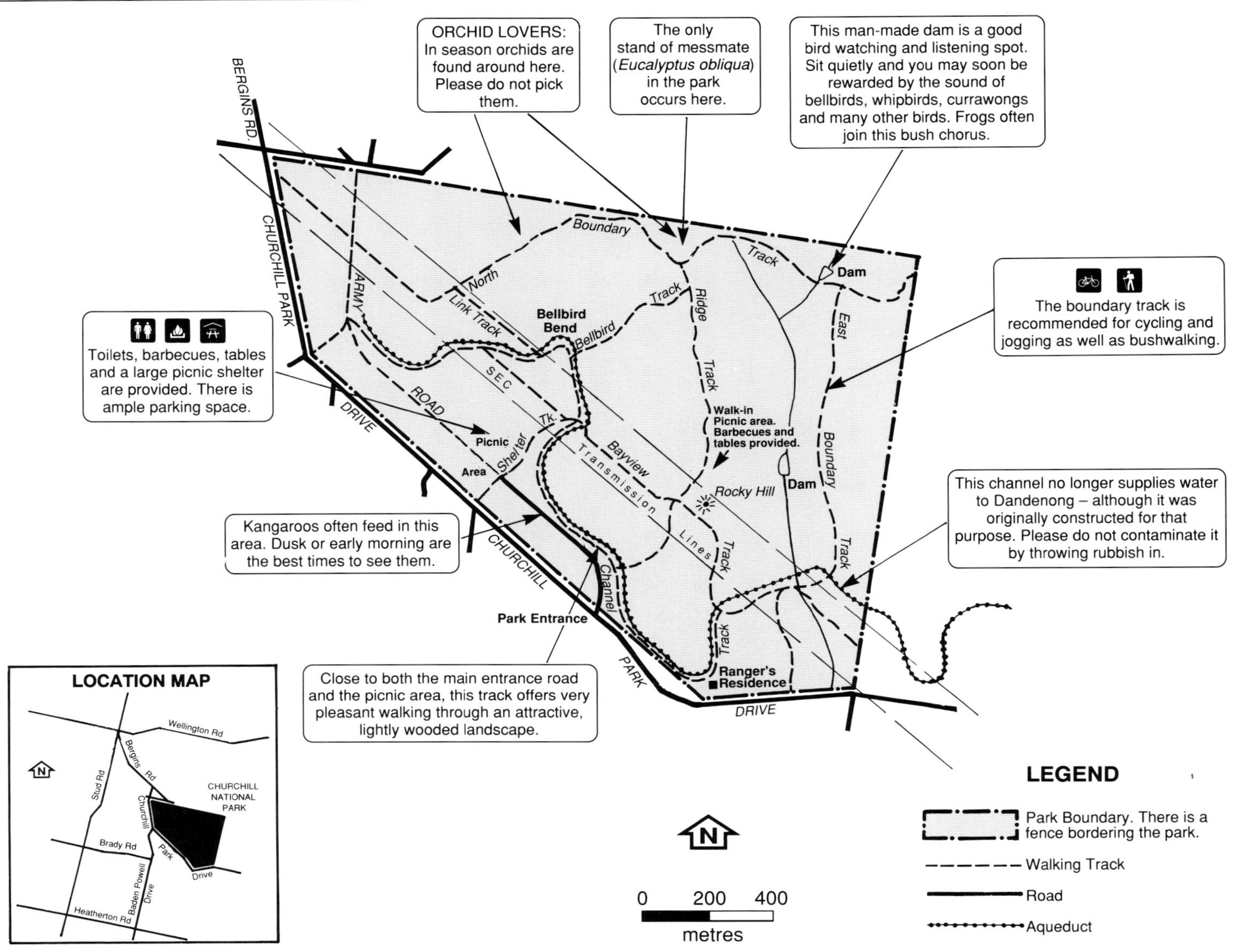

ORCHID LOVERS: In season orchids are found around here. Please do not pick them.
The only stand of messmate (*Eucalyptus obliqua*) in the park occurs here.
This man-made dam is a good bird watching and listening spot. Sit quietly and you may soon be rewarded by the sound of bellbirds, whipbirds, currawongs and many other birds. Frogs often join this bush chorus.
Toilets, barbecues, tables and a large picnic shelter are provided. There is ample parking space.
The boundary track is recommended for cycling and jogging as well as bushwalking.
This channel no longer supplies water to Dandenong – although it was originally constructed for that purpose. Please do not contaminate it by throwing rubbish in.
Kangaroos often feed in this area. Dusk or early morning are the best times to see them.
Close to both the main entrance road and the picnic area, this track offers very pleasant walking through an attractive, lightly wooded landscape.
BERGINS RD.
CHURCHILL PARK DRIVE
CHURCHILL PARK DRIVE
ARMY ROAD
Boundary
North Link Track
Bellbird Bend
Bellbird
Track
Ridge Track
Track
Dam
East Boundary Track
SEC Tk.
Picnic Area
Shelter
Walk-in Picnic area. Barbecues and tables provided.
Bayview
Transmission Lines
Track
Rocky Hill
Dam
Channel
Park Entrance
Track
Ranger's Residence
LOCATION MAP
Wellington Rd
Bergins Rd
Stud Rd
CHURCHILL NATIONAL PARK
Churchill Park Drive
Brady Rd
Baden Powell Drive
Heatherton Rd
N
0 200 400 metres
LEGEND
Park Boundary. There is a fence bordering the park.
Walking Track
Road
Aqueduct

35 French Island State Park

Physical features: 8 300 ha. The coastline is varied, the land uniform and sandy. Mt Wellington is only 96 m high. French Island lies within the Port Phillip Sunkland, a down-faulted trough which resulted from earth movements about 20–30 million years ago. Like Phillip Island, it is part of a high ridge that stands above the drowned sunkland.

Plants and animals: Just over half the Island is State Park and much of this remains as undisturbed woodland and heathland such as can be found on Mt Wellington. More than 500 species of native plants have been found, including 82 orchids. To the north there are mangrove mudflats and saltmarshes which are excellent bird habitat. In all about 200 birds have been recorded. Among the more unusual are the White-breasted Sea-Eagle, Blue-winged Parrot and Tawny-crowned Honey-eater, and rare Orange Bellied Parrots visit the Island each autumn and winter. French Island also has one of Victoria's breeding colonies of Australian Pelicans. As with other island populations, the differences between the mammals and plants of the mainland and those of the Island are of considerable scientific interest. Koalas, introduced here in the 1880's, are free of the disease *Chlamydia* that is affecting Koalas in many places, so they breed well and are often used for restocking other sites in Australia.

Human history: The explorer George Bass was the first to chart this area, although he did think that French Island was joined to the mainland. It was the Frenchman Baudin who established that it was an island and named it Ile des Francais, and Phillip Island, Ile des Anglais. Settlement followed from the 1850's, including a short-lived Industrial Settlement set up in 1894 to help Melbourne's unemployed. It is from this that names such as Perseverance date. Another short-lived venture was salt-farming which failed largely because of difficulties in drying the salt, even with large timber-fired drying vats. Today there are few large trees on the island, a legacy of timber-harvesting for these kilns.

Things to do: Walking; cycling; picnicking; and camping. For ferry timetables contact Victour, Melbourne, phone (03) 619 9444. The ferry does not take motor vehicles and there is no public transport on the island, so you need to take a bicycle or walk. There are three picnic sites within the Park, including one on the western coast. Each of these has camping facilities and water. Water is not available elsewhere.

Best season to visit: Spring for wildflowers; otherwise any, although cycling and walking can be hot in summer.

Special features: Being on an island; views, especially from the Pinnacles; the Island's flora.

Relevant reading:
Land Conservation Council (1973) *Study Report Melbourne Area.*

Further information:
Park Office, Bayview Rd, Tankerton, Vic 3921. Phone (059) 80 1294.
Friends' Group: Phone (03) 791 2315.

Koala *CFL*

French Island

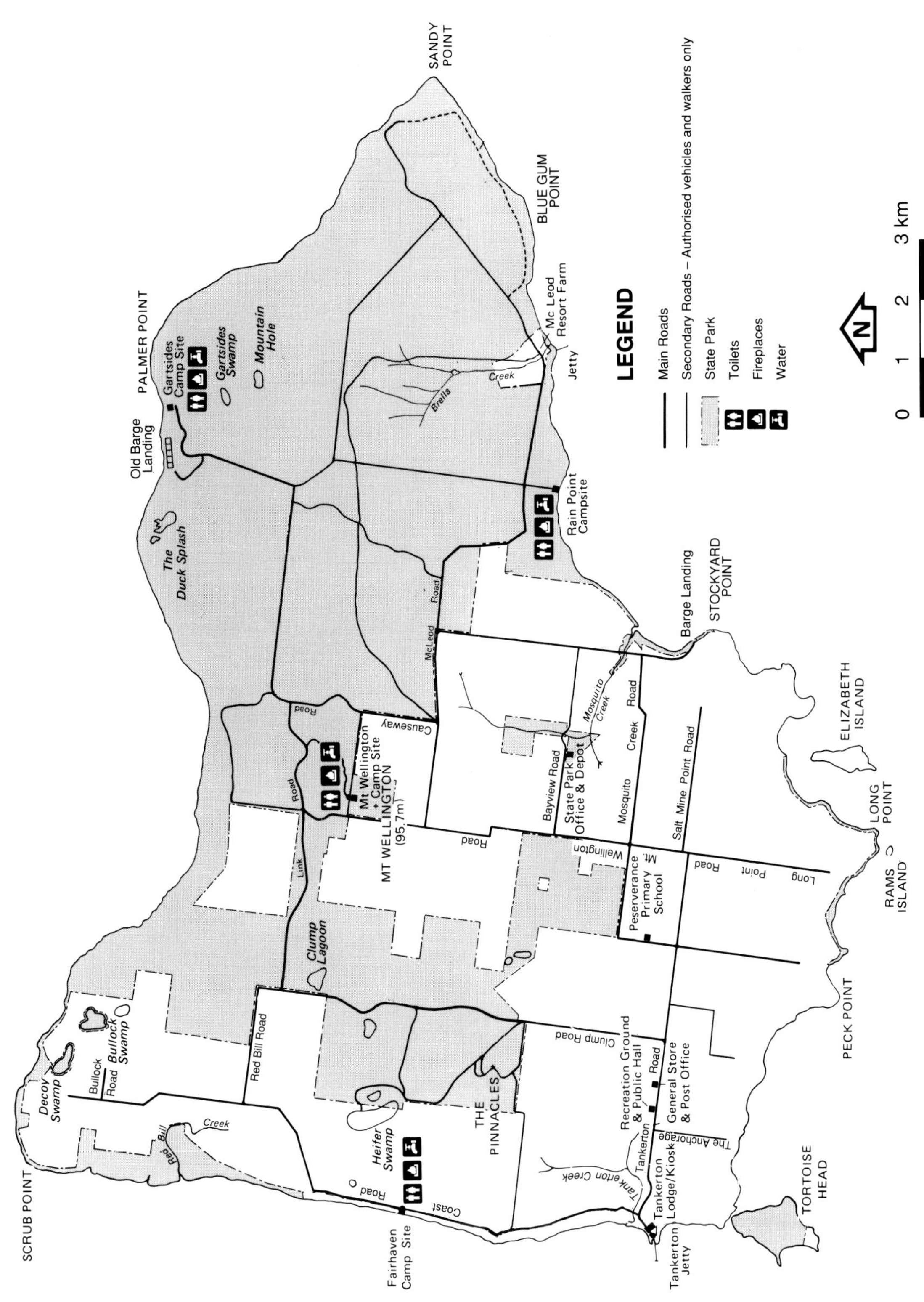

36 Phillip Island Penguin Reserve

Physical features: 300 ha. This account of Phillip Island has been widened to include some of its many other interesting features as well as the Penguin Reserve. The Reserve is at the western end of Phillip Island, a small basaltic island that lies across the entrance to Western Port. As on the Mornington Peninsula, the northern or bay coastline is gentle with sandy beaches, while the southern or ocean coastline is generally cliffed and rocky, although Summerland Beach, where the Penguin Parade takes place, is on the south of Phillip Island and is a pleasant sandy beach between rocky headlands. Phillip Island is actually a composite island made up of a number of 'tied islands' such as Cape Woolamai tied by a sandy isthmus, and the Nobbies tied by a rock platform exposed at high tide. Churchill Island and Pyramid Rock, on the other hand, are 'untied islands'. Most of the island is made up of dark coloured basalt, about 50 million years old, which erodes easily in the salt water. In some parts of the island up to five different flows can be seen, and in some cases there are beautiful crystalline formations in cavities in the basalt. The pink granite at Cape Woolamai and Pyramid Rock is from the Devonian Era and therefore much older. It was used in the beautiful old Colonial Mutual Life building at the corner of Collins and Elizabeth Streets in Melbourne, but like so many other buildings from Melbourne's boom era late last century, this was demolished in the 1960's to make way for larger premises. The granite erodes quite differently from the basalt and forms magnificent jagged rock stacks with sea caves and gulches, and imposing boulder beaches. In all, what we see today is the result of interactions between earth movements, erosion, deposition of sand and sediments, and sea-level changes over the ages.

Plants and animals: There is little native vegetation left on Phillip Island, except for some typical coastal species, including a fine stand of White Mangroves near Rhyll. Most of the remainder of the Island has been cleared for agriculture and settlement. Phillip Island is best known for its Little Penguins, but close behind them come the Koalas, easily seen in some of the trees along the roadsides. There are also Australian Fur Seals at the Nobbies, and many thousands of Mutton-birds (Short-tailed Shearwaters) which, like the penguins, nest here. Cape Barren Geese and Magpie Geese have been re-introduced and can now be seen as well.

The Little Penguins that nest at Phillip Island number some 6 000 breeding pairs, with as many again at Gabo Island in the far east of the State, and at Wilsons Promontory. They are only 33 cm tall, the smallest of the world's penguins, and are the only ones to nest on the Australian mainland. Over the last 80 years penguins have become less and less common at Phillip Island, due largely to loss of habitat and death (including road deaths) through human activity, predation by foxes, dogs and cats, and starvation. Numbers are known to have almost halved over the last 10 years alone. Now there is a major program to try to halt this decline. Measures include reclamation of penguin habitat that has been built over – currently almost a quarter of the residential allotments have been bought back and are being rehabilitated; vermin control; and research into the penguins' life cycle, breeding and feeding behaviour. In some years there is a massive mortality among Little Penguins, and current research indicates that starvation, when their preferred diet of anchovies and pilchards is in short supply, is the major cause of death in adult birds, while younger birds tend to die of parasite infestations.

Human history: Presumably the Aborigines had little trouble in reaching this island of plenty, where they feasted on birds and their eggs, seals, and shellfish from the rocks. The remains of such feasts are now exposed in sandy middens. Certainly oysters were common in the Bay, until over-exploited by fishermen early this century. Sealers and whalers also would have known of the muttonbird rookeries and come here to collect the young, fat-rich birds as they lay in their burrows. Until the San Remo bridge was built the only way across to the Island was by horse at lowtide, or by boat from Stony Point near Hastings on the western side of the Mornington Peninsula. Many of these early visitors were 'egging parties' coming to harvest the large, rich eggs of the muttonbirds, using a long staff of wood with a wire crook at the end for hooking them out of the burrow. These burrows were sometimes inhabited by snakes as well, so it was wise to listen for any hissing when

Phillip Island

Walk to Point Sambell

This track leads through open grassland to Point Sambell. A number of tracks lead to the rock shelves and beaches below. Views extend to Flinders and Cape Schanck on the mainland and tiny Cowrie Beach below. A variety of birds may be seen here, including the Silver, Pacific and Lesser Black-backed Gulls, Nankeen Kestrel, Brown Falcon and Brown Goshawk.

Beach access

There are a number of car parks with access tracks leading to Cat Bay's popular swimming and surfing beaches. The beachscape of this bay varies to include sandy sweeps, rocky points and intertidal rock platforms. Recent work by the National Parks Service has included the fencing of eroded areas to help dune stabilization and revegetation as well as protect bird colonies.

The Nobbies

The Nobbies are two rocky islands seen from Point Grant. The larger is known as Round Island. They are joined to Point Grant by a rocky shore platform of basalt which is covered by the rising tide.

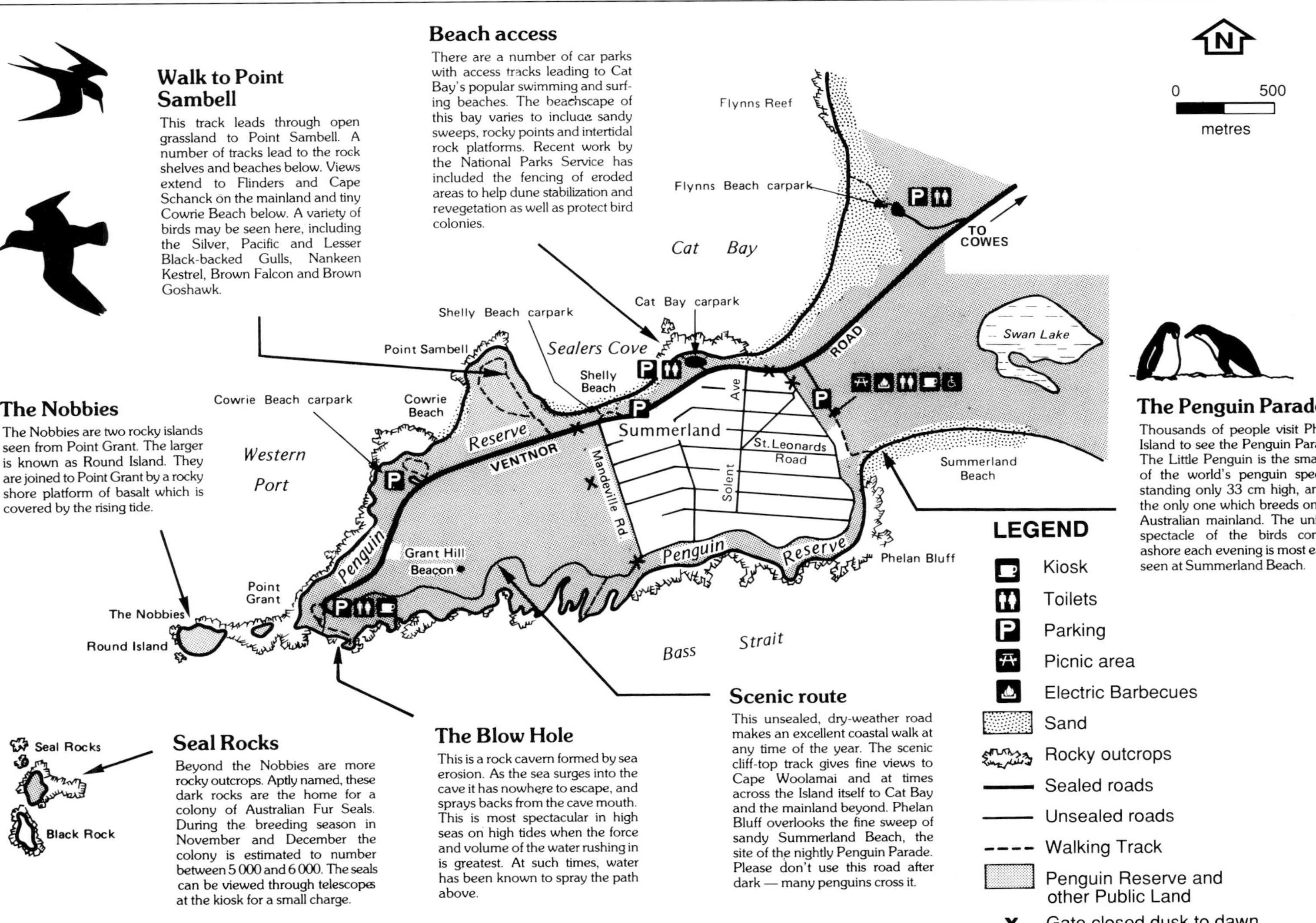

The Penguin Parade

Thousands of people visit Phillip Island to see the Penguin Parade. The Little Penguin is the smallest of the world's penguin species, standing only 33 cm high, and is the only one which breeds on the Australian mainland. The unique spectacle of the birds coming ashore each evening is most easily seen at Summerland Beach.

Seal Rocks

Beyond the Nobbies are more rocky outcrops. Aptly named, these dark rocks are the home for a colony of Australian Fur Seals. During the breeding season in November and December the colony is estimated to number between 5 000 and 6 000. The seals can be viewed through telescopes at the kiosk for a small charge.

The Blow Hole

This is a rock cavern formed by sea erosion. As the sea surges into the cave it has nowhere to escape, and sprays backs from the cave mouth. This is most spectacular in high seas on high tides when the force and volume of the water rushing in is greatest. At such times, water has been known to spray the path above.

Scenic route

This unsealed, dry-weather road makes an excellent coastal walk at any time of the year. The scenic cliff-top track gives fine views to Cape Woolamai and at times across the Island itself to Cat Bay and the mainland beyond. Phelan Bluff overlooks the fine sweep of sandy Summerland Beach, the site of the nightly Penguin Parade. Please don't use this road after dark — many penguins cross it.

LEGEND

- Kiosk
- Toilets
- Parking
- Picnic area
- Electric Barbecues
- Sand
- Rocky outcrops
- Sealed roads
- Unsealed roads
- Walking Track
- Penguin Reserve and other Public Land
- X Gate closed dusk to dawn

the staff first went in. Gradually over the years though, the emphasis has shifted from collecting to just watching and enjoying, particularly the delightful sight of the adult Little Penguins waddling their way up the beach at dusk, each intent on reaching its own burrow. An imposing new Visitor Centre has just recently been opened to service what is now one of Australia's most popular tourist attractions – more than 500 000 visitors each year. In this Centre, as well as the usual facilities, there are videos and displays with information about how penguins live, both while at sea and on land; the history of the Reserve and its management; and current research and management strategies.

Things to do: Viewing the Penguin Parade, and do allow plenty of time to see the excellent displays; koala-spotting – just look for a group of people peering up into a tree; walking, on tracks and beaches (if you're interested in geology, check the reference below first); exploring the rock pools at Cat Bay – named thus because, in 1798, as Matthew Flinders' men 'were putting ashore in search of fresh water, pussie sprang first into the scrub, and was never seen again', probably the first of the many cats that have done so much damage to the wildlife on this island.

Best season to visit: The Penguin Parade is open all year and the walking is good in any season; an extra attraction in late September are the dark 'clouds' of thousands upon thousands of mutton-birds returning to their nesting sites after the long journey south from Siberia.

Special features: Rocky coasts and spectacular scenery; the apparent total disregard of the penguins for curious humans.

Relevant reading:
Clark I. & Cook B. (eds) (1988) *Victorian Geology Excursion Guide.*
Conservation, Forests and Lands (1989) *Phillip Island Penguin Reserve Management Plan.*
Land Conservation Council (1973) *Study Report Melbourne Area.*
Stahel C. and Gales R. (1987) *The Fairy Penguin in Australia.*
Victorian Naturalist (1899) Vol. XVI, No. 3, pp. 45–9, and (1903–4) Vol. XX, pp. 166–173.

Further information:
Penguin Reserve, Summerlands, Phillip Island, Vic 3922. Phone (059) 56 8300.
Penguin Friends: Phone (059) 56 8300.

Little Penguins *CFL*

37 Point Nepean National Park

Physical features: 2 680 ha. Much of this newly-declared Park will already be familiar as the former Cape Schanck Coastal Park and as the Highfield and Greens Bush areas of what was Nepean SP. The remainder, Point Nepean itself, is an exciting new addition, and is the reason for the change in status from state and coastal (with a high recreation emphasis) to national (with a high conservation emphasis) park.

Point Nepean NP embraces most of the southern coastline and the eastern tip of the Mornington Peninsula. The centre of the Peninsula, in which Greens Bush and Highfield lie, is part of the Mornington Uplands which are bounded by two fault lines. To the east of the Uplands are the Western Port Lowlands, and to the west the Port Phillip Lowlands of which the Nepean Peninsula is a major part. These fault lines still occasionally make their presence felt as earth tremors on the Mornington Peninsula. The Nepean Peninsula has developed over the last million years as water, alternately frozen and released in a series of glacial periods, invaded the Yarra floodplain, forming what we now know as Port Phillip Bay. The Peninsula was formed largely from coastal dunes by deposition of secondary limestone from the dissolved shelly material in the sands. This secondary limestone makes up the rugged cliffs along the southern ocean shore of the Peninsula, and also the strange 'cylinders' of limestone seen in the cliffs and along the beaches. These latter structures are formed when a plant stem or root acts as a nucleus for limestone deposition, and then later rots away. At Cape Schanck the rocks are obviously different, being dark and basaltic, and what we are seeing is actually a series of lava flows hundreds of metres thick. The beautiful reddish banding is the result of weathering and therefore of soil formation in between lava flows.

Plants and animals: The Peninsula today is of course very different from that which greeted the first Europeans. Peter Good, gardener on Matthew Flinders Voyage to Terra Australis 1801–03, recorded his impressions of the Nepean Peninsula in his diary:

> This neck of land has a very pleasing appearance, having much resemblance to a Gentlemans Park in England, being covered with fine Green grass and numerous Trees and Bushes in pleasing irregularity, and so far apart as to admit the whole surface to be covered with Grass, with gentle rising hills and little vallies; the soil is rather sandy but is probably the best that we had seen in New Holland and the only place that we had found the surface covered with Grass & which had preserved its verdure through the Dry Season.

The Nepean Peninsula and across towards Bushrangers Bay would once have been covered with an open woodland of Drooping She-oak, Coast Banksia and Moonah; some fine old Moonahs can still be seen in the new part of the Park. On the coast proper the vegetation is shrubby with typical coastal plants such as Coast Wattle, Beard-heath and Tea-tree, and the low, bluish Cushion-bush which adds so much visual appeal to the landscape. This coastal vegetation is extremely vulnerable to people-pressure, but it is vital in preventing erosion. An excellent example of the rehabilitation of a damaged and badly eroded surface can be seen down at Cape Schanck, where a boardwalk has been built from the carpark to the point. In the Greens Bush and Highfield sections of the Park there are tall open forests of Messmate and other eucalypts, with an understorey of often colourful shrubs, and treeferns in the sheltered moist gullies. There is now none of the original forest left on the Mornington Peninsula. Only a few isolated trees older than 150–200 years remain; otherwise all is secondary or even tertiary regrowth.

The animal and bird life has also been greatly altered. Early reports spoke of Eastern Grey Kangaroo, Swamp and Red-necked Wallaby, Echidna, Wombat, Koala, and of possums, gliders and native rats, most of which have now gone or are only rarely seen. Many birds were recorded also, including Emus which are no longer found here, and others which are now rare, although the oceans, coastal heaths and bushland are still good areas to see a variety of birds.

Many of the ocean beaches have excellent rock platforms with a fascinating assortment of seaweeds and marine creatures in the rockpools. Sadly though, they too have suffered badly from people-pressure, and it is only when you are fortunate enough to visit an isolated coast well away from people that you realise just how depauperate many of our rockpools and shorelines have become.

Point Nepean

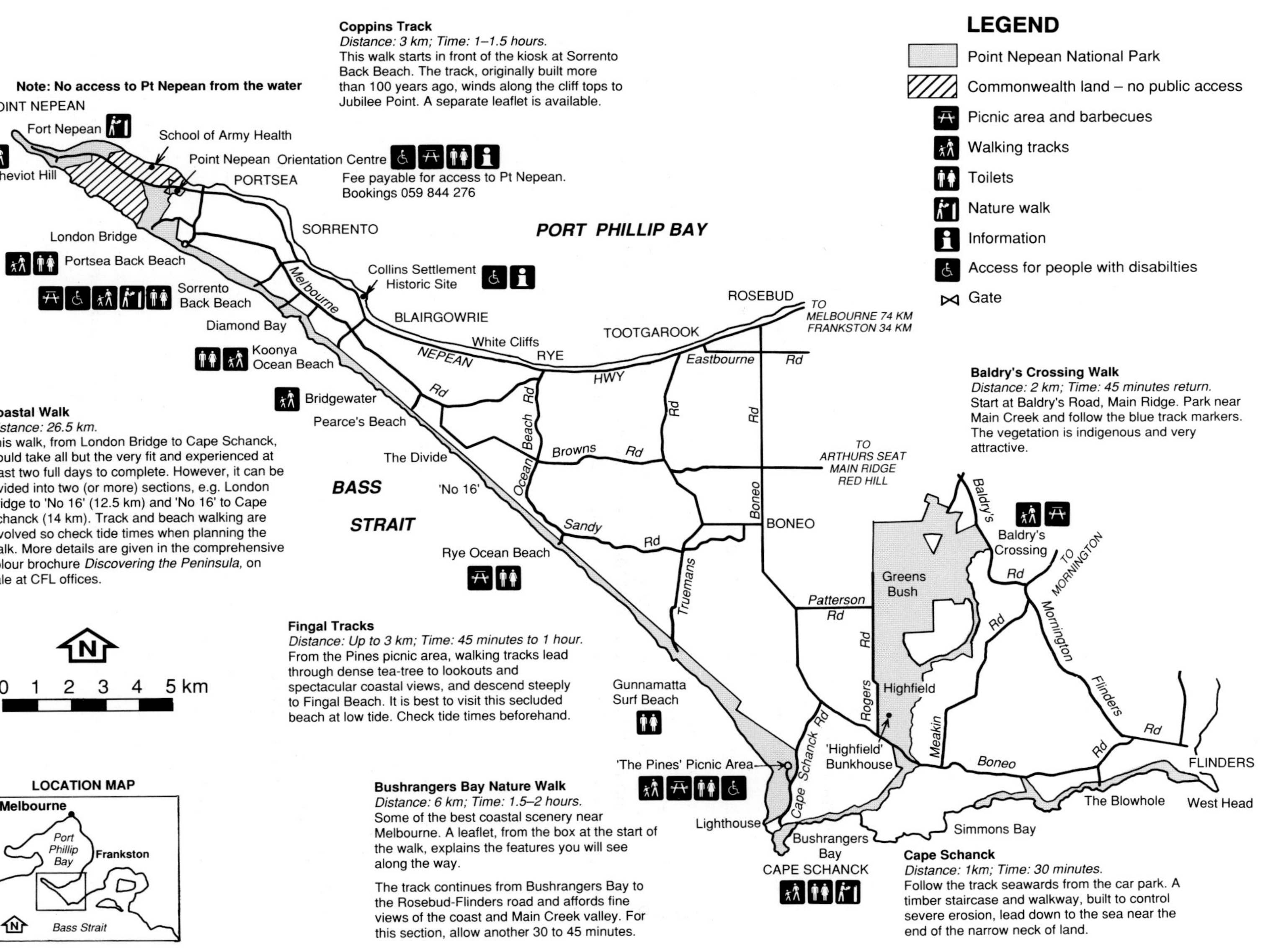

Coppins Track
Distance: 3 km; Time: 1–1.5 hours.
This walk starts in front of the kiosk at Sorrento Back Beach. The track, originally built more than 100 years ago, winds along the cliff tops to Jubilee Point. A separate leaflet is available.

Coastal Walk
Distance: 26.5 km.
This walk, from London Bridge to Cape Schanck, would take all but the very fit and experienced at least two full days to complete. However, it can be divided into two (or more) sections, e.g. London Bridge to 'No 16' (12.5 km) and 'No 16' to Cape Schanck (14 km). Track and beach walking are involved so check tide times when planning the walk. More details are given in the comprehensive colour brochure *Discovering the Peninsula,* on sale at CFL offices.

Fingal Tracks
Distance: Up to 3 km; Time: 45 minutes to 1 hour.
From the Pines picnic area, walking tracks lead through dense tea-tree to lookouts and spectacular coastal views, and descend steeply to Fingal Beach. It is best to visit this secluded beach at low tide. Check tide times beforehand.

Bushrangers Bay Nature Walk
Distance: 6 km; Time: 1.5–2 hours.
Some of the best coastal scenery near Melbourne. A leaflet, from the box at the start of the walk, explains the features you will see along the way.

The track continues from Bushrangers Bay to the Rosebud-Flinders road and affords fine views of the coast and Main Creek valley. For this section, allow another 30 to 45 minutes.

Baldry's Crossing Walk
Distance: 2 km; Time: 45 minutes return.
Start at Baldry's Road, Main Ridge. Park near Main Creek and follow the blue track markers. The vegetation is indigenous and very attractive.

Cape Schanck
Distance: 1km; Time: 30 minutes.
Follow the track seawards from the car park. A timber staircase and walkway, built to control severe erosion, lead down to the sea near the end of the narrow neck of land.

Even so, it is worth timing a beach walk for lowtide and seeing what you can find, but remember all marine life along the shore is now protected and must not be collected. Also, please remember to replace any rocks or pieces of wood and seaweed as you found them – exposure quickly kills most marine and intertidal creatures.

Human history: The Bunurong tribe of Aborigines, largely a coastal people, inhabitated this fertile area at the time Australia was discovered. As well as shellfish from the shore, fish from the sea, and an abundance of birds and game, there were also plenty of plant foods such as grass and wattle seeds which were ground into flour, rushes and many orchids with succulent roots, Cherry Ballart, fungi, and the nectar of banksia trees. A variety of middens and artefacts has been discovered, some of which have since been destroyed by road-making, house building, soil removal and similar activities. One large site, near Cape Schanck, had good fresh water and appears to have been a permanent campsite, a sure indication of an abundance of food.

In 1802, Lieutenant John Murray, in the *Lady Nelson*, discovered and entered Port Phillip Bay, followed a few weeks later by Captain Matthew Flinders in the *Investigator*. By 1803, the First Settlement was established near Sorrento, but both this and an even earlier settlement at Churchill Island in Western Port were short-lived and it was not until the 1840's that the Peninsula saw lasting settlements established. The face of the land changed as pastures were established, limestone extracted and burnt to form mortar for buildings in the rapidly growing city of Melbourne, timber cut to fire the bakers' ovens in Melbourne, and wattle trees stripped of their bark for tannin. As the original vegetation was removed and the land disturbed, Coast Tea-tree, which till then had been just that, a coastal species, began to rapidly colonise further inland until now it makes up much of the native vegetation. With the rapid expansion of Melbourne, the Peninsula steadily gained in popularity as a holiday destination (one such holiday-maker in the 1880's was Laura in Henry Handel Richardson's *The Getting of Wisdom*).

Much of the popularity of the Sorrento region was due to the efforts of the theatrical entrepreneur, George Coppin, after whom Coppins Track is named. He built limestone and clay tracks, using local materials, shelter sheds and elegant rotundas, and as well operated paddle steamers between Melbourne and the Peninsula. At first there was sea access only, then as cars became more frequent roads were built, and from then on holiday houses proliferated throughout the Peninsula.

Some of Coppin's tracks form the foundation of tracks still in use today, as do the numbered tracks along the back beach near Blairgowrie that were built in the late 1800's to facilitate life-saving crews reaching ships wrecked along the notorious ocean beaches. One of the best known shipwrecks along the Point Nepean coast was that of the *Cheviot*, after which Cheviot beach was named.

The newly opened Point Nepean section has a fascinating history, but because it has been a military reserve for over 100 years, it has been inaccessible to most people. From 1840 the land was grazed, but then in 1852 the emigrant ship *Ticonderoga* arrived at the Heads with 100 of its 800 passengers having died of typhus, dysentery and scarlet fever. The Government of Victoria was suddenly faced with a pressing quarantine problem. Facilities were hastily moved out to the Point from Elwood to deal with the situation, and a permanent Quarantine Station was established a few years later. Many of the hospital buildings are still there today, as are the graves of those who died at the hospital, or in shipwrecks around the coast, or simply of old age. The Station's last major use for quarantine purposes was in 1919 when soldiers returned from World War I suffering from the severe influenza outbreak that was ultimately to kill more people than the war itself. Today the Station is the School of Army Health, open to the public at certain times.

The Point's military usage began in 1882 when there was a major scare that Australia was about to be invaded by the Russians. Fortifications were constructed, heavy artillery emplaced and barracks and parade grounds built. Many of these are now semi-derelict and are not open to the public for safety reasons. The first Allied shots of both world wars were fired from here. The first across the bows of a German ship attempting to leave Port Phillip Bay within minutes of the declaration of war; the second across a small Bass Strait freighter which needed prompting to give the appropriate recognition signal! In 1908, the Victorian Government was requested to allot the Commonwealth

Government 170 ha as a military reserve. Now the land is back with the people of Victoria as their newest national park and has been developed with a grant from the Bicentennial Authority. Cape Schanck Coastal Park, on the other hand, was created in 1975 largely to prevent further degradation of the coast by uncontrolled human access.

Things to do: This is a diverse Park, with a wide range of coastal activities – swimming; surfing; diving; fishing; exploring rockpools; beachcombing; and hang gliding from the cliffs. There are many attractive walks, two of the more popular being those at Baldrys Crossing and to Bushrangers Bay. (For the The Two Bays Walk, see Arthurs Seat SP.) Horseriding is also possible in some areas. At Highfield there is a bunkhouse available to schools and to environmental studies groups. And last, but by no means least, there is visiting Point Nepean itself. At present, access is strictly controlled, and it is essential to check and book first.

Best season to visit: Any.

Special features: Rugged and spectacular coastlines; the chance to see one of the least altered parts of the now highly modified Mornington Peninsula; the sense of history.

Relevant reading:

Australian Broadcasting Commission (1969) *Bass Strait.*
Calder W. (1986) *Peninsula Perspectives.*
Conservation, Forests and Lands (1987) *Point Nepean: a Proposed National Park.*
Field J. (1959) *These Joyous Sands.*
Land Conservation Council (1973) *Study Report Melbourne Area.*
National Trust of Victoria (February 1987) *Trust News.*
Garnett S. et al (1986) *Birds of Port Phillip Bay.*
Conservation, Forests and Lands *Discovering Historic Point Nepean.*
Victorian National Parks Association and Conservation, Forests and Lands (1989) *Discovering the Peninsula* (map).

(See also Langwarrin Flora and Fauna Reserve.)

Further information:
Point Nepean NP, PO Box 117, Sorrento, Vic 3943. Phone (059) 844 276.
Friends of Nepean Parks: Phone (03) 25 3244.

Pied Cormorant *CFL*

◀ Rock-climbing at Kooyoora SP *EW*

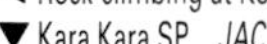
▼ Kara Kara SP *JAC*

◀ Platypus *ARI*

▼ River Red Gums at Barmah SP *CFL*

38 Arthurs Seat State Park

Physical features: 350 ha. Arthurs Seat, 314 m, is the highest point on the Mornington Peninsula and is one of three granite prominences along the length of the Peninsula, the others being at Olivers Hill, near Mornington, and at Mt Martha. They are all from late Devonian lava flows with medium grain granite which can easily be seen in roadside cuttings. This granite weathers to a sandy clay containing quartz crystals. The summit of Arthurs Seat is flat, and is probably a degraded remnant of an ancient surface which is now very eroded. To the south of the mountain the soils are deeper and more fertile, and so have mostly been cleared for orchards and farms.

Plants and animals: Although the vegetation here, as on the rest of the Peninsula, is largely regrowth, much of it, such as the coastal form of Manna Gum on Arthurs Seat, is very attractive, and there is a particularly beautiful fern gully in Waterfall Gully south of *Seawinds*. Almost all these treeferns are quite young though, since many were removed during the Depression to make fern baskets. Much of the the lower part of Arthurs Seat has now been invaded by the South African shrub Boneseed, which arrived in Victoria in 1858 as a garden plant. Unfortunately, it found local conditions very much to its liking, and without the pests and predators of its homeland it has now become a invasive noxious weed. Recently, local C&E staff and volunteers have been clearing some of the tracks of Boneseed, and have had the satisfaction of seeing native plants such as small lilies, violets and orchids start to reappear. More help though, is urgently needed. As the native plants return, so the habitat is improved for native birds and other animals, many of which are dependent on food chains that cannot exist in the deep shade that Boneseed creates.

Human history: The land around Arthurs Seat was taken up by Andrew McCrae in about 1844. McCrae took timber from the tall forests on the eastern, sheltered side of the mountain, leaving the drier Port Phillip side uncleared, but in 1852 the summit was cleared to give an unobstructed view from the newly built tower. As the Mornington Peninsula became more popular with visitors, so did Arthurs Seat with its commmanding views across the bay, which on a good day stretch south to the Otways and north to Mt Macedon. Sadly, much of the mountain has now been scarred, by quarrying, gravel extraction and of course fire and clearing.

Seawinds, another major component of this Park, is just south of the summit of Arthurs Seat. Its 34 ha consist largely of ornamental gardens dominated by a row of massive cypress trees about 100 years old. The property was purchased by the State Government in 1975, but before this its owners bought a number of clay sculptures by the noted Dandenongs sculptor, William Ricketts. These can now be seen around the gardens. Many visitors to *Seawinds* are somewhat puzzled that such splendid gardens lack an equally splendid house, but somehow, although the plans were drawn up, the house was never built.

Since 1975 and the creation of Nepean SP (much of which is now incorporated into Arthurs Seat SP), there has been a program of buying back private land as it became available, including parts of Greens Bush, and adding it to the existing parks.

Things to do: Picnicking; horseriding; camping; walking – the first section of the 30 km Two Bays walking track which will ultimately link Bushrangers and Port Phillip Bays is from Dromana to Waterfall Gully, and is already open. The remainder of the track, from Waterfall Gully to Greens Bush and Main Creek will be completed as soon as possible.

Best season to visit: Any, although *Seawinds* may be closed in wet weather during winter.

Special features: Panoramic views; an unexpectedly unpeopled part (except at the summit of Arthurs Seat) of one of Melbourne's most popular playgrounds.

Arthurs Seat

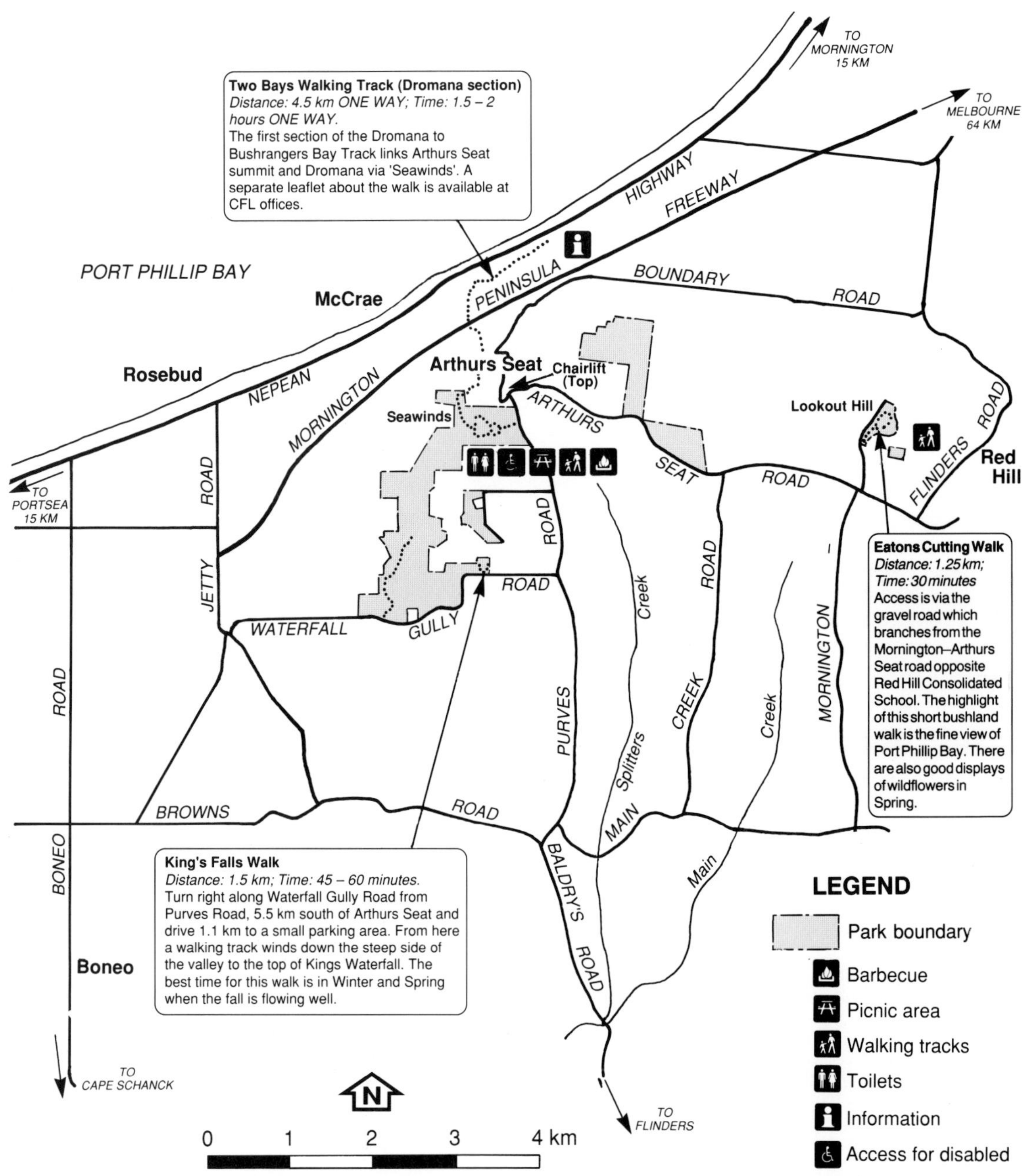

Relevant reading:
Calder W. (1986) *Peninsula Perspectives.*
Land Conservation Council (1973) *Study Report Melbourne Area.*
Victorian National Parks Association and Conservation, Forests and Lands (1989) *Discovering the Peninsula* (map).

Further information:
C&E Office, Nepean Hwy, Dromana, Vic 3936. Phone (059) 87 2755.
Friends of Nepean Parks: Phone (03) 25 3244.

Ivy-leaf Violet *MS*

NORTH EAST AND CENTRAL PARKS

This part of Victoria is remarkably diverse and its parks correspondingly range from riverine woodlands on the Murray River which are frequently flooded, through dry ranges to high plateaux and granite mountains. A number of the parks fall within the 'golden triangle' and have a history that is closely bound up with that of gold and its mining during the boom years of the 1850's and 1860's. In these parks, therefore, there are often interesting examples of regeneration as the bush slowly heals the scars that were left on the face of the land well over one hundred years ago.

	Page No.	*Entrance Fee*	*Information Centre*	*Multilingual Information*	*Picnic Areas*	*Fireplaces*	*Toilets*	*Disabled Access*	*Walking Tracks*	*Nature Walk or Drive*	*Swimming*	*Climbing*	*Horseriding*	*Fishing*	*Boating*	*Camping*	*Caravans*	*Km from Melbourne*	*Date Declared*
Barmah	133		■		■	■	■		■		■		■		■	■	■	225	1987
Beechworth	142				■	■	■		■	■								270	1980
Burrowa-Pine Mtn	145				■	■	■		■	■			■			■		350	1978
Cathedral Range	150				■	■	■		■			■	■			■	■	115	1979
Chiltern	141				■	■	■		■				■			**R**		275	1978
Eildon	155					■	■				■			■	■	■	■	135	1980
Fraser	152	■			■	■	■	**P**	■	■	■			■	■	■	■	150	1958
Kamarooka	125				■	■			■									175	1986
Kara Kara	131				■	■	■		■					■		■		175	1986
Kooyoora	130				■	■	■		■							■		220	1985
Mount Lawson	147												■			■		330	1988
Mount Samaria	149				■	■	■		■							■		130	1979
Reef Hills	138				■	■												200	1986
Terrick Terrick	134				**x**■	■	■		■							■		225	1988
Warby Range	137				■	■	■		■	■			■			■		250	1979
Whipstick	123				■	■	■		■							■		160	1986
Wychitella	127				■	■			■						■	■		235	1985

R = Restricted **P** = Proposed **x** = No Water

Walkers would do well to avoid such innocent looking mounds, each of which marks a nest of ants ready to defend their territory against all comers *JAC*

Yellow Box, a tree which produces excellent honey *JAC*

39 Whipstick State Park

Physical features: 2 300 ha. This Park is in gently undulating country of thinly-bedded and tightly-folded Ordovician shales, slates and sandstones. Soils are skeletal, impermeable and easily eroded. Annual rainfall is about 500 mm, with warm dry summers and cool wet winters.

Plants and animals: Whipstick SP is dominated by open forests of Red Ironbark, Yellow Gum and Grey Box, with some mallee areas of Blue, Green and Bull Mallee. The mallee here and in Kamarooka SP further north, is unusual in that it occurs on rocky soils, rather than on sand as in northern Victoria. The Whipstick's renowned wildflowers are best seen in the open forests where colourful shrubs, including the Whirakee Wattle, make an unforgettable picture against the dark trunks of the ironbark eucalypts. The mallee vegetation is denser and less colourful than that of the forests, but has many interesting plants such as the rare Whipstick Westringia. Because it is so dense and provides so many good nesting sites, the mallee is especially valuable bird habitat. The songbirds are a particular delight, with Crested Bellbirds, Grey Shrike-thrushes and Gilbert's Whistlers all making their presence obvious. A number of mammals are also found in the Whipstick, including Echidnas, Swamp Wallabies and Eastern Grey Kangaroos.

Human history: Aboriginal axe-heads and grinding stones were found here by eucalypt cutters but Europeans had little contact with the Whipstick until gold was discovered here in 1857. Much of the timber was then removed to provide wood for the mines, and later for the expanding rail network. The industry for which the Whipstick is best known, eucalyptus oil distillation using the easily harvested and cineole-rich Blue Mallee, has now all but ceased.

Efforts to create a Whipstick reserve began in the 1880's when the Field Naturalists' Club of Victoria visited the area, but the real push has been in the last 30 years, during which time much of the initiative has come from the Bendigo Field Naturalists' Club, which, along with the VNPA, proposed the formation of a Whipstick national park. The FNC surveyed and mapped the area, and both they and their opposition lobbied the Government vigorously. A turning point was in 1972 when the Whipstick Forest Park was declared. Additional protection came in 1974 with an Interim Development Order (IDO) that prevented further land clearing. This IDO means that there is now a wildlife corridor linking the Whipstick with Kamarooka SP. In 1973 the Whipstick was classified by the National Trust. Whipstick State Park was declared in 1986.

Things to do: Sightseeing including relics of goldmining and eucalyptus oil distilling; studying natural history; walking; cycling; picnicking; fossicking (in restricted areas only).

Best season to visit: Spring for the wildflowers and birds.

Special features: Spectacular wildflower displays; a wealth of birds.

Relevant reading:

Conservation, Forests and Lands (1989) *Whipstick Public Lands Proposed Management Plan.*
Land Conservation Council (1978) *Study Report North-central Area.*
Perry W. (1978) *Tales of the Whipstick.*
Ellis P. 'Conservation History of the Whipstick', *Whirakee* (June 1987 to Sept 1988).

Further information:
C&E Regional Office, 31 Mackenzie St, Bendigo, Vic 3550. Phone (054) 43 8911.

Whipstick and Kamarooka

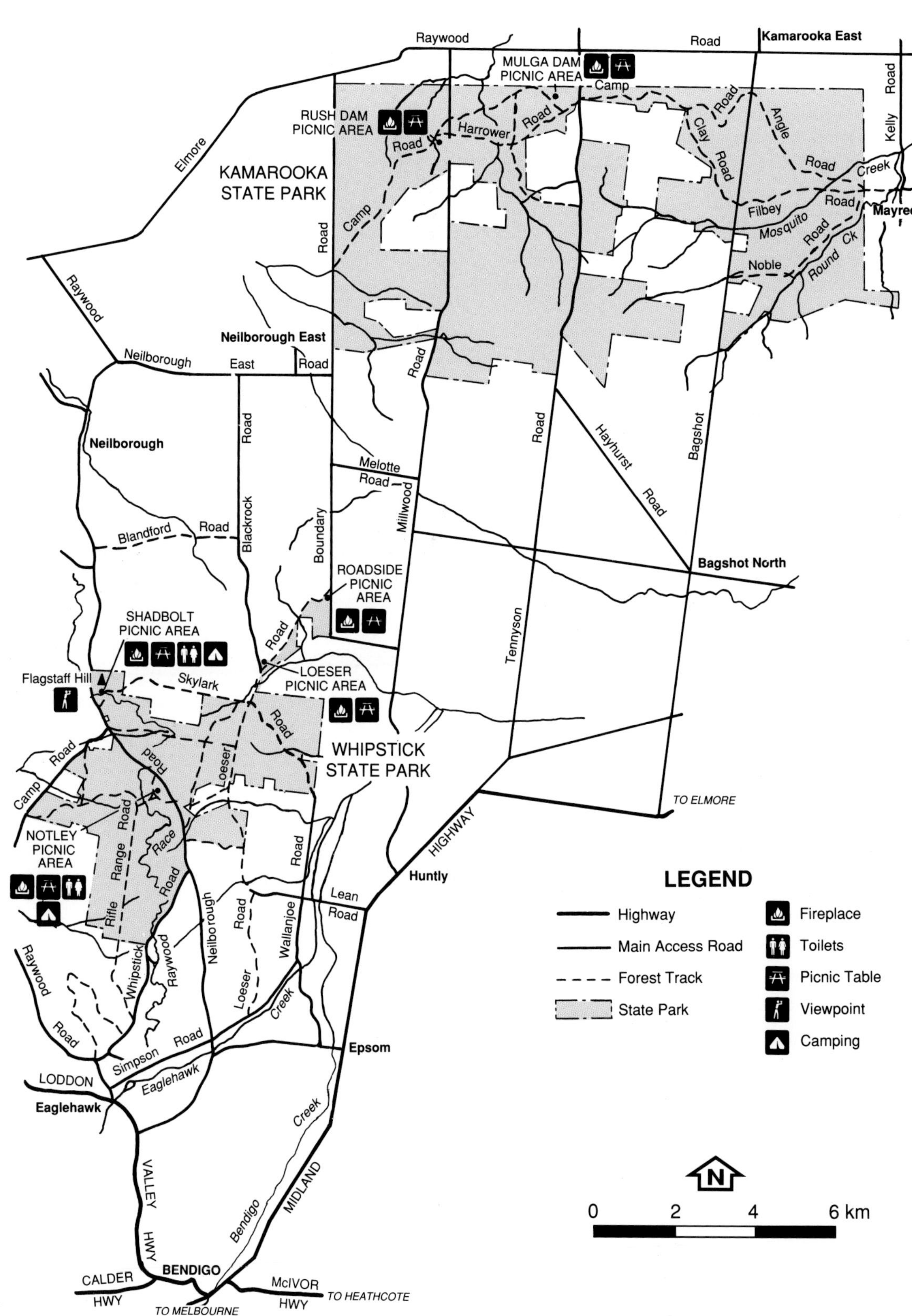

40 Kamarooka State Park

Physical features: 6 300 ha. Kamarooka SP is in that part of Victoria where the western highlands and the riverine plains of the Murray meet. Generally, the geology, soils and climate are similar to those of the Whipstick, except that the gold here occurred in sandstone rather than in the more usual quartz. The average annual rainfall is slightly less at Kamarooka than at Whipstick.

Plants and animals: There are two quite distinct vegetation types in Kamarooka. First, on areas of alluvial sediments there are open forests of Grey Box and Yellow Gum with many plants, such as Murray Pine, Quandong, Berrigan, Turkey-bush, Boobialla and Desert Cassia, which are characteristic of the northern plains flora. One particularly colourful and interesting shrub here is Eutaxia, one of the 'egg and bacon' peas, which in Kamarooka grows into a neat round bush rather than the low spiny mat which is its more usual growth habit. The other major vegetation type is that of mallee scrub, which here contains all the mallee eucalypts for the area – Blue, Green, Bull and the rare Kamarooka Mallee. At first sight all mallee eucalypts may seem alike, but when you look more closely you can quite easily pick out the large leaves of Bull Mallee, the small blue-grey leaves of Blue Mallee, the bright shiny green of Green Mallee and finally the unusual squared-off fruits and buds of Kamarooka Mallee.

The birdlife here is rich, both because the understorey has good shelter and nesting sites, and because there is an overlap between typically northern birds such as the Ringneck Parrot and Shy Heathwren, and typically southern ones such as the Brush Bronzewing and Rose Robin.

Human history: This is similar to that of the Whipstick except that here gold was not discovered until seven years later, in 1863. As well as the remains of eucalyptus-oil distillery sites, there are some relics of the goldmining days and of later forestry activities. Kamarooka was declared as a state park because it is one of the few remnants of the once-widespread northern plains flora, now largely cleared in all other places.

Things to do: Walking; cycling; birdwatching; perhaps a little quiet fossicking for gold (restricted areas only). There are only minimal picnic facilities in this Park, and main roads are unsealed which means that Kamarooka is pleasantly unfrequented and quiet.

Best season to visit: Spring for wildflowers and birdwatching.

Special features: The occurrence of all four mallee eucalypts together; wattles in spring.

Relevant reading: See Whipstick State Park.

Further information: See Whipstick State Park.

Kamarooka Mallee *MS*

Wychitella

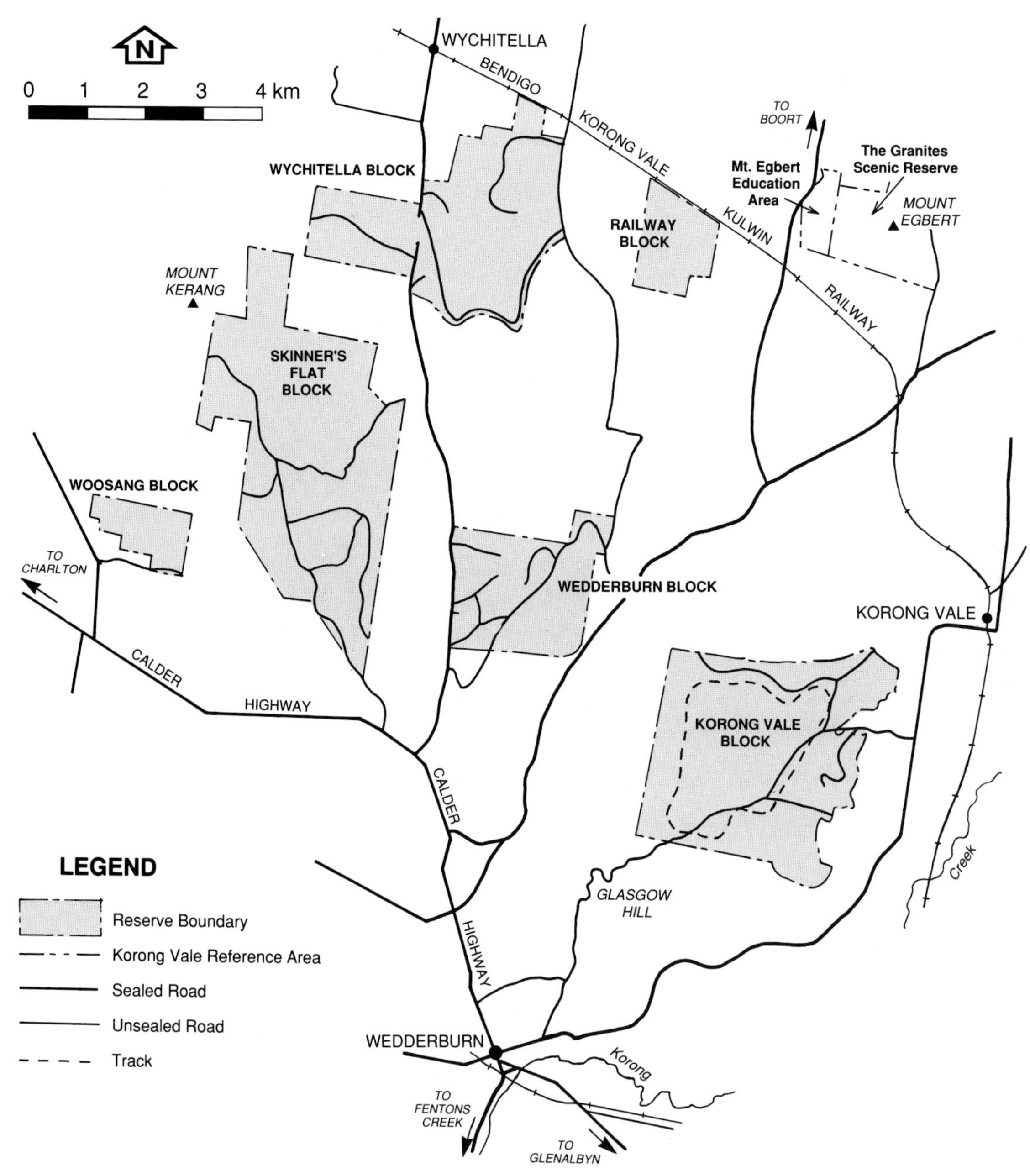

N
0 1 2 3 4 km
WYCHITELLA
BENDIGO
KORONG VALE
KULWIN
RAILWAY
TO BOORT
Mt. Egbert Education Area
The Granites Scenic Reserve
MOUNT EGBERT
WYCHITELLA BLOCK
RAILWAY BLOCK
MOUNT KERANG
SKINNER'S FLAT BLOCK
WOOSANG BLOCK
TO CHARLTON
WEDDERBURN BLOCK
KORONG VALE
CALDER
HIGHWAY
KORONG VALE BLOCK
CALDER
HIGHWAY
GLASGOW HILL
Creek
LEGEND
Reserve Boundary
Korong Vale Reference Area
Sealed Road
Unsealed Road
Track
WEDDERBURN
Korong
TO FENTONS CREEK
TO GLENALBYN

41 Wychitella Flora and Fauna Reserve

Physical features: 3 780 ha. This Reserve of gentle hills and ridges consists largely of tightly folded marine shales, slates and mudstones laid down about 500 million years ago, which often show evidence of contact metamorphism when they are adjacent to areas of igneous activity. The soils are generally impermeable and tend to erode easily. Mt Kerang, 398 m, just outside the Reserve, is the highest point in the district. Annual rainfall is 416 mm, which is considerably lower than for places nearer the Great Dividing Range. Summers are hot and dry, winters cool and wet.

Plants and animals: To see Wychitella, or for that matter any mallee region, at the end of a long, dry summer is to wonder why it is regarded as so special, but come again in spring and the richness and diversity of this fragile environment are there for all to see. For a start, there are four different mallee eucalypts, one of which, the Kamarooka Mallee, is regarded as a threatened species. One of the many wattles that enriches Wychitella, the Bent-leaf Wattle, is also restricted in its distribution, while a number of other plants are more typically found in north-western Victoria. These include the Sweet Quandong, used by early settlers to make a delicious jam, and the delicate Blue Boronia. There are a number of orchids too which somehow manage to push through the hard soil and add their colour and beauty to the springtime display. Wychitella is an extremely important area for birds also, especially the fascinating Malleefowl, a vulnerable species. (See section on the Little Desert for more about Malleefowl.) Some of the other mallee birds, such as the Southern Scrub-robin and various honeyeaters, are much less shy and readily betray their presence by their calls.

Human history: There is no evidence as to Aboriginal use of Wychitella, unlike the Europeans who left behind relics of goldmining, timber harvesting, eucalypt-oil distillation and water channels. But, most importantly, rocky mallee is poor farming land so it was not cleared. Now, with state park status, these precious remnants of a highly specialised type of vegetation are protected and there for all to enjoy.

Things to do: Recreation has been a minor use of the Reserve, and it is generally not intended to increase the few facilities that are available. The main visitors are natural history groups.

Best season to visit: Spring for wildflowers and birdwatching.

Special features: The extraordinary richness of the natural history of this superficially inhospitable environment.

Relevant reading:
Simpson G. et al (1988) *Wychitella Flora and Fauna Reserve Resource Inventory* and (1988) *Proposed Management Plan.*
(See also Whipstick SP.)

Further information:
C&E Regional Office, 31 Mackenzie St, Bendigo, Vic 3550. Phone (054) 43 8911.

Eucalyptus distillery boiler *FWSP*

Eucalyptus distillery *FWSP*

Harvesting eucalyptus for distillation *FWSP*

Underground eucalyptus vat *FWSP*

Kooyoora

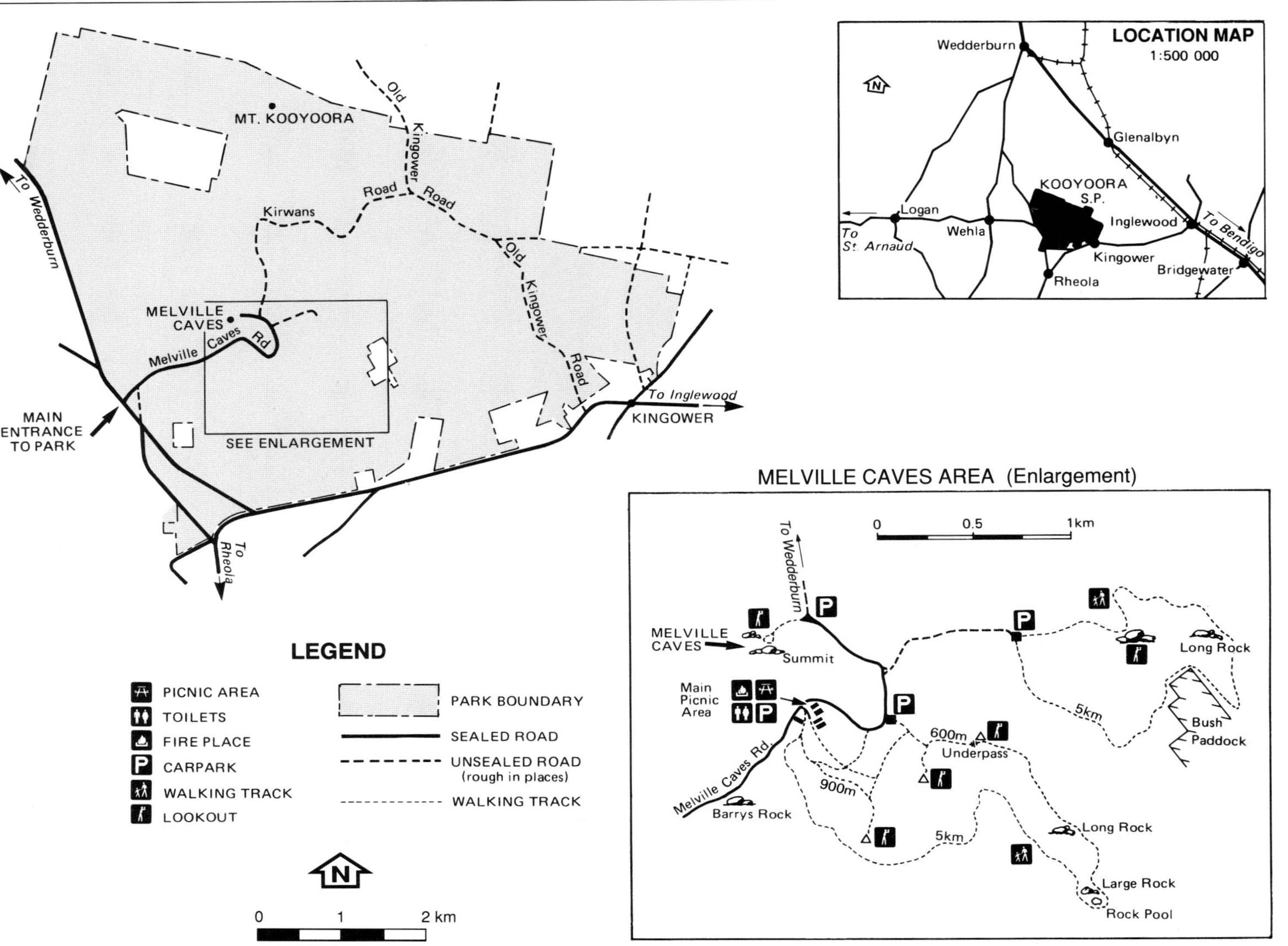

LOCATION MAP
1:500 000
Wedderburn
Glenalbyn
KOOYOORA S.P.
Inglewood
To Bendigo
Kingower
Bridgewater
Rheola
Logan
Wehla
To St. Arnaud
MT. KOOYOORA
Old Kingower Road
Kirwans Road
Old Kingower Road
MELVILLE CAVES
Melville Caves Rd
SEE ENLARGEMENT
To Inglewood
KINGOWER
To Wedderburn
MAIN ENTRANCE TO PARK
To Rheola
LEGEND
PICNIC AREA
TOILETS
FIRE PLACE
CARPARK
WALKING TRACK
LOOKOUT
PARK BOUNDARY
SEALED ROAD
UNSEALED ROAD (rough in places)
WALKING TRACK
0 1 2 km
MELVILLE CAVES AREA (Enlargement)
0 0.5 1km
To Wedderburn
MELVILLE CAVES
Summit
Main Picnic Area
Melville Caves Rd
Barrys Rock
600m
Underpass
900m
5km
5km
Long Rock
Bush Paddock
Long Rock
Large Rock
Rock Pool

42 Kooyoora State Park

Physical features: 3 593 ha. A granite outcrop surrounded by a zone of metamorphosed rock makes up almost the entire Park and forms an abrupt contrast to the surrounding sedimentary hills. The highest point is Mt Kooyoora, 480 m, with sheer rock cliffs and massive exposed boulders. Typically for granite, many of these boulders are split and fissured, forming shallow caves and overhangs. The annual rainfall is about 520 mm, and while there are no permanent creeks, several springs provide a permanent water supply. Winters are cool and wet; summers warm and dry.

Plants and animals: Much of the Park is of open woodlands with a grassy understorey. Blakely's Red Gum, here at its westernmost limit, occurs on the granitic soils. In the east of the Park, on the sedimentary and metamorphic soils, are Grey Box, Yellow Gum, Red Stringybark and Red Ironbark. Much of the understorey is colourful with wattles, bush-peas and the shrubby Grey Everlasting. Many of the gentler slopes are quite wet and mossy with an attractive mix of small plants such as lilies, orchids, sundews and bladderworts. More than 100 birds have been recorded, including the Ring-necked Parrot, here near its southern limit. Rainbow Bee-eaters are also here and are easy to find because of their spectacular colouring and their characteristic purring call. Echidnas, kangaroos and wallabies are still common today, and judging from the remains of Aboriginal feasts held in some of the caves, many other animals, including the now endangered Brush-tailed Rock-wallaby, were once found nearby.

Human history: The Kooyoora caves have yielded stone tools, charcoal and animal remains and show that this area, with its generous supplies of food, water and shelter, was well used by the Aborigines, presumably the Jaara people within whose territory Kooyoora lies. But it is not because of these people that the caves are best known, but because of a bushranger, Captain Melville, who is reputed to have used the caves as a hide-out. Alluvial gold has been mined in Kooyoora, as have mica and the clear quartz crystals once used in crystal wireless sets. The remains of these activities can still be seen. The Park was declared because of its scenic value and its wide range of forest types.

Things to do: Walking; picnicking; camping; sightseeing; enjoying natural and human history.

Best season to visit: Spring for a colourful spread of wattles; otherwise any season.

Special features: Both panoramic views and attractive close-up granite landscapes.

Relevant reading:
Halls F. (1981) *Kooyoora Country by Road and Track.*
Land Conservation Council (1978) *Study Report North-central Area.*

Further information:
C&E Regional Office, 31 Mackenzie St, Bendigo, Vic 3550. Phone (054) 43 8911.
Friends' Group: Phone (054) 38 8222.

Scented Sundew *CFL*

43 Kara Kara State Park

Physical features: 3 840 ha. This Park lies towards the southern end of the north to south running St Arnaud Range. Most of the Park is rugged ridges, some up to 600 m high, formed from sediments which were laid down in the Cambrian/Ordovician Eras. Exact dating is difficult, however, because of a lack of fossils. At the northern and eastern sides of Kara Kara the land is flatter, especially around the Teddington Reservoir. Annual rainfall is about 600 mm. Winters are cool and wet, and summers warm and dry. Access is from the Sunraysia Highway, either about 15 km north of Avoca, (look for the Park sign) or via Stuarts Mill (about 20 km S of St Arnaud) to Teddington Reservoir.

Plants and animals: On the east of the Park the vegetation is sparse and the effects of grazing and of earlier timber harvesting are still quite obvious, but as you climb up the ridges this becomes less apparent, and there are many fine, old trees. Red and Yellow Box and Red Ironbark all give an attractive bluish appearance to the slopes. On the higher ground are Blue Gums and Messmate Stringybarks. The understorey is generally sparse, though there are a number of wattles and smaller plants such as lilies, orchids and sundews. Along the streams are typical wetland plants including Australian Buttercup and White Purslane. Frogs are plentiful throughout much of the Park and keep up a soothing run of plops and bonks in the background. The birdlife too is both prolific and noisy, especially in early spring when whistlers and Grey Shrike-thrushes call loudly from all around, and pardalotes and Mistletoe-birds add their gentler calls. Dominating everything else, though, is the continual agitated screeching of Sulphur-crested Cockatoos. Because there are many mature trees with good nesting hollows, Kara Kara is an excellent breeding area for these and many other birds and arboreal marsupials.

Human history: Aborigines are known to have been here, but they have left no trace. Europeans brought stock into the area in the 1840's and sheep are still grazed in the Park. Stumps and coppice regrowth show where some trees have been cut, but those mature trees that remain have considerable conservation value, especially in this part of Victoria which has been, and still is, extensively used for timber production. In some parts there are signs of quite recent gold-fossicking, though the Park as a whole has escaped the nearby gold fever.

Things to do: Camping; picnicking; fishing; walking; birdwatching; sightseeing (some of the tracks are 4WD rather than 2WD); visiting the nearby Historic Area (gold) of Stuart Mill.

Best season to visit: Any.

Special features: Kara Kara is still little known, but is certainly worth visiting, including perhaps a stay at the very pleasant Teddington Reservoir camping area; good birdwatching.

Relevant reading:
Land Conservation Council (1978) *Study Report North-central Area.*

Further information:
C&E Office, 2 Napier St, St Arnaud, Vic 3478. Phone (054) 95 1115.

Jacky Winter *RAOU*

Barmah

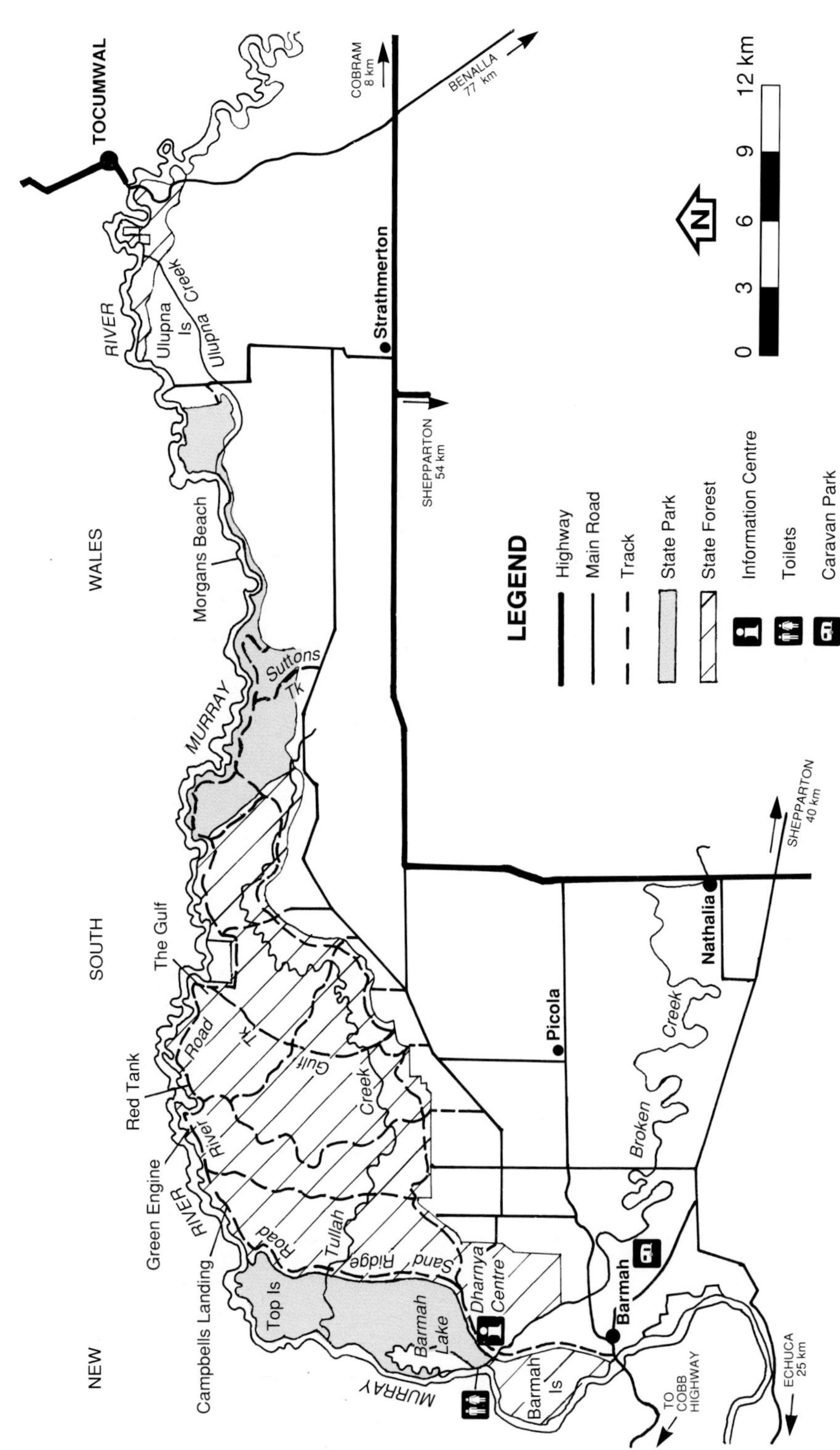

TOCUMWAL
COBRAM 8 km
BENALLA 77 km
Strathmerton
SHEPPARTON 54 km
RIVER
Ulupna Is
Ulupna Creek
NEW
SOUTH
WALES
Morgans Beach
MURRAY
Suttons Tk
The Gulf
Red Tank
Green Engine
Campbells Landing
RIVER
River Road
Gulf Tk
Creek
Tullah Road
Sand Ridge
Dharnya Centre
Top Is
Barmah Lake
Barmah Is
MURRAY
Picola
Nathalia
SHEPPARTON 40 km
Broken Creek
Barmah
TO COBB HIGHWAY
ECHUCA 25 km
LEGEND
Highway
Main Road
Track
State Park
State Forest
Information Centre
Toilets
Caravan Park
N
0
3
6
9
12 km

44 Barmah State Park

Physical features: 7 900 ha. This Park lies in a young alluvial plain of the Murray River, with lunettes from around older swamps and lakes, and levee banks which represent older river heights. The soil is leached topsoil over clay. Rainfall is about 500 mm a year, and summers are generally hot and winters mild.

Aboriginal legend tells how Biami, a powerful ancestral being, sent his lubra down from the high country to dig for food on the waterless plain. He also sent along a giant snake to keep an eye on her. As she walked dragging her stick behind her, the snake slithered in and out of this line, forming the curves of the river bed. The water came when Biami spoke in a voice of thunder, the lightning flashed and torrents of rain fell, filling the mighty Tongala (Murray).

Plants and animals: The ecology of Barmah is a complex web closely linked to the Murray River and its flooding regime. Most of the Park, a wetland rated as being of world significance, is River Red Gum forest with trees up to 300 years old and a grassy/swampy understorey. Barmah is not only on a major flight path for migratory waterfowl, but is also a vitally important breeding area for many birds.

Human history: Barmah, with its wide range of plant and animal foods, was a rich hunting ground for the Aborigines, and reminders of this can be seen in scarred tree trunks where the bark was cut away to build canoes. For the white settlers the main harvest was timber, a resource which has, at times, been ruthlessly exploited. Grazing, also not always well managed, has been important too. Both of these activities are still allowed in Barmah. For many years, the waters of the Murray River have been harvested for irrigation, and this has meant a major alteration, both in timing and in frequency, to its flooding regime, away from that to which the forest is adapted. The detrimental effects of this alteration to the flood pattern to which the Barmah forest is adapted have been sadly apparent over recent years. The problem of adequate water, appropriately timed, is now being addressed.

Things to do: Visiting the Dharnya Centre; enjoying the Forest Drive (but check road conditions first); photography; fishing; camping; canoeing; swimming; birdwatching.

Best season to visit: This rather depends on your method of transport! Many roads are flooded in winter so a small boat becomes the ideal way to move around the Park.

Special features: The magnificent and wonderfully varied River Red Gums; tranquillity; the Dharnya Centre which in 1987 received the Westpac Museum of the Year award.

Relevant reading:
Conservation, Forests and Lands (1989) *Towards a Strategy for Managing the Flooding of Barmah Forest.*
Fahey C. (1988) *Barmah Forest – a history.*
Land Conservation Council (1983) *Report of the Murray Valley Area.*
Parkwatch No. 103, (November 1975).
Victorian Naturalist (1908) Vol. XXV, No. 4, pp. 60–68 .

Further information:
C&E Regional Office, 22 Bridge St, Benalla, Vic 3672. Phone (057) 62 2466.
Dharnya Centre, Sandridge Rd, Barmah, Vic 3639. Phone (058) 69 3302.

45 Terrick Terrick State Park

Physical features: 2 493 ha. This Park, in gently sloping land, has a number of outcrops of ancient Palaeozoic granite, including Mt Terrick itself. The soils are shallow, reddish-brown sandy loams of granitic origin. There is an annual rainfall of 400 mm, with hot summers and mild winters.

Plants and animals: Terrick Terrick protects a significant remnant of northern plains vegetation, which is dominated by White Cypress-pine, almost all of which is regrowth less than 100 years old. Eucalypts, Grey Box and Yellow Box are found on the higher ground. On the rocky knolls there is Deane's Wattle, an attractive species very similar to Silver Wattle, and like it often heavily infested with Grey Mistletoe, a beautiful plant well worth looking at closely when it is in flower. Below the trees are the green-flowered Rock Correa and richly coloured Nodding Blue-lily. Some of the granite slopes have small circular depressions where there are miniature gardens of plants like Early Nancy, Onion-orchid, succulents, and mosses which die back during the heat of summer.

This Park is excellent for birds, and because the vegetation is so open it is generally much easier to see them than in denser areas. One particular pleasure is the delightful little Red-capped Robin, a bird typical of the dry northern interior. This robin has a distinctive way of watching for its prey, often fluttering near the ground to startle insects and then darting down to capture them. The granite outcrops with their crevices and warm surfaces provide good habitat for a number of different reptiles, and Grey Kangaroos are often seen feeding on the grassy understorey.

Human history: Aborigines are known to have used this area, though there is now little evidence of this. By the 1880's, when much of the land in the area had been cleared for agriculture, local people requested that some of the remaining forest should be set aside as a reserve to protect the pines and their durable termite-resistant timber. The eucalypts, cleared so that more pines would grow, are now regenerating, even though cattle still graze in some parts of the Park. To judge from the clear browse line on the pines, these trees are very palatable to stock. State Park status was conferred in order to protect what is now a very important remnant of the northern plains flora, including Victoria's largest area of native pines.

Things to do: Climbing 'Mount' Terrick for extensive views over the surrounding farmland; picnicking; walking; camping. There is no water available, so make sure you bring all you need.

Best season to visit: Any, although the height of summer can be very hot.

Special features: The native pines; the special character and warmth of granite.

Relevant reading:
Land Conservation Council (1983) *Report of the Murray Valley Area.*

Further information:
C&E Regional Office, 31 Mackenzie St, Bendigo, Vic 3550. Phone (054) 43 8911.

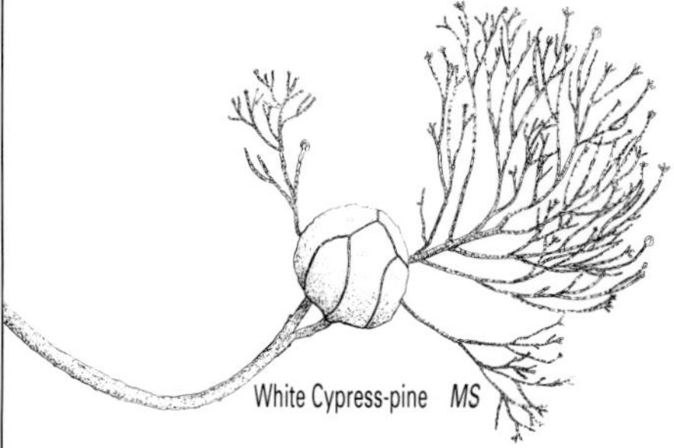
White Cypress-pine *MS*

Terrick Terrick

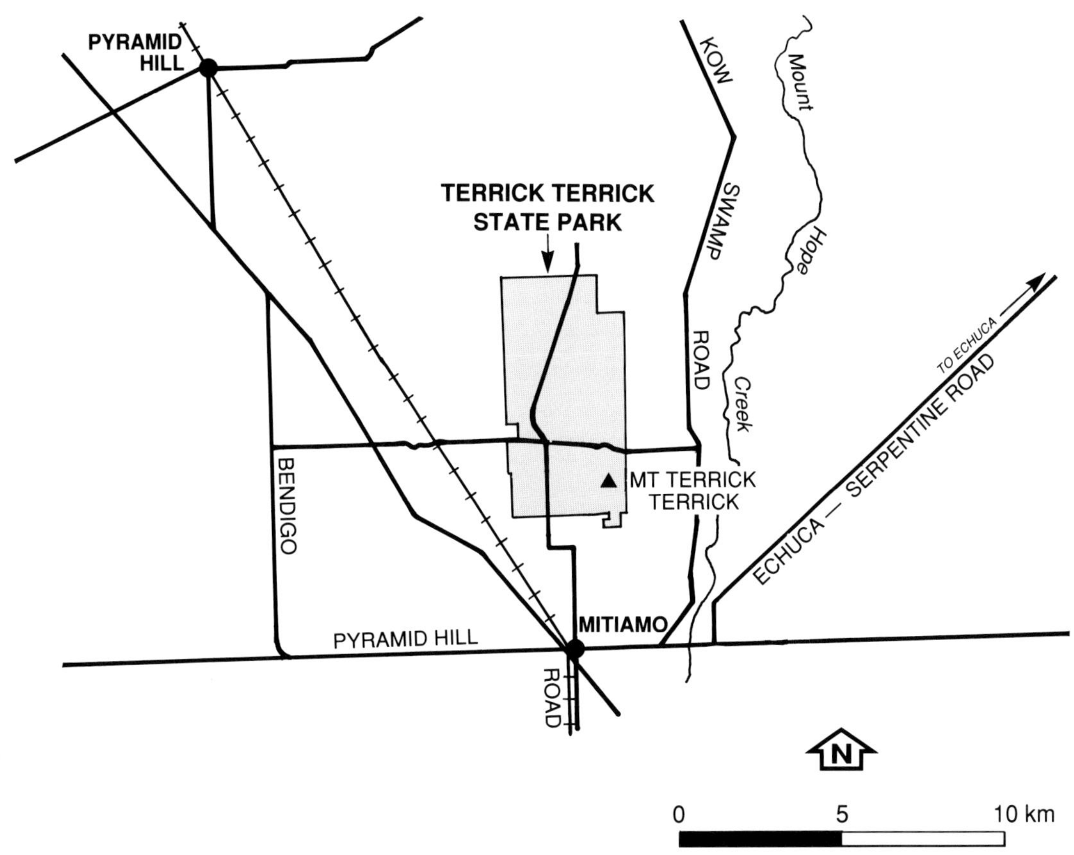

Warby Range

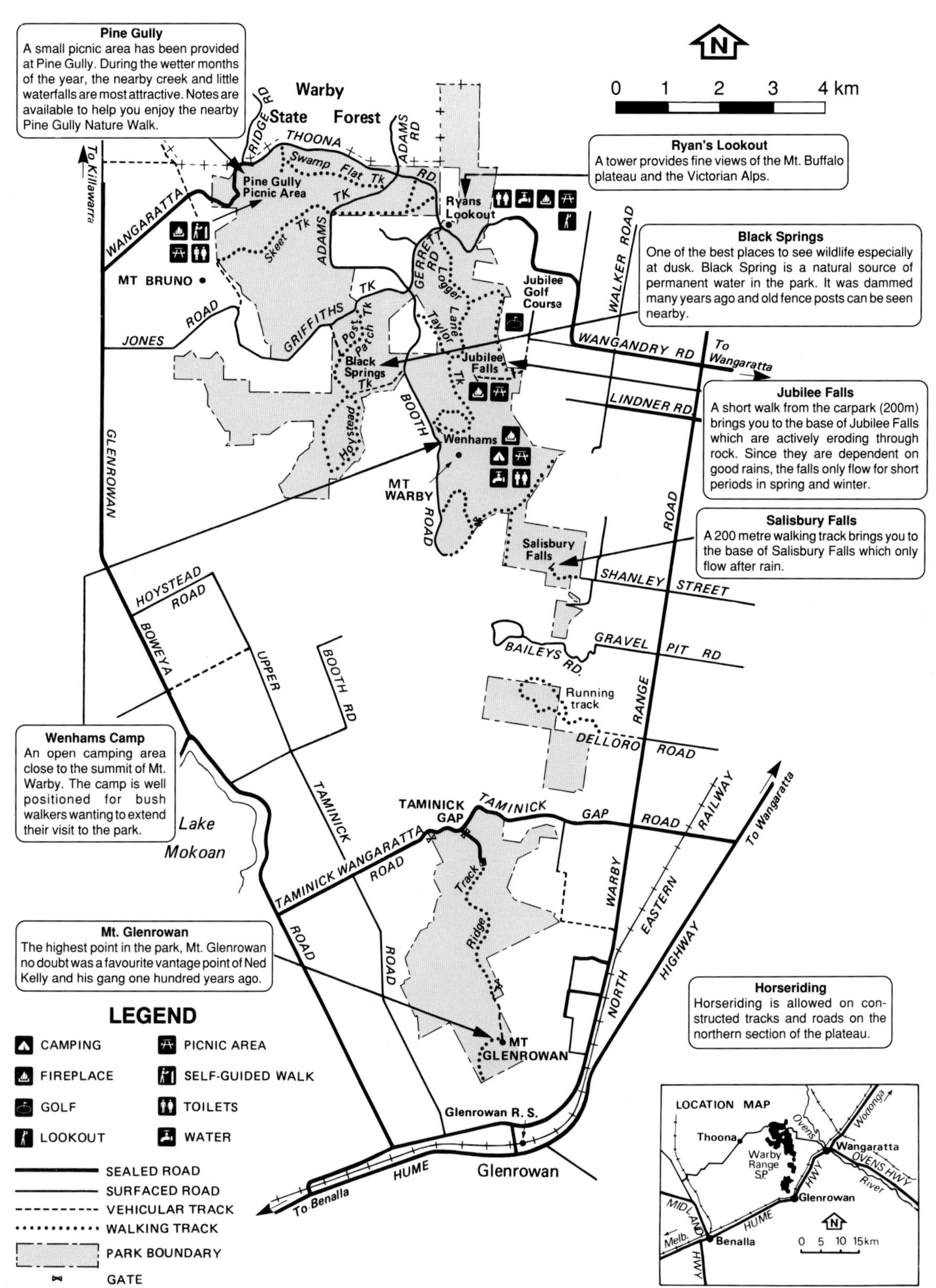

Pine Gully
A small picnic area has been provided at Pine Gully. During the wetter months of the year, the nearby creek and little waterfalls are most attractive. Notes are available to help you enjoy the nearby Pine Gully Nature Walk.
Ryan's Lookout
A tower provides fine views of the Mt. Buffalo plateau and the Victorian Alps.
Black Springs
One of the best places to see wildlife especially at dusk. Black Spring is a natural source of permanent water in the park. It was dammed many years ago and old fence posts can be seen nearby.
Jubilee Falls
A short walk from the carpark (200m) brings you to the base of Jubilee Falls which are actively eroding through rock. Since they are dependent on good rains, the falls only flow for short periods in spring and winter.
Salisbury Falls
A 200 metre walking track brings you to the base of Salisbury Falls which only flow after rain.
Wenhams Camp
An open camping area close to the summit of Mt. Warby. The camp is well positioned for bush walkers wanting to extend their visit to the park.
Mt. Glenrowan
The highest point in the park, Mt. Glenrowan no doubt was a favourite vantage point of Ned Kelly and his gang one hundred years ago.
Horseriding
Horseriding is allowed on constructed tracks and roads on the northern section of the plateau.
N
0 1 2 3 4 km
Warby State Forest
Pine Gully Picnic Area
Ryans Lookout
MT BRUNO
Jubilee Golf Course
Black Springs
Jubilee Falls
Wenhams
MT WARBY
Salisbury Falls
Running track
TAMINICK GAP
MT GLENROWAN
Glenrowan R. S.
Glenrowan
Lake Mokoan
To Killawarra
To Wangaratta
To Benalla
LEGEND
CAMPING
PICNIC AREA
FIREPLACE
SELF-GUIDED WALK
GOLF
TOILETS
LOOKOUT
WATER
SEALED ROAD
SURFACED ROAD
VEHICULAR TRACK
WALKING TRACK
PARK BOUNDARY
GATE
LOCATION MAP
Thoona
Warby Range S.P.
Wangaratta
Glenrowan
Benalla
Melb.
0 5 10 15km

46 Warby Range State Park

Physical features: 3 540 ha. The Warby Range, which dominates the western skyline between Benalla and Wangaratta, is a granitic plateau about 400 million years old. It rises nearly 200 m above the surrounding plain to 514 m at the highest point, Mt Glenrowan. Slopes are quite steep, especially on the eastern (scarp) face, and there are a number of creeks and springs which run only after heavy or prolonged rain. The soil is generally shallow and sandy; there is only a moderate rainfall of about 600 mm. Summers are hot and winters are frosty, all of which means that this is a rather specialised environment.

Plants and animals: Because of the harsh climate here, many of the plants and animals are more typical of the arid country further north. Much of the vegetation is a mix of Blakely's Red Gum and Red Stringybark, with some Red and Long-leaved Box, and, in the gullies, White Box, a handsome tree with white waxy leaves and buds. Among the more northern plants are the Spur-wing and Western Silver Wattles, both found nowhere else in Victoria, and the Northern Sandalwood. The birdlife is prolific and of great interest, especially the rare Turquoise Parrot. Other interesting animals include Burton's Legless Lizard, the Carpet Snake (non-venomous) and the Tuan, a small carnivorous marsupial. Most of the Warbys has not been burnt for many years, as shown by the huge skirts on the Grass-trees. Many of these strange-looking plants are very tall and graceful, indicating great age.

Human history: The Warbys were grazed from the 1840's onwards, which has led to some alteration in the vegetation. Most of the the timber species here are hard and durable, and were harvested for fence posts and to fuel the furnaces of Wangaratta Hospital. Gravel and stone were also taken from the Warbys – some of the pink-toned granite was used to build Wangaratta Cathedral. These exploitative activities are now no longer carried out in the Park.

Things to do: Walking; orienteering; horse and cycle riding; scenic driving; camping (but check with a ranger first).

Best season to visit: Late winter and spring for wildflowers; all other seasons except high summer for more energetic activities.

Special features: Wildflowers; Pine Gully Nature Walk; views of the Great Dividing Range.

Relevant reading:
Land Conservation Council (1983) *Report of the Murray Valley Area*.

Further information:
C&E Regional Office, Ford St, Wangaratta, Vic 3677. Phone (057) 21 5022.

Spur-wing Wattle *CFL*

47 Reef Hills Park

Physical features: 2 040 ha. The hills rise to about 300 m and are of folded Devonian-Silurian sedimentary rock through which run a number of dykes and quartz reefs, and which have been mined for gold. In the southern part of the Park there are much younger alluvial deposits. The soil is generally a sandy loam poorly drained and swampy in some parts, especially in winter when most of the 650 mm of rain falls. Summers can be very hot and winters frosty. There are no spectacular landscape features, apart from the SEC transmission line!

Plants and animals: There are three main types of vegetation in the Park, each dominated by different types of eucalypts, most of which are box-barked, giving a generally dark appearance to the trees. Among these eucalypts is Red Box with its attractive rounded, almost blue leaves which form a striking colour contrast to the yellow-green of the Box Mistletoe and the Cherry Ballart, both of which are common. Even in winter there are splashes of colour, particularly from the Golden Wattle and the guinea-flowers. But it is in spring that Reef Hills really comes into its own with spectacular displays of wildflowers, especially small ground orchids, throughout the Park.

The animal life is rich, with 17 different mammals, including the uncommon Tuan and Squirrel Glider and more than 100 different birds, especially the Turquoise Parrot, Dollar-bird and Bush Thick-knee. There are also many interesting amphibians and reptiles, particularly the Spotted Burrowing Frog and the Lace Lizard. Unfortunately, there are problems too, such as cats, dogs, rabbits and foxes, and the mice in the piles of, as yet, uncleared rubbish.

Human history: Reef Hills probably had little appeal to the Aborigines since Broken River with its more ample supplies of food and particularly water was not far away. Both Hume and Hovell and Major Mitchell's exploration parties went through the area early in the 19th century and no doubt took back word of the grazing country nearby. But it was the discovery of gold in 1860 that made the most impact on Reef Hills, both because of the mine workings and because of the timber that was cut for use inside and outside the mines. The deepest recorded mine is the Lion which went down to 76 m. Timber has continued to be harvested from Reef Hills for firewood, fencing and the production of charcoal. This means that much of what we see today is regrowth over the last 120 years. Bees are also kept in the Park and there are some parts that are set aside for gun clubs, but these are clearly marked for the protection of the public. The park was declared because its forest is an important remnant of northern plains vegetation and because of the wide range of plant and animal life found here.

Things to do: Scenic driving; walking; cycling; horseriding; enjoying the birds and the plants.

Best season to visit: Spring and autumn.

Special features: The wildflowers, especially along Tower and Four Mile Roads; the rich variety of animals in this small and apparently unpromising Park.

Relevant reading:
Conservation, Forests and Lands (1987) *Reef Hills Park Management Plan.*
Land Conservation Council (1973) *Report North-east 2 Area.*

Further information:
C&E Regional Office, 22 Bridge St, Benalla, Vic 3672. Phone (057) 62 2466.

Reef Hills

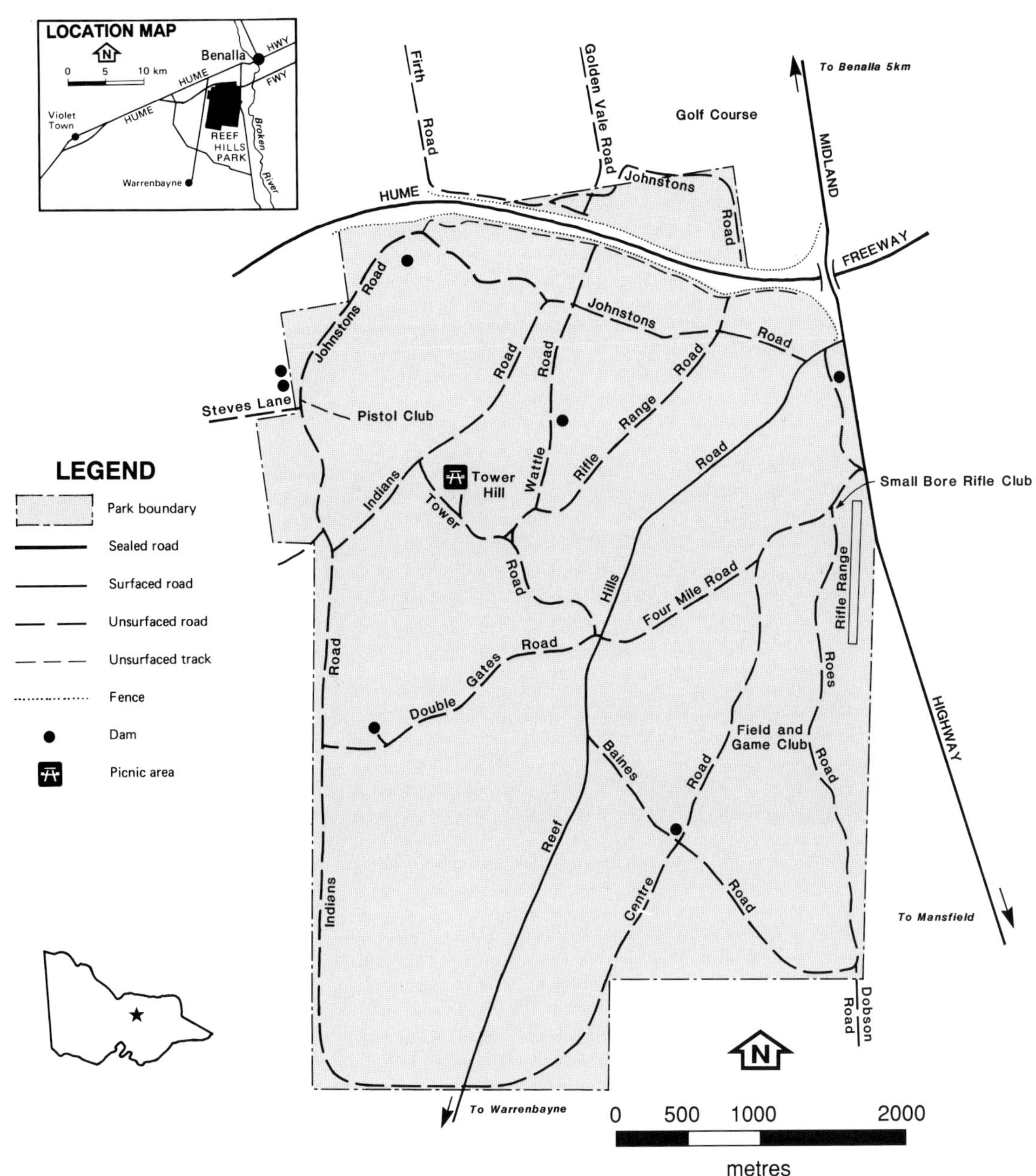
LOCATION MAP
N
0 5 10 km
Benalla
HWY
HUME
FWY
Violet Town
HUME
REEF HILLS PARK
Broken River
Warrenbayne
LEGEND
Park boundary
Sealed road
Surfaced road
Unsurfaced road
Unsurfaced track
Fence
Dam
Picnic area
Firth Road
Golden Vale Road
To Benalla 5km
Golf Course
MIDLAND
HUME
Johnstons
Road
FREEWAY
Johnstons Road
Johnstons
Road
Steves Lane
Pistol Club
Road
Road
Rifle Range Road
Wattle
Tower Hill
Indians
Tower Road
Road
Small Bore Rifle Club
Hills
Four Mile Road
Rifle Range
Road
Double Gates Road
Roes Road
HIGHWAY
Field and Game Club
Baines Road
Road
Reef
Centre
Indians
To Mansfield
Dobson Road
N
To Warrenbayne
0 500 1000 2000
metres

Chiltern

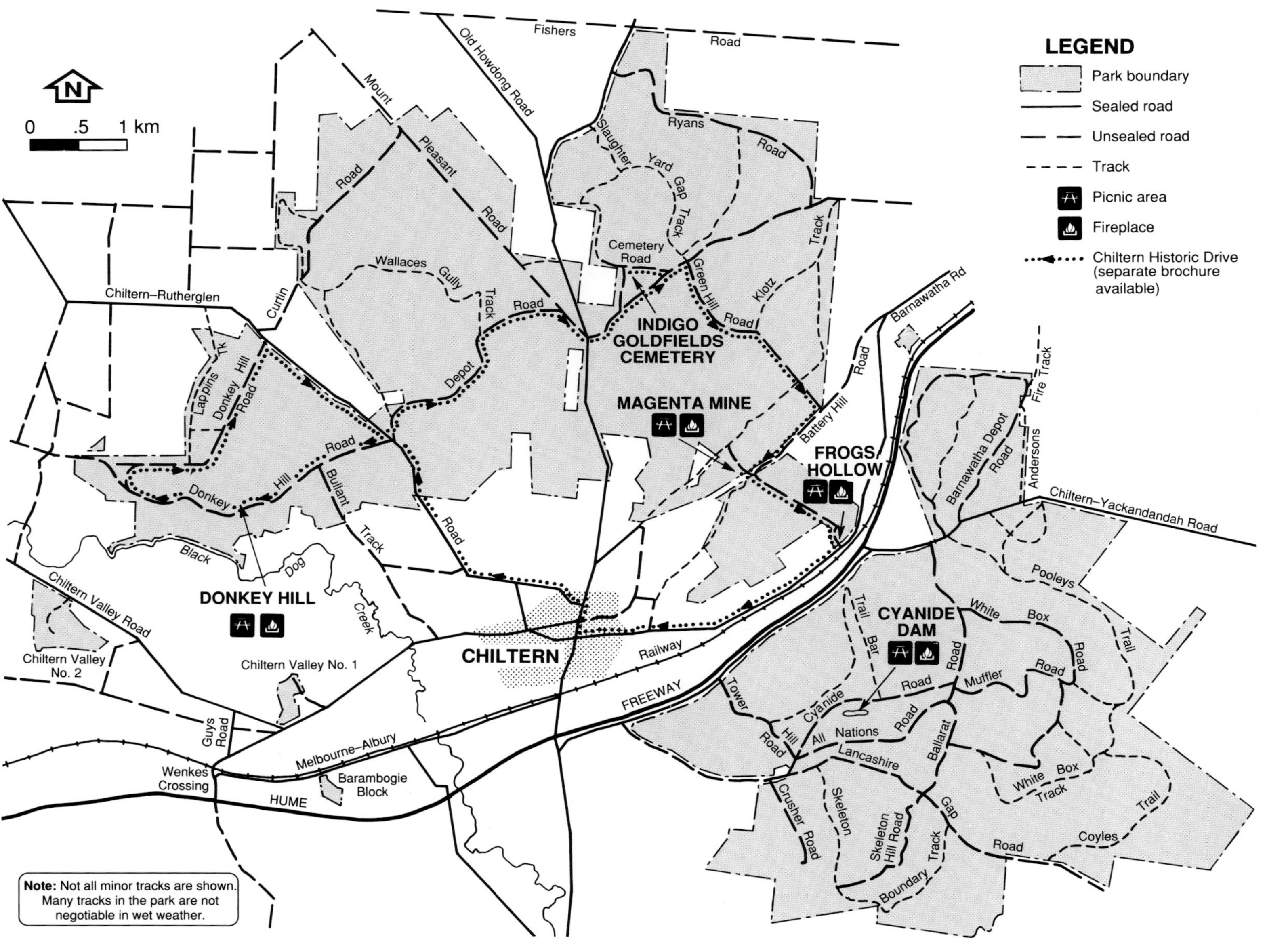

LEGEND
Park boundary
Sealed road
Unsealed road
Track
Picnic area
Fireplace
Chiltern Historic Drive (separate brochure available)
0 .5 1 km
N
Fishers Road
Old Howdong Road
Mount Pleasant Road
Road
Ryans Road
Slaughter Yard Gap Track
Cemetery Road
Green Hill Road
Klotz Track
Wallaces Gully Track
Depot Road
Curtin
Chiltern–Rutherglen
Lappins Tk
Donkey Hill Road
Donkey Hill Road
Bullant Track
Road
INDIGO GOLDFIELDS CEMETERY
MAGENTA MINE
FROGS HOLLOW
Battery Hill Road
Barnawatha Rd
Barnawatha Depot Road
Andersons Fire Track
Chiltern–Yackandandah Road
Black Dog Creek
DONKEY HILL
Chiltern Valley Road
Chiltern Valley No. 2
Chiltern Valley No. 1
CHILTERN
Railway
FREEWAY
Guys Road
Wenkes Crossing
Melbourne–Albury
Barambogie Block
HUME
CYANIDE DAM
Pooleys Trail
White Box Road
Road
Trail Bar
Tower Hill Road
Cyanide Road
All Nations Road
Muffler Road
Ballarat
Lancashire
Gap Road
White Box Track
Coyles Trail
Crusher Road
Skeleton
Skeleton Hill Road
Boundary Track
Note: Not all minor tracks are shown. Many tracks in the park are not negotiable in wet weather.

48 Chiltern State Park

Physical features: 4 300 ha. This Park is in two main sections, one either side of the main Sydney to Melbourne road and rail links. There are also some other very small outliers. Most of Chiltern is of Ordovician sediments such as sandstones and siltstones, with a small outcrop of younger metamorphic rock in the southern part and patches of recent alluvial deposits. The soils are moderately fertile and are generally easily eroded. Rainfall is about 700 mm per year.

Plants and animals: The strong contrast between the dark, rough trunks of the Red Ironbarks and the characteristic grey-green foliage of many of the other trees gives this Park a distinctive appearance at any time of year. In the spring there is a wealth of wildflowers, from the colourful to the more subtle, including many different species of orchids. But it is the birds that are of special interest here, more than 150 species having been recorded. This diversity is due in part to the fact that Chiltern SP is at the junction of the drier inland, or Eyrean, and the cooler southern, or Bassian, faunal regions. There are many different honeyeaters, including the elegantly-patterned Regent Honeyeater, and many parrots and cockatoos of which the small and uncommon Turquoise Parrot is of particular interest. A number of the mammals and reptiles are important too, including the Squirrel Glider, possibly the rarest species of possum in Victoria.

Human history: The nearby township of Chiltern was once a staging post for mail coaches. In 1858 gold was discovered and from then on the fortunes of the town lay largely with gold. The story of this phase of Chiltern can be seen during the Historic Drive which takes you to the old Pioneer Cemetery, now just a few posts in the ground, the Magenta Mine, a dramatic testimony to human effort, and the State Battery site now gently dominated by frog calls from the nearby dam.

Things to do: Enjoying the fascinating Chiltern Historic Drive; camping (by prior arrangement); walking; cycling; picnicking, but this is an old goldfield, and there are still some deep shafts. *Lake View*, an historic home in the Chiltern township where Henry Handel Richardson lived for a short time, is also worth visiting.

Best season to visit: Late winter/spring for flowers and for birds feeding on eucalypt nectar; a wet winter may mean muddy tracks, while summer can be too hot for easy walking or cycling.

Special features: Morning or evening light highlighting the effect of dark trunks and grey-green leaves; the dramatic Magenta Mine workings; the rare and unusual birds and animals.

Relevant reading:
Land Conservation Council (1974) *Report of the North-east Areas 3,4,5.*

Further information:
C&E Office, High St, Chiltern, Vic 3683. Phone (057) 26 1234.
Friends' Group: Phone (060) 20 8668.

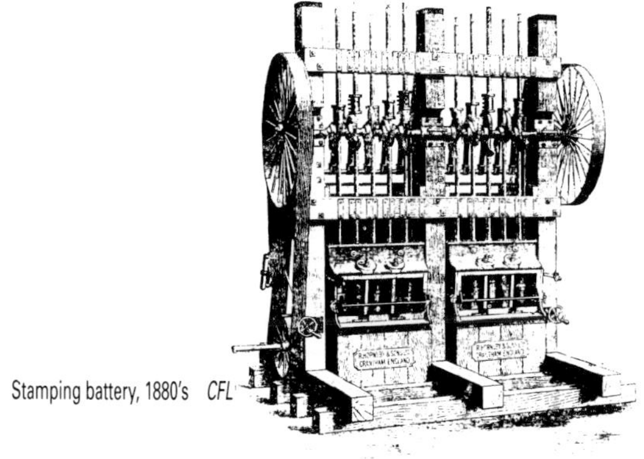

Stamping battery, 1880's *CFL*

49 Beechworth Historic Park

Physical features: 1 130 ha. Most of the Beechworth area consists of Devonian granite, and much of the landscape is very scenic with bold outcrops and massive tors. There are some metamorphic schists and gneisses at the junction of the granite and surrounding older sedimentary rocks. The area has proved extremely rich in gold, and gemstones have also been found in the creeks, including alluvial diamonds from an as yet unknown source. The climate can be quite severe with cold winters and hot summers. Rainfall is around 700 mm a year.

Plants and animals: This granite country has a distinctive and appealing character, heightened by the suprising number of plants, as well as animals and birds, including many different honeyeaters, that are found here. Like Chiltern, Beechworth lies at the overlap between the southern and arid faunal regions, and one of Victoria's rarest snakes, the distinctively striped, non-venomous and largely nocturnal Bandy Bandy, is known only from these areas. Blakely's Red Gum is common along the creeks, and Black Cypress-pines often create some dramatic effects as they grow out of narrow cracks in the granite. The wattles are a beautiful sight in spring against the grey lichened rocks, but in summer there is little colour, since many plants, including the ground orchids, are dormant and only reappear in spring. Other plants, such as the 'resurrection' mosses which grow on the granite, are experts at endurance and although they appear to be quite dead and blackened for most of the summer, they quickly revive when they are wetted. Within seconds they are bright green and actively functioning.

Human history: Settlers arrived in the 1840's, but it was the discovery of gold in 1852 that really saw Beechworth boom. Within months there was a town of 40 000 people eager for their share in the bounty of one of Victoria's richest goldfields – 85 tonnes of gold in 14 years! Many of the features along the historic walks and drives are related to Beechworth's mining history, and there are good interpretative leaflets available for these on site.

Things to do: Scenic driving and walking, including some outside the Historic Park, such as the Beechworth Forest Drive and the walking track between Lakes Kerferd and Sambell; fossicking, for gold and gemstones (in some creeks only); exploring the nearby Ned Kelly country.

Best season to visit: Spring for wildflowers; otherwise any.

Special features: The attractive granite landscapes; the tranquillity of this scene today in contrast to the bustle of a mining settlement; relics of goldmining days.

Relevant reading:
Griffiths T. (1987) *Beechworth: an Australian Country Town and its Past.*
Woods C. (1985) *Beechworth: a Titan's Field.*
Land Conservation Council (1974) *Report of the North-east Areas 3,4,5.*

Further information:
C&E Office, Ford St, Beechworth, Vic 3747. Phone (057) 28 1501.

Poppet head *CFL*

Beechworth

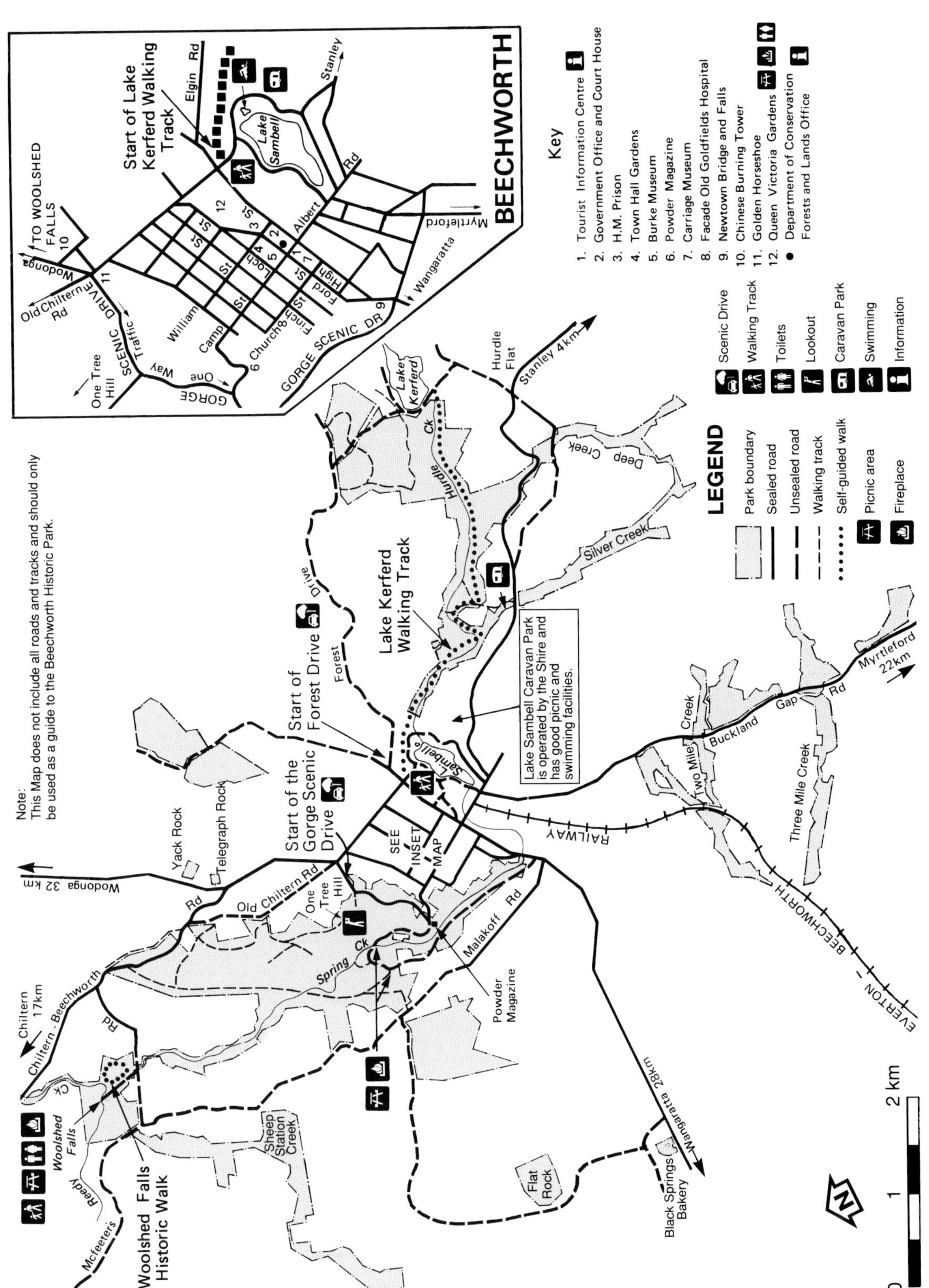
Note:
This Map does not include all roads and tracks and should only be used as a guide to the Beechworth Historic Park.
BEECHWORTH
Key
1. Tourist Information Centre
2. Government Office and Court House
3. H.M. Prison
4. Town Hall Gardens
5. Burke Museum
6. Powder Magazine
7. Carriage Museum
8. Facade Old Goldfields Hospital
9. Newtown Bridge and Falls
10. Chinese Burning Tower
11. Golden Horseshoe
12. Queen Victoria Gardens
● Department of Conservation Forests and Lands Office
LEGEND
Park boundary
Sealed road
Unsealed road
Walking track
Self-guided walk
Picnic area
Fireplace
Scenic Drive
Walking Track
Toilets
Lookout
Caravan Park
Swimming
Information
Start of Lake Kerferd Walking Track
TO WOOLSHED FALLS
Lake Sambell
Lake Kerferd Walking Track
Start of Forest Drive
Start of the Gorge Scenic Drive
SEE INSET MAP
Lake Sambell Caravan Park is operated by the Shire and has good picnic and swimming facilities.
Woolshed Falls Historic Walk
Woolshed Falls
Yack Rock
Telegraph Rock
Wodonga 32 km
Chiltern 17km
Powder Magazine
Flat Rock
Black Springs Bakery
Wangaratta 28km
Stanley 4km
Myrtleford 22km
EVERTON - BEECHWORTH RAILWAY
Hurdle Flat
Deep Creek
Silver Creek
Three Mile Creek
Sheep Station Creek
0 1 2 km

Burrowa-Pine Mountain

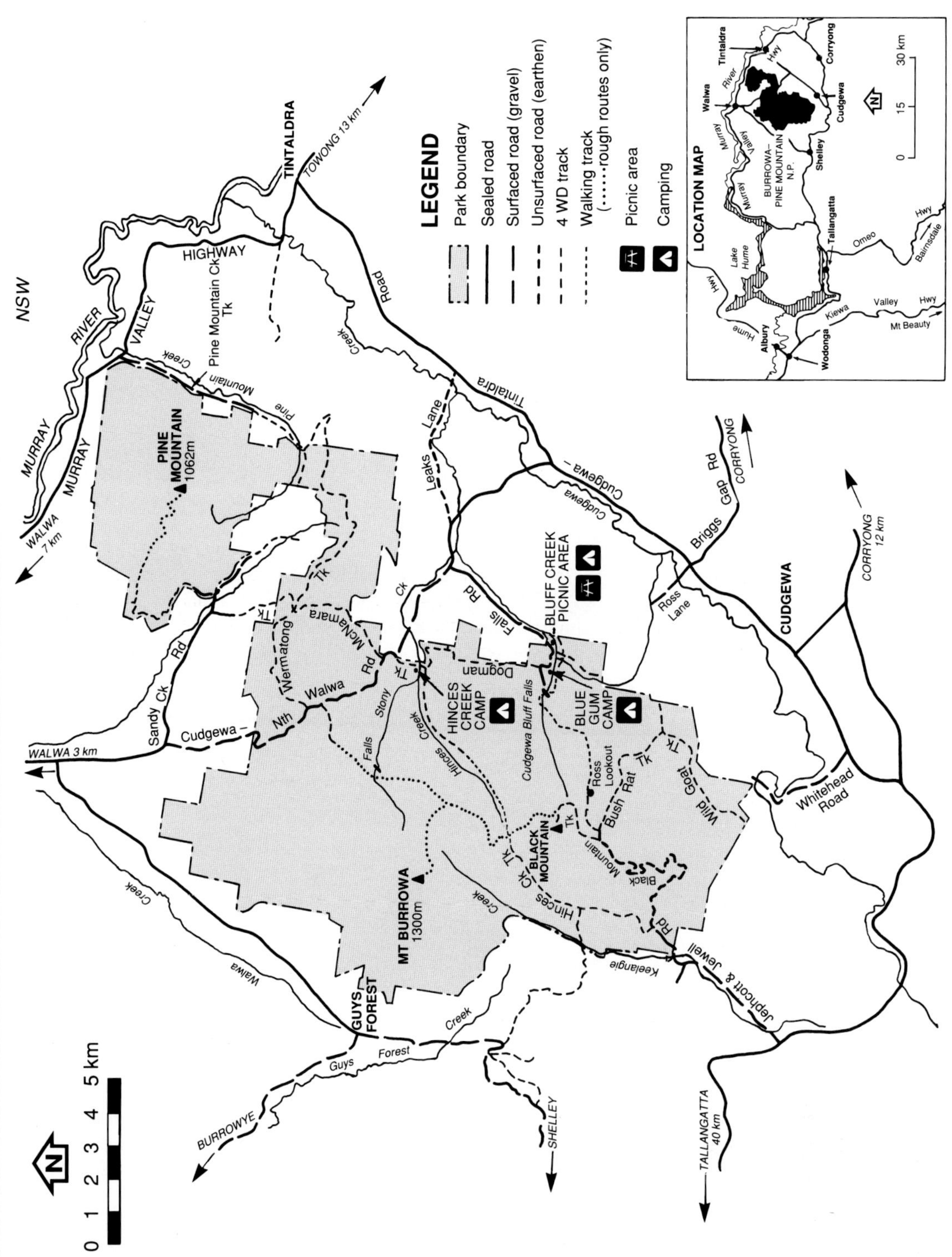

50 Burrowa-Pine Mountain National Park

Physical features: 18 400 ha. This Park is in two distinct sections linked by a narrow L-shaped corridor which runs along a low ridge bordered by cleared farmland. To the north there is the smaller section of the Park, dominated by the massive red granite dome of Pine Mountain (1 062 m). To the south is the Burrowa rhyolite massif, an eroded volcanic remnant with a number of higher peaks such as Black Mountain and Mount Burrowa (1 300 m), the highest point in the Park. (See Cobberas-Tingaringy section for more on the formation of this massif.) Both rhyolite and granite are similar in that they are acid volcanic rocks formed from molten magma that originated deep within the earth's crust, but whereas granite cooled slowly beneath a thick insulating layer of surface rock to form large crystals, rhyolite cooled more quickly nearer the surface, resulting in smaller crystals. Where the hot, volcanic rock 'cooked' the adjacent sedimentary rocks there are mineral-rich seams which have been mined for lead and silver. The Burrowa-Pine plateau as a whole is rugged and has a distinctive outline, with sharp peaks which change their relationship when viewed from different places. Both mountains have considerable areas of exposed rock. The surface of this is subject to extreme temperature changes between day and night and shatters readily to form scree slopes of rock debris.

Rainfall is significantly different between the two parts of the Park – 1 000 mm annually on Mt Burrowa, 700 mm on Pine Mountain. This is not only because of the rainshadow effect of Mt Burrowa on Pine Mountain, but also because of the difference in height between the two. Because of the nature of the landscape, the drainage is often radial or more or less circular, with streams draining essentially northwards into the Murray, some via waterfalls. Winter is cold and summer warm.

Plants and animals: Differences in geology, aspect and rainfall have led to very different types of vegetation in the two parts of this Park. Pine Mountain (named from the Black Cypress-pine here) with its drier climate and generally more adverse conditions, has a number of plants which are considered rare or endangered. These include the rare Phantom Wattle discovered as late as 1964, and then not located anywhere else until 1977 when it was found as a single plant (now destroyed by fire) in the Dora Dora State Forest in New South Wales. Other rare plants are the Branching Grevillea with very divided leaves and small white flowers, and the attractive Green Grevillea with flowers of pale green and deep red. The vegetation of the Burrowa block is diverse, and rather more typical. Here, at lower altitudes, there are peppermint and gum-barked eucalypts along with wet gully plants such as the delicate Victorian Christmas-bush and showy Tall Oxylobium. As you climb higher these give way to dry and then to wet eucalypt forests and finally to Snow Gum on the tops. As in other areas, the open rocky outcrops of both parts of the Park have an especially appealing character; here this is heightened by sweeps of white Button Tea-tree, Violet Kunzea and pink Small Crowea. The spring wildflower display is at its best in the dry open forests, the saddle-link between the two sections of the Park giving a particularly fine display.

The animal life in Burrowa-Pine is abundant and diverse. There are the usual larger mammals such as kangaroos and Swamp Wallabies, while the presence of wombats is obvious too, both from their large burrows and from their territorial markers – droppings on prominences along the tracks. Greater Gliders are here also, though as they are nocturnal, you are unlikely to see them except on a spotlighting walk. They are the largest of the gliding possums, and like Koalas are superbly adapted, feeding almost entirely on eucalypt leaves and seldom if ever needing to drink. Their glide can cover up to 100 metres horizontal distance, and as the animal lands with all four feet extended in a braking position it leaves obvious scratch marks on the tree trunks. Greater gliders feed over well-established routes so a scratched tree could be worth revisiting at night if you want to see one of these animals. More than 180 birds have been recorded here, and for an area essentially without waterbirds, that is a remarkable number. Some of these though, such as the Dollar Bird and Rainbow Bee-eater, are migratory rather than permanent residents, and are only seen when they pass through the Park. Many of the birds, like the various cockatoos, are large and vociferous; others are smaller and more subtle, but the bush is seldom without some chattering and calling.

Human history: Parts of the Park have been logged so there are some access tracks, but the country was felt to be too inhospitable for farming and was left uncleared. Both silver and lead have been mined from Pine Mountain, but there is little evidence of this today. Burrowa-Pine NP was declared as a result of LCC Recommendations that the flora was of particularly high conservation value, and perhaps because of this, use of the Park has increased considerably over recent years, until now there are now nearly 15 000 visitors each year. Many of these are school groups taking advantage of the excellent interpretation programs, including spotlighting and nature walks, which are run by the Ranger.

Things to do: This Park is still largely undeveloped, with only a few, simple facilities provided at the camping ground; bush camping is also allowed by arrangement with the Rangers; walking; horseriding; birdwatching; and, for those with a botanical interest, enjoying the many special plants.

Best season to visit: Spring for exceptional wildflower displays; otherwise any.

Special features: Remoteness; spring flowers; the richness of birdlife; Cudgewa Falls in full spate.

Relevant reading:
Land Conservation Council (1973) *Study Report North-east Area 2.*

Further information:
C&E Office, 8 Jardine St, Corryong, Vic 3707. Phone (060) 76 1655.

This log obviously serves another purpose besides that of deterring four wheel drivers *CFL*

51 Mount Lawson State Park

Physical features: 13 150 ha. Mt Lawson SP lies just south of a loop of the Murray River and of the Murray Valley Highway between Granya and Burrowye, and is reached from this road. Most of the Park falls within the Koetong Uplands, a dissected surface of many small plateaux, bounded to the north, east and west by steep montane slopes rising to 1 020 m at Mt Lawson. The bedrock is Devonian granite, often in large outcrops, and there are some older metamorphic schists at the northern edge of the uplands. Soils are sandy and erosion-prone. Rainfall is about 1 140 mm a year. Winters are cold, occasionally with snow on the high ground, and summers warm to hot.

Plants and animals: On the uplands around Mt Lawson there are open forests of Narrow-leaved Peppermint on the plateaux and moister sites, and Broad-leaved Peppermint is found on the drier, more open sites. North of Mt Lawson, on the steepest, driest slopes, there are stands of Black Cypress-pine, and on the less dry slopes Red Stringybark and Long-leaved Box. As well as these more usual plants, there are a number of rare or uncommon species such as the Kurrajong and the rare, but locally common, Crimson Grevillea. Further research is needed on the fauna of Mt Lawson but many birds have been recorded, and it is likely that the Tiger Quoll still occurs here.

Human history: There is some Aboriginal rock art (though its locality is not yet publicised) within the Park, so Mt Lawson presumably was an important area to the local Aborigines. After European settlement timber was harvested, and there has also been mining for gold, tin, copper, bismuth, molybdenum and tungsten. Bees are brought into the Park, especially when the Red Stringybarks flower, and it is currently recommended that this use continue. The creeks draining the uplands feed into the Murray and so into the Hume Weir. This catchment will continue to be protected.

Things to do: This newly declared Park has no facilities at present, and is awaiting funds for the development of a management plan and interpretative displays, a walking track and other facilities. Meanwhile there are opportunities for sightseeing; walking; fishing; rockclimbing; and remote camping. It is also an excellent chance to watch a park as it develops, right from the start.

Best season to visit: Spring for wildflowers; otherwise any.

Special features: The waterfall and gorge on Flaggy Creek; cascades on Koetong Creek.

Relevant reading: See Burrowa-Pine Mountain NP.

Further information:
C&E Regional Office, 9 Jack Hore Place, Wodonga, Vic 3690. Phone (060) 24 2788.

Kurrajong *FvM*

Mount Samaria

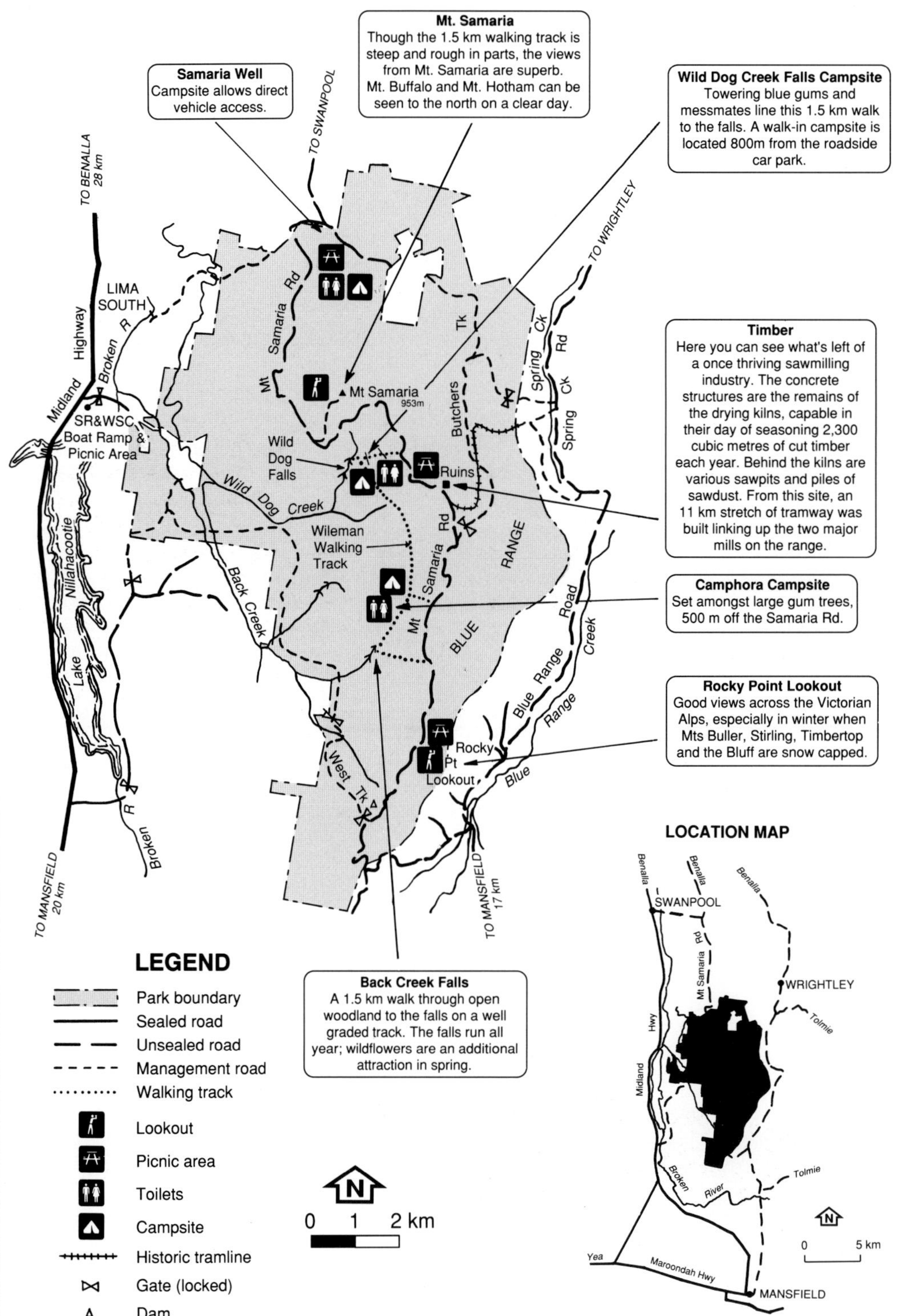

52 Mount Samaria State Park

Physical features: 7 600 ha. Mount Samaria plateau, the dominant feature as you drive up the Midland Highway towards Benalla, is steepest to the east and is generally 700–800 metres high. Mt Samaria itself is 967 m. The plateau is mostly late Devonian granite intruded into marine sandstones and mudstones, which can be seen in the north of the Park. Erosion followed the igneous activity that formed these granites, and then faulting squeezed up the central block between two faults as the Mount Samaria block. The climate is quite harsh; dry in summer, cold and often misty in winter.

Plants and animals: Nearly 400 different plants have now been recorded in this Park. There is a variety of aspects, soils and fire history leading to different environments reflected in the types of trees and particularly in the marked changes in understorey growth. The northern spurs with their Red and Long-leaf Box and Red Stringybark are dry and harsh. The understorey here is sparse and contains a number of drought-tolerant shrubs, such as Cat's Claw, which together make for a beautiful and colourful spring display. There are many creeks in the Park, often with waterfalls, and around these the vegetation is lush with ferns and mosses – the valley wall opposite Back Creek Falls is particularly lovely with a waterfall of vivid green moss tumbling down its face.

In the poorly-drained parts of the plateau are swampy heaths and forests of Mountain Swamp Gums. These can be seen at the Camphora camping ground. At the southern end of the Park are treeless herbfields where the wildflowers are particularly impressive. From the southern or Mansfield approach, as you ascend to enter the Park proper, the road goes past a pine plantation and you are treated to the dramatic contrast of a monoculture with no understorey on one side and the rich diversity of an open eucalypt forest on the other. Birds and reptiles are abundant and varied at Mt Samaria, from Lyrebirds in the wet gullies to Wonga Pigeons on the lower slopes.

Human history: Little is known of the Aboriginal occupation of the area, but by 1840 much of the Park was grazed, probably by bushrangers' stolen stock as well as by that of the legitimate farmers. Timber on the plateau was harvested throughout the 1920's, and remains of a mill, drying kilns, and sawdust heaps, as well as some interesting historical photos, can be seen beside the road in the centre of the Park. From this site, a tramway took the timber down to the mills in the valley below.

Things to do: Scenic driving; picnicking; camping; walking.

Best season to visit: Spring for wildflowers; any season for walking.

Special features: Wildflowers; waterfalls; views across to the Alps from lookouts, especially from Mt Samaria itself.

Relevant reading:
Land Conservation Council (1978) *Study Report North-east Area 2.*

Further information:
C&E Regional Office, 22 Bridge St, Benalla, Vic 3672. Phone (057) 62 2466.

Cat's Claw *MS*

53 Cathedral Range State Park

Physical features: 3 577 ha. Once you have crossed the beautiful Black Spur, travelling north from Healesville, the seven kilometre long Cathedral Range is the dominant feature of the landscape, both by virtue of its dramatic outline and its comparative isolation. It is a jagged ridge of Silurian sandstone which rises sharply to 814 m from the nearby farmland. Unlike some ridges which are wide enough to seem quite secure once you are up on them, this one is a veritable razorback. It is barely two metres wide in places with steep drops to either side. Geologically this whole area is fascinating since it is on the edge of the Cerberean Cauldron, a classic subsidence cauldron with radial and circular faults, some infilled with granitic intrusions. Soils are poor and prone to erosion. Up to 1 200 mm of rain falls on the tops, along with frequent fogs and occasional snow.

Plants and animals: Eleven different vegetation alliances have been recorded here, from Snow Gum woodlands on the higher peaks to tall forest in the wet gullies on the eastern and southern faces, and dry open woodland on the exposed northern and western faces. This variety of habitats means that there is an excellent variety of birds and animals, including lyrebirds. These delightful birds, have, by their mimicry of domestic animals far below on the valley slopes, earned one of their preferred haunts the name of The Farmyard.

Human history: The mountain dwellers and river dwellers of the Tuangurong group of Aborigines are known to have lived in this area, although no evidence now remains of either. The Taggerty run, which included what is now Park, was selected and grazed from the mid-1840's until the 1930's when sheep losses to wild dogs made grazing uneconomic. From the 1930's logging was carried out in the Little River and Storm Creek catchments. Cooks Mill (now a popular camping site) operated from 1940–53. After this logs were taken to Thornton and Marysville, until 1973, when all logging in the area ceased. The remains of trestles built across creeks to reach an early mill outside the Park can still be seen near the SW corner of the Park. Walking clubs began to use this rugged range in the 1930's, and by 1947 the Tigris became the first formally recorded climb in Victoria. Huts were built at Sugarloaf in 1952.

Things to do: Picnicking; walking; rockclimbing; orienteering; camping; fishing; scenic driving, though check the roads first. Some hang gliding and horseriding is also possible.

Best season to visit: Spring for the natural rock gardens on the higher slopes; otherwise any, although roads may be difficult in winter.

Special features: Precipitous country, with a strong contrast between east and west.

Relevant reading:

Algona Guides (1976) *Cathedral Range* (map with walks).
Busby R. (1960) *Melbourne Walker.*
Conservation, Forests and Lands (1984) *Cathedral Range SP Plan of Management.*
Land Conservation Council (1973) *Report of the North-east Area 2.*

Further information:

C&E Regional Office, 46 Aitken St, Alexandra, Vic 3714. Phone (057) 72 1633.

Cathedral Range

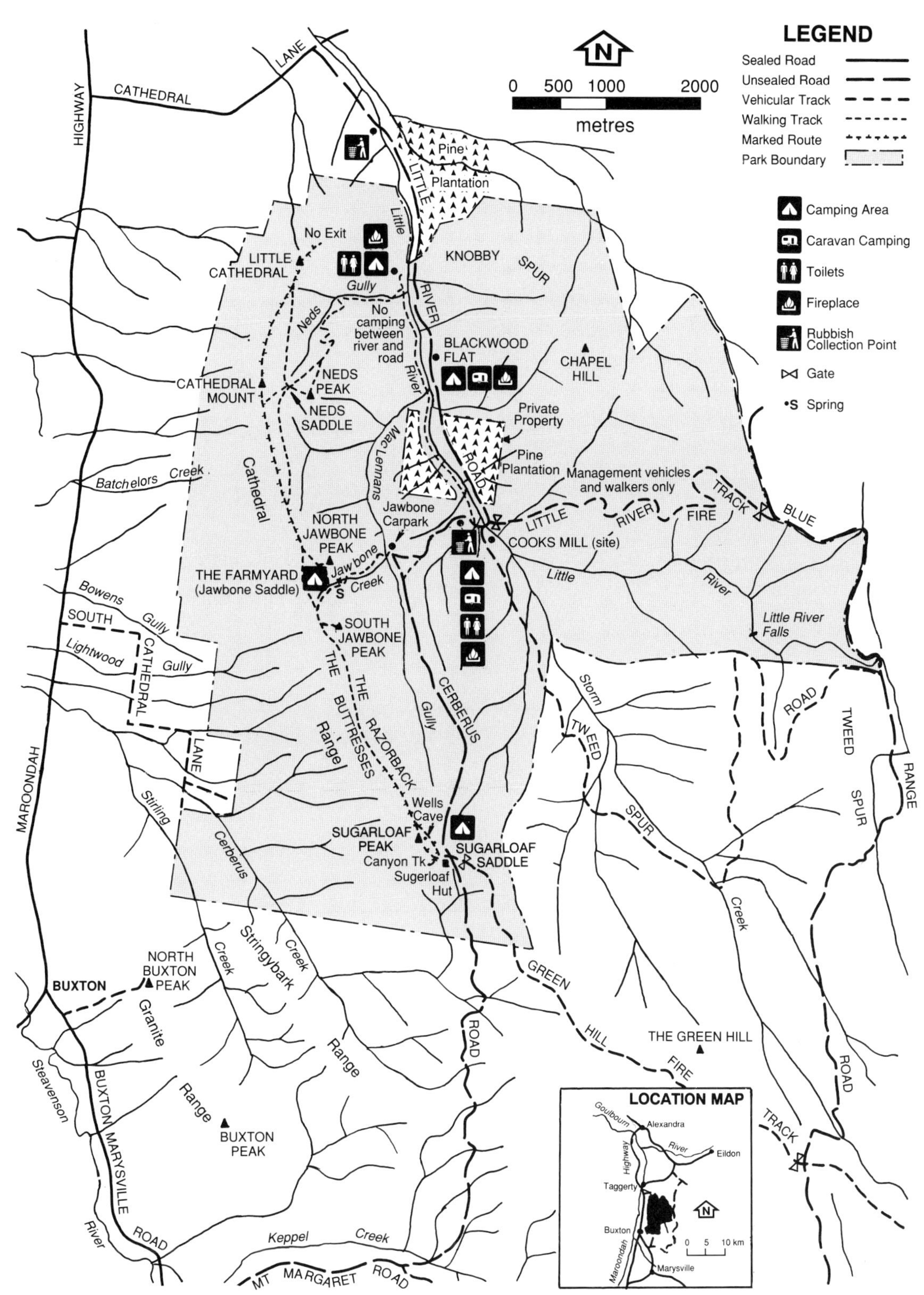

54 Fraser National Park

Physical features: 3 750 ha. Like Eildon SP, this Park borders, and is dominated by, Lake Eildon which reached its final size in the late 1950's after the completion of the Eildon Dam in 1955. The storage capacity is nearly 4 million megalitres, second only in Victoria to the Dartmouth Dam. Although Lake Eildon has a maximum depth of 79 m, the slope of the land is not particularly steep, so large areas of the lake bed may become exposed during periods of prolonged drought, such as in 1968 and 1983 when drowned buildings began to reappear. The actual water frontage, nearly 500 km, comes under the jurisdiction of the Rural Water Commission, including that which falls within the boundary of Fraser NP. The waters are used for irrigation in the Goulburn Valley and some electricity is generated as the water is released from storage.

Both Fraser and Eildon Parks lie within an old dissected plateau of Silurian sandstones, mudstones and shales laid down about 400 million years ago in a vast marine basin. Many of these sediments, including fine examples of upwardly warped anticlines and downward, bowl-shaped synclines, are now exposed in road cuttings and are easy to see. The sediments have also revealed important fossils (mostly outside the Parks) including some of the oldest known woody plants in Australia. During a period of uplift and folding that followed the laying down of these sediments, the release of pressure in the earth's crust was sufficient to allow molten magma to escape through faults in the sedimentary layers and so form dykes of igneous material which now can be seen running across the earlier sedimentary strata. These dykes contain gold and were mined from 1867 onwards. There are also some beds of conglomerate, or pudding-stone, which are a little younger. To the south of the Parks, the landscape is dominated by the ranges of the Cerberean Cauldron (see also Cathedral Ranges SP).

Plants and animals: Although there are small areas of the original vegetation left in Fraser NP, such as around the Lakeside campground, almost all of what we see today is regeneration since the Park was declared in 1957. The original woodlands and forests were cut for timber, especially for the mines, and then cleared for farming. On the evidence of this regrowth and of the surrounding country, the original open woodlands would presumably have been Red Stringybark, peppermint and box with some Candlebark Gums, and also would have had a greater diversity of both plants and animals than they do today. Candlebark Nature Walk is a good place to compare different eucalypt types, especially their barks – the smooth white trunks of the gums; the fine, fibrous bark of the peppermints; the coarse, rough stringyness of the Red Stringybark trunks; and the in-between bark of the Red Box. This last tree is easily recognised by its notched, almost round bluish leaves, and the fact that it grows in particularly dry, hard soils. The most obvious form of animal life is the Eastern Grey Kangaroo, large numbers of which graze on the grassy slopes near the Lakeside camping ground. The birds are varied, with waterbirds and waders such as herons and ibis, and many different bush birds, some of which indicate that you are now well and truly north of the Great Dividing Range – the magpies are black, not white, backed, and there are Friar-birds and, in summer, Dollar Birds.

Human history: When white settlers arrived in this area in 1839 it was inhabited by the Yauung Illam Baluk tribe, known as the 'black devils' to at least one early observer, mystified by their corroborees and ceremonies. Gold was discovered in 1867, and many reminders of this remain, both in relics such as the trenches and remains of old huts on the Candlebark Gully walk, and in names like Auriferous Spur and UT Creek. This last was Ultima Thule, the back of beyond, and as it was a three day walk out for supplies, that name no doubt felt all too appropriate.

Although the goldfields were never very rich they provided a living for men such as Bob Briers, the hermit of Italian Gully who arrived in the 1920's and lived his chosen lonely life there until his death in 1953. A very different story is that of the Merlo family after whom Italian Gully and Italian Bay are named. John Merlo came to Victoria in 1861, and after some years on other Victorian goldfields he and his family moved in 1880 to what is now the eastern boundary of Fraser NP, where he worked the Solferino Mine. From there they moved into the Delatite Valley and developed *Glen Hope*, a

Fraser

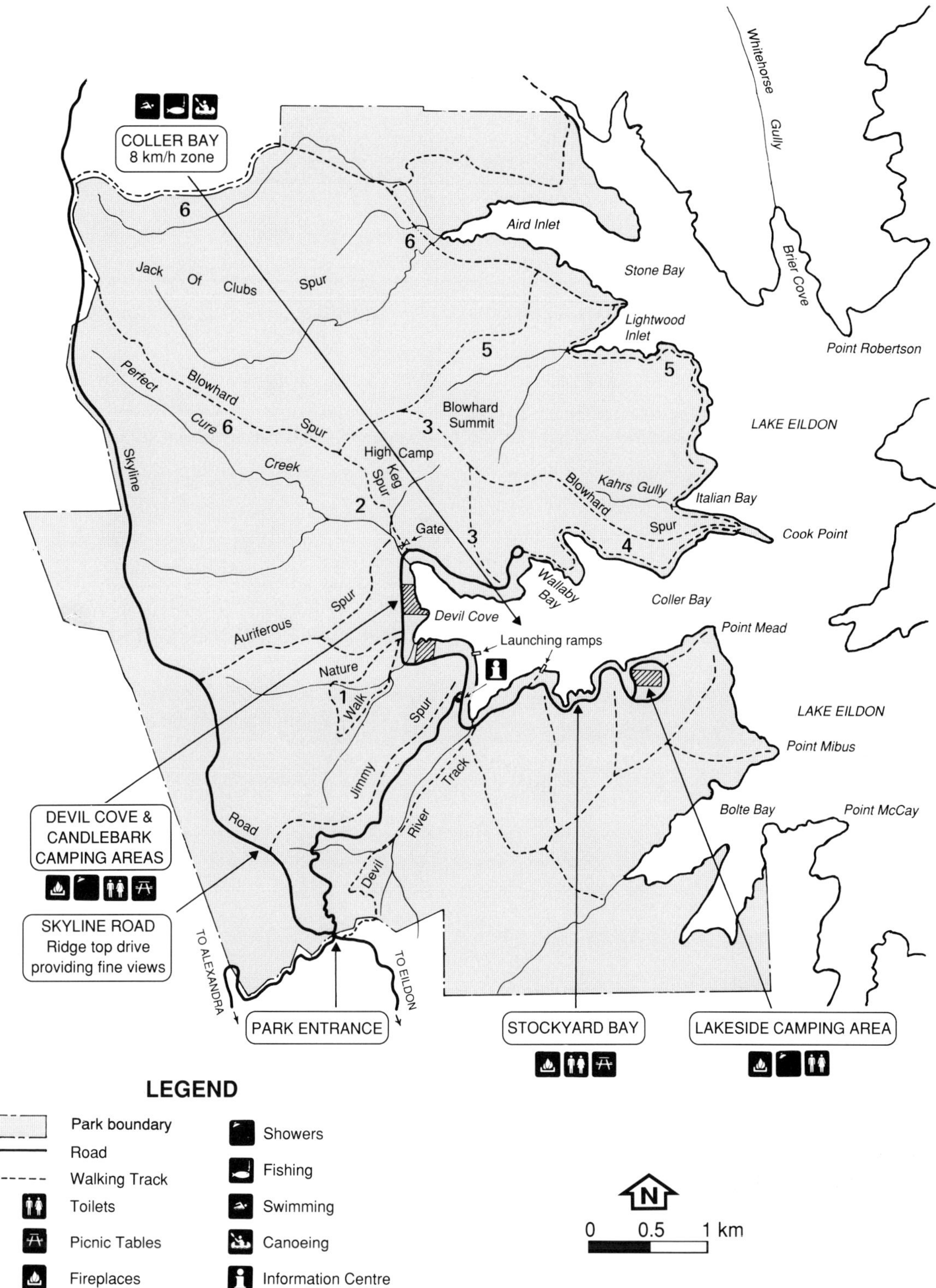

COLLER BAY
8 km/h zone
Whitehorse Gully
Aird Inlet
Stone Bay
Brier Cove
Lightwood Inlet
Point Robertson
Jack Of Clubs Spur
Perfect Cure Creek
Blowhard Spur
Blowhard Summit
High Camp
Keg Spur
Skyline
LAKE EILDON
Kahrs Gully
Italian Bay
Blowhard Spur
Cook Point
Gate
Wallaby Bay
Coller Bay
Auriferous Spur
Devil Cove
Launching ramps
Point Mead
Nature Walk
Jimmy Spur
River Track
Devil
LAKE EILDON
Point Mibus
Road
Bolte Bay
Point McCay
DEVIL COVE & CANDLEBARK CAMPING AREAS
SKYLINE ROAD
Ridge top drive providing fine views
TO ALEXANDRA
TO EILDON
PARK ENTRANCE
STOCKYARD BAY
LAKESIDE CAMPING AREA
LEGEND
Park boundary
Road
Walking Track
Toilets
Picnic Tables
Fireplaces
Showers
Fishing
Swimming
Canoeing
Information Centre
N
0 0.5 1 km

productive farm and vineyard, building first one house, then a second to accomodate their large family. After John's death and some years on the land on her own, his widow sold to Herbert Coller, whose family renamed the property *Benara*, and built it into a successful grazing property. In 1952, *Benara* was resumed by the State Rivers and Water Supply Commission in anticipation of the filling of Lake Eildon. During the 1968 drought *Benara* emerged, shingle roof still intact, and then again in 1983 it re-appeared from the drowned valley, now considerably more decayed. It is unlikely to have survived the re-drowning that inevitably followed.

National park status was conferred on this area when the problem arose of what to do with the land that had been resumed during the building of the Eildon Dam and the flooding of the valleys. Forested catchments are more successful than unforested, and natural regeneration seemed a suitable solution. Thus Fraser NP has no history of concerned individuals and groups pushing for the protection of what they saw as worth preserving. Rather, it was a political answer to an immediate problem. And so the National Parks Authority, then only weeks old, not only gained its first new park, but also one in whose name its Chairman, The Hon. A.J. Fraser, was duly honoured.

Things to do: Walking; swimming and other water sports; fishing; camping (but you must book ahead at busy times). The Upper Goulburn Historic area nearby is also well worth visiting.

Best season to visit: Any.

Special features: Regeneration of native bush; the kangaroos near the camping ground; tranquil, lakeside camping.

Relevant reading:
National Parks Service (1971) *Fraser NP Master Plan.*
Land Conservation Council (1973) *Report of the Melbourne Area.*

Further information:
Ranger-in-Charge, Fraser NP Park Office, Park Rd, Alexandra, Vic 3714. Phone (057) 72 1293.

Merlo family, 'Glen Hope' farm, 1909 *CFL*

'Benara', 1955 *CFL*

55

Eildon State Park

Physical features: 24 000 ha. This Park, similar in character to Fraser NP, is in three parts, each separated from the others by the waters of Lake Eildon. Of these three, the part immediately south-east of Eildon township has the highest point, Rocky Peak, 1 059 m. Lake Eildon lies in the valley of the Goulburn River and its major tributaries, the Big, Howqua and Delatite Rivers. The country is deeply dissected, giving the Lake a total shoreline of nearly 500 km and the landscape an extremely scenic character. There are also some excellent look-out points with wide views across to the Baw Baw Plateau and the High Country. The geology, described under Fraser NP, is of considerable interest.

Plants and animals: On the drier slopes the open forest has a mix of various box, stringybark and peppermint eucalypts, often with a colourful spring understorey, and Blue Gum in the wetter areas. The animals are typical for this type of country and are similar to those which would be seen in Fraser NP.

Human history: (See also Fraser NP.) When Lake Eildon was completed in 1955, some of the catchment area became Fraser NP, and much of the remainder was designated as Eildon State Forest. As a result of Land Conservation Council Recomendations in 1977, this State Forest became State Park and so received a higher level of protection and a greater emphasis on conservation and recreation values.

Things to do: Like the rest of the Lake, Eildon SP has high recreational potential. Watersports are very popular as are fishing; swimming; bushwalking; studying natural history; and camping (you need to book for busy times). Hunting for Sambar Deer, but not with dogs, is allowed in season.

Best season to visit: Summer is the most popular season because so many activities are water-based, but the Park has an appeal at any time of year, especially for walking and picnicking.

Special features: The fascinating variation in colour of the eucalypts, especially when the young tips of the stringybarks are bright red; the clear, ringing calls of the currawongs – a characteristic sound of Victoria's hill country.

Relevant reading: See Fraser NP.

Further information:
C&E Regional Office, 46 Aitken St, Alexandra, Vic 3714. Phone (057) 72 1633.

Drowned trees *AB*

Eildon

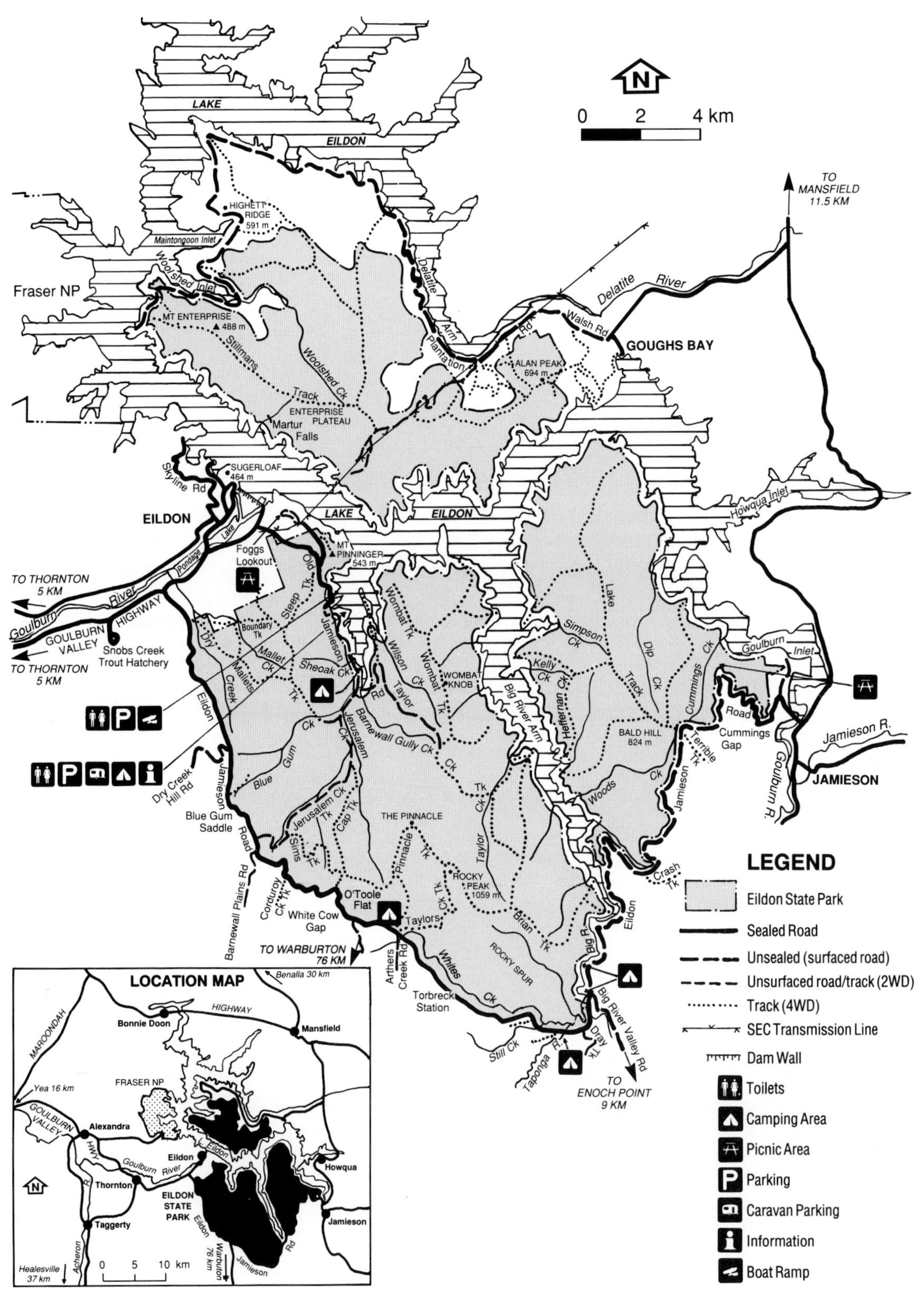

LAKE
EILDON
0 2 4 km
TO MANSFIELD 11.5 KM
HIGHETT RIDGE 591 m
Maintongoon Inlet
Fraser NP
Woolshed Inlet
MT ENTERPRISE 488 m
Stillmans
Track
Woolshed Ck
Delatite Arm
Plantation
Delatite River
Walsh Rd
GOUGHS BAY
ALAN PEAK 694 m
ENTERPRISE PLATEAU
Martur Falls
SUGERLOAF 464 m
Skyline Rd
EILDON
Howqua Inlet
Foggs Lookout
MT PINNINGER 543 m
TO THORNTON 5 KM
Goulburn River
GOULBURN VALLEY HIGHWAY
Snobs Creek Trout Hatchery
Pondage
Boundary Tk
Old Steep Tk
Jamieson Ck
Mallet Ck
Malletts Creek
Dry Creek
Sheoak Ck
Wombat Tk
Wilson Ck
Wombat Tk
WOMBAT KNOB
Taylor Rd
Simpson Ck
Kelly Ck
Heffernan Ck
Big River Arm
Lake Dip Track
Cummings Ck
Goulburn Inlet
Road
Cummings Gap
Jamieson R.
Goulburn R.
JAMIESON
BALD HILL 824 m
Terrible Tk
Woods Ck
Jamieson
Eildon Jamieson Road
Jerusalem Ck
Barnewall Gully Ck
Blue Gum Ck
Dry Creek Hill Rd
Blue Gum Saddle
Jerusalem Ck Tk
Cap Tk
Sims Tk
THE PINNACLE
Pinnacle Tk
Taylor Ck
Tk
ROCKY PEAK 1059 m
Brian Tk
Crash Tk
Barnewall Plains Rd
Corduroy Ck Tk
O'Toole Flat
White Cow Gap
Taylors Ck Tk
TO WARBURTON 76 KM
Arthers Creek Rd
Whites Ck
ROCKY SPUR
Torbreck Station
Big R.
Eildon
Big River Valley Rd
Dray Tk
Still Ck
Taponga R.
TO ENOCH POINT 9 KM
LOCATION MAP
Benalla 30 km
HIGHWAY
MAROONDAH
Bonnie Doon
Mansfield
Yea 16 km
FRASER NP
GOULBURN VALLEY
Alexandra
HWY
Goulburn River
Eildon
Eildon
Howqua
Thornton
EILDON STATE PARK
Taggerty
Eildon Rd
Jamieson
Warburton 76 km
Jamieson
Healesville 37 km
Acheron
0 5 10 km
LEGEND
Eildon State Park
Sealed Road
Unsealed (surfaced road)
Unsurfaced road/track (2WD)
Track (4WD)
SEC Transmission Line
Dam Wall
Toilets
Camping Area
Picnic Area
Parking
Caravan Parking
Information
Boat Ramp

◀ Lake Eildon SP *JAC*

▼ Grass-trees, Warby Ranges *DMC*

▲ Rufous Whistler *ARI*

▶ Flight of Ibis, Barmah SP *CFL*
▼ Phantom Wattle *JW*

▲ View across Fraser NP *JAC*

ALPINE PARKS

As of December 1989, Victoria has a magnificent new national park – the long awaited Alpine National Park. This Park embraces 646 000 ha and links the protected High Country of Victoria, New South Wales and the Australian Capital Territory. Because of the size and diversity of the Alpine NP, it has been treated here as a series of different areas each of which was once a separate park. The Alpine NP is now managed as a group of four units: Bogong, Wonnangatta-Moroka (incorporating Wabonga Plateau), Cobberas-Tingaringy and Dartmouth. Also included in this section are three other parks: Snowy River NP which is contiguous with the new Alpine NP; and Mt Buffalo NP and Baw Baw NP which, although separate from the main line of the Alps, are very much part of Victoria's 'winter playground'. The geology for all the alpine parks is covered here.

The Great Dividing Range is never particularly high. Mt Bogong, the highest point, only reaches 2 000 m. Nonetheless, the Range is truly majestic. It has been formed by four main processes – sedimentation, intrusion, erosion and uplift. The sedimentation began 500 million years ago when sediments were deposited in a vast marine basin across much of eastern and south-eastern Australia. These strata were later folded and compressed by earth movements, setting up stresses which allowed molten magma to well up from the earth's interior and intrude into the earlier sediments. Magma cooled slowly beneath overlying layers of rock to form the Devonian granites of Mt Buffalo. The heat and pressure of this folding, and the igneous activity, metamorphosed some of the rock into the slates that outcrop at Mt Feathertop and the schists and gneisses of the Bogong High Plains.

Following the intrusive activity there was a period of stability for 300 million years, and the land was eroded to an almost level plain. Then, about 90 million years ago, a period of uplift in what is now the Australian Alps began gradually to elevate the land. Streams and rivers cut down through the land, wearing away the softer sediments more quickly than the harder granitic and metamorphic rocks. In some cases, gorges, dropping steeply down through 1 000 m, resulted. The 'alps' also saw a further period of igneous activity when lava flows filled the developing valleys and other low-lying areas. This basalt was harder than the surrounding sediments, and as they eroded away, the lava-filled valleys were left as prominences such as Mt Loch and Mt Jim on the Bogong High Plains. Where the original valley was deep, the lava mass cooled slowly into hexagonal columns such as those at Ruined Castle above Falls Creek. (See also Organ Pipes NP.)

Over the last 20 000 years cold and ice have made their erosive presence felt. An interesting effect has been the rock rivers (blockstreams) of boulders, seen in many parts of the Alps. These are river-like masses of large blocks of rock, often basalt, which crack off and then slowly move downhill as the result of successive freezing and thawing.

Today, standing on some vantage point, it is often difficult to see an overall pattern to the Alpine landscape, just an east to west trend of range after range stretching away into an ever bluer distance. A relief map, however, soon shows that the Victorian High Country is really an enormous plateau broken into three large blocks, separated from each other by deep valleys caused by erosion, often along fault lines. West Kiewa, one of the more impressive valleys, is the result of a fault grinding a 1.5 km strip of land into rock flour.

Our Alps today, for all their rugged vastness, are an extremely fragile part of our heritage. However we enter them, be it on foot, on horseback or by vehicle, they deserve our respect and reverence.

Relevant reading:

Conservation, Forests and Lands *Common Ground* (December 1989).
Conservation, Forests and Lands *Dartmouth Unit Proposed Management Plan* (1989).
Gould League of Victoria (1970) *Birds of Victoria: the Ranges.*
Johnson R. (1974) *The Alps at the Crossroads.*
Land Conservation Council (1977) *Report on the Alpine Study Area* and (1974) *Report on the East Gippsland Study Area.*
McCann I.R. (1987) *The Alps in Flower.*
Mosley G. (1988) *Australian Alps World Heritage Nomination Proposal.*

Alpine

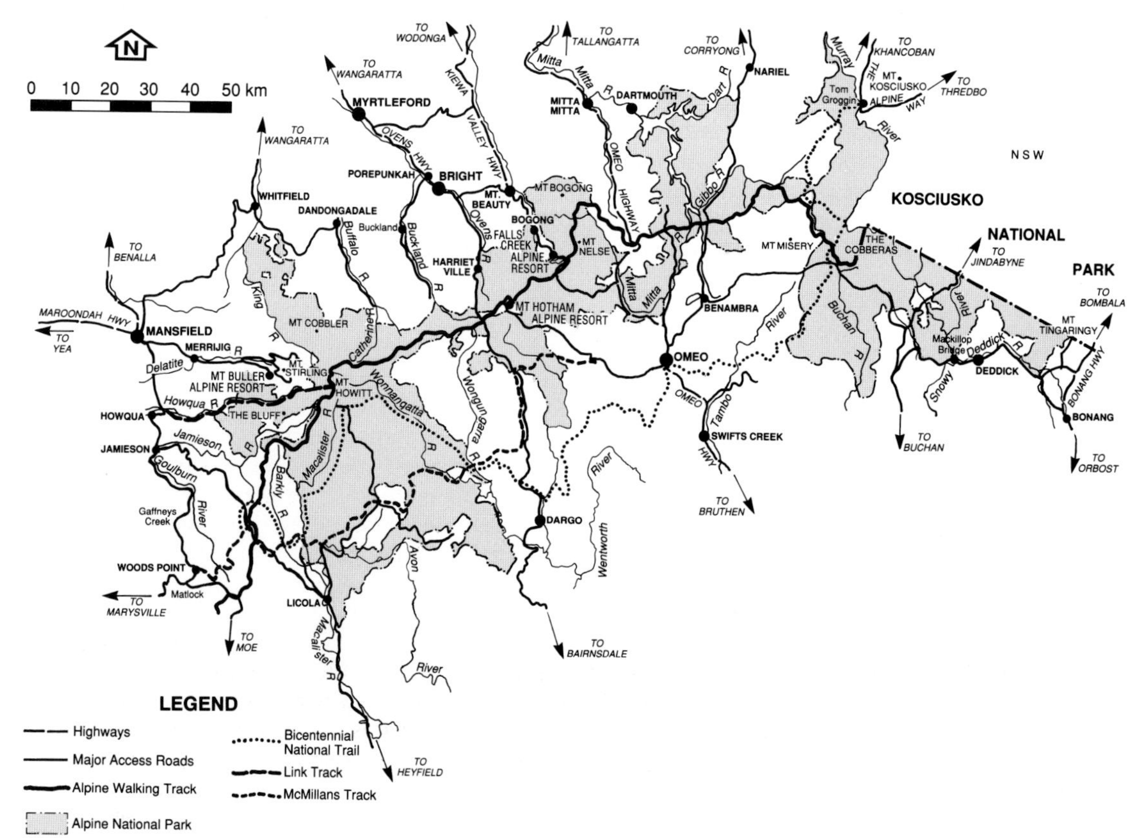

	Page No.	Entrance Fee	Information Centre	Multilingual Information	Picnic Areas	Fireplaces	Toilets	Disabled Access	Walking Tracks	Nature Walk or Drive	Swimming	Climbing	Horseriding	Fishing	Boating	Skiing	Camping	Caravans	Km from Melbourne	Date Declared
Avon	168											■		■			■		200	1987
Baw Baw	181	■			■	■	■		■	■			■	■	■	■	■		180	1979
Bogong	161				■	■	■		■				■	■	■	■	■		340	1981
Cobberas-Tingaringy	173										■		■	■	■		■		450	1979
Mount Buffalo	182	■	■		■	■	■	■	■	■	■	■	■	■	■	■	■		335	1898
Snowy River	174					■	■		■		■	■	■	■	■	■	■		390	1980
Wabonga Plateau	170				■	■	■		■				■				■		270	1980
Wonnangatta-Moroka	165					■			■		■	■	■	■		■	■		230	1982

56 Alpine NP – Bogong

Physical features: 81 200 ha. There is often some confusion between Mt Bogong and the Bogong High Plains; both lie within the central block of the Victorian High Country, but because of deep valleys running away to the north-west, Mt Bogong is isolated from the rest of the plateau. Most of the high points, including Mt Bogong, a granodiorite massif, are somewhat disappointing as 'mountains', since apart from a few, like Feathertop, they appear not as spectacular peaks but as rounded prominences. Often, though, there are some impressive cliffs such as those below the summit of Bogong. (See also Alpine Introduction.)

Plants and animals: Victoria's most notable botanist, Baron Ferdinand von Mueller, was the first person to systematically collect in this area and reveal the riches of our alpine flora. He began his expeditions in 1853, soon after his appointment as Victorian Government Botanist, and returned a number of times, exploring both the northern and the southern High Country, often on his own. He had a deep love of all plants, never failed to be moved by the magnificence of our eucalypt forests and constantly urged others to protect and venerate them also.

Just as von Mueller did, today's traveller ascends typically through the dry open forests of the lowlands with peppermints, stringybarks and boxes, up through forests of Blue Gum, Messmate and Candlebark, then towering Mountain Ash, followed by Alpine Ash, on through Mountain Gum and White Sallee, and finally into the rugged Snow Gums. Every one of these is a eucalypt, and every one has its own character printed on the landscape. For the last 4 000 to 8 000 years the snowline has been at about 1 700 m but this varies considerably, not only with latitude but also with aspect and therefore sun and wind. Frost hollows into which the cold air drains and is then unable to escape from, occur frequently. Although treeless, these are rich with shrubs, grasses and other small plants, and it is here and above the snowline that the best wildflower displays are seen. Often these hollows are poorly drained, and contain gentle creeks and boggy pools surrounded by sundews, bladderworts and Sphagnum Moss. This is the country that is so vulnerable to damage from trampling by stock or people, and which, in its pristine state, is an enormously valuable reservoir of summer water, releasing it slowly into creeks and rivers. Over the last 50 years, studies have been made of the effects of cattle grazing in the Alps, and it is now recognised that cattle cause considerable damage, not only to the bogs, but to the soils and to the flora generally. Cattle grazing is not compatible with the primary objective of a national park, that of conservation, and it is therefore proposed to phase out grazing from the more sensitive areas of the High Country.

Animal life in the Alps is surprisingly rich and diverse, although only one mammal appears to be fully adapted to the alpine environment. This is the Mountain Pygmy-possum, or Burramys, which can go into a state of torpor to conserve energy during the cold weather. Until 1966 when a live animal was found in a ski hut at Mt Hotham, this delightful little animal was only known from fossils, but fortunately it thrives and breeds in captivity so its biology is now becoming better understood. It is currently known from only two quite small alpine areas near Mt Hotham and Mt Kosciusko, which are well separated from each other by the broad lowland valley of the Mitta Mitta River. It is found above 1 350 m altitude, often in rock rivers where it moves freely among the snow-covered boulders. Much more easily seen than Burramys are the wombats, which often move through heavy snow, and Echidnas, which can sometimes be seen during the summer, foraging under the Snow Gums.

During the summer a number of birds visit the alpine areas on a fairly regular basis, although usually only some ravens stay throughout the winter, and it is these birds which have learnt to exploit a new food resource – that provided by the ski resorts. In summer the ravens have to rely on a more natural diet, including large numbers of Bogong Moths, a favourite food also of the currawongs which move up from lower altitudes. Other altitudinal migrants include the vivid Flame Robin, always a joy to see, and Richard's Pipit, Gang Gangs, Yellow-tailed Black-Cockatoos and a number of honeyeaters. A rather less expected summer visitor is the Japanese Snipe, a summer migrant from the northern hemisphere. There are a number of distinctive insects here, especially

Bogong

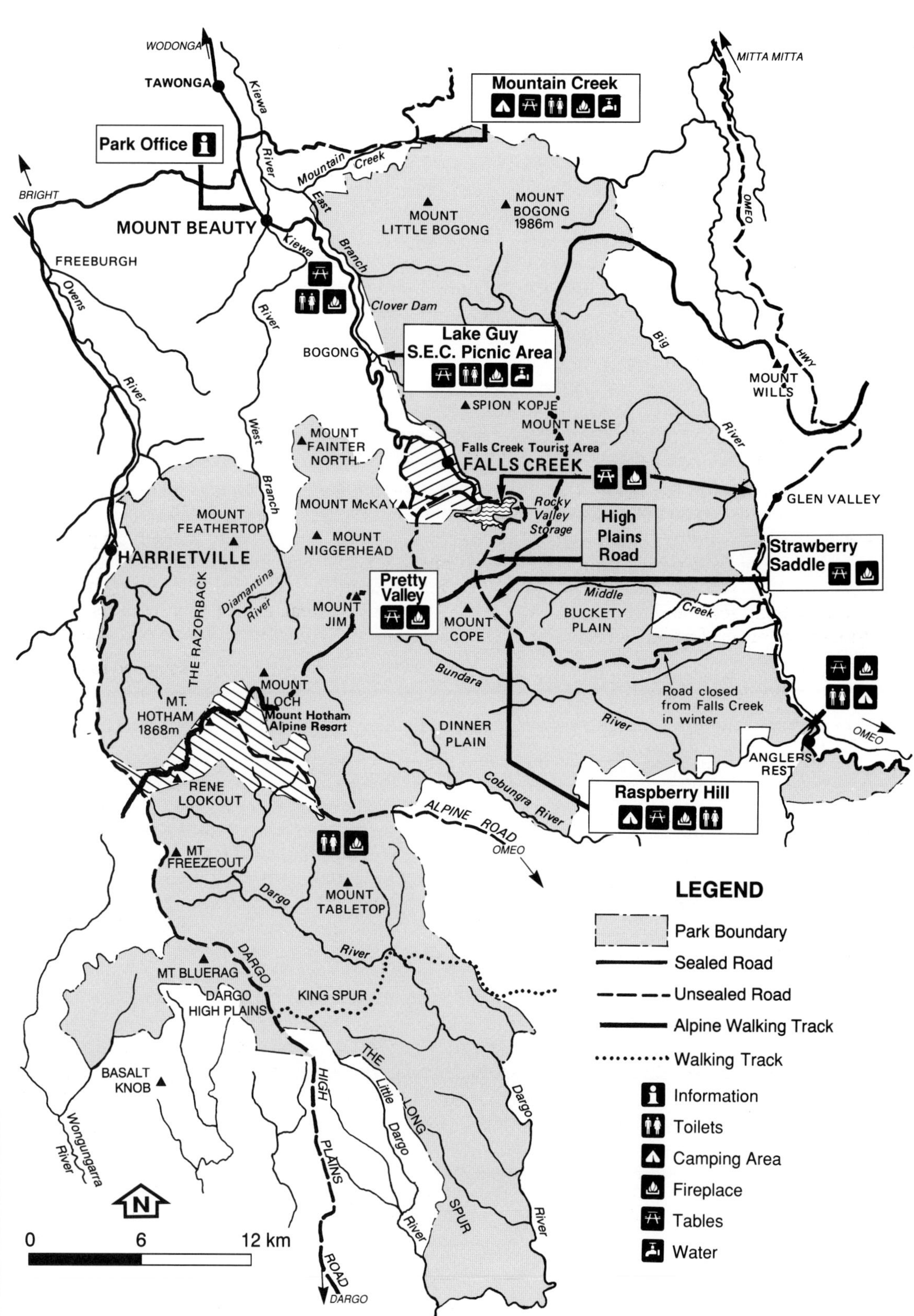

WODONGA
TAWONGA
Park Office
BRIGHT
MOUNT BEAUTY
FREEBURGH
Mountain Creek
MITTA MITTA
MOUNT LITTLE BOGONG
MOUNT BOGONG 1986m
OMEO
Clover Dam
BOGONG
Lake Guy S.E.C. Picnic Area
MOUNT WILLS
SPION KOPJE
MOUNT NELSE
Falls Creek Tourist Area
FALLS CREEK
MOUNT FAINTER NORTH
MOUNT McKAY
Rocky Valley Storage
High Plains Road
GLEN VALLEY
Strawberry Saddle
MOUNT FEATHERTOP
HARRIETVILLE
MOUNT NIGGERHEAD
Pretty Valley
MOUNT JIM
MOUNT COPE
BUCKETY PLAIN
THE RAZORBACK
Road closed from Falls Creek in winter
MOUNT LOCH
Mount Hotham Alpine Resort
MT. HOTHAM 1868m
DINNER PLAIN
ANGLERS REST
OMEO
Raspberry Hill
RENE LOOKOUT
ALPINE ROAD
OMEO
MT FREEZEOUT
MOUNT TABLETOP
MT BLUERAG
DARGO HIGH PLAINS
KING SPUR
BASALT KNOB
THE LONG SPUR
HIGH PLAINS ROAD
DARGO
N
0
6
12 km
LEGEND
Park Boundary
Sealed Road
Unsealed Road
Alpine Walking Track
Walking Track
Information
Toilets
Camping Area
Fireplace
Tables
Water

the grasshoppers with their yellow and black spots, the warning effect of which is heightened further when they jump by bright orange startle markings on their legs. Probably the best known insects though are the Bogong Moths. These small brown moths arrive in the summer in their millions to aestivate (over-summer) in cracks and crevices among boulders and under bark, where they remain for three to four months.

Human history: The High Country was familiar to the Aborigines, with many groups travelling there each summer to harvest Bogong Moths, a significant part of their diet. The moths were scooped out of their hiding places and stirred in hot ashes to remove their wings before being sieved and eaten, either as they were or ground into a highly nutritious paste. The annual moth harvest was also used as an occasion for trading and marriage, since a man was not allowed to marry within his own family group.

Although the Alps formed a major barrier to early settlers seeking new pastures for their stock, George McKillop travelled south from Monaro in NSW, to the Omeo Plains in 1835, followed six years later by Angus Macmillan who found a way through to Corner Inlet near Wilsons Promontory. Summer grazing appears to have begun in the Victorian High Country in the 1850's, about 20 years later than in NSW. Next came goldmining, from the 1850's onwards. The last mine in the Bogong area, the Red Robin mine near Mt Loch, closed only recently. Perhaps the most lasting legacy of the miners was their introduction of skiing, with all that it has meant in terms of tourism and recreation. Now, the major downhill ski resorts in Victoria are under the control of a separate body, the Alpine Resorts Commission, unlike the situation in NSW where the ski resorts are within the Kosciusko NP and where there is therefore a greater emphasis on conservation within these resorts.

Timber harvesting too, has been a major issue in the Alps. Massive cutting took place in the alpine regions after the 1939 bushfires wiped out most of the good timber closer to Melbourne. Many of the roads now in use in the Alps are old logging roads, and have done much to open up previously inaccessible country. Unfortunately though, this can well lead to erosion and degradation. In some areas, since incorporated into national parks, the highly controversial once-only logging has been allowed, leaving scars and erosion that will take many years to heal. It will be many years too before these logged forests return both to the condition which so delighted Baron von Mueller,

> ...those sentiments of veneration which amongst all the grand works of nature, an undisturbed forest region is most apt to call forth.

and to the condition appropriate to a great national park.

For a number of years now, attempts have been made to create an Alpine National Park that will link with Kosciusko NP and so truly protect this extremely important part of Australia. This importance was highlighted by the nomination late in 1988 of the Australian Alps for World Heritage listing. The basis for the nomination was the Alps' distinctive sclerophyll (hard-leaved) vegetation, centred around 50 species of eucalypts which here are a living laboratory of how speciation has occurred in the 50 million years since Australia separated from the rest of Gondwana. There are four criteria which must be satisfied for World Heritage listing. These concern the earth's geological and biological evolution, the presence of rare, beautiful or exceptional natural formations, and habitat for rare or endangered species. Every one of these criteria is met by our magnificent Australian Alps.

Things to do: Obviously recreation in the Alps is seasonal. Many keen skiers, both downhill and cross-country, never go near the High Country in summer, and many walkers never ski, but for a growing number of people the appeal is a year-round one – scenic driving; camping; photography and sketching, especially of the picturesque old mountain huts; and just enjoying the special character and atmosphere. Horse-trekking is now becoming a popular way to see more country in a short time.

Best season to visit: Any, depending on your interests. Wildflowers are at their best from November onwards, with those of the highest country being most spectacular in mid to late January.

Special features: Views, on a clear day, you can see if not forever, at least as far as Mt Kosciusko across the NSW border; the change in tree types as you go up into the High Country; wildflowers, especially the Silky Daisy which often grows in running water; brilliant grasshoppers.

Relevant reading:
Siseman J. and Brownlie J. (1986) *Bogong National Park.*
Conservation, Forests and Lands (1989) *Alpine Area Bogong Planning Unit Proposed Management Plan.*
(See also Alpine Introduction.)

Further information:
C&E Office, Kiewa Valley Hwy, Mt Beauty, Vic 3699. Phone (057) 57 2693.
Friends' Group: Phone (03) 560 8766.

Burramys *CFL*

57 Alpine NP – Wonnangatta-Moroka

Physical features: 107 000 ha. This section of the Alpine NP straddles the Great Dividing Range and contains the headwaters of many rivers, including the Howqua and King to the north and the Macalister and Wonnangatta to the south. It falls within the most easterly of the three high blocks that make up the Victorian Alps, and can be divided into three further sections: a northerly area of dramatic scenic features such as the highly descriptive Crosscut Saw and Razor; a high plateau embracing the the plains country; and finally the river valleys, some with spectacular gorges and waterfalls. Generally the land is not particularly high. Mt Howitt, 1 742 m, is the highest point and not really a 'proper' peak at that; The Cobbler, 1 620 m, is more isolated and rugged. It is not so much the actual height that creates dramatic visual effects but rather the way in which the land suddenly falls away in precipitous bluffs and chasms. Much of Wonnangatta-Moroka is sedimentary rock, with the oldest (non-marine) sediments being in the east. There is also some conglomerate, and igneous areas such as the basalt cappings and fascinating rock rivers. At Snowy Bluff, near the junction of the Moroka and Wonnangatta Rivers, are high cliffs which expose a good sequence of inter-bedded sedimentary and volcanic rocks. The landscape that we see today is largely the result of quite recent uplift, erosion and deposition.

Plants and animals: Because there is such a variety of altitude, slope and aspect here, there is a wonderful richness of plant and animal life, with more than 1 300 plants and 180 birds, not to mention a number of fish, amphibia, reptiles and mammals such as Swamp Wallabies, gliders and possums, Antechinus and native rodents. Those streams and rivers that are quiet and undisturbed are ideal habitat for the Platypus.

The valleys are deeply wooded with a formidable array of Prickly Tea-tree and saw sedges along the streams, then up through tall eucalypts to open forests of stringybarks, boxes and peppermints, according to aspect, and finally to montane forests of Snow Gums and open alpine herb fields above the snowline. It is in the flowers of the herbfields and Snow Gum woodlands that the beauty of the Alps is there for all to see, starting with wide expanses of Rusty Pods and Purple Eyebright in November, and ending with Mountain Gentian and Small Crowea in March. In winter the Snow Gums add their own colour, with richly marked trunks of red, green and silver against a backdrop of snow. Along the alpine bogs and streams there are patches of Sphagnum Moss, which, when undamaged, retains the meltwater from the winter snow.

Human history: This country was part of important trade routes for the Aborigines, who were also known to come up into the Alps when there was a plentiful supply of the protein and fat-rich Bogong Moths.

The first European known to have explored the area was the eminent Victorian botanist, Baron Ferdinand von Mueller, who, soon after his appointment as Victorian Government Botanist in 1853, recognised that no one had yet collected in the Alps and that here was a chance to make his name. In 1860, Alfred Howitt explored the area in search of gold. This he found in a tributary of the Wonnangatta, thus starting the rush that led to the now derelict boom towns of Grant and Talbotville (in the Grant Historic Area which adjoins Wonnangatta-Moroka). The early prospectors stayed almost entirely along the stream beds, and it was the cattlemen who, recognising the value of the High Country for summer grazing, moved out on to the tops in search of pasture. Sheep were also grazed there for a time, but the depredations of the dingos soon made this unworkable. One of the most notable of the early cattlemen families was that of the Bryces, who until 1914 lived at the historic Wonnangatta Station, the homestead of which was burnt down in 1957. The site is still a popular destination for walkers and 4WD-ers, many of whom are fascinated by the small family cemetery, and by the still unsolved Barclay murders. Barclay, the station manager, was murdered in 1918, and for many months it was assumed that the cook, who had disappeared, was guilty, until his body too was discovered in a partly burnt-out woodpile. Now Wonnangatta Station has been bought and added to Wonnangatta-Moroka Unit, and its heritage is there for all to share.

Wonnangatta-Moroka

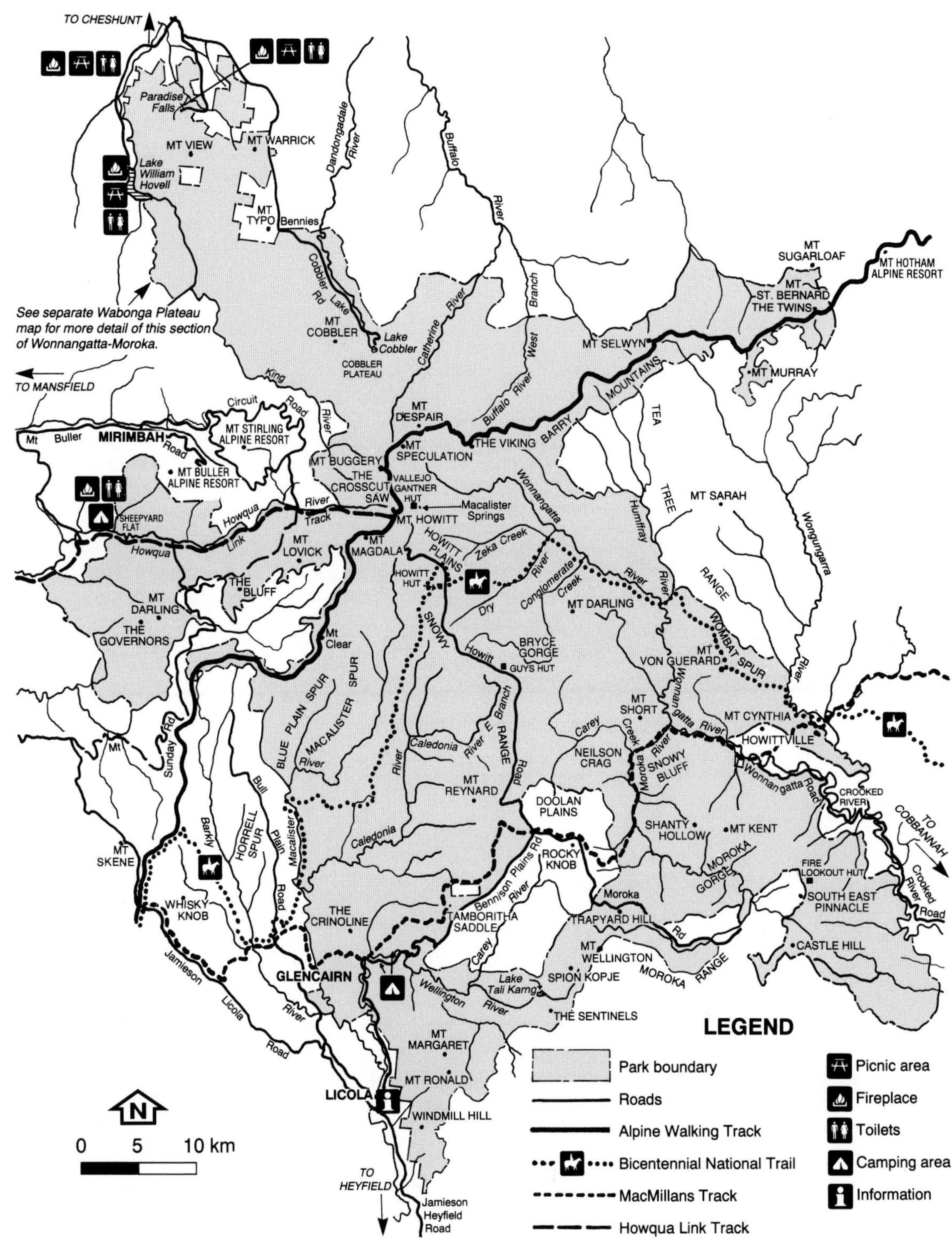

Last of all came the timber-getters, particularly after the 1939 fires burnt out so much of the more accessible timber nearer Melbourne. Harvesting of timber has now ceased, though it will be some time yet before all the scars have healed, especially where the regeneration work was inadequate and where logging took place on slopes over the prescribed 30°.

Things to do: Because of timber-harvesting over the years, there is a network of tracks throughout the Park, which are popular for 4WD (not that all are always open, you do need to check first). Many are also accessible to 2WD vehicles. There are many good walking tracks, including significant parts of the Alpine Walking Track, which runs for 400 km from Walhalla to Tom Groggin on the NSW border; and McMillans Track which was put in as a pack route in 1860 to link the gold settlements of Woods Point and Omeo, and which has recently been restored as a Bicentennial project. There are also excellent opportunities for many short day walks, such as those to the very beautiful Conglomerate Falls, and from Lake Cobbler to Mt Cobbler. Bush camping is popular, as are horseriding and visiting the Historic Areas and old huts. Because of the wonderful light effects, there are also many attractive challenges for photographers and artists generally. Conditional hunting and fishing are allowed.

Best season to visit: Obviously winter for skiing; otherwise November to March for wildflowers, with the peak, on the highest country, being late December to late January; spring through to autumn for walking and general touring.

Special features: The ethereal effect of clouds in the valleys with peaks projecting above, especially on an autumn morning; the spectacular and constantly changing wildflowers; sitting on a peak and watching swifts and perhaps butterflies too, skimming past.

Relevant reading:
Siseman J. (1985) *Wonnangatta-Moroka National Park.*
Mortimer W.M. (1981) *The History of Wonnangatta Station.*

Further information:
C&E Office, Pearson St, Heyfield, Vic 3858. Phone (051) 48 2355.
Friends' Group: Phone (03) 795 4629.

Wombat *CFL*

58 Avon Wilderness

Physical features: 40 000 ha. Most of the Avon Wilderness is made up of freshwater Carboniferous sediments, similar to those of Mitchell River NP. There is also some basalt. The Avon River rises below Mt Wellington (1 600 m), the highest point. Tali Karng, the beautiful little jewel of a lake, so often associated with the Avon, is not in the Wilderness but is included in the Alpine NP.

Plants and animals: The montane forests here are of outstanding botanical importance and have a number of significant species, including an endemic buttercup, *Ranunculus eichlerianus.* There are many birds and other animals known too, but more comprehensive surveys are needed. One group of animals often overlooked is the native fish, such as Blackfish. These are now attracting more interest as it becomes apparent that they can seldom compete successfully with introduced trout. Wilderness areas can therefore be particularly important as habitats for these and other species.

Human history: There has been limited exploitation of this area; some timber harvesting and chromite mining have taken place, and some areas have been grazed. All these activities have now ceased, allowing the following ideals to be more completely fulfilled:

> The wilderness experience involves the perception of being part of nature, of an environment unaltered by human intervention, of isolation, and of being exposed to the challenge of the elements.
>
> The main elements of appeal of the wilderness are:
> - spiritual refreshment and an awareness of solitude arising from close contact with the uninhabited, substantially undisturbed, natural environment
> - the knowledge that there still exists a large natural area in which plants, animals and soils can survive with minimal interference by Man
> - refuge from the pressures, sights and sounds of modern urban life
> - the adventure and challenge of putting one's powers of endurance and self-reliance to the test in substantially undisturbed natural environments.
>
> 1979 LCC Final Recommendations for the Alpine Area.

Things to do: Camping; bushwalking; rockclimbing; fishing; enjoying natural history. Wilderness means no tracks, other than for management, and no facilities, so you must be self-reliant, taking in all supplies and bringing out all rubbish.

Best season to visit: Any, although you should also be aware of unpredictable weather and sudden river risings.

Special features: The wilderness experience; the view of Tali Karng (although not actually in the Avon), especially with mist rising from it.

Relevant reading:
Preece K. and Lesslie R. (1987) *Survey of Wilderness Quality in Victoria.*

Further information:
C&E Office, 8 Pearson St, Heyfield, Vic 3858. Phone (051) 48 2355.

Avon

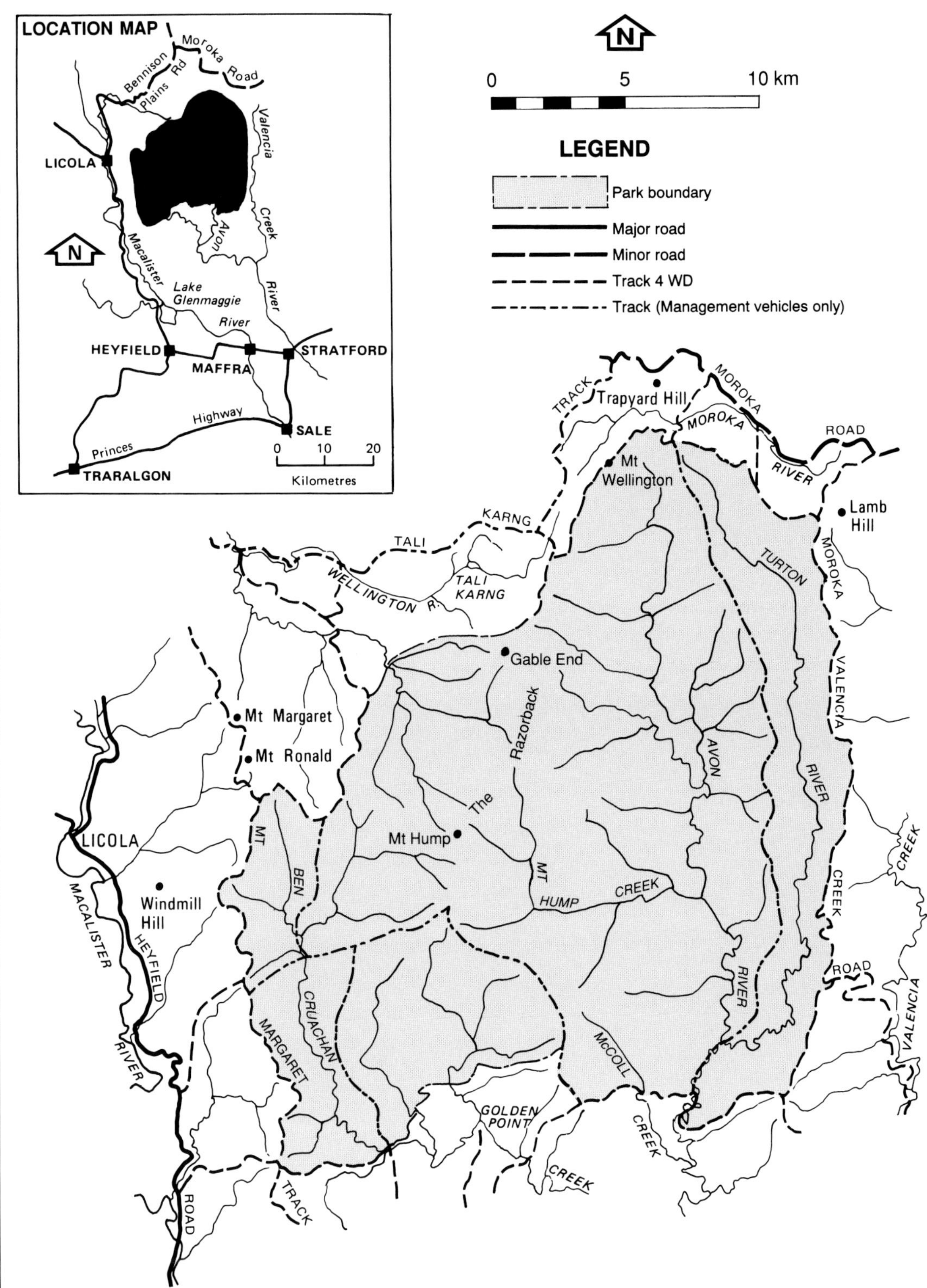

LOCATION MAP
Moroka Road
Bennison Plains Rd
Valencia Creek
LICOLA
Avon
Macalister
Lake Glenmaggie
River
River
HEYFIELD
MAFFRA
STRATFORD
Highway
SALE
Princes
TRARALGON
0 10 20
Kilometres
N
0 5 10 km
LEGEND
Park boundary
Major road
Minor road
Track 4 WD
Track (Management vehicles only)
TRACK
Trapyard Hill
MOROKA
MOROKA
ROAD
RIVER
Mt Wellington
Lamb Hill
KARNG
TALI
TALI KARNG
WELLINGTON R.
TURTON
MOROKA
Gable End
VALENCIA
The Razorback
Mt Margaret
Mt Ronald
AVON
RIVER
LICOLA
MT BEN
Mt Hump
MT HUMP CREEK
CREEK
CREEK
Windmill Hill
MACALISTER
HEYFIELD
ROAD
CRUACHAN
MARGARET
RIVER
McCOLL
VALENCIA
RIVER
GOLDEN POINT
CREEK
CREEK
TRACK
ROAD

59 Alpine NP – Wabonga Plateau

Physical features: 21 200 ha. Wabonga Plateau is bounded to the west by the King River; the Rose River, which starts below Mt Cobbler in Wonnangatta-Moroka NP, runs through part of Wabonga before turning east to flow along the edge of the Buffalo Plateau. The Plateau is Upper Devonian/ Lower Carboniferous in age (360–300 million years old), and consists of both non-marine sediments and volcanic deposits. It is extensively dissected and has steep ridges and cliffs, some of which expose both the sedimentary and the volcanic formations. There are also large rock outcrops which are of considerable geological interest. The Plateau is best known for Paradise Falls on Stony Creek, another tributary of the King River. These falls are extremely scenic (when there is plenty of water flowing) particularly so since you can easily walk behind the water and look out through a liquid curtain. This is because the lip of the Falls is considerably harder than the underlying strata, which have therefore eroded away. Wabonga Plateau is on the western edge of the High Country and catches the rain and southerly winds, so the weather can sometimes be unexpectedly severe.

Plants and animals: Most of the Plateau is covered with open forest of peppermint with some Messmate and Alpine Ash in more sheltered areas, and Snow Gum and Mountain Gum on the higher land. The heathy understorey is dense in parts with peas, grevilleas, dogwoods, wattles, grasses and ferns. Many of these are showy and well worth seeing in spring. Echidnas, wallabies, kangaroos and wombats are all quite common and there is a rich variety of birds and reptiles. Detailed studies of the flora and fauna have not yet been made.

Human history: The first land grant on Wabonga was in 1886, but only a small block in the centre of the Park has been cleared, and this is still privately owned. The area was grazed and logged before its reservation. Logging has now ceased and grazing will have stopped by July 1991.

Things to do: Dispersed (bush) camping; bushwalking; fishing; exploring by 4WD or trail bike but *please* keep to the formed tracks – the area is fragile and easily damaged.

Best season to visit: Spring for wildflowers; otherwise any time, although Paradise Falls can be rather meagre unless there has been recent rain. Beware of sudden weather changes.

Special features: Paradise Falls; imposing cliffs; scenic landscapes.

Relevant reading:
Land Conservation Council (1974) *Report on the North-east Areas 3,4,5.*

Further information:
C&E Regional Office, Ford St, Wangaratta, Vic 3677. Phone (057) 21 5022.

Galaxid *CFL*

Wabonga Plateau

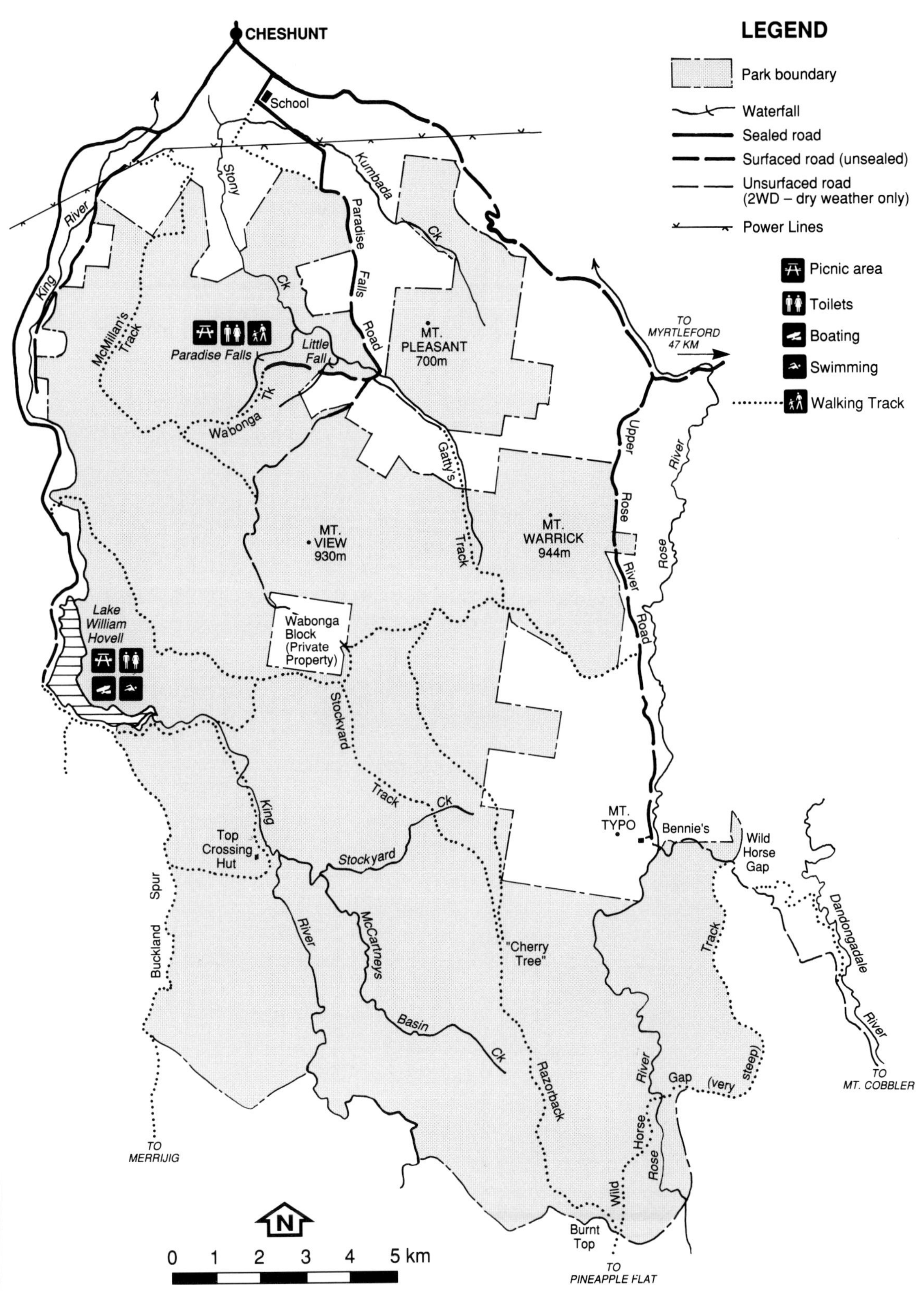

Cobberas-Tingaringy

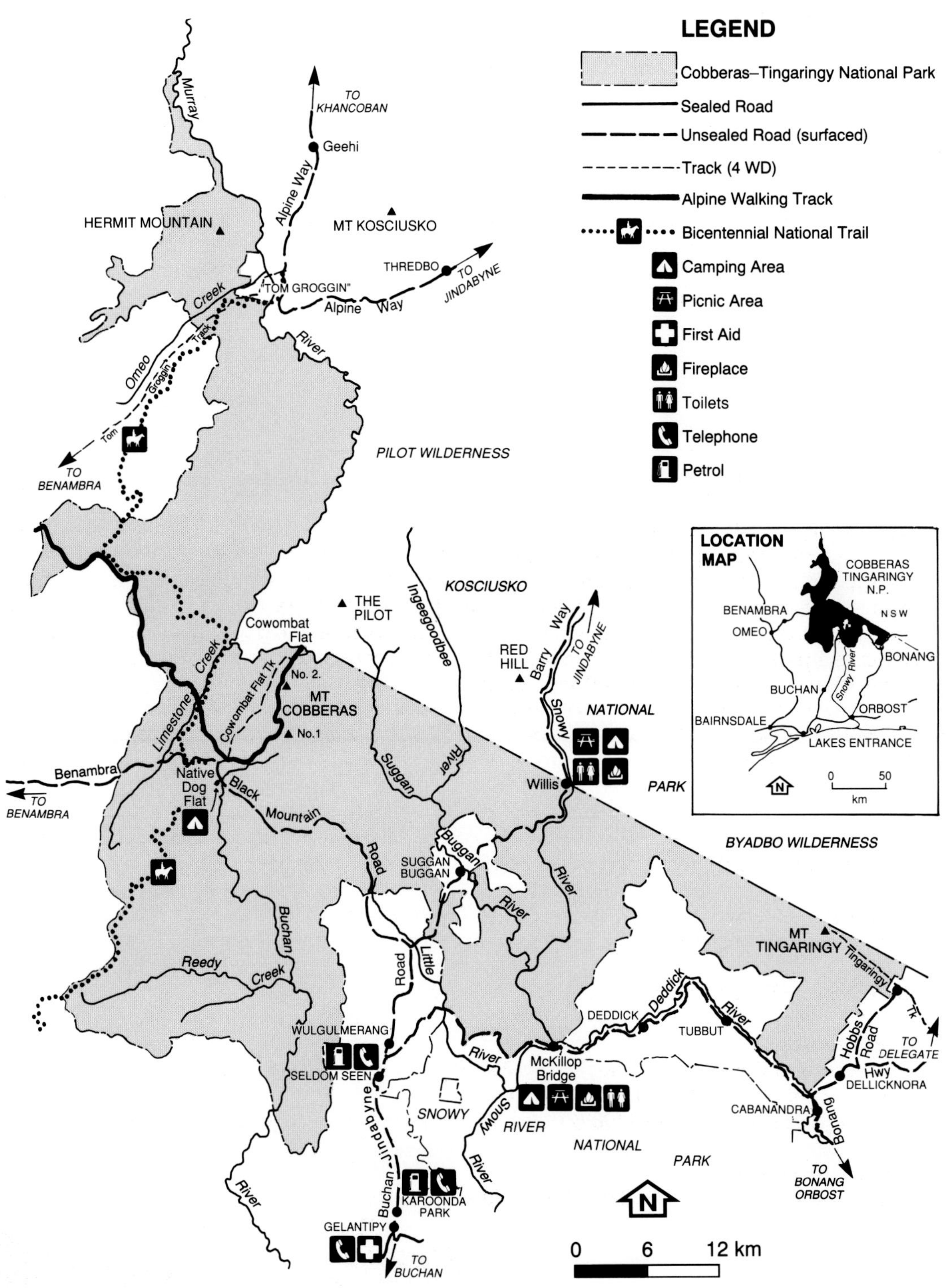

60 Alpine NP – Cobberas-Tingaringy

Physical features: 154 600 ha. This area, one of our largest and most remote and rugged, is in the Great Dividing Range and is named from Mt Cobberas No 1 (1 838 m) and Mt Tingaringy (1 448 m). Two other national parks border it; Snowy NP in Victoria and Kosciusko NP in New South Wales (NSW). Together they protect some of Australia's most spectacular scenery and form the very heartland of the Alpine National Park. Like Mt Burrowa to the north and the Cerberean Cauldron near Marysville, Cobberas was formed by crustal subsidence creating a circular fissure which was then in-filled with Devonian granitic material. The massive granitic plateau that was formed when the surrounding sedimentary rocks eroded away is now deeply dissected by rivers such as the Buchan, Suggan Buggan and Snowy. It also includes the most extensive blockstreams in mainland Australia (see Alpine Introduction). There are minerals and marble in the area, and until recently there was a possibility that mining of these might be allowed in a section of then unproclaimed Park, a possibility which caused considerable conflict with the paramount objectives of national park management.

Plants and animals: There are many similarities with Snowy River NP (see this section also) but there is also an unusual and, as yet, little understood vegetation community known as Red Wattle. Because it forms such a dense canopy, Red Wattle has been likened to a 'dry rainforest'. This Red Wattle community, together with a constant group of associated species, ranges in form from dense scrub in the Alps to tall trees along rivers and the edges of true rainforest.

Human history: The Buchan Valley, one of the Aborigines' access routes to the High Plains and the annual Bogong Moth feast, was also these people's last refuge as they were driven off their land by the early settlers. The high mountains formed important landmarks for the cattlemen and miners coming south from Monaro in NSW in search of new pastures and new wealth. Runs were taken up in the 1840's but the higher land was little used except for some summer grazing. Proposals for protection as a park began in 1935 when Myles Dunphy proposed a Primitive Area of nearly 4 000 square kilometres. As a result of his efforts, Kosciusko NP, including primitive areas, was declared in 1944, but in Victoria the pressure of conflicting interests delayed protection for any of our Alps, apart from Mt Buffalo, until 1979. When protection did come, many saw it as a compromise and certainly there are still problems needing to be resolved before the Alps receive the protection that they so clearly warrant.

Things to do: Some parts are negotiable by 2WD, but it is more a place for the adventurous and those who are thoroughly competent in bushcraft, including navigation by map and compass.

Best season to visit: Winter for cross-country skiing; otherwise spring for wildflowers and any for walking, but beware of sudden floods and weather changes.

Special features: Expansive views; rugged scenery; the sense of isolation.

Relevant reading:
Land Conservation Council (1977) *Report on the Alpine Study Area* and (1982) *Supplementary Report for the Alpine Area Special Investigation*.
Conservation, Forests and Lands (1989) *Cobberas-Tingaringy Unit Proposed Management Plan.*

Further information:
C&E Office, Main St, Bendoc, Vic 3888. Phone (064) 58 1456.

Brumbies *AW*

61 Snowy River National Park

Physical features: 95 400 ha. Snowy River NP is dominated by the river that gives it its name. Although nearly half the flow is diverted westwards by the Snowy Mountains Electricity Scheme, the Snowy can still turn on some impressive floods that, over time, have polished and sculptured the limestone outcrops in its bed. This limestone, and its associated caves, is only a small part of the Park. The larger part is of Snowy River volcanics several thousand metres thick, with interbedded sandstones and conglomerates. The river has now cut through this plateau, forming a series of highly scenic gorges and waterfalls. Much of the Snowy country lies within a marked rainshadow.

Plants and animals: This Park has a great range of vegetation. The combination of isolation, size, height and aspect, with their obvious effects on shelter and rainfall, means that there are unspoiled riverine communities: dry open forest, including the visually very appealing cypress pines and White Box on the dry red soil of the rainshadow areas; pristine tall wet forests; small areas of warm and cool temperate rainforests; and patches of heath and mallee. The plants are extremely varied too, from true East Gippslanders like Sweet Pittosporum and Kanooka to typical Mallee shrubs such as Desert Phebalium and Slender Westringia. A number of endemic plants were found within the Snowy Gorge when the area was first thoroughly examined in 1950. This Park is also the Victorian stronghold of the once-widespread Brush-tailed Rock-wallaby, now only otherwise known from a few localities in East Gippsland and from a small part of Grampians NP.

Human history: See Cobberas-Tingaringy NP for general background. Silver has been mined in what is now Park, along the Silver Mine walking track, downstream from Mackillops Bridge.

Things to do: Bush walking and canoeing are undoubtedly the Snowy's best known attractions, and rightly so; both are exhilarating here, but require careful preparation and a proper degree of skill. There are also roads suitable for scenic driving, though some need extreme care. On the gentler side, the Snowy has beautiful sandy beaches for camping, swimming and fishing.

Best season to visit: Spring for flowers, especially wattles; otherwise any, although do check road conditions and river heights, and be prepared for sudden and dramatic changes in the weather.

Special features: This is a Park of superlatives – spectacular, magnificent, awe-inspiring and many others can be applied to the scenery, especially the gorges, and the forests. Everything is so much on the grand scale that it is easy to miss the more intimate beauty that is here too.

Relevant reading:

Da Costa G. (1988) *Car Touring and Bush Walking in East Gippsland.*
Helman P. (1979) *Snowy River Study.*
Wakefield N.A. 'Snowy River Gorge', *Victorian Naturalist* (1957), No. 74, pp. 49–54.

Further information: See Cobberas-Tingaringy.

White-water rafting *RH*

◀ Mountain Pygmy-possum *ARI*
▼ Mt Lawson NP *RL*

▲ Summer on the High Plains, Bogong *GT*

▼ Ovens Valley from Mt Buffalo *JP*

▲ The Bluff, Wonnangatta-Moroka *EW*

▲ Small Crowea *JW*

▲ Misty morning, Wabonga Plateau *P&LJA*

▲ Snow Gums, Mt Bogong *P&LJA*
◀ Mt Buffalo NP *JP*

Snowy River

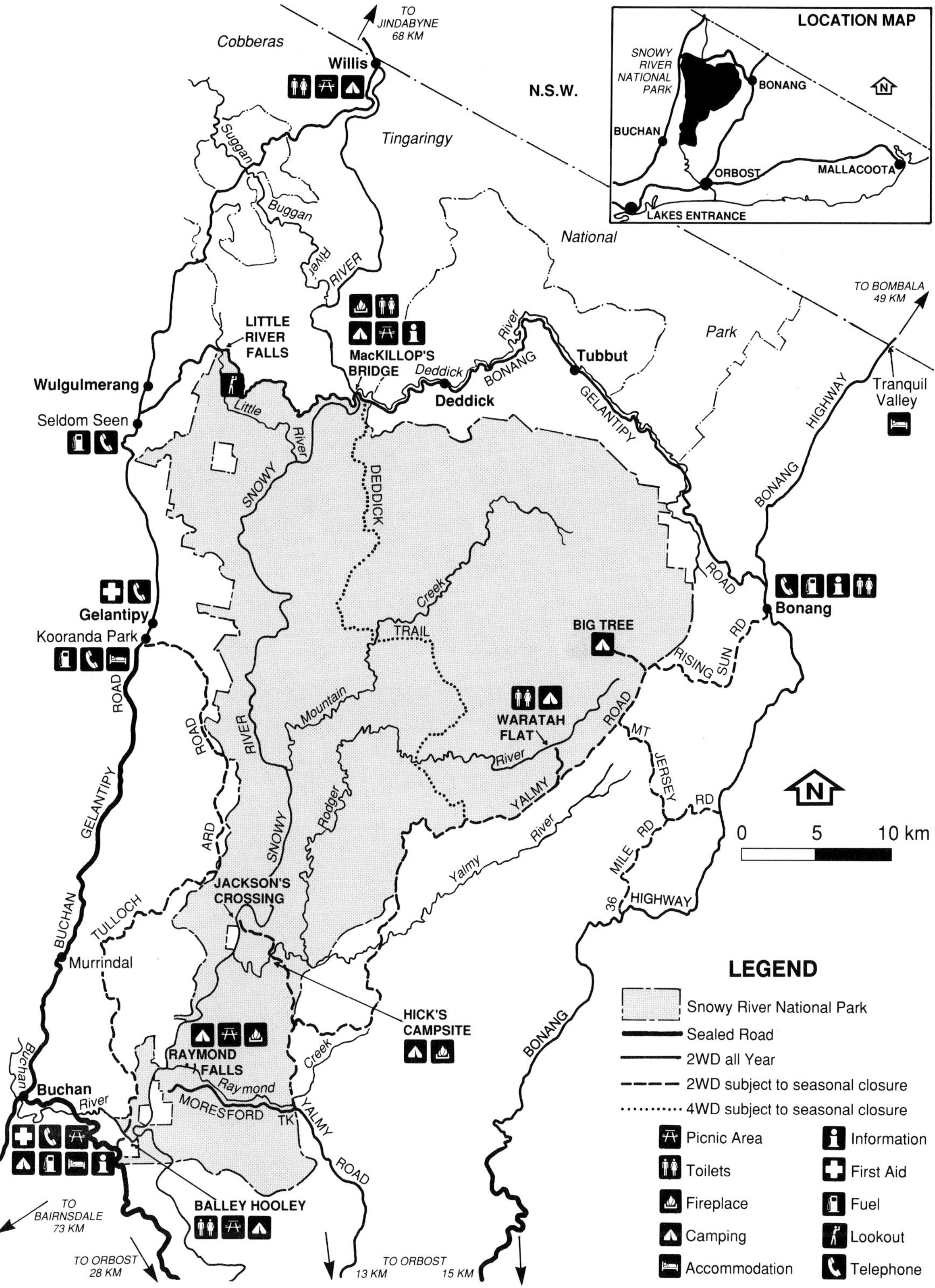

LOCATION MAP
SNOWY RIVER NATIONAL PARK
BONANG
BUCHAN
ORBOST
MALLACOOTA
LAKES ENTRANCE
TO JINDABYNE 68 KM
Cobberas
Willis
N.S.W.
Tingaringy
National
Park
TO BOMBALA 49 KM
Tranquil Valley
LITTLE RIVER FALLS
MacKILLOP'S BRIDGE
Deddick
Tubbut
Wulgulmerang
Seldom Seen
Gelantipy
Kooranda Park
Bonang
BIG TREE
WARATAH FLAT
JACKSON'S CROSSING
HICK'S CAMPSITE
Murrindal
RAYMOND FALLS
Buchan
BALLEY HOOLEY
TO BAIRNSDALE 73 KM
TO ORBOST 28 KM
TO ORBOST 13 KM 15 KM
0 5 10 km
LEGEND
Snowy River National Park
Sealed Road
2WD all Year
2WD subject to seasonal closure
4WD subject to seasonal closure
Picnic Area
Toilets
Fireplace
Camping
Accommodation
Information
First Aid
Fuel
Lookout
Telephone

Baw Baw

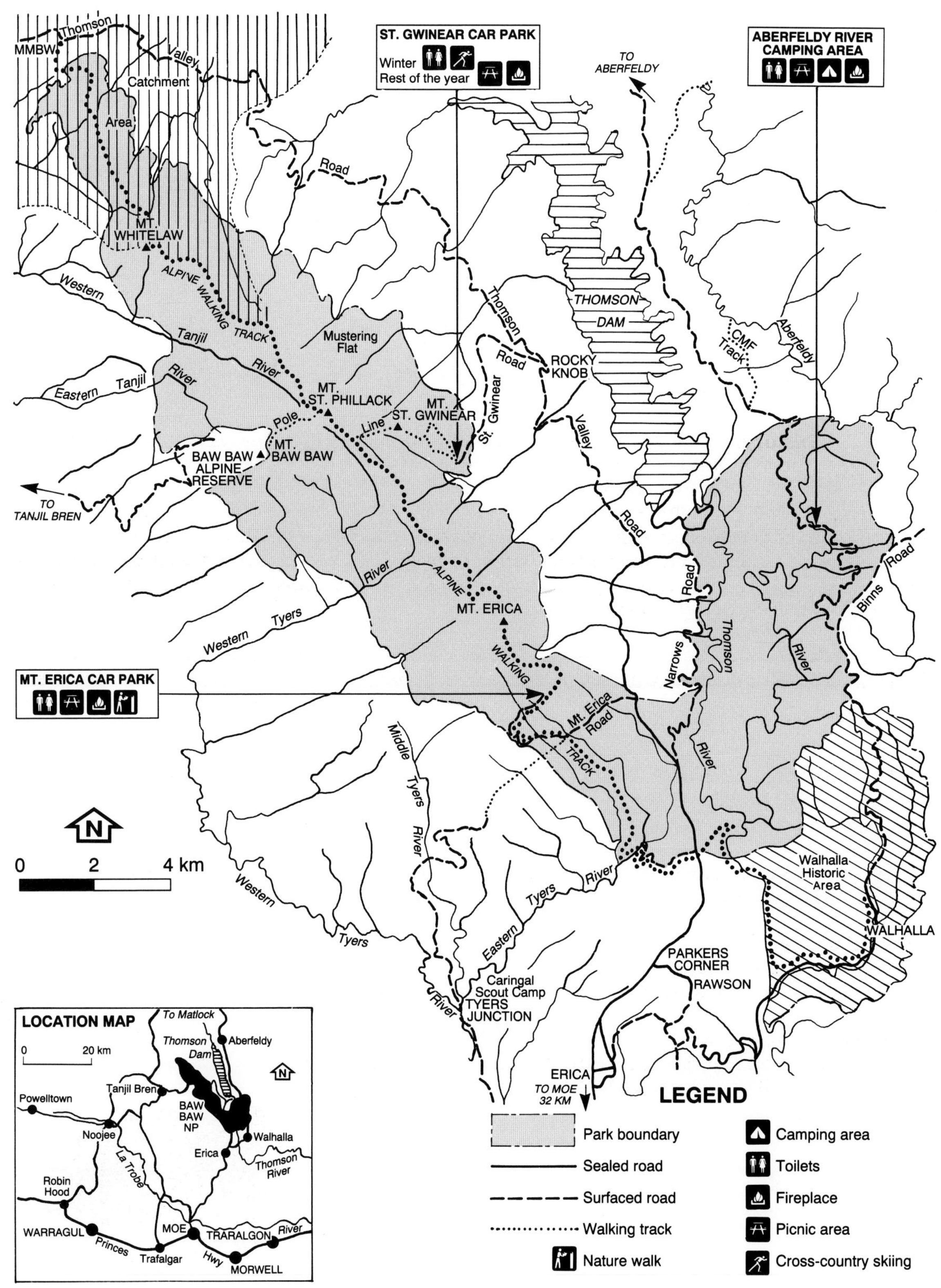

ST. GWINEAR CAR PARK
Winter
Rest of the year
ABERFELDY RIVER CAMPING AREA
TO ABERFELDY
MMBW
Thomson
Valley
Catchment
Area
Road
MT. WHITELAW
ALPINE WALKING TRACK
Western
Tanjil
River
Mustering Flat
THOMSON DAM
ROCKY KNOB
Thomson Road
CMF Track
Aberfeldy
Eastern
Tanjil
River
MT. ST. PHILLACK
MT. ST. GWINEAR
St. Gwinear
Pole
Line
Valley
BAW BAW ALPINE RESERVE
MT. BAW BAW
TO TANJIL BREN
Road
Road
Binns
Road
River
ALPINE
MT. ERICA
Western
Tyers
WALKING
Narrows
Thomson
River
MT. ERICA CAR PARK
Mt. Erica Road
TRACK
Middle Tyers River
River
Walhalla Historic Area
0
2
4 km
Western
Tyers
Eastern
Tyers
River
WALHALLA
PARKERS CORNER
RAWSON
Caringal Scout Camp
TYERS JUNCTION
River
ERICA
TO MOE 32 KM
LOCATION MAP
0
20 km
To Matlock
Thomson Dam
Aberfeldy
Tanjil Bren
Powelltown
BAW BAW NP
Walhalla
Noojee
La Trobe
Erica
Thomson River
Robin Hood
WARRAGUL
Princes
Trafalgar
MOE
TRARALGON
River
Hwy
MORWELL
LEGEND
Park boundary
Sealed road
Surfaced road
Walking track
Nature walk
Camping area
Toilets
Fireplace
Picnic area
Cross-country skiing

62 Baw Baw National Park

Physical features: 13 300 ha. Much of this Park lies in a massive, elliptical granodiorite plateau, an offshoot of the Great Dividing Range, the remainder is along the valleys of Thomson and Aberfeldy rivers. The highest point is Mt St Phillack, 1 566 m; Baw Baw itself is 1 564 m. Rainfall is high, and because of exposure to the south, snow often falls earlier here than elsewhere. A number of rivers arise on the plateau, including the Thomson to the north and the Tanjil and Tyers to the south. The ski village is not included in the Park, but is run by the Alpine Resorts Commission.

Plants and animals: The time that has elapsed since the onset of the Tertiary Ice Ages has allowed a distinctive Australian alpine flora to evolve. Some of the alpine flora elements are Gondwanaland species, such as members of the myrtle, heath and protea families, which were able to adapt to the increasing cold; others, such as gentians and plantains, are immigrants that came down from the north across land bridges via the mountains of Indonesia and New Guinea, or across from South America. Much of the natural history is similar throughout the alpine area, but Baw Baw, perhaps because of its isolation and unusual climatic conditions, does have two particularly interesting species: the Baw Baw Berry – one of only two 'ericas' in Australia – and the Baw Baw Frog, both of which have a very limited distribution. In the Aberfeldy valley, the vegetation is typical dry open forest, which contrasts strongly with the wet gullies and tall forests of the plateau itself.

Human history: Although artefacts have been found in the foothills, the Aborigines were apparently fearful of this high country because of a fabled yellow snake which was highly venomous, and a boiling chasm. The massive bulk of the plateau was a barrier to early goldminers trying to reach the rich fields further east, and it was only gradually that tracks were constructed. The best known of these was the tourist Baw Baw Track which ran from Walhalla to Warburton, and was enormously popular with walkers until burnt out by the 1939 fires. Much of the tall forest, especially the Mountain Ash, has previously been logged. Skiing has developed steadily since the 1940's, mostly in the resort area rather than the Park.

Things to do: Because it is close to Melbourne, this Park is a popular with day-visitors in winter, many people coming to toboggan, throw snowballs and just enjoy what might be their first ever contact with snow. Others come to cross-country ski and to snow camp. There are also many good walks, both long and short.

Best season to visit: Like other alpine parks, Baw Baw is now popular throughout the year. Winter sports July–September (provided there is snow); walking throughout the year; wildflowers December–January.

Special features: Ease of access; the wonderful colour of Snow Gum trunks in winter; summer wildflowers; picturesque walking, including the Beech Gully Nature Walk.

Relevant reading:

Adams J. (1980) *Mountain Gold.*
Waters W.F. 'The Baw Baws', *The Melbourne Walker* (1966).

Further information:

C&E Office, Main Rd, Neerim South, Vic 3825. Phone (056) 28 1401.
Friends' Group: Phone (051) 92 4335.

Baw Baw Frog *AW*

63 Mount Buffalo National Park

Physical features: 31 000 ha. Mt Buffalo is a massive granite plateau which extends for 12 km NS and 7 km EW. It rises abruptly for 1 000 m from the surrounding land, most of which is cleared. The Horn, the highest point, is 1 723 m. Many of the plateau walls are extremely steep, such as that of the Gorge directly below the Chalet, and the Back Wall and Wall of China at the southern end of the Park. Up on the plateau much of the ground is undulating, punctuated by dramatic granite tors and boulders, which makes for easy and scenic walking. Some of the tors, such as the Monolith, now have wooden steps and so can easily be climbed.

Plants and animals: The vegetation is typically alpine as described for the Bogong area, but there is the additional interest of three endemic species – the Mt Buffalo Sallee, a 'willow-leaved' eucalypt, the Fern-leaf Baeckea and the Buffalo Sallow Wattle. The wildflowers are particularly attractive here, and there is a delightful account of the first Field Naturalists' Club of Victoria excursion to Mt Buffalo in 1903–4 when just getting to Buffalo was quite a challenge:

> One who visits the Australian Alps at Christmas will find ... nature there presenting us with an awakening spring, which has again and again filled the hearts of men with greatest delight. But spring in the Alps must be seen not only from the depths of the valleys – it must be viewed from the heights of the mountains, for there is the kingdom of the Alpine flowers, where beauty of form is competing with splendour of colour or perfume.

An added pleasure when walking is to look for some of the many fungi that spring up, especially in the autumn. If you find a clump of rather dirty, white, irregular toadstools growing at the base of a tree, it is worth going back to the spot at night to see if it is one of the ghost fungi which glow eerily in the dark, supposedly with enough light to read by. Birds are plentiful except in the depths of winter, and they and the other animals are similar to those described for Bogong (except there are no Mountain Pygmy-possums at Buffalo).

Human history: Bogong Moths come here in the summer, and therefore the Aborigines came too, presumably up Goldies Spur on the mountain's southern flank, for many years the only way up the mountain. In 1853, Ferdinand von Mueller, the newly appointed Government Botanist, and John Dallachy, superintendent of the Melbourne Gardens, climbed up the Buffalo plateau and made the first recorded ascent of The Horn. Among the plants they collected and named was the Royal Grevillea, named in honour of Queen Victoria. Three years later the Manfield brothers, miners from the nearby Buckland River, began bringing groups up to the plateau, and from then on Buffalo's fame spread steadily. Both winter and summer parties made the long journey up Goldies Spur and across to near the Gorge, where simple accommodation was provided from the 1880's onwards. Thanks to the mountain's popularity and obvious appeal, it was set aside as a national park in 1898, one of the first areas in Victoria to be so protected. Further milestones were the construction of a proper road in 1908 along Straker's Track, made some years earlier and now the route of today's access road; and the building of the Government Chalet in 1910. In 1924, following its purchase by the Victorian Railways, the Chalet was remodelled to more or less the building we see today.

Many of those who were active in the Buffalo area around the turn of the century are remembered now in the names of landmarks: James Manfield, guesthouse proprietor and guide; Dr J.F. Wilkinson, a local doctor and keen walker and skier; Sir Thomas Bent, the Premier of Victoria who opened the 1908 road; and Carlo Catani who constructed the road, and built Lake Catani in 1910. (Catani was also the man responsible for draining the Koowerup swamp south-east of Melbourne.)

One tourist development that fortunately did not eventuate at Mt Buffalo was the Tatra Inn project. In addition to the Inn, an artificial lake for skating and a multi-storied hotel/motel were to be built at Dingo Dell. More than ten years of lobbying from the public and the Victorian National Parks Association ensued before this development (begun in 1964) was stopped. But those were an eventful ten years for Victorian conservation during which time the Little Desert controversy and the setting up of the Land Conservation Council had made the public aware that they did have a voice and that politicians could be made to listen to that voice.

Mount Buffalo

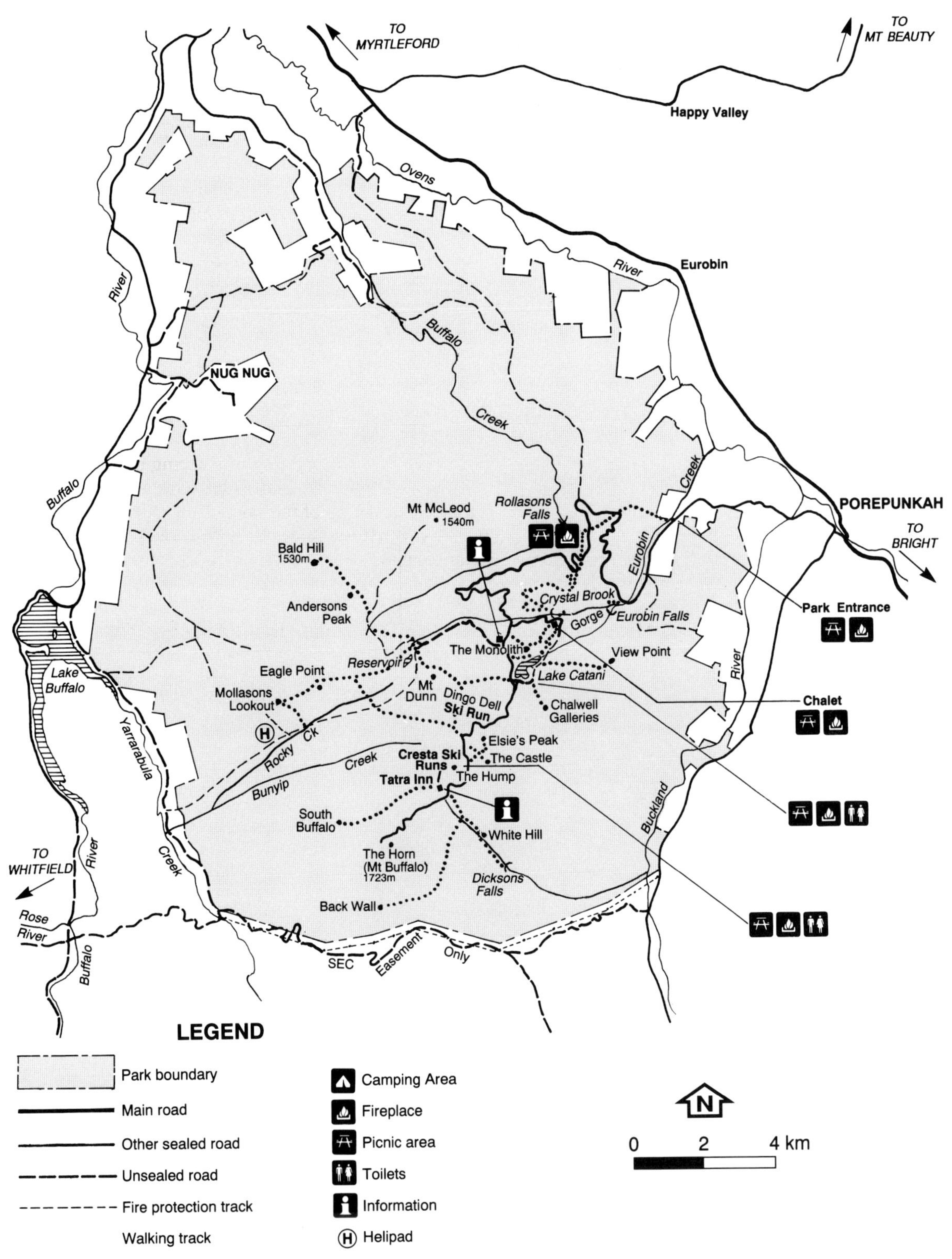

Things to do: Tobogganing; cross-country and beginners' downhill skiing; walking on the 70 km of tracks, including self-guided nature walks and the historic track from the Buckland Valley up Goldies Spur in the steps of the Aborigines, explorers, goldminers and early tourists; enjoying the Nature Drive up from the Park entrance; bicycling; horseriding; and for the really adventurous, rockclimbing on the Gorge Wall or hang gliding in the north of the Park.

Best season to visit: Winter for snow sports; summer for wildflowers; autumn, summer and spring for walking, bicycling and horseriding.

Special features: Spectacular scenery both intimate and long distance; excellent walking, often with the constant accompaniment of calls from lyrebirds, currawongs, shrike-thrushes and many other birds.

Relevant reading:
Algona (1972) *Mt Buffalo National Park* and (1984) map of same.
Boadle P.R. (1982) *Action Plan for Development Areas Mt Buffalo NP.*
'The Buffalo Mountains Camp-out', *Victorian Naturalist* (1904) Vol. XX, No. 11, pp. 144–156.

Further information:
Mt Buffalo Park Office, Park Rd, Mt Buffalo, Vic 3745. Phone (057) 55 1466.
Friends' Group: Phone: (057) 56 2331.

Alpine scene *JST*

SOUTH EAST PARKS

To the east and south-east of Melbourne is Gippsland, an area with considerable diversity of landscape and climate. The Strzelecki Ranges in the western part of the region are in the path of rain-bearing westerly winds and have a high rainfall. By the turn of the century most of this heavily timbered country was cleared by a combination of the axe and summer burning, and the tall forests replaced by dairy farms. In the Eastern Strzeleckis, however, native scrub regenerated readily and this, along with a short growing season, rabbits, comparative isolation, poor economic returns and finally the loss of many of the young men to the Great War, meant that many families simply walked off the 'heartbreak hills' and left it all behind them. A later exodus occurred when the 1939 bushfires devastated so much of Victoria. Today, many of these once deserted and weed-infested farms are now a productive part of a major re-afforestation program, using pines and eucalypts. In contrast to the heavily forested parks are a number of 'dry' parks along the La Trobe Valley, noted for their wildflower displays. To the south is the isolated granite mass of Wilsons Promontory with its spectacular coastlines. Further east are not only the tranquil Gippsland Lakes with their mild climate and high potential for tourism, but also the magnificent Mitchell River.

	Page No.	*Entrance Fee*	*Information Centre*	*Multilingual Information*	*Picnic Areas*	*Fireplaces*	*Toilets*	*Disabled Access*	*Walking Tracks*	*Nature Walk or Drive*	*Swimming*	*Climbing*	*Horseriding*	*Fishing*	*Boating*	*Camping*	*Caravans*	*Km from Melbourne*	*Date Declared*
Gippsland Lakes	214	■			■	■	■		■		■		■	■	■	■		250	1979
Holey Plains	193				■	■	■		■	■			■	■		■		190	1977
Mitchell River	207				■	■	■		■		■				■			300	1986
Moondarra	212				■	■	■				■			■		■		160	1986
Morwell	203				■	■	■		■	■								170	1967
Mount Worth	204				■	■	■		■									125	1979
Nyerimilang	214				■	■	■		■	■								390	1980
Sth Gippsland M&CP★	190	■			■			P	■		■		■	■	■	■	■	200	1986
Tarra-Bulga	194		P		■	■	■	P	■	■			■					195	1986
The Lakes	214	■	■	■	■	■	■	■	■	■	■			■	■	■	■	285	1927
Tyers	210				■	■	■		■		■	■	■	■		■		160	1986
Wilsons Prom	186	■	■	■	■	■	■	■	■	■	■	■		■	■	■	■	226	1905

P = Proposed ★ = Facilities available some parks only

64 Wilsons Promontory National Park

Physical features: 49 000 ha. There are essentially two components to the Prom, as it is affectionately known: granite and sand. The impressive masses of granite formed from molten rock which welled up from the earth's interior approximately 375 million years ago and cooled deep beneath an insulating layer of rock, now eroded away. The sand that forms the beaches and the Yanakie Isthmus extends down the western side as far as Darby River. As this sand built up, it blocked the outlets of the streams which then formed extensive swamps, such as those leading into Sealers Cove. At one time, Tasmania and the Prom were joined, but as the sea level rose after the last Ice Age, Tasmania became isolated, and perhaps for a time the Prom was also an island.

Plants and animals: The combination of the geological and fire histories of the Prom has led to a wide variety of habitats – beaches, variously of rock, sand and mud, estuaries and freshwater creeks, heathlands, open and closed forests, and rocky outcrops. This diversity is reflected in the fact that more than 700 native plants are found here. Most of the trees along the entrance road are various types of stringybark eucalypts, with some coastal Manna Gum. In very sheltered places, there are patches of closed forest containing plants characteristic of both warm temperate rainforest (Lilly-pilly, here at its westernmost limit in Australia) and cool temperate rainforest (Myrtle Beech). On the drier sandy slopes, often on headlands like that of Tongue Point, Casuarina woodlands create an atmosphere of their own where the sound of the sea is muffled and the ground is carpeted with dropped 'leaves'. Woodlands of grasstrees and Saw Banksia (the unmistakable Bad Banksia Men!) are particularly striking, but it is probably the open heathlands that have the greatest appeal, since it is here that the best wildflower displays are found. A springtime walk to Millers Landing can reward you with at least a dozen orchids in flower. At Millers Landing itself are the world's southernmost mangroves – the White Mangrove.

There is a variety of animals too, the larger of which – wombats, kangaroos, wallabies and Koalas – are easily seen. Fur seals are common on the offshore islands, such as the Glennies. An interesting aside is that more than 20 native animals are known to have been released at the Prom between 1900 and 1941. Some, such as possums and wombats, were quite common and perhaps understandable; others, including tree kangaroos which are animals of the northern tropical rainforests, were less so. A number of non-Prom native plants like Cabbage Fan-palms were also introduced about the same time. Today we see national parks as refuges for indigenous flora and fauna, and it is fortunate that many of these introduced animals failed to survive.

For many people, one of the most vivid Prom memories is that of the Crimson Rosellas. Hundreds of these charming and gentle little parrots are now so used to being fed by people that they will perch on anyone who looks to have a ready handout. Of course there is an abundance of other bird life too, such as water birds on the beaches and rivers, honeyeaters working the nectar-rich flowers of the heathlands, and a multitude of small bush birds in the gullies.

Human history: To judge from the number of Aboriginal middens scattered around the coast, this place was a favourite site with the Brataualong group of the Gippsland Kurnai who occupied this area and knew it as Wanoom. Evidence suggests that the Aborigines harvested shellfish and fish, and that they collected nesting seabirds and eggs from offshore islands. During the winter they moved further inland to more protected areas where there were plenty of game and edible plants.

The earliest Europeans to see Wilsons Promontory were George Bass and his crew of six oarsmen during their epic voyage from Sydney in an open whaleboat in 1798. Sealers and whalers came soon after, and what a tragically different picture Sealers Cove must have presented then from the peace of today. Timber was also taken from the Prom, via Sealers Cove, and for a brief period tin was mined at Mt Hunter in the northern part. The Prom, with its fearsome cliffs, outlying islands and hidden reefs, has wrecked many ships, and even today, despite modern navigational aids and good lighthouses, ships still go aground. The lighthouse on South East Point, destination of one of the most popular long walks, was built of local granite by convict labour in 1859.

Wilsons Promontory

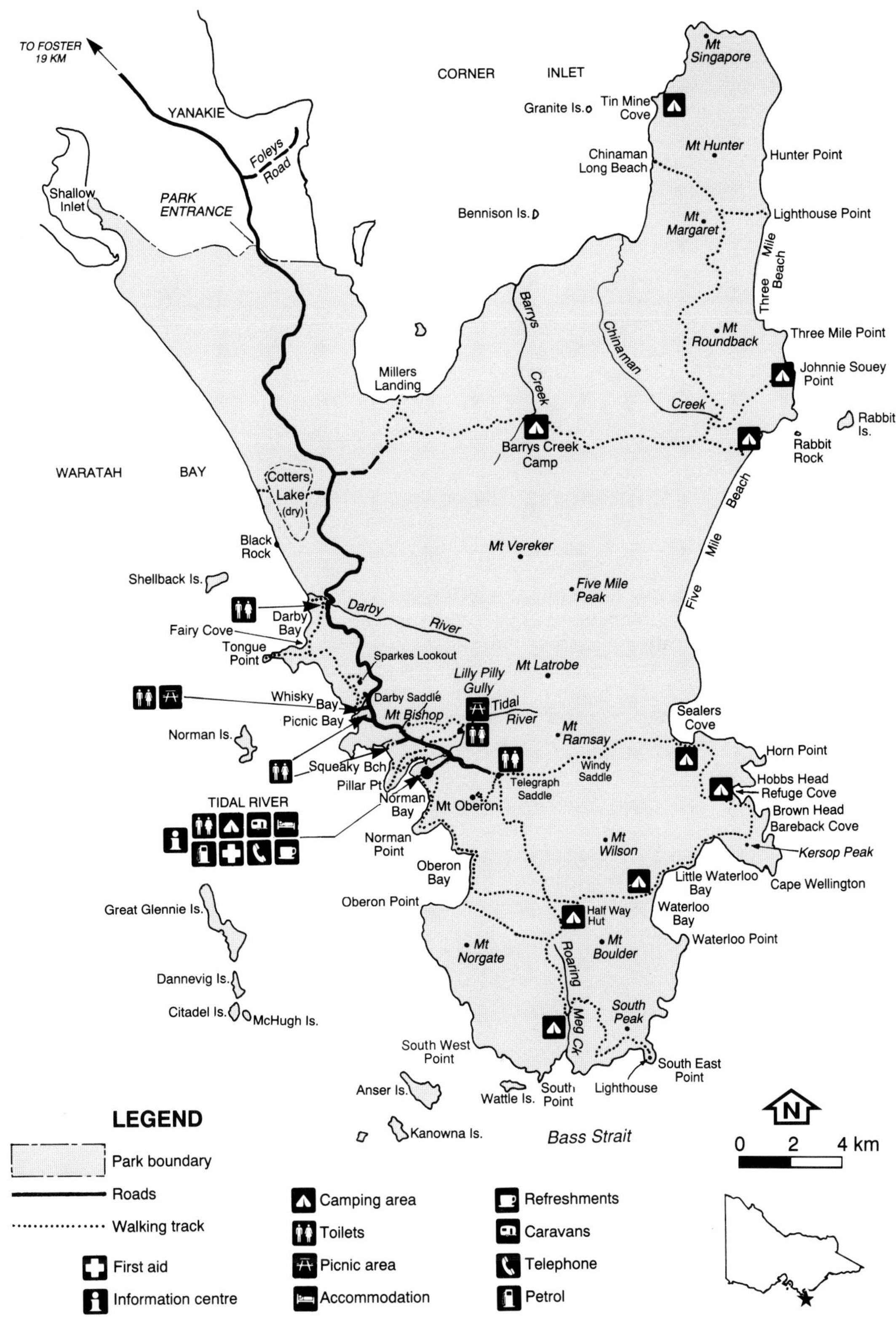

By the late 19th century moves were made to have the Prom set aside as a national park, largely by Arthur Lucas and John Gregory, members of the Field Naturalists' Club of Victoria, whose names are now commemorated by group lodges at Tidal River. In 1898, a small area of the Prom was reserved for public use, and then in 1905 over 30 000 ha were reserved as a national park. This time one of the chief protagonists was Baldwin Spencer, a Melbourne University professor, after whom the third group lodge is named. But the battle was not yet won – those precious 30 000 ha had no shoreline because of the exclusion of a half kilometre strip around the coast. In 1908 that strip too was added and now Victorians could be rightfully proud of 'The National Park' as it became known. To quote a 1912 newspaper article:

> All is wild and beautiful in this sanctuary, where one must name the birds without a gun. Here there is a truce between man and nature, a truce which is to last forever. The ring of the axe is not heard in the forests, and no gun is discharged to wake the echoes. The quail leads her brood through the grass without fear.

Others besides naturalists and walkers soon realised the charms of this wild and isolated area, though for many years getting there was an adventure in itself. Originally, the only accommodation at the Prom was the 'Committee Cottage', built for the use of the Park's Committee of Management at Darby River. In 1923 this was enlarged into an accommodation house, the Darby Chalet. The revenue from the Chalet helped to run the park, along with fees for the agistment of cattle and a small government grant. Life at the Chalet was not always idyllic – one family remembers not only an infestation of bedbugs but also being sent out to collect dry cow dung, which was burnt to help keep away the mosquitoes. There were three possible ways to get to Darby River: the first was to go by train to Fish Creek, and then, on the next day, continue either by wagon along Darby Beach or by boat to Darby River; the second was by boat from Welshpool to Millers Landing, then on foot to Darby River; or the third, by steamer to the lighthouse and then walk. But of course it was well worth all that effort once you arrived, even if only for a cup of tea! One bus load, after their journey along the beach, were seen to pile out of the bus and into the Chalet, drink their tea, and then, without so much as looking around them, get back into the bus and drive away. Shades of some of today's coach tours? Most people of course stayed far longer to enjoy swimming at Darby Beach, walking, and horse or pushbike riding along the network of tracks. These tracks had been put in when the Prom was surveyed last century with a view to selling blocks of land. One scheme planned to bring in Scottish crofters and set up a fishing industry; another to grow vegetables at Refuge Cove; and yet another to develop a settlement, Seaforth, at Singapore Peninsula. Other proposals for the Prom were the Forests Department's beautification scheme of poplars, oaks and pines at Chinamans Creek (removed by a timely bushfire) and a hotel at Tidal River (blocked by an angry public, alerted by the then infant Victorian National Parks Association).

By 1925, huts at Tidal River and Sealers' Cove also provided accommodation. In 1941 the Prom was taken over by the Army for commando training, and it was their huts that later formed the Tidal River settlement, though sadly, the Chalet itself was in such poor condition that it had to be demolished (some of its timbers were later used in flats at Tidal River). Today there are strict limits on the number of people who can stay at the Prom, and in this way the essential charm and character of the place is retained to a quite remarkable degree considering its enormous popularity.

Things to do: From the simple soul-food of watching waves crashing on granite boulders far below, to long distance walking, the Prom has it all – camping; swimming; sunbathing; surfing; beachcombing; boating; fishing; photography; painting; gentle or energetic walking on the 80 km of tracks; and a whole host of interesting plants, animals and landscapes to enjoy. Even a drenching day has its compensations in that it provides time to explore the Information and Education Centre and its displays and exhibits, many of them 'hands-on'. Within six months of its opening this Centre had received the 1983 Best New Exhibition award for both Victoria and Australia. A day visit to the Prom is an excellent introduction, if only to make you realise how much there is to come back for next time!

Best season to visit: There isn't one! It is a park for all seasons, with a different appeal to different people. To walk along a Prom beach in the teeth of a winter gale is an exhilarating experience, as is standing on some high point watching the southerly squalls chase each other landwards in rapid succession. For flowers, it would have to be late winter or spring when the air is heavy with the honey scent of White Kunzea and the heathlands are bright with wildflowers. This 'Prom-ophile' has counted more than 30 different plants in flower on a patch of heathland not ten minute's walk from the camping ground. Summer, though, sees by far the highest usage, and campsites are in such demand that they are available only by ballot. Group lodges are taken as soon as bookings open, regardless of the season. There are also some motor cabins and flats available.

Special features: It is hard to single out any particular feature – the Prom has an atmosphere and a magic that is there whether you are visiting it for the first time or whether, like so many others, you have long ago lost count. Certainly it must have captivated almost everyone who has been there.

Relevant reading:

Brownlie S.& J. (1971) *Wilsons Promontory National Park.*
Conservation, Forests and Lands (1987) *Wilsons Promontory NP Management Plan.*
Cooper R.P. (1975) *Wilsons Promontory National Park and its Avifauna.*
Garnet J.R. (1971) *The Wildflowers of Wilsons Promontory National Park.*
Land Conservation Council (1980) *Report of the South Gippsland Area 2.*
Victorian National Parks Association and Conservation, Forests and Lands (1989) *Discovering the Prom on Foot.*

Further information:
Park Information Centre, Tidal River, Vic 3960. Phone (056) 80 8538.
Friends' Group: Phone (03) 853 8923.

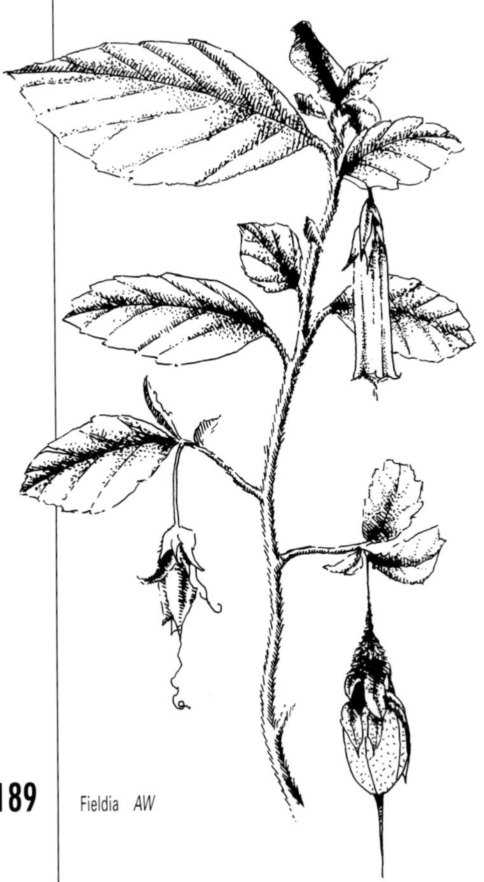

Fieldia *AW*

65 South Gippsland Marine and Coastal Parks

General features: There are five reserves included under this title and together they protect the shoreline of Wilsons Promontory and adjacent inlet areas. They are: Wilsons Promontory Marine Reserve; Wilsons Promontory Marine Park; Shallow Inlet, Corner Inlet, and Nooramunga Marine and Coastal Parks.

The Wilsons Promontory Marine Reserve generally covers the shoreline of the Promontory and 300 m out to sea from low-tide mark, and the offshore islands between Refuge Cove in the east and Norman Bay in the west. This Reserve has the highest level of protection. Much of it is spectacularly rocky; the other reserves generally have sandy and muddy beaches. Together they protect a diversity of coastal and marine communities, as well as historic sites such as Old Settlement Beach and a number of important shipwrecks including the *Clonmel* wrecked near Port Albert in 1841. The natural communities include rocky shores and underwater cliffs, sandy coasts, mudflats with mangroves and seagrasses, salt marshes, and coastal vegetation. The mudflats and adjacent land are vitally important as fish nurseries, and as feeding and roosting grounds for migratory waders such as the Short-tailed Sandpiper and the Red-necked Stint, both of which breed in arctic Siberia and then fly south each northern winter. Other important birds include the Ground Parrot (rare), the Orange-bellied Parrot (endangered), and the Cape Barren Goose (rare in Victoria). Asian Hog Deer (almost extinct in Asia) live on some islands and coasts.

Things to do: The calm shallow waters of the inlets are popular for water sports and camping. Amateur fishing varies from none at all in the Marine Reserve to fishing and flounder-spearing in Nooramunga. Some seasonal hunting of Hog Deer is allowed. Anyone wishing to fish or hunt should check the appropriate regulations. The Marine Reserve has spectacular underwater scenery with clear water, steep cliffs, rocky ledges, and a variety of colourful and interesting creatures to rival those of the Great Barrier Reef. For birdwatchers, the three Coastal and Marine Parks offer the richest variety; migratory birds are often there in their thousands. Setting aside these five reserves created considerable controversy over their impact on commercial and amateur fishing, and therefore on local tourism. It is hard to imagine, though, that such a superb area, with such a wide range of activities, would be anything other than a magnificent drawcard for tourists.

Best season to visit: September–April for migratory birds (by March some may be in breeding plumage); April is usually the calmest for diving; the fishing is good any time.

Special features: The tranquillity of the land and sea.

Relevant reading:

Conservation, Forests and Lands (1984) *Wilsons Promontory Marine Parks Proposed Management Plan.*
The Gould League of Victoria (1983) *Coastal Survival.*
Legg, D., Chapman A., and Danns P. (1987) *Andersons Inlet – Waders and Waterbirds.*
South Gippsland Conservation Society (1985) *Beach and Bush Day Trips.*

Further information:
C&E Regional Office, 310 Commercial Rd, Yarram, Vic 3971. Phone (051) 82 5755.
Friends' Group: Phone (03) 386 1029.

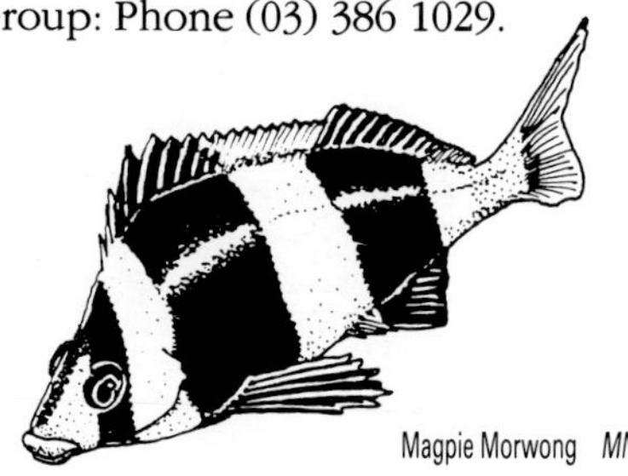

Magpie Morwong *MN*

South Gippsland Marine and Coastal

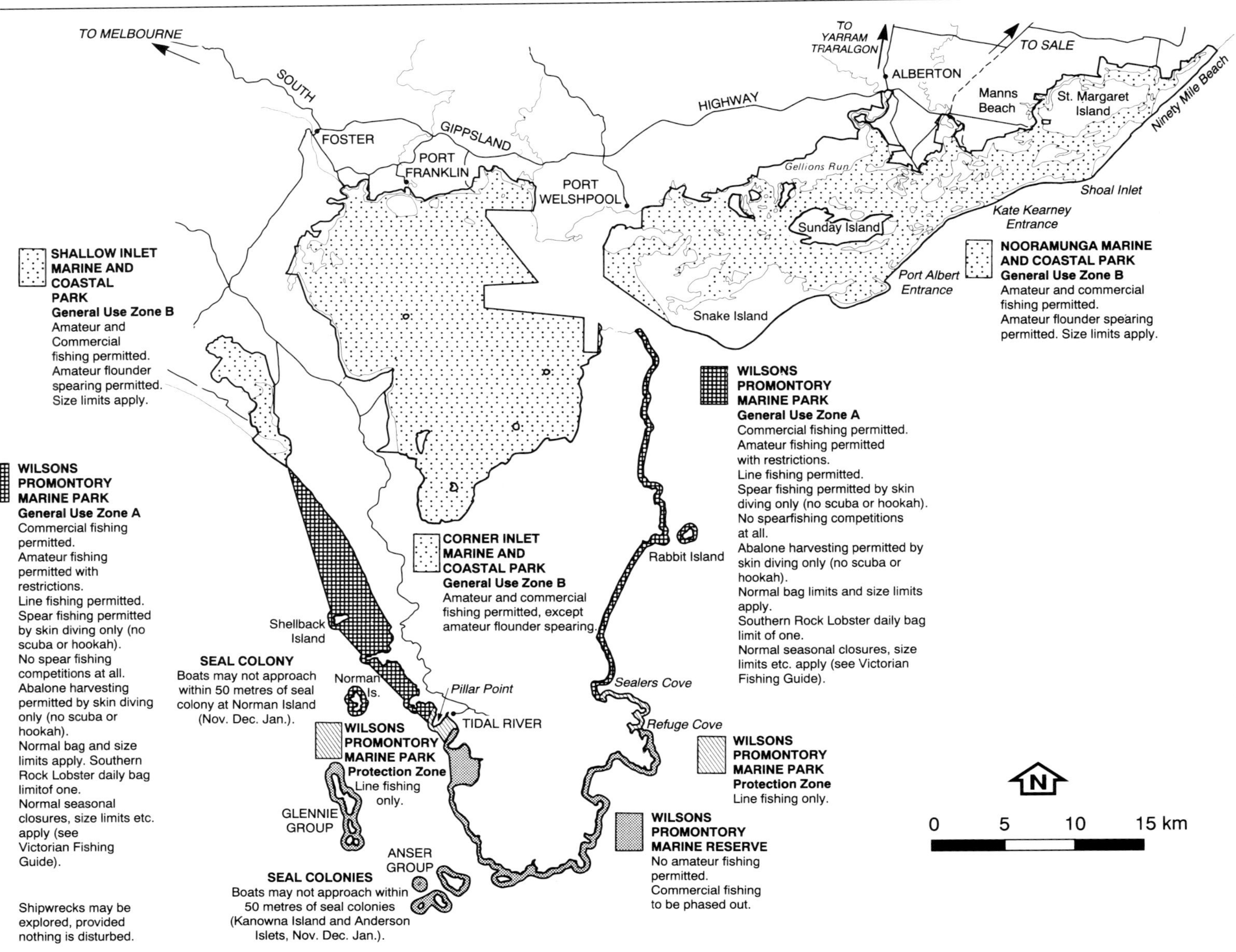

Holey Plains

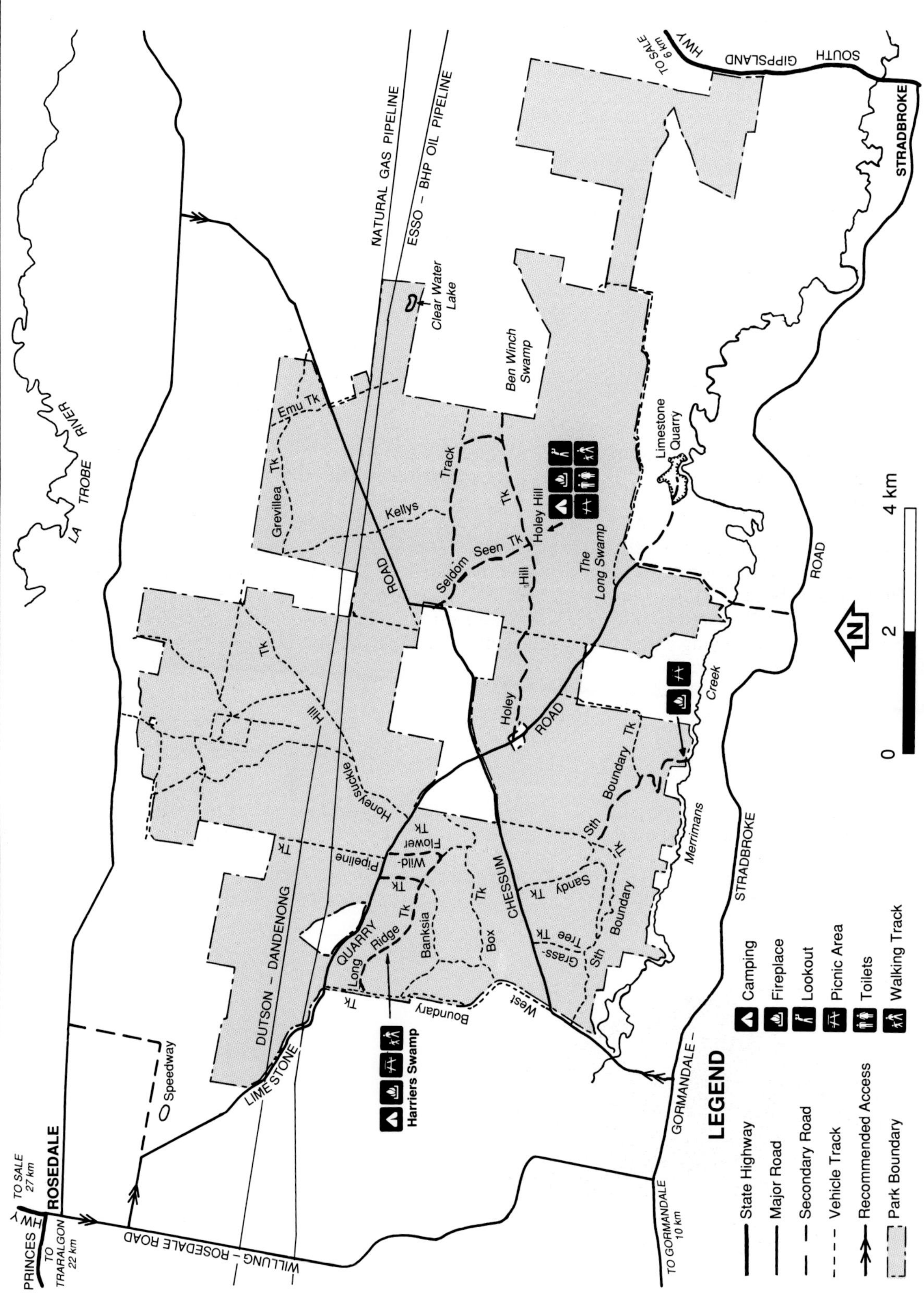

66 Holey Plains State Park

Physical features: 10 576 ha. This Park is in generally young, undulating, sandy country. In the older limestone areas in the south, the land shows concentric slumping where the underlying limestone has dissolved away, leading to sunklands. In almost all of Holey Plains SP and nearby land, the limestone is underlain by deposits of brown coal similar to those elsewhere in the La Trobe Valley. There are a number of interesting swamps at different successional stages in the Park, as well as the very beautiful Clear Water Lake. Annual rainfall is about 600 mm. The highest point is Holey Hill, 218 m, where there is a fire tower with a view over the surrounding countryside.

Plants and animals: This Park was declared because of its high conservation value. Twenty-nine different vegetation associations have been identified, and there are some rare and interesting plants, including the Winter Greenhood orchid, and new plants not yet properly named: a Helichrysum, a Prostanthera and a Pomaderris. Much of the woodland is of Shining Peppermint/Saw Banksia, a rare association found on leached soils with a cemented layer just below the surface. Dense bracken and shrubs make up the understorey, which in turn provides good food and shelter for many birds and other animals. Common Bronzewings, although generally rather cautious birds, can often be seen feeding along the open tracks. The almost incessant calls of cuckoos accompany you in the late winter and spring. Apparently, the male cuckoo makes himself conspicuous to distract potential hosts from the female while she lays her egg. Grey Kangaroos, Swamp Wallabies, Koalas and various possums and native rats are also quite common. At least 12 different reptiles, including the Freshwater Tortoise, and ten different frogs are found in this Park.

Human history: There are at least two Aboriginal sites known at Holey Hill. The Park was once part of a grazing run, but because of poor soils it has not been intensively farmed. Pines are planted on a small area now surrounded by Park, and on much of the adjacent land. The setting aside of Holey Plains began in 1963 when the Rosedale Shire Council created a small reserve. Later, the La Trobe Valley Field Naturalists' Club campaigned for the full protection of this very special conservation area, surveying it and preparing plant and animal lists, and by 1977 their efforts were rewarded by the creation of Holey Plains SP.

Things to do: Walking; observing the fascinating plant and animal life; photography.

Best season to visit: Any, although winter can be quite cold.

Special features: Swamps; birdlife, including migrants moving down from the mountains; rare plants; there are also some excellent wetlands near Sale, which are also managed by C&E.

Further information:
C&E Regional Office, 71 Hotham St, Traralgon, Vic 3844. Phone (051) 74 6166.

Freshwater Tortoise *AW*

67 Tarra-Bulga National Park

Physical features: 1 230 ha. Tarra and Bulga are only 3 km apart but have different characters brought about by the different terrain. Both are in the Strzelecki Ranges and on Mesozoic sandstones about 150 million years old, but in Bulga more pronounced faulting has meant higher and steeper, and therefore wetter, slopes. Fog and mist are common to both areas, as are deep and fertile soils.

Plants and animals: This is one of the most lushly vegetated of all the parks within easy reach of Melbourne. Your attention is torn between following the trunk of a Mountain Ash up and up for literally hundreds of metres, or staying nearer the ground and revelling in the luxuriance of tree-ferns all around. Once you step onto the cleverly sited Corrigan's suspension bridge across Macks Creek, there can be no doubt – it is the tree-ferns that claim your attention. Standing suspended above a continuous floor of brilliantly green Soft Tree-fern crowns is a truly entrancing experience.

This type of bush is described as a closed cool temperate rainforest, and certainly, when you look upwards, little if any open sky can be seen. In Tarra-Bulga the upper storey is typically of Mountain Ash, and below this are relics of the ancient forests that once covered much of Australia – Southern Sassafras, Austral Mulberry and Banyalla, along with the majestic bulk of Myrtle Beech, the dominant canopy tree. Below these are typical wet gully shrubs such as Mountain Correa and Victorian Christmas-bush, and the tree-ferns themselves. And everywhere in these lower layers there are ferns and mosses, all contributing to the rich variety of green and yet more green. Unlike warm temperate rainforest, there are few climbers here (see also East Gippsland Parks).

The few flowers that are to be seen have almost all fallen from the trees and, although often very beautiful in form, are usually coloured white, muted greens or yellows. Among the creamy flowers is the bell-shaped Fieldia which grows on tree trunks, and is the sole Victorian representative of the otherwise near-tropical family that includes the African Violet. Such flashes of colour as do occur generally come from the birds or the fungi, some of which are vivid purples, reds and oranges.

This is a rich environment for birds and other animals. At the heart of this richness is the soil itself – a teeming world of bacteria, fungi and small invertebrates such as worms and insect larvae that feed birds like the Australian Ground-thrush, the Lyrebird and its companion, the Pilotbird. Most of the mammals, ground-dwellers such as the native rats, bandicoots and Antechinus, and the arboreal possums and gliders, are nocturnal and so not easily seen. There's little difficulty though in seeing many of the birds – Pink, Rose, Flame, Scarlet and Yellow Robins, parrots and Golden Whistlers are all brightly coloured and are easy to see, as are the less conspicuous honeyeaters and thornbills. Two groups of biologically fascinating 'creepy crawlies' found here deserve a special mention. One is a little known 'missing link' group, the peripatids, whose lineage goes back for more than 500 million years. They are intermediate between the worms and the jointed-leg invertebrates such as insects and spiders. The other group is the leeches. Many people have a fear and horror of leeches quite out of proportion to the damage they do. Any leech will leave its human feeding ground very smartly if sprinkled with salt, leaving a small wound that may dribble blood for a while. Certainly some people are allergic to leech bites, but then so are some to bee-stings!

Human history: The dense wet bush that clothed these hills was less attractive to the local Kurnai Aborigines than the coasts and more open country not far away. There, food was plentiful and the living more comfortable, although the early European settlers did report seeing native artefacts in the deep bush. Certainly Strzelecki, an early explorer here, had cause to be grateful to the hunting skills of an Aborigine, Charlie Tarra, who accompanied him in 1840. Today's traveller, driving along the Grand Ridge Road in a weatherproof vehicle, can only try to imagine what it was like for this party pursuing Strzelecki's straight line route all the way to Western Port.

One question for many visitors to Tarra-Bulga is how these small precious jewels of parks escaped the wholesale slaughter of most forests in the area. Standing on Corrigan's Bridge over Macks Creek in Bulga is an appropriate time to remember with gratitude men such as Frank Corrigan of the

 Piemans Falls, Wonnangatta-Moroka *JP*

▼ Campsite, Alpine Walking Track, Baw Baw NP *P&LJA*

▼ Summit view of Mt Tingaringy, Cobberas-Tingaringy NP *CFL*

▲ Rafting in the Snowy River NP *GS*

◀ Damage by Black-Cockatoos searching for wood borers, Avon Wilderness *MT*

Granite cliffs, Wilsons Promontory NP *JAC*

▼ View from the Amphitheatre, Mitchell River NP *JAC*

▲ Lilly Pilly Gully, Wilsons Promontory NP *CFL*

◀ Tarra Bulga NP *JAC*

Tarra-Bulga

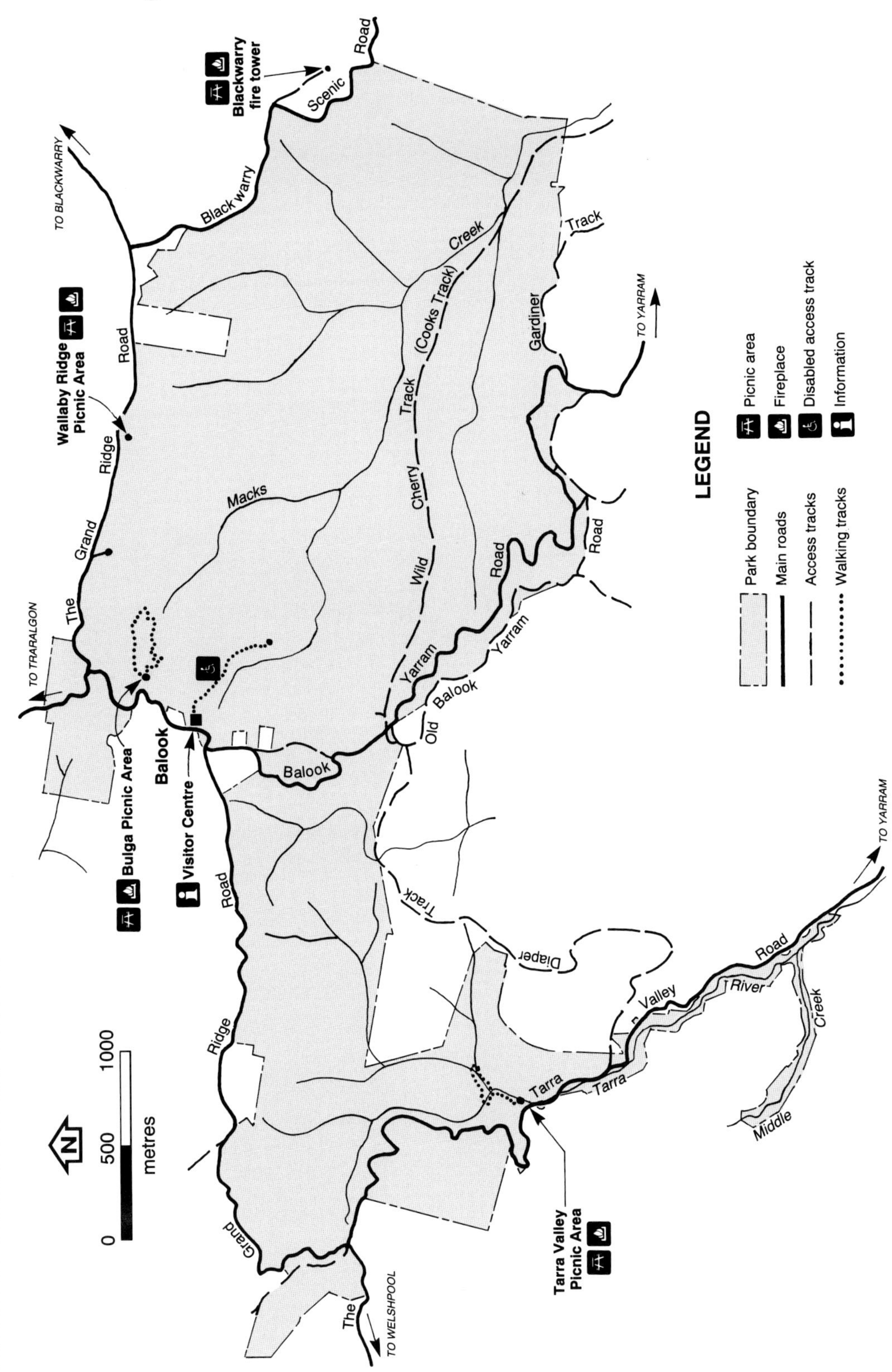

Blackwarry fire tower
Scenic Road
TO BLACKWARRY
Blackwarry
Wallaby Ridge Picnic Area
Ridge Road
The Grand
Macks
Creek
Track
(Cooks Track)
Cherry
Wild
Gardiner
TO YARRAM
TO TRARALGON
Bulga Picnic Area
Balook
Visitor Centre
Yarram
Road
Old Balook
Balook
Road
Track
Diaper
Valley
River
Road
Creek
Middle
Tarra
Tarra
TO YARRAM
Tarra Valley Picnic Area
Ridge
Grand
The
TO WELSHPOOL
0
500
1000
metres
N
LEGEND
Park boundary
Main roads
Access tracks
Walking tracks
Picnic area
Fireplace
Disabled access track
Information

Alberton Shire Council who, early this century, initiated the setting aside of both Tarra and Bulga National Parks, now combined into the one Park. At a time when large-scale felling and firing of the forests was generally considered little short of a duty, the foresight of such men bequeathed us the riches that we enjoy today. As with all our parks, they are *our* parks and it is we who have the responsibility to care for them and nurture them. Small parks like these are especially vulnerable to people-pressure and to that of domestic and feral animals.

Things to do: Tarra-Bulga has a very special character best appreciated by going quietly and tuning in with all your senses to what is around you – looking at the variety of plant form and subtlety of colour, the flashes of bright birds flying past; listening to the water in the streams (and probably from the wet vegetation), the sounds of birds and other animals; smelling the damp bush and aromatic plants such as the Victorian Christmas-bush; feeling the change in temperature on your skin as you pass through different micro-climates; gently stroking the filmy ferns clothing the treeferns and enjoying the smooth coolness and strength of a mighty eucalypt trunk.

Best season to visit: Any season but as the Park receives over twice Melbourne's annual rainfall be prepared for rain. There is an attraction in seeing these Parks in rain and mist though, and in trying to visualise what life must have been like for those early pioneers.

Special features: Cyathea Falls at Tarra; the Bulga suspension bridge and the site of Wills farm further down Macks Creek.

Relevant reading:

Garnet J.R. in *Victorian Naturalist* (1960) Vol. 77, No. 3, pp. 78–80, and No. 4, pp. 106–7.
Land Conservation Council (1980) *Report of the South Gippsland Area 2.*
Noble W.S. (1986) *The Strzeleckis: a new future for the heartbreak hills.*
South Gippsland Development League (1922) *Land of the Lyrebird.*

Further information:

C&E Office, Balook Rd, Balook, Vic 3971. Phone (051) 96 6127.

Mountain hut, Strzéleckis *CFL*

Morwell

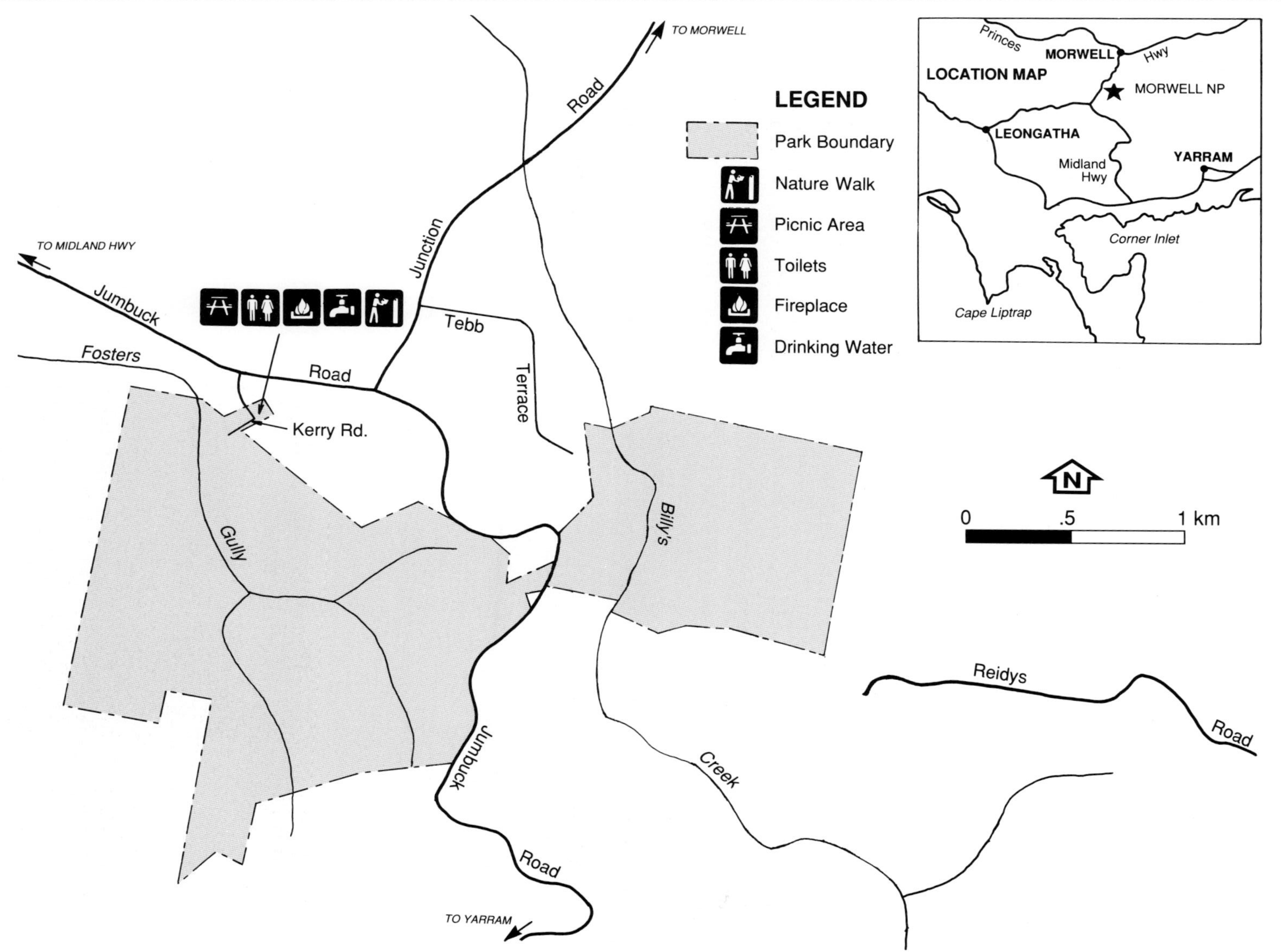
LEGEND
Park Boundary
Nature Walk
Picnic Area
Toilets
Fireplace
Drinking Water
LOCATION MAP
Princes
MORWELL
Hwy
MORWELL NP
LEONGATHA
Midland Hwy
YARRAM
Corner Inlet
Cape Liptrap
0
.5
1 km
N
TO MORWELL
Junction
Road
TO MIDLAND HWY
Jumbuck
Road
Fosters
Tebb
Terrace
Kerry Rd.
Gully
Billy's
Creek
Reidys
Road
Jumbuck
Road
TO YARRAM

68 Morwell National Park

Physical features: 283 ha. This Park is mostly made up of sandstones and siltstones some 100 million years old. In some parts these sedimentary rocks are bordered by younger igneous rock. The land is hilly, up to 174 m, and there are some very steep slopes. Most soils are fertile clay loam over deep clay. Rainfall is about 1 000 mm, and extremes of temperature are uncommon.

Plants and animals: Morwell NP is mostly 80–100 year old regrowth, and because of the variety of aspects and the steep slopes, the vegetation varies from typical wet gully plants such as ferns, Blanket-leaf and Victorian Christmas-bush to peppermint eucalypts and ground orchids in the dry open forests. The Butterfly Orchid, which grows on tree trunks and which was once common over much of Victoria, is still found here, and was one of the main reasons for the declaration of the Park. Koalas are quite common, and can often be seen snoozing the day away in a convenient tree. Bird life is abundant, with gully birds such as Lyrebirds and Eastern Whipbirds, both of which are far more easily heard than seen, to many less shy bush birds, some of which are only too happy to share both the picnic ground and your picnic with you.

Human history: Much of the Park was logged until 1956, and Billy Creek, in the new part of the Park, was used from 1914 to supply water to Morwell and Hazelwood (Churchill). The old water main can still be seen. Moves to create a national park from privately-owned land were begun by local people in the early 1960's when nearby land was being subdivided. Much of the credit, as is the case with so many of our parks, belongs to dedicated and enthusiastic people who put posterity before short-term profit. This dedication is still apparent in the support shown to the Park by its hard-working Friends' Group, which is currently raising money to develop the newly-added Billy Creek area.

Things to do: Walking; picnicking.

Best season to visit: Spring for wildflowers in the drier open forests; otherwise any time.

Special features: The Butterfly Orchid; the walking tracks; Lyndons Clearing; river scenery along Billy Creek; the wonderful background sound of birdcalls.

Relevant reading:
Land Conservation Council (1980) *Report of the South Gippsland Area 2.*

Further information:
Park Office, Jumbuk Rd, Churchill, Vic 3842. Phone (051) 22 1478.
Friends' Group: Phone (051) 22 2597.

Derelict milling machinery *JAC*

69 Mount Worth State Park

Physical features: 1 040 ha. Mt Worth SP is in the Western Strzeleckis, a huge block which was upthrust along the Yarragon fault which runs south-west to north-east. The bedrock is of mudstone and sandstone laid down about 150 million years ago. Rainfall is high, over 2 000 mm annually (nearly three times that of Melbourne) and the soils are very fertile. The dominant landmark in the area is Mt Worth, 518 m, which is close to but not actually in the Park. Mt Worth SP is bordered to the west by the Grand Ridge Road and the east by the West Tarwin River, the headwaters of which rise in the Park. There are also some small waterfalls in the Park. Most of the Western Strzeleckis have been cleared or are planted to pines, making Mt Worth SP especially valuable.

Plants and animals: The plant life here reflects the high rainfall. There is an abundance of ferns, especially treeferns, and in the gullies plants such as Austral Mulberry, Blanket-leaf and Sassafras. Further up the slopes there is a profusion of other plants such as Silver Wattle, various daisy-bushes and Cassinias, Mountain Correa, Banyalla, Victorian Christmas-bush and Privet Mock-olive. Towering over these smaller trees is a variety of eucalypts particularly Mountain Ash, and some Manna Gum. There are the usual bush animals too – Swamp Wallabies, gliders, Bush and Water Rats, Antechinus, Bandicoots and Platypus, but perhaps the most interesting and unusual animal is a somewhat unexpected one, for this is the home of the Giant Gippsland Earthworm. These animals grow to more than two metres in length and are as thick as a human thumb. They are not found in any other state or national park in Victoria; this is the only area in which they receive this level of protection. Not that you are likely to see one – they are only found underground – but if you listen carefully you may hear their characteristic gurgling sound as they move through the wet soil.

Birds are abundant too, including the highly colourful but surprisingly well-camouflaged Crimson Rosella, the very vocal Lyrebird, and the rare Sooty Owl, a bird whose breeding cycle is closely tied in with that of one of its chief prey animals – the Brown Antechinus. All the males of this particular small marsupial species die soon after mating. This means that there is an excellent protein boost for Sooty Owls about to lay their eggs. Many of the female Antechinus die after weaning their young. This time the bodies are a convenient meal for fledgling Sooty Owls.

Human history: As in the case of Tarra-Bulga, this heavily timbered country was probably less used by the Aborigines than the more open areas, although a possible tribal meeting place has been located on Mt Worth, near the picnic ground. Again, as in the Eastern Strzeleckis, the slopes that were not too steep were largely cleared by the European settlers. Fourteen sawmill sites have been found within the Park, and evidence of timber harvesting in the 1930's and '40's can be seen in the old sawmill site and sawdust heaps at Trevorrow's Mill on the Giants Circuit Track. Felling timber was a dangerous job. An important reason for building the West Gippsland Hospital at Warragul was to cope with the many injuries that occurred in the timber mills throughout the Strzeleckis.

Moves to have this precious remnant of vegetation protected began in 1970 when the Shire of Warragul and the local Field Naturalists' Club began working for the preservation of Moonlight Creek valley. Without their efforts it is probable that we would see a pine plantation here today. Mt Worth SP is now the only significant area of native vegetation in the Western Strzeleckis.

Things to do: Picnicking; sightseeing; walking; and enjoying the plant, animal and bird life. There are good walking tracks, from steep and rugged to very gentle and suitable for any age.

Best season to visit: Any, though perhaps not midwinter.

Special features: The Standing Giant, a magnificent Mountain Ash tree which is over two metres in diameter above the buttresses of its trunk and which is probably more than 300 years old; a wonderful luxuriance of treeferns; and the views from the lookouts along McDonald's Track. This Park has a particularly active Friends' Group, and the tracks and bridges in the Park are largely the work of this small but dedicated group of people.

Mount Worth

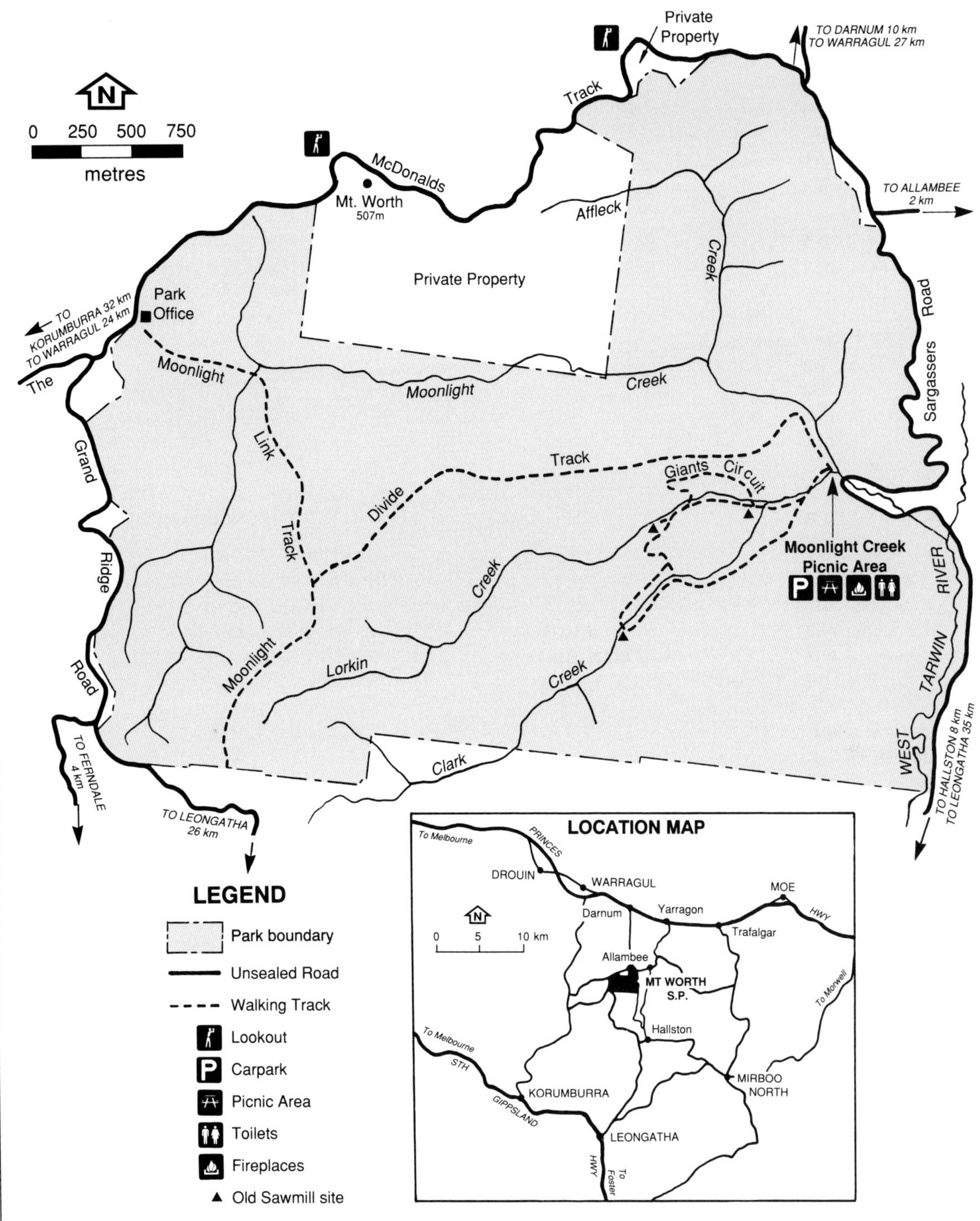

0 250 500 750
metres
Private Property
TO DARNUM 10 km
TO WARRAGUL 27 km
Track
McDonalds
Mt. Worth
507m
Affleck
TO ALLAMBEE
2 km
Private Property
Creek
Park Office
TO KORUMBURRA 32 km
TO WARRAGUL 24 km
Road
Sargassers
The
Moonlight
Moonlight
Creek
Grand
Link
Track
Giants Circuit
Divide
Track
Ridge
Moonlight Creek
Picnic Area
Creek
RIVER
Moonlight
Lorkin
Road
Creek
TARWIN
WEST
TO HALLSTON 8 km
TO LEONGATHA 35 km
TO FERNDALE
4 km
Clark
TO LEONGATHA
26 km
LEGEND
Park boundary
Unsealed Road
Walking Track
Lookout
Carpark
Picnic Area
Toilets
Fireplaces
Old Sawmill site
LOCATION MAP
To Melbourne
PRINCES
DROUIN
WARRAGUL
MOE
HWY
Darnum
Yarragon
Trafalgar
0 5 10 km
Allambee
MT WORTH
S.P.
To Morwell
Hallston
To Melbourne
STH
MIRBOO
NORTH
KORUMBURRA
GIPPSLAND
LEONGATHA
HWY
To Foster

Relevant reading:
Conservation, Forests and Lands (1978) *Mt Worth SP Proposed Management Plan.*
Land Conservation Council (1980) *Report of the South Gippsland Area 2.*
Narracan Shire (1988) *Tracks Through Time.*
(See also Tarra-Bulga NP.)

Further information:
Park Office, McDonalds Track, Seaview via Warragul, Vic 3820. Phone (056) 26 4227.
Friends' Group: Phone: (056) 23 1563.

Giant Gippsland Earthworm *AB*

70 Mitchell River National Park

Physical features: 11 900 ha. The dominant feature of this Park is the contrast between the high land of a once vast plateau and the deep river valleys and gorges that have dissected this plateau since it was uplifted about five million years ago. In parts of the Mitchell River Gorge, layers of sandstones, mudstones and conglomerates laid down 350 million years ago can clearly be seen where the river has carved its way down through the nearly horizontal layers of rocks. These rocks contain freshwater fossils, and many of them have been stained by iron oxide to varying shades of pinks and reds, which makes the cliffs even more impressive. The contrast in the rate of weathering of the harder sandstone and the softer mudstone has led to the formation of the Park's best-known feature, the Den of Nargun. This is an eerily beautiful place where Woolshed Creek tumbles down a precipitous valley and then over a resistant sandstone lip into a dark pool below. Behind the pool a sizeable cave has been formed where the splashing water has carved out the underlying mudstone. The mouth of the Den is guarded by stalactites and stalagmites, many of which are now broken.

Plants and animals: The Den of Nargun is appealing for its rock formations alone, but the effect is greatly heightened by the surrounding vegetation which is a typical East Gippsland 'jungle' of warm temperate rainforest (WTRF). There are no eucalypts. Instead, there are liane vines looping up and down through trees such as Kurrajong, Lilly-pilly, Muttonwood and Blue Olive-berry, and massive Kanookas with their pale papery bark. Everywhere there are lichens, mosses and ferns in luxuriant profusion. Altogether it is a rather surprising collection of plants in an area where the rainfall is only about 700 mm per annum, but of course the answer is micro-climate – the closed canopy of the forest, growing deep in a sheltered gully, retains moisture and creates the humidity necessary for such plants to grow. The dramatic contrast in climate and vegetation as you climb down into or up out of Woolshed Creek is almost unbelievable, especially on a hot summer's day. Up at the car park and picnic ground, the vegetation is sparse and offers little protection from the heat, but down in the gully, along the creek, all is cool and shady.

The WTRF is at its worldwide southern and western limits in this area (apart from a small occurrence at Wilsons Promontory) and correspondingly, some of the rainforest birds, such as the Black-faced Monarch, an elegant fly-catcher, are seldom found further west. A number of the WTRF plants have large succulent fruits, a feature not common among Victorian plants, and these attract birds such as King Parrots and Satin Bower-birds. The latter are clever mimics and are well-known for the bower of grass and sticks that the male bird builds. These bowers are decorated, not only with any blue objects that the bird can find, but also with a mixture of saliva and charcoal that he paints on with a stick. This bower is not a nest, but a mating ground. After mating the female builds the nest and raises the young on her own, as does the Lyrebird, also found in this Park. There are many other bush birds in the Park, and both the gullies and the drier country above are good for bird-watching. In open areas there is suitable habitat for the Grey Kangaroo and Emu, while Swamp Wallabies and Wombats are likely to be seen in more sheltered areas. You may also be lucky enough to see a Goanna, or even, when walking quietly beside the water, a Gippsland Water Dragon sunning itself on a tree branch over the water.

Human history: Very few Aboriginal relics have been found in this area, probably because of the Narguna. Aboriginal legends tell how the Narguna, a fearsome creature with human arms, hands and breast, but otherwise of stone, lived in caves in the Mitchell River area, and would leap out and catch passers-by and drag them into the cave. It was futile to try to shoot or spear the Narguna because it simply turned the missile back on its tracks and wounded the would-be assailant. The first European to see this area was probably Alfred Howitt, who surveyed the Mitchell River in 1875, and who, as a competent geologist and naturalist, made notes and sketches of what he saw. Howitt had come down-river from Tabberabbera in bark canoes built by the two Aborigines who accompanied him. The rapids in the Mitchell proved too much for them, however, and they abandoned the canoes and continued overland, striking up Woolshed (Deadcock) Creek where they soon came across the Den of Nargun. This valley forms an impressive contrast to the surrounding country at

Mitchell River

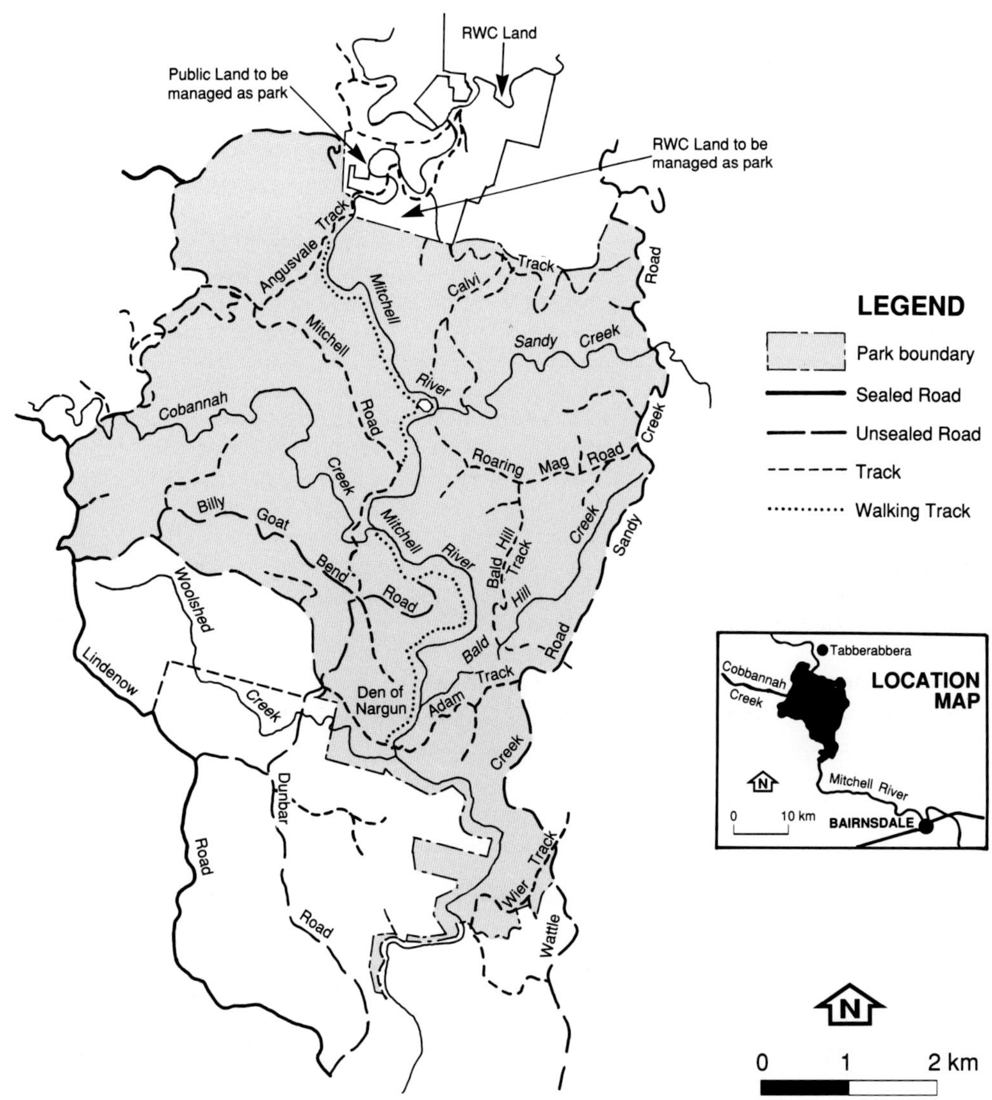

any time, but it must have been particularly dramatic on that day, as bushfires were raging in the dry country above them while they, and large numbers of frightened birds and animals, remained protected in the valley below. The Den formed an apparently total block to further progress, but the Aborigines soon felled a tree so that it leant against the overhang of the cave. They then cut steps in the tree, and all were able to proceed. Meanwhile, Howitt busied himself with 'a slight sketch' of 'this wonderfully picturesque and beautiful spot'. For many years after the only people likely to have visited this wild and lonely river were prospectors looking for alluvial gold and stockmen seeking cattle which might have strayed from the runs on the plateau above. From 1904, after a group of naturalists visited the Den, it became steadily better known and in 1938, after pressure by the Field Naturalists' Club of Victoria, Woolshed Creek was declared a sanctuary. In 1963, Australian Paper Manufacturers Ltd donated additional land and the Glenaladale National Park was formed. Finally, in 1986, a massive increase in area took in the Mitchell River Gorge also, and the name was changed to the more appropriate Mitchell River National Park.

Things to do: Walking, both easy and challenging; 4WD (or robust 2WD!) driving; white-water canoeing; pottering for mining relics; swimming; camping (restricted to canoeists and hikers).

Best season to visit: Any, but the contrast of dry scrub and rainforest will be best in summer.

Special features: The Den of Nargun; the red cliffs where Woolshed Creek joins the Mitchell River; the breath-taking lookout over the Amphitheatre.

Relevant reading:
Croll R.H. (1928) *The Open Road.*
Progress Report of the Geological Survey of Victoria 4 (1877) pp. 118–26.

Further information:
C&E Regional Office, 210 Main St, Bairnsdale, Vic 3875. Phone (051) 52 6211.

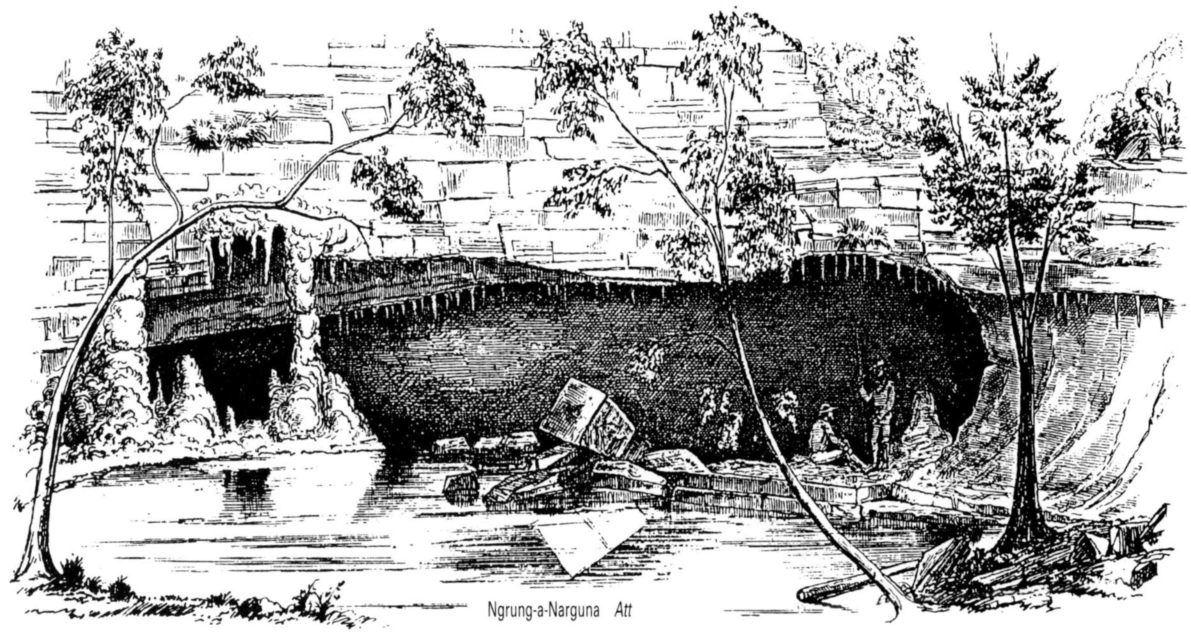

Ngrung-a-Narguna *Att*

71 Tyers Park

Physical features: 1 810 ha. Tyers Park is in the foothills to the north of the La Trobe Valley, and is based around the Tyers River, which runs between the walls of the Tyers Gorge for much of the Park. The rocks include limestone and conglomerate (puddingstone). The latter, seen at road cuttings and at Petersons Lookout, formed the bed of an ancient river which was then uplifted. The limestone contains both plant and animal fossils, and was mined in areas now included in the Park.

Plants and animals: Most of the Park is covered with open forest and woodlands that include many different eucalypts, one of which, Silvertop, is a tall tree with a dark ironbark-like trunk, topped by small white branches and very red young leaves. Colourful wildflowers are plentiful in spring, particularly the Common Correa, numerous wattles and a number of different types of Pomaderris. Orchids are abundant, as are birds. Nearly 100 different bird species are recorded for the Park. As in other gorges, there is a particular delight in being able to stand on a high point, in this case Petersons Lookout, and watch birds such as Peregrine Falcons and eagles fly past below. Much of the river is quiet, ideal habitat for that very shy animal, the Platypus, which has been aptly described as 'arguably the most uniquely Australian mammal and certainly the most improbable'.

Human history: Timber was cut for pulping and some gold mined around Tyers Park. The land on which the La Trobe Valley Water and Sewerage board constructed their pipeline to bring water from Moondarra Reservoir to the La Trobe Valley runs through natural bushland originally owned by the State Electricity Commission. Thanks to the efforts of the La Trobe Valley Field Naturalists' Club (LVFNC) over the years, this land has now been handed over to the Crown, allowing its inclusion in Tyers Park. One of the highspots of Tyers Park, Petersons Lookout, also has a special significance for the LVFNC – Jim Peterson was a keen member and office-bearer of the Club for many years. When he died, Club members gathered rocks from the high country that Jim loved so much, and built a memorial cairn at what is now the Lookout.

Things to do: Scenic driving but check the tracks first on the Park map – some of them are closed to public vehicles; walking along some excellent tracks; swimming; fishing; studying natural history, especially birdwatching.

Best season to visit: Spring for wildflowers; any season for walking and birdwatching.

Special features: Petersons Lookout; the Wirilda walking track.

Relevant reading: See Moondarra SP.

Further information:
C&E Office, School Rd, Erica, Vic 3825. Phone (051) 65 3204.

Peripatus *CFL*

Tyers

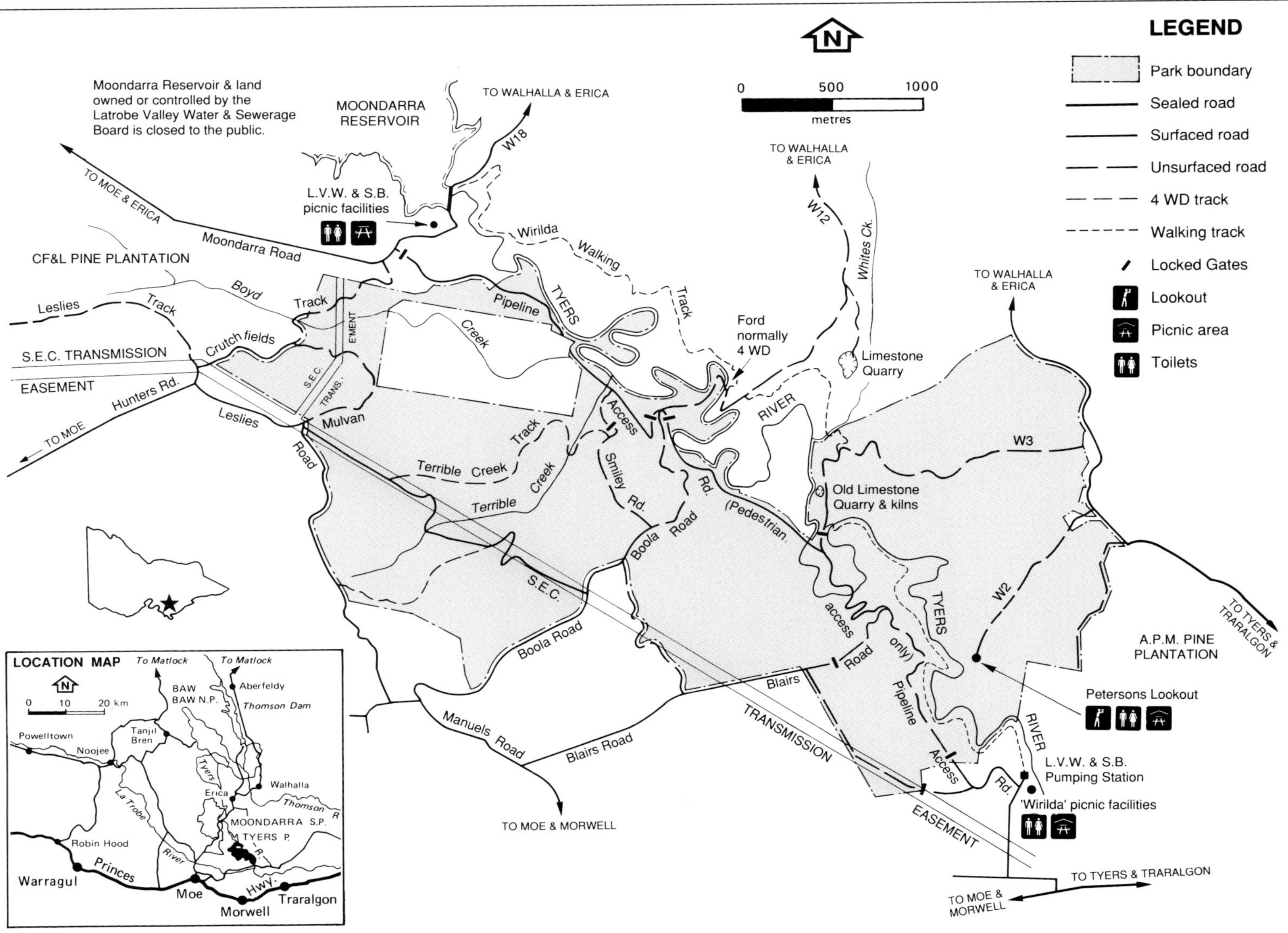

LEGEND
Park boundary
Sealed road
Surfaced road
Unsurfaced road
4 WD track
Walking track
Locked Gates
Lookout
Picnic area
Toilets
N
0 500 1000
metres
Moondarra Reservoir & land owned or controlled by the Latrobe Valley Water & Sewerage Board is closed to the public.
MOONDARRA RESERVOIR
TO WALHALLA & ERICA
W18
L.V.W. & S.B. picnic facilities
TO MOE & ERICA
Moondarra Road
CF&L PINE PLANTATION
Leslies Track
Boyd Track
Crutch fields
S.E.C. TRANSMISSION EASEMENT
Hunters Rd.
TO MOE
Leslies Road
S.E.C. TRANS. EMENT
Mulvan
Wirilda Walking Track
Pipeline
TYERS RIVER
Creek
Terrible Creek Track
Terrible Creek
Access
Smiley Rd.
Boola Road
Rd. (Pedestrian access only)
S.E.C.
Boola Road
Ford normally 4 WD
TO WALHALLA & ERICA
W12
Whites Ck.
Limestone Quarry
Old Limestone Quarry & kilns
W3
TO WALHALLA & ERICA
W2
TYERS
Road
Pipeline
Blairs
TRANSMISSION
EASEMENT
Access Rd.
Manuels Road
Blairs Road
TO MOE & MORWELL
TO TYERS & TRARALGON
A.P.M. PINE PLANTATION
Petersons Lookout
RIVER
L.V.W. & S.B. Pumping Station
'Wirilda' picnic facilities
TO TYERS & TRARALGON
TO MOE & MORWELL
LOCATION MAP
To Matlock
To Matlock
0 10 20 km
BAW BAW N.P.
Aberfeldy
Thomson Dam
Powelltown
Noojee
Tanjil Bren
Tyers
Walhalla
Thomson R
Erica
MOONDARRA S.P.
TYERS P.
R.
La Trobe River
Robin Hood
Warragul
Princes Hwy.
Moe
Morwell
Traralgon

72 Moondarra State Park

Physical features: 6 292 ha. Moondarra SP, like Tyers Park, is on the northern edge of the La Trobe Valley, but because of differing aspect and elevations, each has a surprisingly different character. The soil is derived from the Tertiary and Palaeozoic sediments of the Moondarra Plateau and is often poorly drained, creating swampy areas, even on the hillsides. As Henry Tisdall, a Walhalla schoolteacher and naturalist, said of the area in 1883:

> The vegetation changes from bad to worse, first stringybark ranges ... thin out gradually, and at length nothing is to be seen but heaths and a variety of herbs which gladden the heart of the botanist but make a selector shudder as he gazes knowing full well that their presence indicates poor sandy waste ground.

Plants and animals: Seventeen different eucalypts have been recorded from Moondarra and there are five different forest types, from Manna and Swamp Gum along the Tyers River, up to Mountain Grey Gum and Messmate Stringybark on the ridges. Much of the understorey is shrubby and very colourful in spring, with Banksias, Hakeas and Tea-trees as well as many other smaller plants, including orchids. Many of the trees have mistletoe growing on them. This plant, while detrimental to the host tree, is a rich source of nectar for honeyeaters, fruit for the Mistletoe Bird, and food for caterpillars of the beautiful Imperial and Wood White Butterflies.

Human history: Moondarra was grazed in the past, and timber was taken both for sawlogs and for pulping up until about the 1960's. The remains of timber tramways can still be found in the northern section of the Park. The narrow gauge railway line from Moe to Walhalla, constructed early this century to get timber to the mines and general supplies to Walhalla, ran through the southern 'tail' of the Park. The line was dismantled in the 1950's, but some of its course can still be seen. One of the engines that used to run on this line, a G-class Beyer-Garratt, is currently being used on the Puffing Billy line, the popular narrow-gauge tourist attraction in the Dandenongs near Melbourne.

This Park resulted from the Land Conservation Council's recognition of an unusual type of vegetation association not found elsewhere in Victoria – Silvertop/Yertchuk woodland, with banksias and hakeas over a ground layer of spear-grasses, sedges and lilies.

Things to do: See Tyers Park.

Best season to visit: See Tyers Park.

Special features: The wildflowers, particularly along Seninis Road.

Relevant reading:
Adams J. (1980) *Mountain Gold.*
Land Conservation Council (1973) *Study Report Melbourne Area.*

Further information: See Tyers Park.

Imperial White Butterfly *AW*

Moondarra

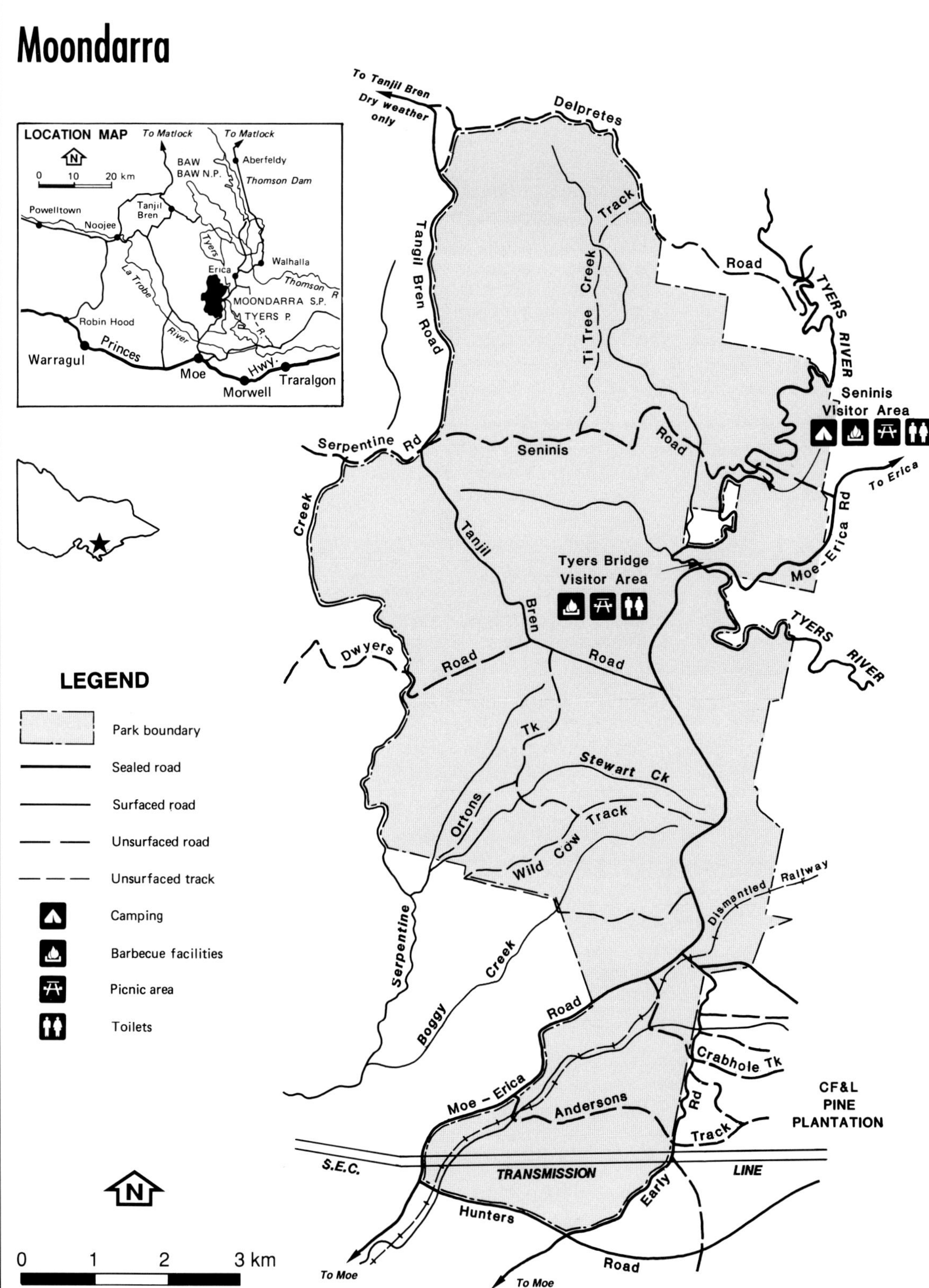

LOCATION MAP
To Matlock
To Matlock
0 10 20 km
BAW BAW N.P.
Aberfeldy
Thomson Dam
Powelltown
Noojee
Tanjil Bren
Tyers
Walhalla
Erica
Thomson R
La Trobe
MOONDARRA S.P.
TYERS P.
Robin Hood
River
Princes
Hwy.
Warragul
Moe
Morwell
Traralgon
To Tanjil Bren
Dry weather only
Delpretes
Track
Road
Tangil Bren Road
Ti Tree Creek
TYERS RIVER
Seninis Visitor Area
Serpentine Rd
Seninis
Road
To Erica
Creek
Tanjil
Tyers Bridge Visitor Area
Moe-Erica Rd
Bren
Dwyers
Road
Road
TYERS RIVER
LEGEND
Park boundary
Sealed road
Surfaced road
Unsurfaced road
Unsurfaced track
Camping
Barbecue facilities
Picnic area
Toilets
Tk
Stewart Ck
Ortons
Track
Wild Cow
Dismantled Railway
Serpentine
Boggy Creek
Road
Crabhole Tk
Moe – Erica
Andersons
Rd
CF&L PINE PLANTATION
Track
S.E.C.
TRANSMISSION
LINE
Early
Hunters
Road
To Moe
To Moe
0 1 2 3 km

73

The Lakes National Park, Gippsland Lakes Coastal Park and Nyerimilang Park

Physical features: 2 390 ha (The Lakes NP); 17 200 ha (Gippsland Lakes CP); 200 ha (Nyerimilang). Since the Gippsland Lakes, in which all three of these parks are situated, are a single system, the three will be described together.

The Gippsland Lakes are more correctly described as coastal lagoons in that they are areas of shallow water which have been sealed off from the sea by the deposition of barriers. There are three main lakes – Lake Wellington in the east and Lake King in the west, with longer, narrower Lake Victoria connecting the two. The Coastal Park includes most of the 90 Mile Beach between Seaspray and Lakes Entrance with its coastal dunes and the water and land that lie immediately behind the beach. The Lakes National Park covers two of the now-stabilised sandy inner barriers – Sperm Whale Head and Rotamah Island. Nyerimilang is a small park on the edge of the cliffs of the original shoreline.

The Gippsland Lakes are geologically young, having formed over the last 100 000 years from a large open bay at the coastal edge of a Miocene limestone plateau. This bay has since become sealed off from the sea by a series of barriers. Most of the area is low-lying and sandy or swampy. The lakes are generally shallow, with the water level being higher and the salinity lower in winter and early spring. Most of the hinterland around the lakes has been cleared for agriculture. Until almost 100 years ago, when a permanent entrance was cut at Lakes Entrance, the outer barrier remained intact until floods or storms caused a break, somewhere east of Lakes Entrance. The rivers flowing into the lakes have, over hundreds of years, deposited some of their load of silt as bordering banks, or silt jetties, as they entered the relatively calm waters of the lakes. The Mitchell River silt jetty, though now quite eroded, is well worth seeing.

The climate is generally mild, with lower summer and higher winter temperatures than in the rest of the State, which has led to the Gippsland Lakes area being dubbed Victoria's Riviera.

Plants and animals: The increased salinity caused by the cut at Lakes Entrance appears to have had a major effect on the ecology of the lakes system. A number of the less salt-tolerant fringing plants have died off, particularly the Common Reed, leaving the shores vulnerable to erosion by wind and wave action. This is very noticeable along the Mitchell River silt jetty, where what was once a continuous bank is now a series of islands. Sadly, some of the power boats using the river choose to ignore the speed limit signs and so exacerbate the problem.

On the ocean side of the sandy dunes there are the typical low-growing and sand-binding coloniser plants such as Sea Rocket, Hairy Spinifex, Variable Groundsel and the introduced Marram Grass. These open coasts are excellent for birds, though you do have to be something of an expert to decide which albatross or petrel it is flying well out to sea. There's no trouble though identifying the gannets as they plunge into the sea in a succession of breathtaking dives.

On the seaward side of the coastal dunes are the shrubby Cushion-bush, Grey Saltbush and Sea-box. Further inland, away from the full intensity of the strong salty winds, there is a dramatic increase in the number of different plants. Coast Banksia and Coast Tea-tree form an overstorey to small shrubs and low-growing plants including a variety of native orchids. Bush birds suddenly appear too, such as whistlers, thornbills, and the Grey Shrike Thrush and White-browed Scrub-wren.

There are also extensive areas of open woodland comprising Saw Banksia and a number of different eucalypts, depending on the soil type and the availability of water. The understorey plants in the woodlands and the heathlands are both diverse and colourful. The road into The Lakes NP passes through the Coastal Park, and in spring, when the Silky Tea-tree is in full flower, it is a lovely sight. For anyone interested in plants it is worth stopping along this road and taking time to explore the floral riches here – the beautiful Blue Dampiera, Golden Grevillea, a particularly vividly coloured Common Correa, and the delicate pink Heath-myrtle. Once into the Sperm Whale Head peninsula, the roadside is white with Ribbed Thryptomene which in Victoria is confined to this area and to nearby Dutson Downs. The richness of the plant life is well-matched by that of the birds –

▼ Sunset over Tyers Park *JAC*

▲ Crimson Berry, Wilsons Promontory NP *DMC*

◀ Underwater life, Wilsons Promontory Marine Reserve *KH*

◀ Underwater boulders, Wilsons Promontory Marine Reserve *JAC*

◀ Diver, Wilsons Promontory Marine Reserve *KH*

Brush Bronzewings are perhaps the most obvious as they fly up in front of you with clattering wings. Honeyeaters, including the dapper Eastern Spinebill, and insect-feeders such as robins and fantails are also numerous.

A totally different community of plants and animals can be seen along the shores of Lake Reeve, much of which is often dry. Here there are expanses of saltmarsh where the plants are low-growing and succulent and often quite red. These plants include Grey and Beaded Glassworts, and Seablite, plants which are food for the Ground Parrot, an uncommon bird that occurs here but is not easy to see (see also Carlisle SP).

There are also a number of swamps and freshwater lakes, including Lake Killarney on Sperm Whale Head, where there is a bird hide with the commoner birds illustrated. Here you can often see, and hear, a number of different ducks, particularly Chestnut Teal with their unexpected chuckling call. But it is on the open water and shorelines, especially where there is a sheltered sandbar, that the richness and beauty of the birdlife is almost overwhelming. Who could forget sunset on a still autumn day when sky, water and the breasts of the preening pelicans and spoonbills are all flushed a delicate pink; or the sight of every convenient navigation marker and dead tree decorated with cormorants drying their wings? Then there are the little clusters of delightfully raffish-looking Crested Terns; the thousands of Coots with their white-bossed beaks floating peacefully on the water; and the groups of grebes constantly diving and reappearing. And to top it all there could well be a White-breasted Sea-eagle flying overhead, or a school of Bottle-nosed Dolphins swimming past, or even a really rare visitor like the Channel-billed Cuckoo which is normally found well north of here. For anyone who loves wildlife, and birds in particular, there is no better way to enjoy the Gippsland Lakes than through a course at the Rotamah Island Bird Observatory (address below). There's always a special charm about islands and Rotamah is no exception – a picturesque old farmhouse with dozens of kangaroos grazing on the front 'lawn', a wealth of birds, hides to watch them from, plus expert guidance on what you are seeing and might yet see. More than 170 species of birds have now been recorded from Rotamah.

Many of the kangaroos at Point Wilson on Sperm Whale Head are used to handouts and now expect visitors to feed them – a strong temptation for most people but one which is much better resisted, both for the sake of the animals which become too dependent on a highly unsuitable diet, and for the sake of future visitors who could well be threatened by large and impatient kangaroos. Besides the kangaroos, wallabies, wombats and possums, there's another shyer and less easily seen animal in these parks – the Asian Hog Deer, (see also South Gippsland Marine and Coastal Parks).

Over the last few years there has been a significant conservation success in the Gippsland Lakes when the local community, led by C&E staff, mounted a well co-ordinated effort to protect the Little Terns nesting near Lakes Entrance. Thanks to many people's dedication, there's been the great satisfaction of seeing these birds increase from a precarious few to a small but thriving colony.

Human history: No doubt the Gippsland Lakes were favourite hunting and fishing grounds for the Aborigines, but the hinterland was good farming country and so the blacks were soon dispossessed of their lands just as happened in other similar situations. Just east of the Gippsland Lakes is the Lake Tyers Aboriginal Settlement, originally set up to accommodate displaced Aborigines from all over Victoria.

Much of what is now protected parkland has been shot over by sportsmen and grazed by cattle. In 1926, when all grazing families except the Bartons had been forced off their land by a lack of stock feed, moves were begun by the Bartons and other naturalists to have Sperm Whale Head set aside as a national park. In 1929 this was realised and a Committee of Management was appointed. As often happened then, it was up to the Committee to finance the running of the Park. In order to do this they sold rights to grazing, bark-stripping from the Black Wattles, exploring for oil and harvesting dolomite, all from within the Park. Remains of the last two activities can still just be seen.

For many years people have been aware of the charm of this very special area, but in 1984 more formal recognition came when the Gippsland Lakes were identified, along with six other parts of Victoria, as having special potential for tourism, and as such to be promoted and developed.

For an understanding of times past in the Gippsland Lakes, a visit to Nyerimilang is a must. This

The Lakes, Gippsland Lakes and Nyerimilang

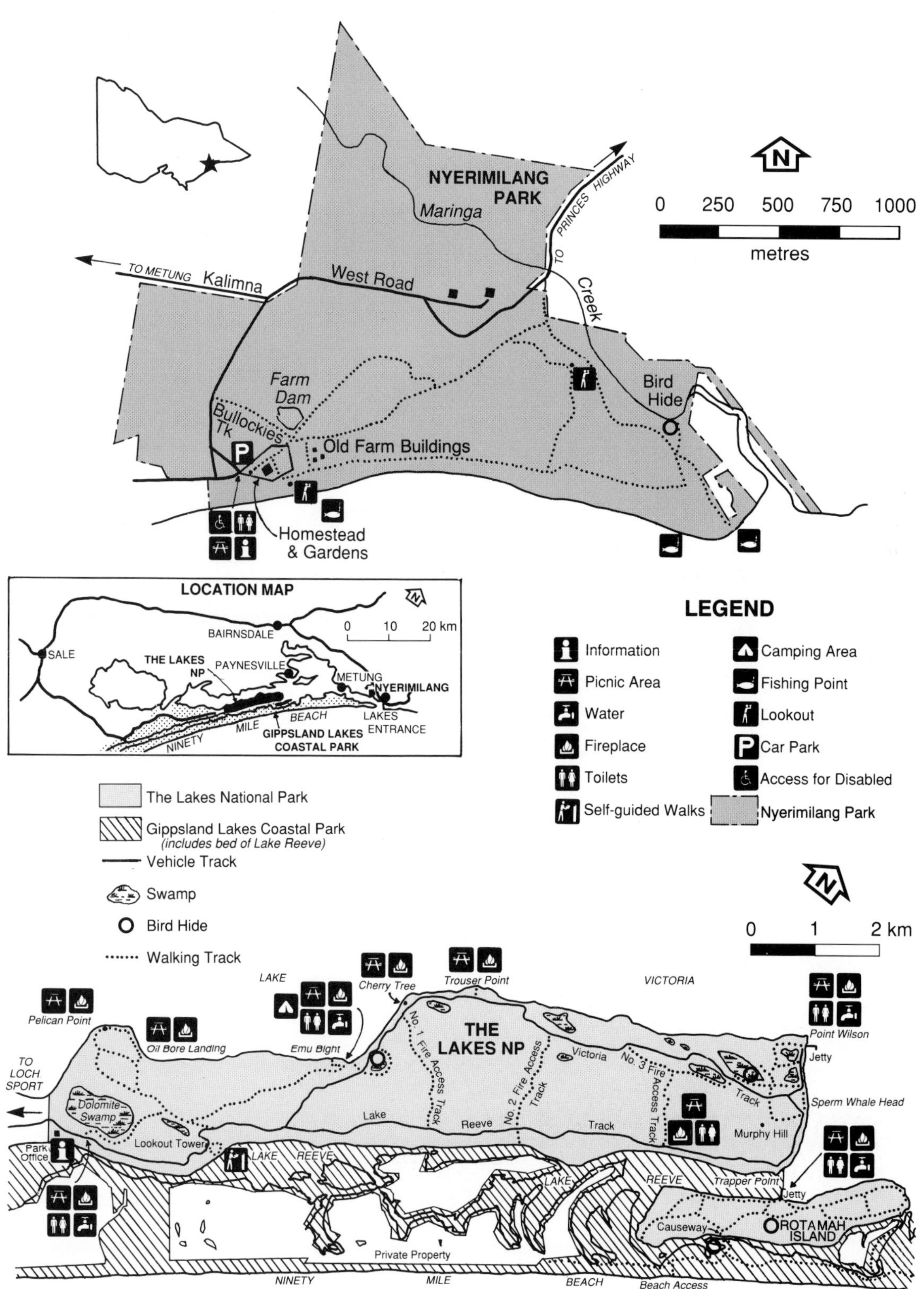

lovely old homestead is 10 km north-west of Lakes Entrance. At present there is only road access, but it is planned to rebuild the jetty and so allow visitors to come in by boat too. Nyerimilang began as a shooting and fishing lodge for a Melbourne family; then in 1936 it became the Boys' Training Farm run by the Anglican church before passing back into private ownership. It was purchased by the Victorian Government in 1976. The homestead has excellent displays on local history and natural history as well as a reference library available to visitors. It also serves as a community resource for meetings and appropriate environmental and historical activities. The garden around the house is parklike with an interesting mix of exotic and native plants, including some magnificent old Kurrajong trees, which here are at the south-eastern limit of their range. Beyond the garden there are walking tracks to native bush and marshland, both of which are good bird habitats.

Things to do: Boating, both sail and power; canoeing; swimming; good fishing, both within the lakes system, and along the 90 Mile Beach. There are many good walking tracks through the woodlands and heathlands. In the early morning the sandy tracks often have a fascinating array of animal tracks, large and small, crossing and recrossing our manmade pathways. Birds too are a major attraction for many people.

Best season to visit: Spring for wildflowers; autumn, and often winter too, for near-perfect weather; summer for water-based activities; any season for birds.

Special features: Tranquillity; the coastal heathlands in spring; a visit to Rotamah Island; the wealth of birdlife.

Relevant reading:
Bird E.C.F (1978) *The Geomorphology of the Gippsland Lakes.*
Land Conservation Council (1972) *Report of the South Gippsland Area 1.*
Le Cheminant M. (1985) *The Story of Nyerimilang.*
National Parks Service (1981) *Nyerimilang Reserve Proposed Management Plan.*

Little Tern *CFL*

Further information:
C&E Office, Loch Sport, Vic 3851. Phone (051) 460 0278.
Rotamah Island Bird Observatory, PO Box 75, Paynesville, Vic 3880. Phone (051) 56 6398.
Friends of Nyerimilang: Phone (051) 56 2573.

Nyerimilang homestead *MvT*

EAST GIPPSLAND PARKS

'East Gippsland' is a term which usually includes all land east of the Snowy River. In this book, those parks which form part of the new Alpine National Park, have been grouped under 'Alpine', leaving only five, all national parks, in East Gippsland. Two – Lind and Alfred – are very small, and if declared today would probably not be *national* parks; a further two, Coopracambra and Croajingolong, are well worthy of their present status; the last, Errinundra, only partly protects the truly magnificent and highly significant forests of this area.

East Gippsland constitutes only about 6% of Victoria's total area, but it has nearly 50% of the State's plants, and comparable proportions of its mammals, birds and amphibians. This diversity is both because it is a meeting point for northern and southern climatic zones, with an even rainfall throughout the year, and also because of the variety of landforms and environments, from coastal to alpine. Many of the waterways have been less modified than elsewhere, so it is a very important area for native fish as well.

One of the things most clearly associated in many people's minds with East Gippsland is rainforest, especially the 'jungle' or warm temperate rainforest (WTRF) in which luxuriant vines scramble over every available tree and shrub. There are, in fact, two types of rainforest in Victoria: WTRF and cool temperate rainforest (CTRF), and both of these are found in East Gippsland.

Rainforest as a whole is defined by the overall vegetation structure:

- a more or less continuous canopy
- trees are generally broad-leaved
- species are able to re-establish below this canopy and are not fire-dependent for regeneration
- vigorous growth of liana climbers, epiphytes and ferns;

and the individual plants which make up the rainforest, within an association of a minimum size.

Victorian WTRF, found only in East Gippsland where it is at its southernmost limit, includes Lilly-pilly, Kanooka, Mutton-wood, Blue Olive-berry, and Sweet Pittosporum, the tree which has become a pest species in the Dandenongs because of its ability to grow in heavy shade and crowd out naturally-occurring understorey species. Small amounts of Leatherwood and Yellow-wood may also be found in WTRF. CTRF, on the other hand, is found in the Otway Ranges, Central Highlands (near Marysville) and the Strzelecki Ranges, as well as in East Gippsland on the Errinundra Plateau. Characteristic CTRF species include Myrtle Beech (not found in East Gippsland), Sassafras, Black Olive-berry and perhaps Blackwood. At and near the Goonmirk Rocks on the Errinundra Plateau there is an unusual type of CTRF of Mountain Plum-pine, in association with Alpine Pepper, Gippsland Waratah, Tree Lomatia, Privet Mock-olive, Banyalla and Forest Geebung.

There are also animals which depend primarily on rainforest as their habitat. These include the Fruit Bat, Sooty Owl, Satin Bowerbird, Black-faced Monarch, Pink Robin and two species of frog.

Relationship to fire is a particularly interesting aspect of rainforests and one which is currently being monitored in Alfred NP and Coopracambra NP, both of which were severely burnt in the 1983 fires, (see these Parks also). If there were no fires where the rainfall is adequate for rainforest to grow (evenly spread and more than 1 500 mm per year in southern Victoria, 700 mm in eastern Victoria), there would probably be more rainforest. But fires do occur over much of the State, and these encourage the germination and establishment of fire-dependent sclerophyll (hard-leaved) trees, usually eucalypts and wattles, at the expense of the rainforest species. Logging and therefore removal of protective buffers of vegetation around areas of rainforest may also cause the rainforest to recede and the fire-prone sclerophyll forest to advance. Thus the area under rainforest can well be altered, and unfortunately, with more frequent fires, that means recession rather than advance of the rainforests. Wattles and eucalypts, both fire-dependent groups, represent the Australian flora that has evolved since Australia broke away from the ancient Gondwana landmass about 45 million years ago and drifted north into warmer drier latitudes; the rainforest represents remnant Gondwana flora which has survived only in moist pockets where the climate is similar to that which prevailed in Gondwana.

All our Australian rainforests urgently require further study; both the 1% that are in Victoria and the more complex, species-rich tropical and sub-tropical rainforests further north. Some aspects, such as vegetation structure, are now becoming better understood, but others like the all important invertebrate fauna, the very basis of so many foodchains, are still in need of further research. To this end, there is now a National Rainforest Conservation Program which is being developed and implemented in co-operation with the relevant states. There is also now a Rainforest Information Centre in Lochiel St, Orbost.

Relevant reading:

Conservation, Forests and Lands (1985) *East Gippsland Floristic Map and Guide to Vegetation Communities.*
Conservation, Forests and Lands (1986) *Victoria's Rainforests.*
Da Costa G. (1988) *Car Touring and Bush Walking in East Gippsland.*
Land Conservation Council (1974) *Report on the East Gippsland Study Area.*
Parkwatch No. 138, (Spring 1984).

	Page No.	*Entrance Fee*	*Information Centre*	*Multilingual Information*	*Picnic Areas*	*Fireplaces*	*Toilets*	*Disabled Access*	*Walking Tracks*	*Nature Walk or Drive*	*Swimming*	*Climbing*	*Horseriding*	*Fishing*	*Boating*	*Camping*	*Caravans*	*Km from Melbourne*	*Date Declared*
Alfred	229					■	■		■									480	1925
Coopracambra	225																	520	1975 (SP) 1988 (NP)
Croajingolong	232				■	■	■		■	■	■			■	■	■		434	1979
Errinundra	223													■				460	1988
Lind	230					■	■		■	■								435	1926

Errinundra

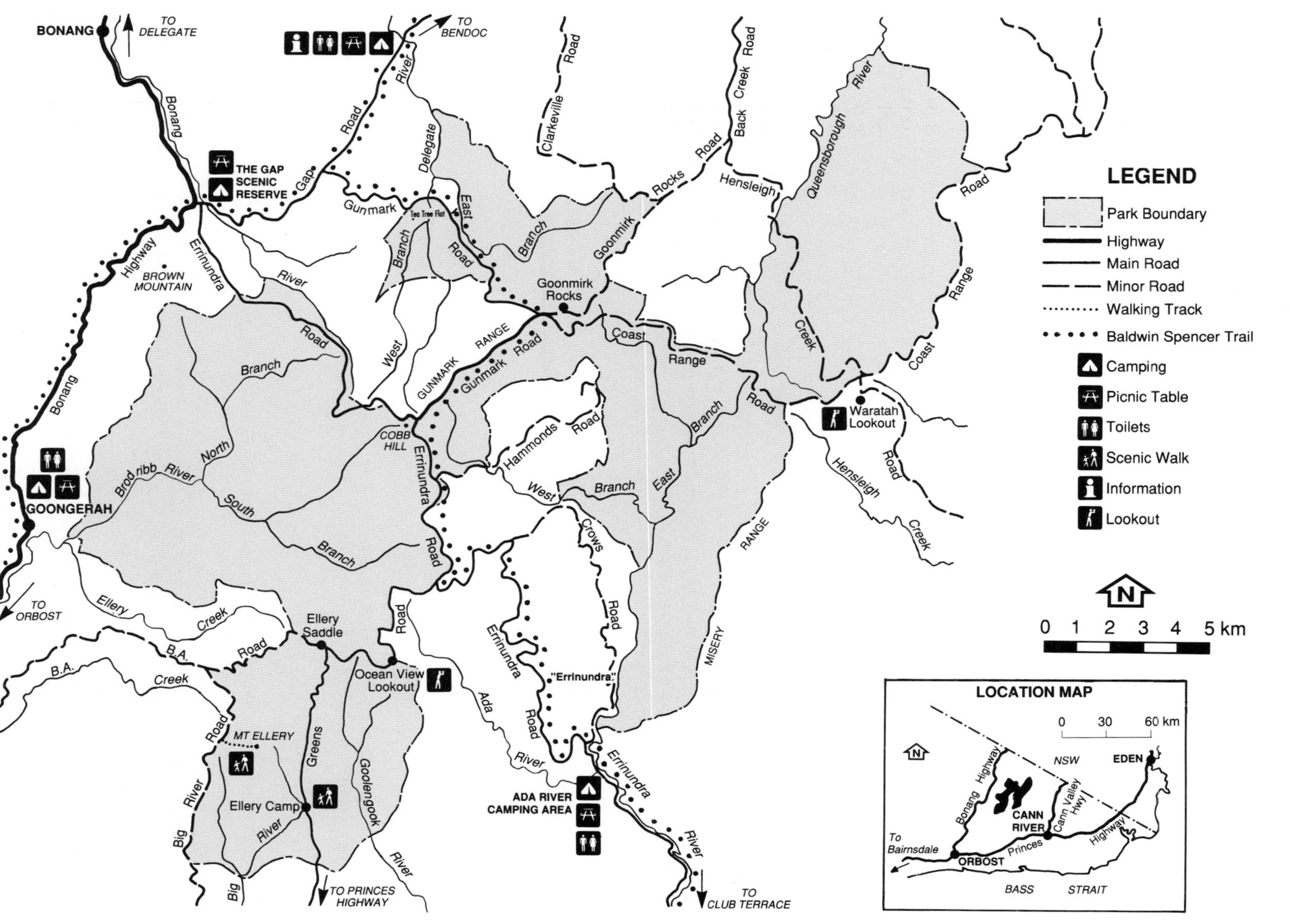
BONANG
TO DELEGATE
TO BENDOC
Bonang
THE GAP SCENIC RESERVE
Gap Road
River
Delegate
Gunmark
Tea Tree Flat
East Road
Branch
Clarkeville Road
Rocks Road
Back Creek Road
Hensleigh
Queensborough River
Road
Goonmirk
Goonmirk Rocks
Highway
BROWN MOUNTAIN
Errinundra
River
Road
West
GUNMARK RANGE
Gunmark Road
Coast Range
Creek
Coast Range
Road
Waratah Lookout
Hensleigh Road
Creek
Branch
North
South
Brodribb River
Branch
COBB HILL
Errinundra Road
Hammonds Road
West Branch
East Branch
RANGE
MISERY
GOONGERAH
TO ORBOST
Ellery Creek
Ellery Saddle
B.A. Road
B.A. Creek
Road
Ocean View Lookout
Crows Road
Ada River
Errinundra Road
"Errinundra"
ADA RIVER CAMPING AREA
Errinundra River
TO CLUB TERRACE
MT ELLERY
Greens
Goolengook River
Ellery Camp
River
Big River
Big
TO PRINCES HIGHWAY
LEGEND
Park Boundary
Highway
Main Road
Minor Road
Walking Track
Baldwin Spencer Trail
Camping
Picnic Table
Toilets
Scenic Walk
Information
Lookout
N
0 1 2 3 4 5 km
LOCATION MAP
0 30 60 km
NSW
EDEN
Bonang Highway
CANN RIVER
Cann Valley Hwy
Highway
Princes
To Bairnsdale
ORBOST
BASS STRAIT

74 Errinundra National Park

Physical features: 25 100 ha. Errinundra NP is one of those magical places that almost everyone in Australia has now heard of, but very few people could find on a map, let alone say that they have actually visited. It lies in a remote area of Victoria east of the Bonang Highway and well west of the Cann River Highway. Much of the Park is a granitic plateau bounded to the east, south and west by steep escarpments and to the north by older Ordovician sediments which are continuous with the those of the Monaro Tablelands of New South Wales. The surface of the plateau is of gently rolling country, rising to over 1 200 m at the granite outcrops of Mt Ellery and the Goonmirk Rocks, two of the Park's best known landmarks. The soils on the plateau are deep and fertile, watered by mist and cloud as well as by a high rainfall. Below the 1 000 m line the country drops steeply away, and in some cases rivers and streams fall through as much as 700 m in 2 km, often by way of spectacular falls and cascades interrupted by clean, clear pools. The northern fall to the Monaro Tablelands is a transition area from the high rainfall plateau up to much drier sub-alpine country, often snow-covered in winter.

Plants and animals: The name Errinundra conjures up visions of tall, tall forests and perhaps rainforest too. Both are characteristic of the Park. About one third of the plateau was originally covered with very old montane forest of Shining Gum and Brown-barrel (Cut-tail) eucalypts with a well-developed understorey, including that floral beauty, the Gippsland Waratah. The rest of the plateau has the largest area in Victoria of cool temperate rainforest (CTRF), here dominated by Sassafras and Black Olive-berry, rather than Myrtle-beech (see East Gippsland Introduction). At the Goonmirk Rocks there is a unique form of CTRF in which Mountain Plum-pine, normally a low-growing shrub of open sub-alpine areas, grows into a tall tree, up to 17.5 m tall which is frequently draped with festoons of delicate moss. These 'cloud-forest' trees have an unmistakably ancient feel about them and may well be as much as 500 years old. (The plum-pines here are sufficiently distinct from those of the Alps and they may ultimately be recognised as a separate species.) As the plateau drops off down the escarpment there is a zone of transition between this cool temperate rainforest and warm temperate rainforest (WTRF). The Northern Fall is also an area of transition, this time between the lush rainforests of the plateau through woodlands of a variety of eucalypts, including an unusual and now uncommon association between Broad-leaved Peppermint and gums, then through Snow Gum woodlands to sub-alpine vegetation. Of particular interest too is that recent pollen studies have shown that Errinundra may well be the only place in Victoria where forests survived the Ice Ages. No wonder the Errinundra plateau is considered botanically important as well as beautiful.

Equally, it is extremely important for the wide variety of birds and other animals that are characteristic of the different habitats, though there is still considerable survey work needed on the fauna of Errinundra. Two of Victoria's rarest frogs, the Giant Burrowing Frog and the Great Barred Frog, are confined to East Gippsland, especially the CTRF of Errinundra. There is also a high diversity of native fish, and as there are few introduced species it is an extremely important reference area where relatively unmodified habitat can be compared with altered waterways elsewhere in the State. In all, the conservation of this area is not just important to Victoria alone, or even south-eastern Australia, but is of national and international importance.

Human history: Since the mid-1960's when logging began on the plateau, over half of the tall forests have been felled and replaced by dense stands of even-age, fire-prone eucalypt regrowth. Errinundra is a comparatively small park, smaller than it should be in relation to the importance of the area in which it lies, especially as some of the area has been declared as National Estate and therefore is recognised by the Australian Heritage Commission to be of outstanding natural value. It seems ironic that, at the same time that East Gippsland is being promoted as a prime wilderness destination for tourists, logging is impinging on and even destroying that very wilderness quality.

At the time of writing this area is also receiving increasing media coverage because of recent proposals for an electrified Very Fast Train with some advantages in terms of shorter overland travel time between major centres, as well as reduced traffic, pollution and accidents on the main highways. Many people, though, are very concerned about the effects of such a train on this important wilderness area. Not only would the line and its necessary safety fencing cut right through sensitive natural environments, but, to judge from overseas experience, it would be very noisy, especially at the high speeds of around 350 km/hr, that are proposed. Then there is the disruption of the actual construction, with erosion and siltation being almost certain. There are serious social considerations too concerning the monopolistic effects on existing, less expensive, passenger services, and the extent to which the public purse will be drawn upon in a supposedly private enterprise. Another espoused benefit is that incoming tourists will be able to reach the major ski fields in a very short time after their aircraft lands, but this raises the question as to how much extra pressure the ski fields, in particular Kosciusko NP can withstand. The sensitive East Gippsland country is still far from adequately understood and other options such as alternative routes or improvements to the existing route surely should be considered.

Things to do: Walking in a walker's paradise, with a variety of experiences from gentle grades leaving plenty of time and energy to marvel at the beauty and magnificence of the tall forests, to slow and arduous, but very rewarding, slogs of 1–2 km covered in a full day.

Best season to visit: Late spring to early summer, especially November–December when the waratah is in flower. Roads may be impassable in winter and very dusty in summer when logging trucks are operating nearby.

Special features: The wilderness quality of much of the country which leaves you with a sense of awe and wonder, especially at the grandeur of the tall forests; the view from Mt Ellery which, on a clear day, stretches from Mt Kosciusko to Mallacoota Inlet; a misty morning at Frosty Hollow; Gippsland Waratah in full bloom.

Relevant reading:
Conservation, Forests and Lands (1989) *Errinundra NP Proposed Management Plan.*

Further information:
C&E Parks and Regional Information Centre, Cann River, Vic 3889. Phone (051) 58 6351.

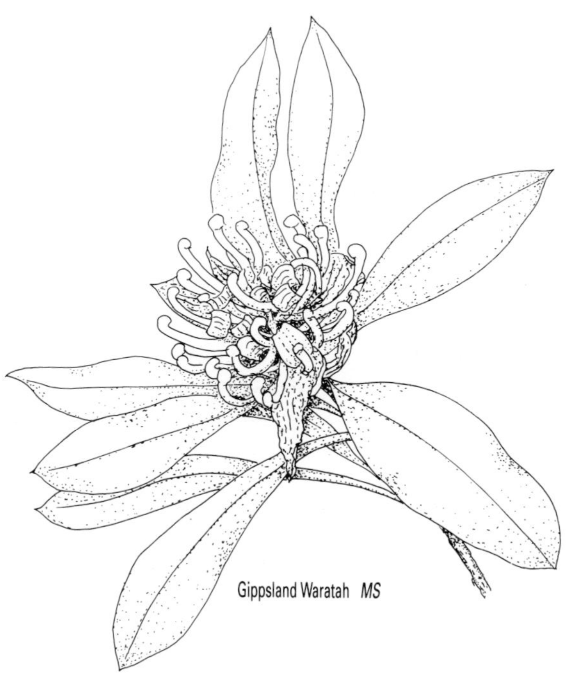
Gippsland Waratah *MS*

75 Coopracambra National Park

Physical features: 35 100 ha. The bedrock here, known as the Genoa River Beds, is of Upper Devonian sediments 345–360 million years old. These beds are about 300 m deep and are of non-marine sandstones and mudstones with some conglomerates which contain boulders up to 30 cm in diameter. Much of the rock is reddish or purplish, which heightens the dramatic effect of formations like the 30 km long Genoa Gorge, where the river has cut deep, steep walls down through the soft sediments. Of particular geological interest here are the earliest known footprints of a terrestrial tetrapod (four-legged) animal in the world. The tracks are similar to those found in Greenland of the earliest type of amphibian, the Ichthyostegalia, and are assumed to have been made by a short-limbed animal 50–100 cm long. There are also a number of plant fossils from the same era which therefore pre-date the evolution of flowering plants by almost 210 million years. Part of the Park adjoins Nungatta NP in NSW, but unfortunately, the headwaters of the Genoa have not been protected and have suffered from clearing for woodchipping and pine plantations.

Plants and animals: This Park is not only visually spectacular but botanically fascinating. Plants from the high country of Tasmania overlap those from eastern NSW and Victoria. Much of the Park is covered with dry open forests of stringybark, gum and box eucalypts, but in sheltered gullies on Mt Merragunegin there are pockets of warm temperate rainforest. Along the river in late spring, the Crimson Bottlebrush is particularly vivid against the red rock of the cliffs, while the round clumps of Rock Orchid against exposed rock outcrops make a beautiful sight, especially when in full bloom. Jones Creek, now included in Coopracambra NP, was the first rainforest to be designated as a reference area because of its pristine condition and rich flora and fauna. This area is unusual in that it has no free surface water, a circumstance which, along with its being on a marked slope, led to Jones Creek rainforest being severely burnt in February 1983. Even the tree-ferns, which normally regenerate easily after fire, were burnt so thoroughly that only an ash-filled hole marked where each had stood. Many of the Lilly-pillies were killed (see also Alfred NP). Whilst early post-fire observations of Jones Creek showed a massive growth of opportunistic plants like Forest Bindweed and various shrubby kangaroo-apples, the regeneration of primary rainforest species such as Lilly-pilly does not appear to be keeping pace with that of eucalypt seedlings. The site is now being monitored on a long-term basis.

Many of the animals and birds are those typical of dry open forest – possums and gliders, bats, Bush Rats, Swamp Wallabies and Antechinus, honeyeaters, thornbills, tree-creepers, kookaburras and owls, with the rather unexpected addition of the White-breasted Sea-eagle, which can sometimes be seen cruising along the Gorge. Among the more unusual animals are, from the Jones Creek area, a new species of robin and a giant earthworm.

Human history: This Park is probably the least visited of all Victoria's parks, both because of its remoteness and because so few people even know of it, but the Wangarabell valley in this general area was once a busy farming community, settled before the rest of East Gippsland. The community was large enough to support its own school and run an agricultural show, and there was also a small butter and cheese factory. Some of the settlers also worked in the nearby Yambulla Creek goldmines.

Coopracambra was declared first as a state park in 1979 as the result of Land Conservation Council (LCC) recommendations as to its high value for nature conservation and remote recreation. In 1980, the Park was burnt by a wildfire which came across the border from forests in NSW. As the result of further studies commissioned by the LCC, Coopracambra State Park was enlarged in 1988 to include Jones Creek, Mt Kaye and Mt Denmarsh to the south, and was also upgraded to national park status.

Things to do: Walking along short walks near the Wangarabell Road (the access road from Genoa in the east). Most of Coopracambra though is wilderness, and therefore remains the territory of the experienced and well-equipped bushwalker. For such people it is a challenging and rewarding area

Coopracambra

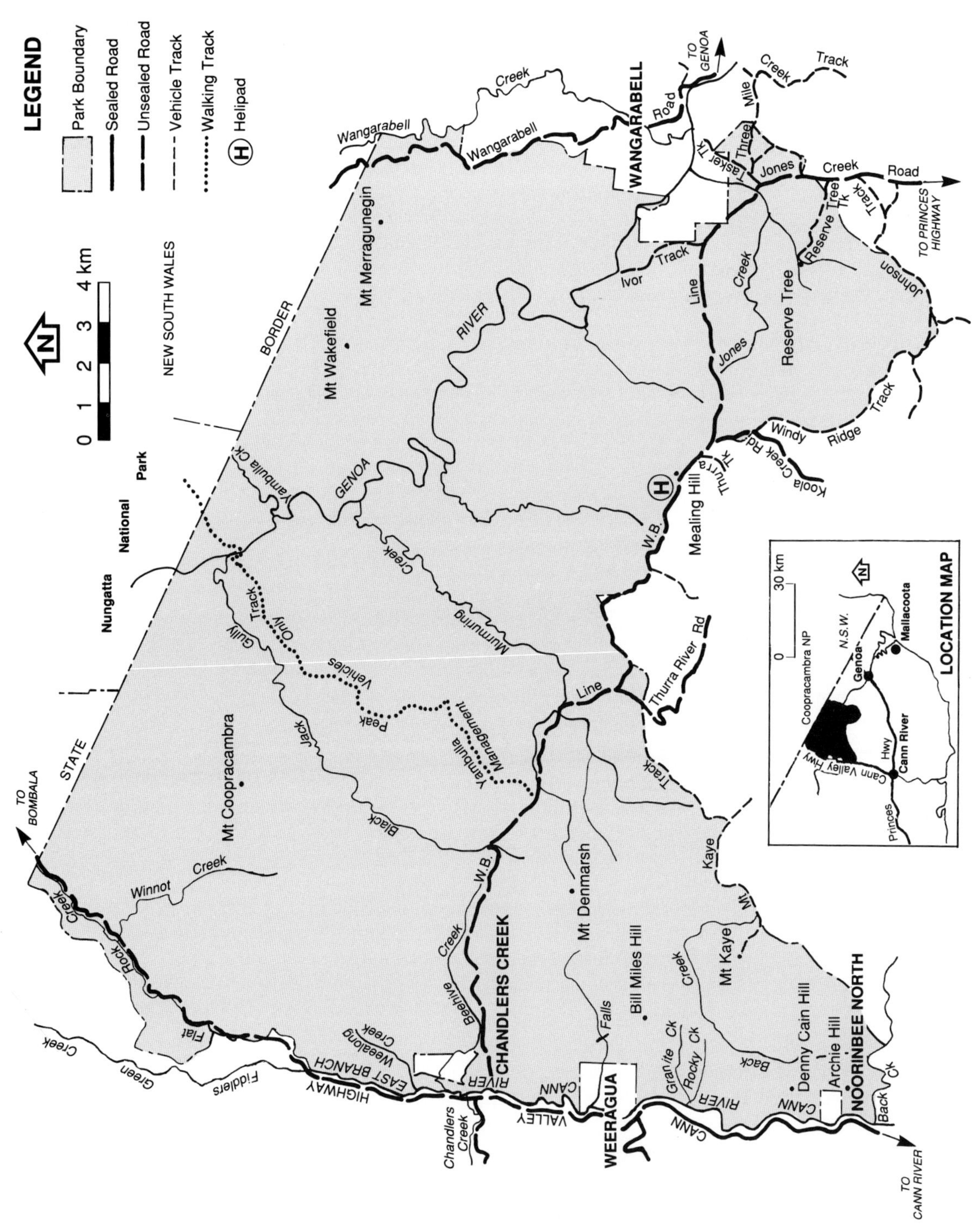

because of its rugged scenery, prominent peaks and general lack of access. One of the best climbs in East Gippsland is that to the summit of Mt Denmarsh, 870 m, in the new addition to the Park. The peak is a granitic cone ringed with impressive cliffs and affords awe-inspiring views across a vast forested area crowned with peaks such as Mt Kaye, 1 001 m, and Mt Coopracambra, 990 m, in Victoria, and Nungatta Mountain and Yambulla Peak across the border in NSW. Mt Kaye and Mt Coopracambra are also hard but rewarding climbs. Horseriding is permitted in some parts; check with C&E staff first.

Best season to visit: Spring for wildflowers; otherwise any, although the river can rise suddenly in any season.

Special features: Remoteness; spectacular scenery, especially Genoa Gorge.

Further information:
C&E Parks and Regional Information Centre, Cann River, Vic 3889. Phone (051) 58 6351.

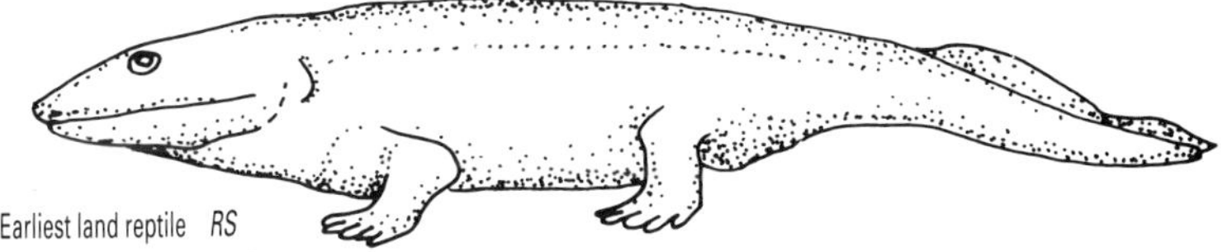

Earliest land reptile *RS*

Alfred

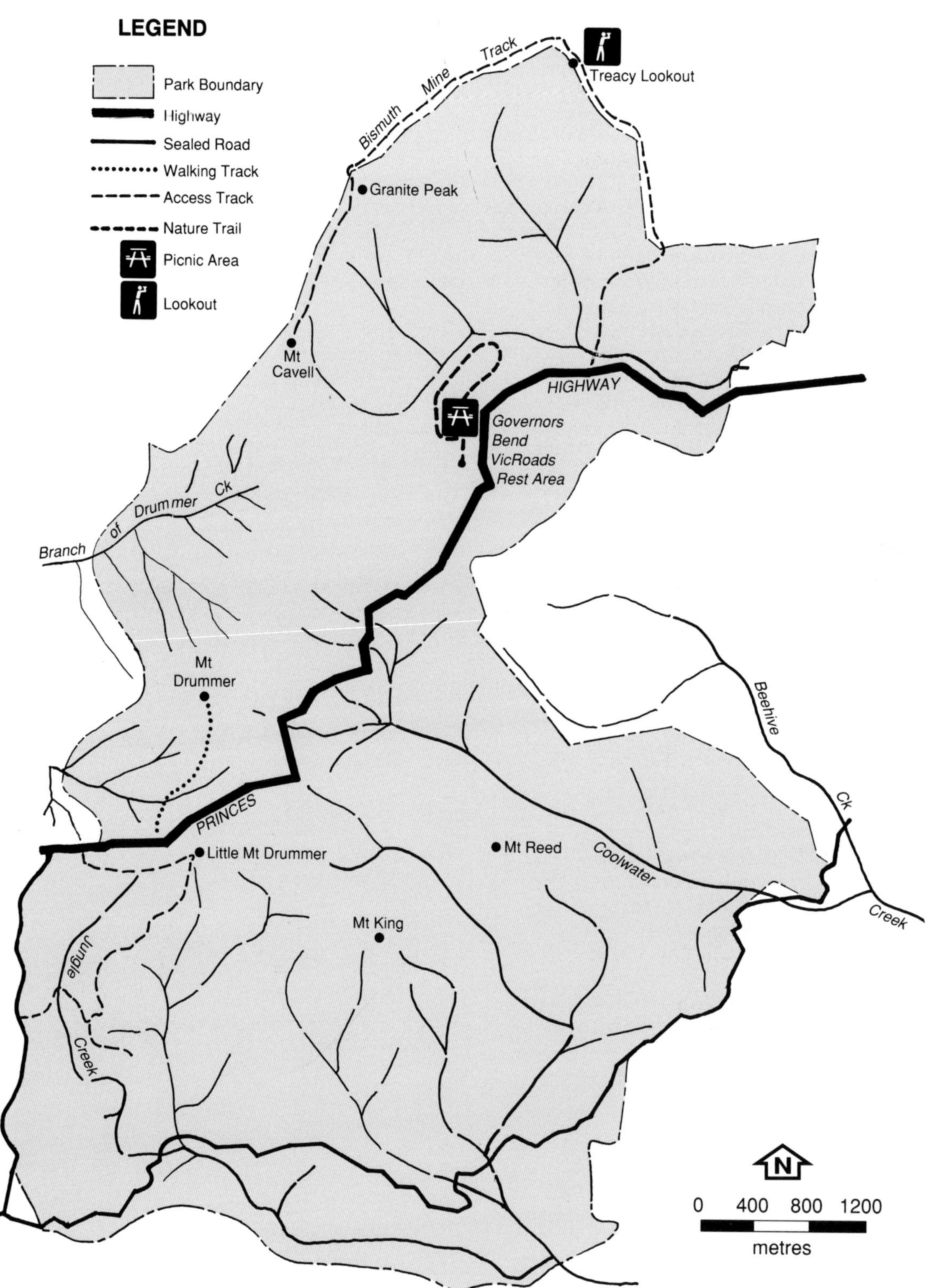

LEGEND
Park Boundary
Highway
Sealed Road
Walking Track
Access Track
Nature Trail
Picnic Area
Lookout
Bismuth Mine Track
Treacy Lookout
Granite Peak
Mt Cavell
HIGHWAY
Governors Bend VicRoads Rest Area
Branch of Drummer Ck
Mt Drummer
Beehive Ck
PRINCES
Little Mt Drummer
Mt Reed
Coolwater Creek
Mt King
Jungle Creek
0 400 800 1200
metres
N

76 Alfred National Park

Physical features: 3 050 ha. The Princes Highway runs right through Alfred NP, but few people take the time to stop here. Much of the Park, of Devonian granites intruded into Ordovician slates, lies along the slopes of a ridge which separates the catchments of the Thurra and Wingan Rivers. This upper part of the Park is steep and hilly with granite outcrops such as Mt Drummer (440 m); the lower part is of Ordovician sediments.

Plants and animals: The Drummer rainforests are the most valuable surviving stands of warm temperate rainforest in Victoria, with a great diversity of species including many which are rare and of broken distribution. All the Victorian tree-ferns grow here; Soft, Prickly, Rough and Slender, plus the Skirted, a probable natural hybrid between the Rough and Slender Tree-fern. Some of these tree-ferns have a wealth of other plants growing on their trunks, including the very primitive Long Fork-fern. The Drummer rainforests are the most accessible to the public, although entry into the rainforest is not easy as there are few walking tracks. Fortunately, whilst the rainforest margins were severely damaged or destroyed by intense crown fires in 1983, much of the closed canopy seems to have survived and the Lilly-pilly and Kanooka trees are regenerating from buds below the bark. Interestingly, one plant, Violet Nightshade, which was thought extinct in Victoria before the fire, has now dramatically increased along the margins of the rainforest. Other plants though, such as the Tangle Orchid, only occur in mature rainforest and may now be extinct at Mt Drummer.

Many of the familiar wet forest birds such as Lyrebirds, Pilot-birds, Wonga Pigeons and Ground Thrushes are here, along with rainforest species such as the Brown Flycatcher and the migratory Monarch Fly-catcher. The dry open areas are particularly rich in honeyeaters when the eucalypts are in flower.

Human history: Alfred NP was established largely as the result of the representations of two prominent naturalists – Charles Daley and Edward Pescott – to the Lands Department in 1924 and 1925. The Minister, Alfred Downard, was sympathetic, and agreed also that the park could bear his name but, as a modest man, he preferred Alfred to Downard NP, apparently declaring that there would be many Alfreds who deserved such a tribute.

Things to do: Walking. There are no access roads, only foot tracks, including a nature trail and the track up Mt Drummer. The rainforest is most accessible near Karlo Creek.

Best season to visit: Any.

Special features: Alfred NP provides a fascinating insight into the changes that occur after fire and will be well worth watching over the years.

Relevant reading:
Landscape Australia 2/85 p. 141–151 and 3/85 p. 238–244.

Further information:
C&E Parks and Regional Information Centre, Cann River, Vic 3889. Phone (051) 58 6351.

77 Lind National Park

Physical features: 1 365 ha. Lind NP is divided almost in two by Euchre Creek, which flows north-west through the Park to join the Bemm River. From 1909 the Princes Highway also ran through the park, but now a realignment takes the road along its southern border. The Park as a whole is leaf-shaped with Euchre Creek as the midrib, and smaller creeks forming the side veins. Between the creeks are dry ridges, the easternmost of which forms both the Park boundary and the watershed between the Bemm and Cann Rivers. Upper Devonian sandstones and siltstones form the bedrock of Lind NP and much of the surrounding State Forest.

Plants and animals: Lind has an interesting mix of vegetation which highlights the importance of micro-climate. Along the drier ridges are tall, open eucalypt forests of Silvertop Ash, Messmate, Grey Gum and White Stringybark with a shrubby understorey that is bright with flowers in spring, especially Pomaderris which is often mistaken for wattle. River Peppermints grow near the creeks; note their typical peppermint smell and small clustered flowers, but atypical white gum-type bark. In the valleys there is warm temperate rainforest, including waratah, as well as more widely-occurring wet gully plants. Lind is still regenerating after being badly burnt in the 1939 fires. (For animals and more detail on rainforest see East Gippsland Introduction and Croajingolong NP.)

Human history: The small settlement of Club Terrace to the north of the Park was once a gold mining town but little evidence of this remains. The Park was declared in 1926 largely to provide an attractive stopping spot along the newly created Princes Highway to Genoa.

In 1986 the Land Conservation Council (LCC) recommended that, because of Lind's small size and the incongruity of its being accorded the same status as places like Wilsons Promontory NP and Mt Buffalo NP, it should be downgraded partly to a scenic reserve and partly to state forest, with logging allowed in the latter. Although this was perhaps logical on the grounds that Lind was not only small but also had no greater conservation merit than other nearby areas, such a step was seen as a very dangerous precedent. Once the principle of revoking national park status and allowing exploitation were established, no park would be safe. Once again, Victorians showed their concern for their parks and rose to defend Lind, and the LCC recommendation was not adopted by the Government.

Things to do: Picnicking; enjoying the Euchre Valley Nature Drive (which runs along the previous route of the Princes Highway); walking.

Best season to visit: December for waratahs; otherwise any, though winter can be rather bleak.

Special features: Easily accessible warm temperate rainforest; Gippsland Waratah.

Further information:
C&E Park and Regional Information Centre, Cann River, Vic 3889. Phone (051) 58 6351.

Long Fork-fern *MS*

Lind

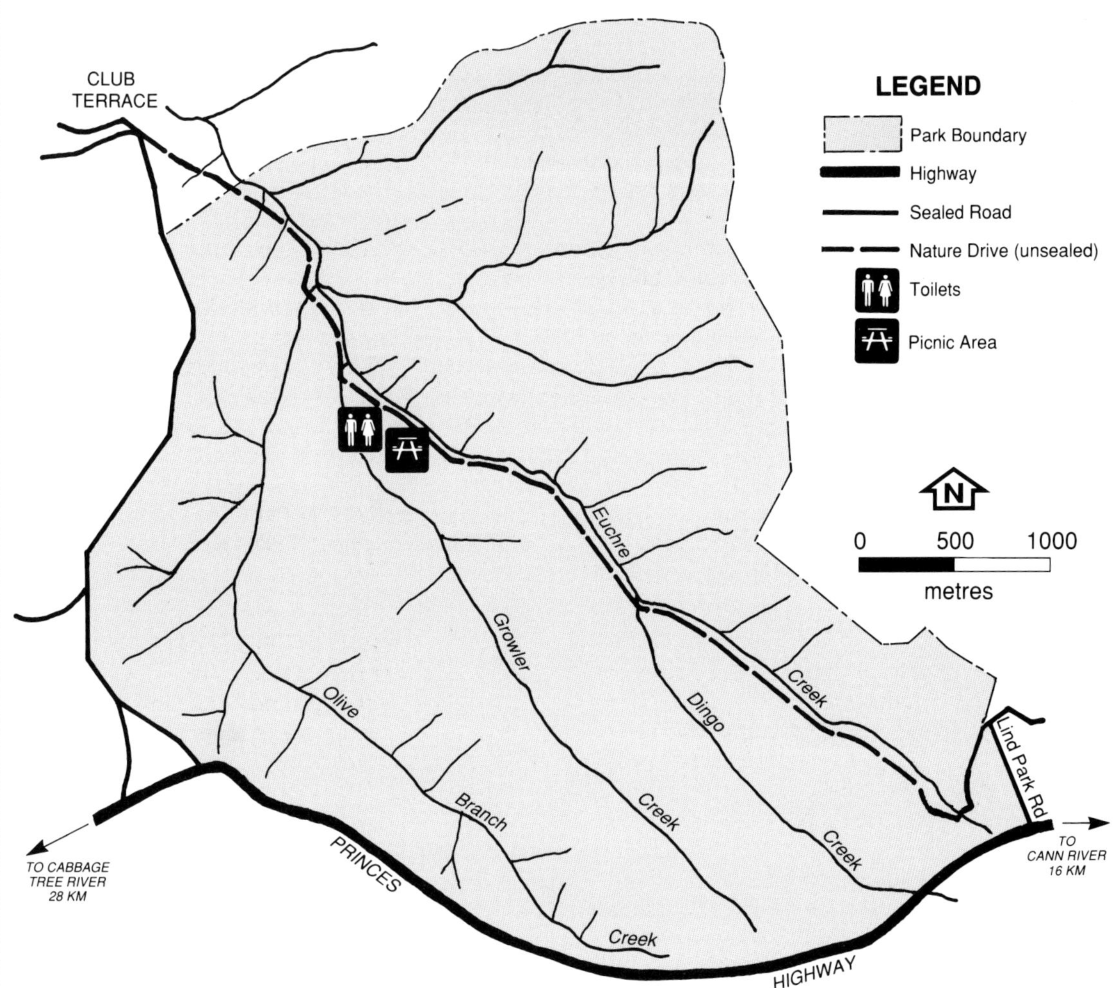
CLUB
TERRACE
LEGEND
Park Boundary
Highway
Sealed Road
Nature Drive (unsealed)
Toilets
Picnic Area
N
0
500
1000
metres
Euchre
Creek
Growler
Creek
Dingo
Creek
Olive
Branch
Creek
Lind Park Rd
PRINCES
HIGHWAY
TO CABBAGE
TREE RIVER
28 KM
TO
CANN RIVER
16 KM

78 Croajingolong National Park

Physical features: 87 500 ha. This 100 km long park, the largest in this region, is generally bounded by natural features such as coast, rivers and ridges, and includes the waters of various inlets along with a number of islands both offshore and within Mallacoota Inlet. There are two main landscape components to the Park: a moderately dissected tableland of Ordovician sediments generally of low relief and north to south bands of Lower Devonian granites, often a reddish colour, which include the higher land such as Mt Everard, Genoa Peak and the Howe Ranges, as well as coastal features such as Point Hicks and Tullaberga Island; and a coastal system, developed from the build-up of much younger sands, which provides largely undisturbed examples of dynamic coastal processes. Features formed in this way include the magnificent mobile dunes at Point Hicks, and the lagoons, which are river basins drowned by recent rises in sea level. The climate is less extreme than that of much of the rest of Victoria, although storms, with spectacular displays of lightning and sudden heavy downpours, are sometimes a feature of the area.

Plants and animals: Not only does Croajingolong have high scenic and landscape values, it is also an extremely important area for a wide variety of plants and vegetation associations, and for birds and other animals. It is here in far East Gippsland that plants characteristic of New South Wales and southern Queensland meet those from further west in Victoria, forming associations not found elsewhere. Anyone familiar with the eucalypts of central Victoria will soon be aware that bloodwoods, Silvertop and Rough-barked Apple have generally replaced stringybark and box eucalypts. Plant communities in Croajingolong range from those typical of coastal environments to patches of warm temperate rainforest in the Howe Ranges and in pockets along the coastal hinterland. These latter are often revealed by local names such as Jungle Creek. The 'jungles' of Croajingolong have the typical structure of this type of vegetation, with many liane vines, ferns and epiphytes (see also East Gippsland Parks Introduction). There are a number of epiphytic orchids here, including the aptly-named Tangle Orchid which has a thick water-absorbing outer layer to its aerial roots. A particularly interesting epiphyte, though this time a plant of the drier eucalypt forests, is the Golden Mistletoe, which is parasitic on another mistletoe, the Long-flower Mistletoe, which in turn feeds off eucalypts – the botanical equivalent of 'big fleas have smaller fleas upon their backs to bite 'em'.

The Croajingolong heathlands are of great importance too, and have a particularly spectacular spring display which includes large numbers of many different ground orchids. In all, the management plan recognises seven areas in Croajingolong as being of particular botanical significance, including the Howe Ranges and nearby areas that are still very isolated.

The heathland and dry open woodlands are particularly sensitive to burning. The correct burning regime, often still poorly understood, is of vital importance to a number of small mammals and birds such as the Long-nosed Potoroo, White-footed Dunnart, the Smoky and the New Holland Mouse, and especially the rare and endangered Ground Parrot, which requires heathland habitat burnt between 3 and 25 years previously.

Croajingolong's wide variety of habitats makes the Park an excellent area for birds, and the 250 or so recorded species include ten classified as rare. Among the more interesting birds are the Ground Parrot, Eastern Bristle-bird, Southern Emu-wren, and the handsome Glossy Black-Cockatoo, a bird not unlike the Red-tailed Black-Cockatoo but without that bird's distinctive crest. The waterbirds are a particular pleasure here and an interesting variety can be seen almost anywhere on the inlets. One that never fails to attract attention is the tiny Azure Kingfisher, often seen just as a vivid flash of blue entering the water. Equally impressive in a very different way is a White-breasted Sea-eagle as it cruises majestically above the water with slow, powerful wing beats. The heathlands and woodlands too are a delight for birdwatchers, with noisy flocks of honeyeaters and Rainbow and Musk Lorikeets as well as many smaller, quieter birds. The wetter bush and rainforest have their bird attractions too, especially the handsome purplish-black Satin Bowerbird with his curiously speckled mate and offspring. Not that they are likely to be seen together, except for a courting pair at the bower; he is a bird of many mates, which in itself indicates that these forests are sufficiently rich in food for a female to rear chicks on her own.

◀ Genoa River, Coopracambra SP *HS*

▲ Red Passion-flower *PBA*

◀ Sassafras trees, Errinundra NP *CFL*

▲ Errinundra NP *PI*

▼ Brush-tailed Phascogale *ARI*

▼ Purple Fan-flower and Shrubby Platysace *GW*

▲ Gippsland Waratah, Errinundra NP *CFL*

No account of Mallacoota's animals would be complete without mentioning those curious modern day 'dinosaurs' – the giant Goannas that frequently form a welcome committee to picnickers at Goanna Bay in Top Lake. These animals have an impressive dignity and presence that you cannot easily ignore. Rather more attractive are the Gippsland Water Dragons, but they are shyer and therefore more difficult to see. There is one animal you should keep a sharp eye out for though – the tiny Scrub or Bush Tick which for those unfortunate enough to be allergic to its bite can be very unpleasant. A quick check of yourself, and especially of children who are more vulnerable because of their smaller size, should be a matter of routine. Don't try to remove an embedded live tick; kill it first with kerosene or meths, then pull it out with tweezers using a twisting action and making sure you remove the head as well as the body.

Human history: Aborigines, members of the Krautungulung (men of the east and baysides), had been in this area for an estimated 17 700 years when Europeans arrived, and they were understandably reluctant to relinquish its rich, productive shores to the incoming settlers. The first of the settlers, Captain John Stevenson, a whaler, settled at Captains Point near today's Mallacoota in 1842 for a few years before moving further inland. Well before, in 1770, Captain James Cook had passed this way and named Point Hicks in honour of his lieutenant who first sighted the Australian mainland here. Other notable early visitors were George Bass and his crew who, during their whaleboat voyage from Sydney, took refuge in Fly Cove and explored Wingan Inlet during a storm in 1797. *HMS Beagle* with Charles Darwin aboard also passed this way in 1843. The coast was often rough and stormy and a number of shipwrecks occurred before the Gabo Island and Cape Everard (Point Hicks) lighthouses were erected in 1862 and 1890 respectively.

Although fishing is an important local industry, agriculture has never been so in far East Gippsland, both because of small local populations and the distance from larger markets. Timber harvesting has been far more significant, particularly post World War II with logging of railway sleepers for export and of saw-logs for local mills. There has also been some grazing, bee-keeping and gravel and sand extraction, most of which has now ceased or is under review (see Management Plan below for further details). There was even a small goldmine, the Spotted Dog Mine, east of Mallacoota, and relics of this 1890's operation can still be seen by those prepared to take a boat across to Cemetery Point, near the site of the first Mallacoota settlement.

This Park was one of many declared by the Victorian Government on 26 April, 1979 to commemorate the centenary of the declaration of Australia's first national park, Royal NP near Sydney. Within the boundaries of Croajingolong NP were included three small existing national parks – Captain James Cook, Wingan Inlet and Mallacoota. The first of these, Captain James Cook, was declared on 20 Apri1, 1970 to commemorate the bicentenary of Captain Cook's first sighting of the Australian continent, but it was a pocket-handerchief of a park, 2 750 ha, far too small for adequate habitat protection, and to make matters worse, some of its boundaries cut right across important ecological associations, dramatically reducing its value.

Together with the adjoining Nadgee Nature Reserve in New South Wales, Croajingolong is now part of the Croajingolong National Park Biosphere Reserve declared under the UNESCO 'Man and the Biosphere Program'. This declaration, though not imposing any legal constraints upon management, does imply an obligation to carry out the principles of the Biosphere Program.

Things to do: Camping (the most popular activity); fishing; boating; swimming; sunbathing; and surfing. There is an excellent range of walks from long, demanding beach and near wilderness walks to easy family walks, especially around the holiday centres. Croajingolong is a wonderful place too for photography, birdwatching and studying natural history generally.

Best season to visit: Any; the climate here is generally milder in summer and winter than elsewhere in Victoria. Spring for wildflowers in the heathlands.

Special features: Idyllic coastal and estuarine scenery, often very uncrowded; the range of walks; flocks of waterbirds on the estuaries and inlets; altogether such an enchanting place that it's hard not to want to keep it to one's self!

Croajingolong

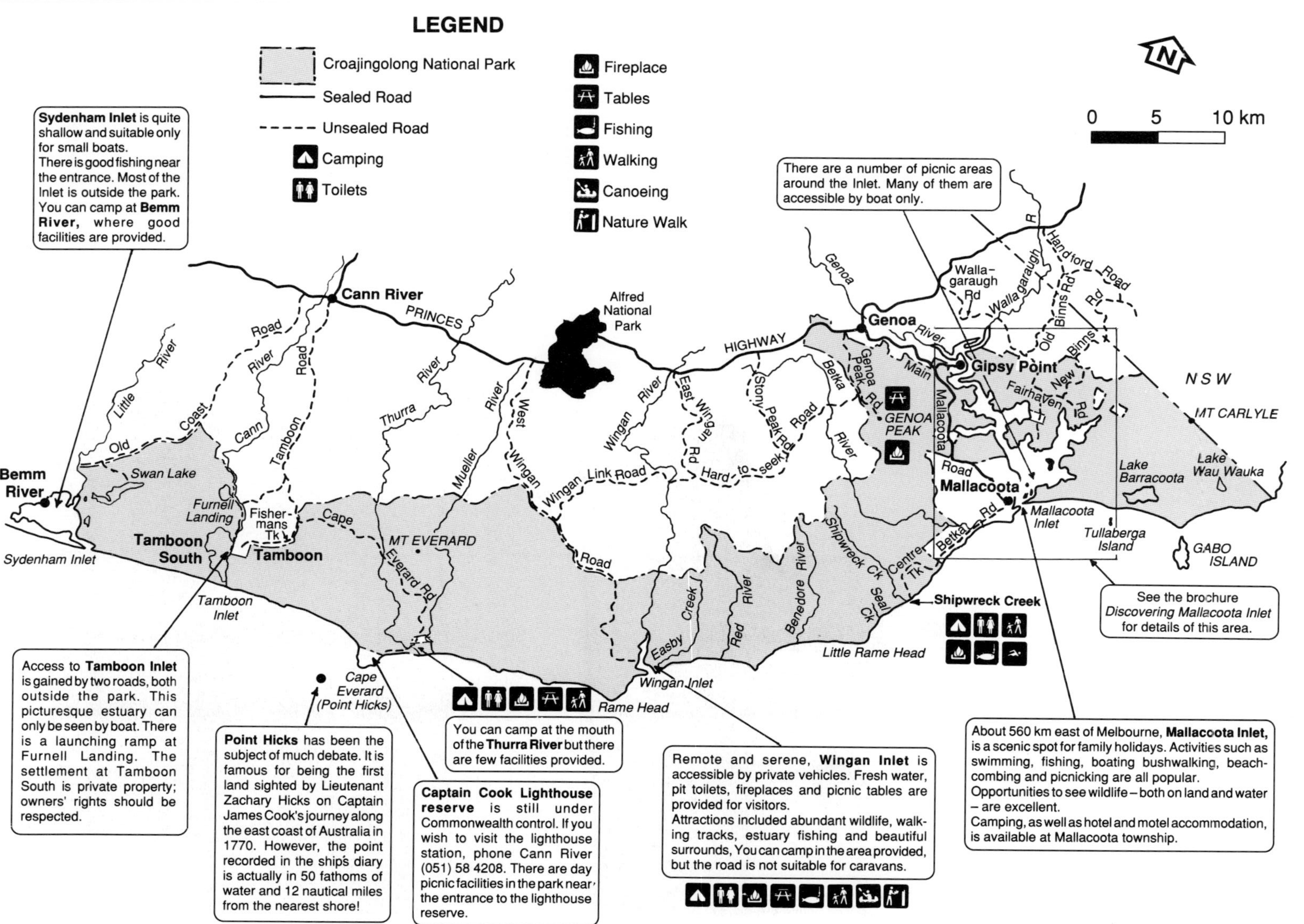

Relevant reading:
Conservation Forests and Lands (1985) *Croajingolong NP Draft Management Plan*.
Friends of Mallacoota (1986) *Stepping Stones: a guide to Mallacoota and District*.
Mallacoota School (1979) *Birds of Mallacoota*.

Further information:
Park Office, Princes Highway, Cann River, Vic 3889. Phone (051) 58 6351.

Wreck of SS Saros, 1937 *CFL*

Appendices

Wedge-tailed Eagle *CFL*

Geological time scale

ERA	MILLIONS OF YEARS AGO	PERIOD	GEOLOGICAL EVENTS IN VICTORIA
Cainozoic	Present ▼ 2	Quaternary	Newer volcanics form vast lava plain in western Victoria. Marine transgression and regression. Uplift of Eastern Highlands and around basins. Sedimentation including aeolian and calcareous stranded dunes. Extinction of Australian megafauna.
	2 ▼ 65	Tertiary	Final fragmentation of Gondwana as Australia separates from Antarctica. Brown coal laid down in the La Trobe Valley. Older volcanics, generally in eastern Victoria.
Mesozoic	65 ▼ 140	Cretaceous	Fragmentation of Gondwana continues. Much sedimentation in the Otway, Bass and Gippsland Basins. Uplift of the Otway Ranges. Flowering plants appear.
	140 ▼ 195	Jurassic	Splitting apart of Gondwana, the southern super-continent, associated with basaltic outpourings and volcanic activity. Warm to cool climate. Wide variety of plant remains.
	195 ▼ 230	Triassic	Much of eastern Australia folded, uplifted and eroded. Cool temperate climate with lagoons and swamps. Dinosaurs and mammals appear.
Palaeozoic	230 ▼ 280	Permian	Most of southern Australia glaciated, rises in sea level as icecaps melt. Long period of stability with erosion and deposition of sediments, including glacial tillite. Coal swamps. First conifers.
	280 ▼ 345	Carboniferous	Eastern Victoria dry, south and west under the sea. Increasing cold with glacial activity to the north. Folding, faulting and erosion of sediments. Reduced diversity of plants and animals. Reptiles appear.
	345 ▼ 395	Devonian	Almost all Victoria above the sea, climate warm. Mountain building and earth movements in the cast. Volcanic activity especially in the cauldrons of central Victoria. Major diversification of fish and land vegetation.
	395 ▼ 435	Silurian	Much of Australia dry but Victoria still largely under water. Erosion of uplifted land. Laying down of Grampians sediments and volcanic activity in western Victoria. First land plants.
	435 ▼ 500	Ordovician	Rocks widespread. Rapid diversification of animals, and deposition of fossil-rich rocks, generally in deep warm seas. Much folding of rocks and mountain building. Gold-bearing rocks formed.
	500 ▼ 570	Cambrian	Most of eastern Australia under deep warm seas. Volcanic activity followed by marine deposition and sedimentation. Oldest known rocks in Victoria, but few outcrops. Wide variety of animals, all plants marine. Few fossils.

Common and scientific names

PLANTS

Fungi

Cinnamon Fungus	*Phytophthora cinnamomi*
Ghost Fungus	*Pleurotus nidiformis*

Mosses, Ferns & Fern Allies

Bristle-fern, Veined	*Polyphlebium venosum*
Fork-fern, Long	*Tmesipteris billardieri*
Skeleton	*Psilotum nudum*
Moss, Sphagnum	*Sphagnum spp.*
Spleenwort, Willow	*Asplenium polyodon*
Treefern, Rough	*Cyathea australis*
Slender	*C. cunninghamii*
Skirted	*C. marcescens*
Soft	*Dicksonia antarctica*

Pines

Cypress-pine, Black	*Callitris endlicheri*
Scrub	*C. verrucosa*
Slender	*C. preissii*
White	*C. glaucophylla*
Pine, Murray (see White Cypress-pine)	
Mountain Plum	*Podocarpus lawrencei*
Oyster Bay	*Callitris rhomboidea*

Flowering Plants

Apple, Rough-barked	*Angophora floribunda*
Ash, Mountain	*Eucalyptus regnans*
Baeckea, Fern-leaf	*Baeckea crenatifolia*
Rosy	*B. ramosissima*
Ballart, Cherry	*Exocarpos cupressiformis*
Banksia, Coast	*Banksia integrifolia*
Hairpin	*B. spinulosa*
Saw	*B. serrata*
Silver	*B. marginata*
Banyalla	*Pittosporum bicolor*
Beard-heath	*Leucopogon sp.*
Beard-heath, Veined	*Leucopogon neurophyllus*
Beech, Myrtle	*Nothofagus cunninghamii*
Berrigan	*Eremophila longifolia*
Berry, Baw Baw	*Wittsteinia vacciniacea*
Crimson	*Cyathodes juniperina*
Bitter-pea, Hop	*Daviesia latifolia*
Blackwood	*Acacia melanoxylon*
Blanket-leaf	*Bedfordia arborescens*
Blue-lily, Nodding	*Stypandra glauca*
Tufted	*Thelionema caespitosum*
Boneseed(*)	*Chrysanthemoides monilifera*
Boobialla	*Myoporum insulare*
Boronia, Blue	*Boronia caerulescens*
Forest	*B. muelleri*
Sticky	*B. anemonifolia*
Bottlebrush, Prickly	*Callistemon brachyandrus*
River	*C. sieberi*

Box, Black	*Eucalyptus largiflorens*
Blue	*E. bauerana*
Grey	*E. microcarpa*
Long-leaved	*E. goniocalyx*
Red	*E. polyanthemos*
Yellow	*E. melliodora*
Boxthorn, African (*)	*Lycium ferocissimum*
Brown-barrel	*Eucalyptus fastigiata*
Buloke	*Allocasuarina leuhmannii*
Bush-pea, Mt Byron	*Pultenaea patellifolia*
Scented	*P. graveolens*
Buttercup, Australian	*Ranunculus lappaceus*
Button-grass	*Gymnoschoenus sphaerocephalus*
Buttons, Wrinkled	*Leptorhynchos gatesii*
Caladenia, Blue	*Caladenia caerulea*
Cardoon (*)	*Cirsium vulgare*
Cassia, Desert	*Cassia nemophila*
Cattle-bush	*Heterodendron oleifolium*
Cat's Claw	*Grevillea alpina*
Christmas-bush, Victorian	*Prostanthera lasianthos*
Clematis, Forest	*Clematis glycinoides*
Cooba, Small	*Acacia ligulata*
Correa, Common	*Correa reflexa*
Mountain	*C. lawrenciana*
Rock	*C. glabra*
White	*C. alba*
Crowea, Small	*Crowea exalata*
Cushion-bush	*Calocephalus brownii*
Cut-tail (see Brown-barrel)	
Daisy-bush, Musk	*Olearia argophylla*
Velvet	*O. pannosa*
Duckweed, Tiny	*Wolffia australiana*
Early Nancy	*Wurmbea dioica*
Eumong	*Acacia stenophylla*
Eutaxia	*Eutaxia microphylla*
Everlasting, Grey	*Helichrysum obcordatum*
Rosemary	*H. rosmarinifolium*
Eyebright, Purple	*Euphrasia collina*
Fan-palm, Cabbage	*Livistona australis*
Fieldia	*Fieldia australis*
Geebung, Forest	*Persoonia silvatica*
Grass, Kangaroo	*Themeda triandra*
Marram (*)	*Ammophila arenaria*
Porcupine	*Triodia irritans*
Grass-tree, Austral	*Xanthorrhea australis*
Greenhood, Winter	*Pterostylis fischii*
Grevillea, Branching	*Grevillea ramossisima*
Brisbane Ranges	*G. steiglitziana*
Golden	*G. chrysophaea*
Green	*G. jephcottii*
Rosemary	*G. rosmarinifolia*
Groundsel, Variable	*Senecio lautus*
Guinea-flower	*Hibbertia sp.*
Gum, Blakely's Red	*Eucalyptus blakelyi*
Blue	*E. globulus*
Candlebark	*E. rubida*

Mountain Grey	*E. cypellocarpa*
Mountain Swamp	*E. camphora*
River Red	*E. camaldulensis*
Shining	*E. nitens*
Snow	*E. pauciflora*
Spotted	*E. maculata*
Swamp	*E. ovata*
Yellow	*E. leucoxylon*
Hardenbergia, Purple	*Hardenbergia violacea*
Heath, Common	*Epacris impressa*
Heath-myrtle	*Micromyrtus ciliata*
Hop-bush, Wedge-leaf	*Dodonea viscosa*
Ironbark, Red	*Eucalyptus sideroxylon*
Kanooka	*Tristaniopsis laurina*
Kunzea, Violet	*Kunzea parvifolia*
Kurrajong	*Brachychiton populneus*
Leatherwood, Eastern	*Eucryphia moorei*
Leek-orchid, Maroon	*Prasophyllum hartii*
Lilly-pilly	*Acmena smithii*
Lily, Pincushion	*Borya mirabilis*
Logania, Oval-leaf	*Logania ovata*
Lomatia, Tree	*Lomatia fraseri*
Mallee, Blue	*Eucalyptus polybractea*
Gippsland	*E. kitsoniana*
Green	*E. viridis*
Yellow	*E. incrassata*
Kamarooka	*E. froggattii*
Bull	*E. behriana*
Slender-leaf	*E. foecunda*
Soap	*E. diversifolia*
Mint-bush, Rough	*Prostanthera denticulata*
Mistletoe, Drooping	*Amyema pendulum*
Golden	*Notothixos subaureus*
Grey	*Amyema quandang*
Mock-olive, Large	*Notolaea venosa*
Privet	*N. ligustrina*
Moonah	*Meleleuca lanceolata*
Morning-flag	*Orthrosanthus multiflorus*
Mulberry, Austral	*Hedycarya angustifolia*
Mutton-wood	*Rapanea howittiana*
Nealie	*Acacia rigens*
Noonflower, Rounded	*Disphyma crassifolium*
Oliveberry, Black	*Elaeocarpus holopetalus*
Blue	*E. reticulatus*
Onion-orchid, Notched	*Microtis orbicularis*
Orchid, Butterfly (see Gunn's Orchid)	
Gunn's	*Sarcochilus australis*
Tangle	*Plectorrhiza tridentata*
Wax-lip	*Glossodia major*
Oxylobium, Tall	*Oxylobium arborescens*
Passion-flower, Red	*Passiflora cinnabarina*
Pepper, Alpine	*Tasmania xerophila*
Peppermint, Broad-leaved	*Eucalyptus dives*
Narrow-leaved	*E. radiata*
Shining	*E. willisii*
Phebalium, Silvery	*Phebalium bullatum*

Common name	Botanical name
Pittosporum, Sweet	*Pittosporum undulatum*
Pomaderris, Hazel	*Pomaderris aspera*
Rusty	*P. ferruginea*
Purslane, White	*Montia australasica*
Quandong, Sweet	*Santalum acuminatum*
Rocket, Sea	*Cakile maritima*
Rusty-pods	*Hovea montana*
Sallee, Mt Buffalo	*Eucalyptus mitchelliana*
White	*E. pauciflora*
Saltbush, Grey	*Atriplex cinerea*
Sandalwood, Northern	*Santalum lanceolatum*
Sassafras, Southern	*Atherosperma moschatum*
Satinwood	*Phebalium squameum*
Scent-bark	*Eucalyptus aromaphloia*
Sea-box	*Alyxia buxifolia*
She-oak, Black	*Allocasuarina littoralis*
Drooping	*A. stricta*
Silvertop	*Eucalyptus sieberi*
Speedwell, Diggers'	*Parahebe perfoliata*
Star-bush, Lemon	*Asterolasia astericophora*
Spinifex, Hairy	*Spinifex sericeus*
Stringybark, Brown	*Eucalyptus baxteri*
Messmate	*E. obliqua*
Red	*E. macrorhyncha*
Silver-leaved	*E. cinerea*
Sundew, Scented	*Drosera whittakeri*
Sunray, Hoary	*Helipterum albicans*
Tea-tree, Button	*Leptospermum micromyrtus*
Coast	*L. laevigatum*
Mallee	*L. coriaceum*
Shiny	*L. nitidum*
Silky	*L. myrsinoides*
Woolly	*L. lanigerum*
Three-corner Jack (*)	*Emex australis*
Thryptomene, Grampians	*Thryptomene calycina*
Ribbed	*T. micrantha*
Turkey-bush	*Myoporum deserti*
Violet, Ivy-leaf	*Viola hederacea*
Waratah, Gippsland	*Telopea oreades*
Water-mat	*Lepilaena sp.*
Wattle, Bent-leaf	*Acacia flexifolia*
Black	*A. mearnsii*
Buffalo Sallow	*A. phlebophylla*
Coast	*A. sophorae*
Deane's	*A. deanei*
Golden	*A. pycnantha*
Phantom	*A. phasmoides*
Red	*A. silvestris*
Rock	*A. rupicola*
Silver	*A. dealbata*
Three-nerve	*A. trineura*
Whirakee	*A. williamsonii*
Wedding Bush	*Ricinocarpos pinifolius*
Westringia, Slender	*Westringia eremicola*
Violet	*W. glabra*
Whipstick	*W. crassifolia*

Wheel-fruit	*Gyrostemon australasicus*
Wonga-vine	*Pandorea pandorana*
Wood-sorrel, Creeping	*Oxalis corniculata*
Yellow-wood	*Acronychia oblongifolia*
Yertchuk	*Eucalyptus consideniana*

MAMMALS

Antechinus, Brown	*Antechinus stuartii*
Swamp	*A. minimus*
Yellow-footed	*A. flavipes*
Bandicoot, Eastern Barred	*Perameles gunnii*
Bobuck, see Mountain Brushtail Possum	
Devil, Tasmanian	*Sarcophilus harrisii*
Diprotodon (E)	*Diprotodon sp*
Dolphin, Bottle-nosed	*Tursiops truncatus*
Dunnart, White-footed	*Sminthopsis leucopus*
Echidna	*Tachyglossus aculeatus*
Fruit-bat	*Pteropus sp.*
Fur-seal, Australian	*Arctocephalus pusillus*
Glider, Feathertail	*Acrobates pygmaeus*
Greater	*Petauroides volans*
Squirrel	*Petaurus norfolcensis*
Sugar	*P. breviceps*
Hog-deer, Asian (*)	*Axis porcinus*
Hopping-mouse, Mitchell's	*Notomys mitchelli*
Kangaroo, Eastern Grey	*Macropus giganteus*
Giant (E)	*Sthenurus sp.*
Red	*Macropus rufus*
Western grey	*M. fuliginosus*
Koala	*Phascolarctos cinereus*
Lion, Marsupial (E)	*Thylacoleo carnifex*
Mouse, New Holland	*Pseudomys novaehollandiae*
Silky	*P. apodemoides*
Smoky	*P. fumeus*
Ningaui, Mallee	*Ningaui yvonneae*
Phascogale, Brush-tailed	*Phascogale tapoatafa*
Platypus	*Ornithorhynchus anatinus*
Possum, Common Brushtail	*Trichosurus vulpecula*
Leadbeater's	*Gymnobelidus leadbeateri*
Mountain Brushtail	*Trichosurus caninus*
Potoroo, Long-footed	*Potorous longipes*
Pygmy-possum, Eastern	*Cercartetus nanus*
Mountain	*Burramys parvus*
Western	*Cercartetus concinnus*
Rabbit-rat, White-footed (?E)	*Hapalotis albipes*
Rat, Bush	*Rattus fuscipes*
Heath	*Pseudomys shortridgei*
Water	*R. lutreolus*
Rock-wallaby, Brush-tailed	*Petrogale pencillata*
Thylacine (?E)	*Thylacinus cynocephalus*
Tree-kangaroo	*Dendrolagus sp.*
Tuan (see Phascogale, Brush-tailed)	
Wallaby, Red-necked	*Macropus rufogriseus*
Swamp	*Wallabia bicolor*
Wombat, Common	*Vombatus ursinus*

BIRDS

Albatross, Wandering	*Diomeda exulans*
Bee-eater, Rainbow	*Merops ornatus*
Bellbird, Crested	*Oreoica gutturalis*
Black-Cockatoo, Glossy	*Calyptorhyncus lathami*
Yellow-tailed	*C. funereus*
Red-tailed	*C. magnificus*
Bower-bird, Satin	*Ptilonorhynchus violaceus*
Spotted	*Chlamydera maculata*
Bristle-bird, Eastern	*Dasyornis brachypterus*
Rufous	*D. broadbenti*
Bronzewing, Brush	*Phaps elegans*
Common	*P. chalcoptera*
Bustard, Australian	*Ardeotis australis*
Cockatoo, Pine	*Cacatua leadbeateri*
Sulphur-crested	*C. galerita*
Coot, Eurasian	*Fulica atra*
Cuckoo, Channel-billed	*Scythrops novahollandiae*
Cuckoo-shrike, Ground	*Coracina maxima*
Dollarbird	*Eurystomus orientalis*
Duck, Blue-billed	*Oxyura australis*
Freckled	*Stictonetta naevosa*
Eagle, Wedge-tailed	*Aquila audax*
Emu	*Dromaius novaehollandiae*
Emu-wren, Southern	*Stipiturus malachurus*
Fairy-wren, Splendid	*Malurus splendens*
Variegated	*M. lamberti*
Falcon, Peregrine	*Falco peregrinus*
Fantail, Grey	*Rhipidura fuliginosa*
Firetail, Beautiful	*Emblema bella*
Friar bird	*Philemon sp.*
Gang-gang	*Callocephalon fimbriatum*
Gannet, Australian	*Morus serrator*
Goose, Cape Barren	*Cereopsis novaehollandiae*
Ground-thrush, Australian	*Zooathera dauma*
Heathwren, Shy (or Mallee)	*Sericornis cautus*
Honeyeater, Black	*Certhionyx niger*
Helmeted	*Lichenostomus cassidix*
Pied	*Certhionyx variegata*
Tawny-crowned	*Phylidonyris melanops*
Yellow-tufted	*Lichenostomus melanops*
Kingfisher, Azure	*Ceyx azureus*
Kookaburra, Laughing	*Dacelo gigas*
Knot, Red	*Calidris canutus*
Lorikeet, Musk	*Glossopsitta concinna*
Rainbow	*Trichoglossus haematodus*
Lowan (see Malleefowl)	
Lyrebird, Superb	*Menura novaehollandiae*
Malleefowl	*Leipoa ocellata*
Magpie	*Gymnorhina tibicen*
Miner, Bell	*Manorina melanophrys*
Monarch, Black-faced	*Monarcha melanopsis*
Mutton bird (see Shearwater, Short-tailed)	
Owl, Boobook	*Ninox novaeseelandiae*
Powerful	*N. strenua*
Sooty	*Tyto tenebricosa*

Parrot, Blue-winged	*Neophema chrysostoma*
Ground	*Pezoporus wallicus*
King	*Alisterus scapularis*
Mulga	*Psephotus varius*
Orange-bellied	*Neophema chrysogaster*
Regent	*Polytelis anthopeplus*
Scarlet-chested	*Neophema splendida*
Turquoise	*N. pulchella*
Pelican, Australian	*Pelecanus conspicillatus*
Penguin, Fairy (see Little Penguin)	
Little	*Eudyptula minor*
Pilot bird	*Pycnoptilus flocculosus*
Pipit, Richard's	*Anthus novaeseelandiae*
Quail, King	*Coturnix chinensis*
Quail-thrush	*Cinclosoma sp.*
Redthroat	*Sericornis brunneus*
Ringneck, Mallee	*Barnardius barnardi*
Robin, Flame	*Petroica phoenica*
Red-capped	*P. goodenovii*
Rose	*P. rosea*
Pink	*P. rodinogaster*
Rosella, Crimson	*Platycercus elegans*
Yellow	*P. flaveolus*
Sandpiper, Short-tailed	*Calidris acuminata*
Scrub-robin, Southern	*Drymodes brunneopygia*
Scrub-wren, White-browed	*Sericornis frontalis*
Sea-eagle, White-breasted	*Haliaeetus leucogaster*
Shearwater, Fluttering	*Puffinus gavia*
Short-tailed	*P. tenuirostris*
Shrike-thrush, Grey	*Colluricincla harmonica*
Shrike-tit, Crested	*Falcunculus frontatus*
Snipe, Japanese	*Gallinago hardwickii*
Stint, Red-necked	*Calidris ruficollis*
Spinebill, Eastern	*Acanthorhynchus tenuirostris*
Stilt, Banded	*Cladorhynchus leucocephalus*
Swan, Black	*Cygnus atratus*
Teal, Chestnut	*Anas castanea*
Tern, Crested	*Sterna bergii*
Little	*S. albifrons*
Thick-knee, Bush	*Burhinus magnirostris*
Thornbill, Samphire	*Acanthiza iredalei*
Thrush, Scaly (see Ground-thrush, Australian)	
Tree-creeper, Brown	*Climacteris picumnus*
Wattlebird	*Anthochaera sp.*
Whistler, Gilbert's	*Pachycephala inornata*
Rufous	*P. olivacea*
Woodswallow	*Artamus sp.*

REPTILES

Bandy Bandy	*Vermicella annulata*
Dragon, Earless	*Tympanocryptis cephalus*
Goanna	*Varanus gouldii*
Lizard, Burton's Legless	*Lialis burtonis*
Monitor, Lace	*Varanus varius*
Python, Carpet	*Morelia spilota*

Shingle-back	*Trachydosaurus rugosa*
Skink, Mourning	*Egernia luctuosa*
Snake, Tiger	*Notechis scutatus*
Yellow-faced Whip	*Demansia psammophis*
Tortoise, Freshwater	*Chelodina longicollis*
Water-dragon, Gippsland	*Phyisgnathus lesueurii howittii*

AMPHIBIANS

Frog, Baw Baw	*Philoria frostii*
Green and Golden Bell	*Litoria aurea*
Long-thumbed	*Limnodynastes fletcheri*
Giant Spotted Burrowing	*Heleioporus australiacus*
Great Barred	*Mixophyes faciolatus*

FISH

Galaxiids	*Galaxias spp.*
Cod, Murray	*Maccullochella peeli*
Sea-horse	*Hippocampus sp.*

INVERTEBRATES

Bogong Moth	*Agrotis infusa*
Butterfly, Imperial White	*Delias harpalyce*
Earthworm, Giant Gippsland	*Megascolides australis*
Snail, Otways Black	*Victaphanta compacta*
Tick, Bush or Scrub	*Ixodes holocyclus*

(*) = introduced
(E) = extinct

Origins of park names

Alfred NP – after Alfred Downard, Minister for Lands and Water Supply at the time of declaration.

Angahook-Lorne SP – 'hook' a projecting headland or sharp river bend, associated with the Anglesea district; Lorne from the Marquis of Lorne.

Arthurs Seat SP – from the similarity Lieutenant Grant saw to Edinburgh Hill, associated with legends of King Arthur.

Avon Wilderness – from Avon River, named by Angus McMillan, perhaps after (Stratford on) Avon.

Barmah SP – Aboriginal *paama,* a meeting place.

Baw Baw NP – was pronounced 'bo-bo'; either Aboriginal *bo-ye* ghost, or *bo-bo* bandicoots. In 1846 Tyers named it Mt Bow Bow – echo.

Beechworth Historic Park – surveyor Smyth's Leicestershire birthplace.

Big Desert Wilderness – from the early settlers' perception of the land's agricultural potential.

Black Range SP – descriptive of its appearance.

Bogong – from the *bugong* moths which migrate here each summer.

Brisbane Ranges NP – after Sir Thomas Brisbane, Governor of NSW from 1821–5.

Burrowa-Pine Mountain NP – from the Aboriginal *burrowye* towards the east; and Pine from the native cypresses here.

Cape Nelson SP – Lieutenant Grant sighted this landmark from the *Lady Nelson* in 1800.

Carlisle SP – either after the northern English city, or politician Joseph Carlisle.

Cathedral Range SP – descriptive of one of the peaks in this rugged range.

Chiltern SP – from the nearby township, named after the Chiltern Hills in England.

Churchill NP – a re-naming of Dandenong NP in honour of Sir Winston Churchill.

Cobberas-Tingaringy – from the Aboriginal *koburra* the head, and *tingira* the sea.

Coopracambra SP – Aboriginal for kookaburra.

Croajingolong NP – from the Aboriginal *krauatungalong* the men of the east and of the bayside.

Dandenong Ranges NP – from the Aboriginal *tanjenong* high mountain.

Discovery Bay Coastal Park – sighted by Major Mitchell in 1836.

Eildon SP – after the three Eildon Hills in Scotland, the reputed burial place of King Arthur.

Errinundra NP – perhaps from the Aboriginal *erraneen* to tattle.

Fraser NP – after the Hon. A.J. Fraser MP, who steered the National Parks Bill through the Victorian Parliament in 1956.

French Island SP – named by either Capt. Baudin or Capt. Hamelin from the 1800 French scientific voyage.

Gellibrand Hill Park – after Joseph Gellibrand who explored the Upper Barwon in 1875.

Gippsland Lakes Coastal Park – after Sir George Gipps, Governor of NSW 1838–46.

Grampians NP – named by Major Mitchell after the Grampians Range in his Scottish homeland.

Hattah-Kulkyne NP – Hattah, probably Scottish, the name of an early property; Kulkyne from Aboriginal for howling dingo.

Holey Plains SP – from the property, pitted with crab holes, of which the Park was once part.

Kamarooka SP – Aboriginal for wait-a-while.

Kara Kara SP – Aboriginal for gold and quartz.

Kinglake NP – after Alexander Kinglake, a surveyor.

Kooyoora SP – uncertain, perhaps from the Aboriginal *koo-o-yoro* a bat, or *koorooro* night.

Lake Albacutya SP – from the Aboriginal *ngelbakutya* place of bitter quandongs.

Langi Ghiran SP – Aboriginal *lar-ne-jeering* home of the Black Cockatoo.

Langwarrin Flora and Fauna Reserve – named Longwaring (long waiting) by William Willoby, a Scot.

Lerderderg SP – from the Aboriginal *lairdedairk*, perhaps *larb* stone house, and *darrk* peppermint gums.

Lind NP – after Sir Albert Lind, a grazier and the Member for East Gippsland from 1920–61 in the Victorian Legislative Assembly.

Little Desert NP – how the early settlers saw it.

Lower Glenelg NP – named by Major Mitchell for the Secretary of State for the Colonies.

Long Forest Flora Reserve – perhaps by Capt. Bacchus after Long Forest on the Welsh border.

Lysterfield Park – from local resident William Lysterfield, a producer of grand opera.

Melba Gully SP – named in honour of Dame Nellie Melba.

Mitchell River NP – named by Angus McMillan after Major Thomas Mitchell.

Moondarra SP – from the Aboriginal *mundara* much rain and thunder.

Morwell NP – from the Shire and nearby town, named after the Morwell rocks in Devon, England.

Mount Arapiles-Tooan SP – after Mt Arapiles in Spain (where Major Mitchell fought under the Duke Of Wellington); and from the Aboriginal *too-an* the tuan.

Mount Buffalo NP – descriptive of the bulky shape of this range.

Mount Eccles SP – a mis-spelling of 'Eeles', a military colleague of Major Mitchell.

Mount Napier SP – named by Major Mitchell after Colonel Napier.

Mount Richmond NP – name of pioneer Stephen Henty's house at Portland and of his son.

Mount Samaria SP – named by a surveyor after the one-time capital of Northern Israel.

Murray-Kulkyne Park – from the Kulkyne property; and the River Murray, named by explorer Charles Sturt for the Secretary of State for Colonies.

Nyerimilang Park – Aboriginal for chain of many lakes.

Organ Pipes NP – from the basalt columns in the Park.

Otway NP – named Cape Albany Otway by Lieutenant Grant in 1800 to honour his friend Capt. William Albany Otway.

Phillip Island Penguin Reserve – this island's name has changed from Snapper Island to Grant Island to Isle of the English. Its final name came from Bass in honour of Captain Arthur Phillip.

Pink Lakes SP – from an orange pigment in microscopic plants living in these salty lakes.

Point Nepean NP – named by Lieutenant Murray after Sir Evan Nepean, Secretary to the Admiralty.

Port Campbell NP – first known as Campbell's Creek after Capt. Alexander Campbell, 'the last of the buccaneers'.

Reef Hills Park – from the low hills, once mined for gold, in this Park.

Snowy River NP – descriptive of the mountains where this river arises.

South Gippsland Marine and Coastal Parks – after Sir George Gipps, Governor of NSW from 1838–46.

Steiglitz Historic Park – from Charles and Augustus von Stieglitz, sons of a squatter.

Tarra-Bulga NP – from Charlie Tarra, an Aborigine, who accompanied the explorer Strzelecki; and Aboriginal *bulga* a high mountain.

Terrick Terrick SP – uncertain, perhaps from Aboriginal for sisters (from two hills there).

The Lakes NP – from the Gippsland Lakes, adjacent to this Park.

Tyers SP – from the surrounding district, named after Commissioner Charles Tyers.

Wabonga Plateau – from the Aboriginal *wabong ngon boojek* trouble.

Warby Ranges SP – originally named Fullers Range by Major Mitchell, then Futters, and finally Warby Ranges after a squatter.

Warrandyte SP – Aboriginal *warren* to throw and *dyte* a target.

◀ Coastal rocks, Croajingolong NP *P&LJA*

▼ Croajingolong NP *P&LJA*

▲ Betka Beach, Croajingolong NP *P&LJA*

◀ Coastal rocks, Croajingolong NP *JAC*

Rainforest, East Gippsland *CFL*

Werribee Gorge SP – probably Aboriginal *wearibi* spine, referring to the tortuous course of the river.

Whipstick SP – from the thin whippy growth of the typical eucalypts here.

Wilsons Promontory NP – after Thomas Wilson, of London, a friend of explorers Bass and Flinders.

Wonnangatta-Moroka – Aboriginal for big water and for sky.

Wychitella Flora and Fauna Reserve – uncertain, perhaps from the Aboriginal for a dry stick, or for a rush-like plant.

Wyperfeld NP – the name of Ellerman's station in 1850, uncertain origin, perhaps by a German settler from his native village, Wipperfeld.

Yea River Park – after Colonel Yea, killed in the Crimean War.

Books of general interest

Access of Natural Areas for the Disabled & National Parks Service (1983) *Outdoor Victoria.*
Australian Conservation Foundation (1973 onwards) *Habitat.*
Bardwell S. (1980) *National Parks of Victoria, and State, Coastal and Historic Parks.*
Cochrane R.G. et al (1968) *Flowers and Plants of Victoria.*
Conservation Forests and Lands (now Conservation and Environment) Management Plans for parks.
Costermans L.F. (1981) *Native Trees and Shrubs of South-eastern Australia.*
Croll R.H. (1928) *The Open Road in Victoria.*
Duncan J.S. (ed) (1982) *Atlas of Victoria.*
Fairley A. (1982) *A Field Guide to the National Parks of Victoria.*
Frood D. and Calder M. (1987) *Nature Conservation in Victoria.*
Galbraith J. (1977) *Wildflowers of South-East Australia.*
Hall T.S. (1911) *Victorian Hill and Dale.*
Land Conservation Council (1988) *Statewide Assessment of Public Land Use Victoria.*
Land Conservation Council Study Reports, now available for all Victoria.
Pizzey G. (1980) *A Field Guide to the Birds of Australia.*
Readers' Digest (1976) *Complete Book of Australian Birds.*
Strahan R. (1983) *Complete Book of Australian Mammals.*
Victorian National Parks Association (1975 onwards) *Parkwatch.*
Willis J.H. (1962, 1972) *A Handbook to Plants in Victoria Vol I and II.*

Victorian National Parks Association

The area of Victoria which is protected by parks has been greatly increased in recent years from less than a million hectares (4%) in 1981, to more than two and a half million hectares (12%) in 1990. As well, 80% of our coastline is protected. Almost all the various landforms are now represented. For beauty and diversity, our parks are unsurpassed.

Behind this wonderful achievement there is more than one hundred years of dedicated work by individuals, conservation groups and governments. We can be as proud of the history of conservation in Victoria as we are of our parks.

Regrettably though, there are still threats to our parks system. The mining industry announced in 1986 that it would campaign against the 'locking away' of land in wilderness and park areas. They will spend 'whatever is necessary' to achieve their aims. Some other destructive uses of parks – grazing, broom-bush cutting, timber getting – continue, despite being widely recognised to be detrimental to both conservation and recreation values. We must also scrutinise proposed tourism developments to ensure that they do not destroy the very areas tourists come to see.

This book is published by the Victorian National Parks Association as a tribute to those parks which are managed under the National Parks Act. Included are all of our national and wilderness parks as well as the most notable of our state, coastal, marine and historic parks. Publication was assisted by a financial grant from the Bicentennial Authority which we gratefully acknowledge.

The Victorian National Parks Association Inc., is a conservation group formed in 1952 to promote the creation of new parks, as well as the good management of existing parks. Those who wish to help in a practical way may join one of our 30 or so Friends' Groups, or become a volunteer helper. Members are encouraged to help in the preparation of reports and submissions which influence government policy. We have regular meetings and members receive a monthly newsletter and a quarterly magazine, *Parkwatch*. We have an extensive and varied bushwalking program, and for those less energetic we have excursions and the aptly named 'Walk, Talk and Gawk' outings.

I invite readers to join the Association and help protect Victoria's magnificent legacy of parks.

Further information and membership enquiries may be made to the Victorian National Parks Association Inc., 1st Floor, 247 Flinders Lane, Melbourne 3000, phone (03) 650 8296.

Joan Lindros
President

Friends' Groups

Many of our parks now have a Friends' Group. Friends' Groups are extremely important to their respective parks, doing things that otherwise would not be done. Anyone can be a Friend; no particular skills are needed.

The objects of a Friends' Group are:

- to provide support and to foster public awareness of the park;
- to assist with special projects selected by Friends in consultation with the Ranger-in-Charge;
- to bring into contact people with a common interest in the park.

A Friends' Group number has been given for the relevant parks. If the contact person changes, or you need general information about Friends' Groups, contact the VNPA office, address above.

Bushwalkers' Code

Keep groups small
Reduce your impact on the area by organising camping and hiking parties ranging from a safe minimum of four to not more than ten people.

Keep to the track
Keep to tracks. Avoid walking over easily damaged areas, but in open untracked country (such as snowgrass plains) spread out to disperse damage. Leave fences and gates as you find them.

Respect flora and fauna
Minimise damage to plants during your walk and at campsites. Use foam mats to sleep on and sandshoes to walk around the campsite.

Protect water resources
Conserve quality of water resources. If you suspect its quality, you should boil drinking water for at least three minutes. Always wash at least 30 metres from streams or lakes and scatter used washing water. Don't use soap where possible and don't dispose of rubbish and food scraps in waterways.

Cook with a stove
Because of a shortage of firewood around some campsites, use portable stoves for cooking. Stoves are cleaner, and safer to use at times of high fire danger.

Keep fires small
If you must light a fire in an emergency, keep it small. If there is plenty of dry fallen timber use it sparingly. Where possible use existing fireplaces. Follow local fire regulations and when you leave make sure the fire is out. Extinguish fire with water and test that it is out by putting your hand in the ashes. Scatter the cold ashes before you leave.

Respect other campers
Whether walking or camping, you should consider other people's wish to enjoy the peace and tranquillity of the bush. Noisy parties disturb other campers.

Bury toilet wastes
Use toilets where they are available. Where they are not, bury faecal waste at least 100 metres from campsites, tracks and water sources. Dig a hole 15 cm deep within the soil's organic layer. Carry out non-degradable items.

Carry out rubbish
Take in the least amount of packaging, tins, plastic etc. Carry out all rubbish, including that left by inconsiderate visitors. No longer 'burn, bash and bury'; the resulting soil disturbance is unacceptable, and the rubbish is likely to be scattered by foraging animals.

Leave campsites tidy
Leave campsites in the same or better condition as when you arrived. Use existing sites or clearings where possible.

Don't depend on huts
Be self-sufficient and do not rely on huts for overnight accommodation. Always carry a tent. If you camp near huts, do so at a reasonable distance away (30 m) to reduce impact.

Be prepared for alpine weather
Take extra care when visiting alpine country; a benign summer's day can quickly become a full-scale blizzard. Be fully prepared with a change of clothing and proper equipment, whatever the season. Let someone know where you are going, and check road conditions first.

Index

About the author

JANE CALDER, B.Sc. Canterbury, New Zealand, is a botanist and biologist. She lectures in Landscape Architecture at the Royal Melbourne Institute of Technology (RMIT) and teaches natural history at the Council of Adult Education (CAE), Melbourne. Jane conducts outdoor education programs for the CAE and for the Victorian National Parks Association. Jane's previous book, *The Grampians – a noble range*, was acclaimed as a rich contribution to our national parks literature.

JAC

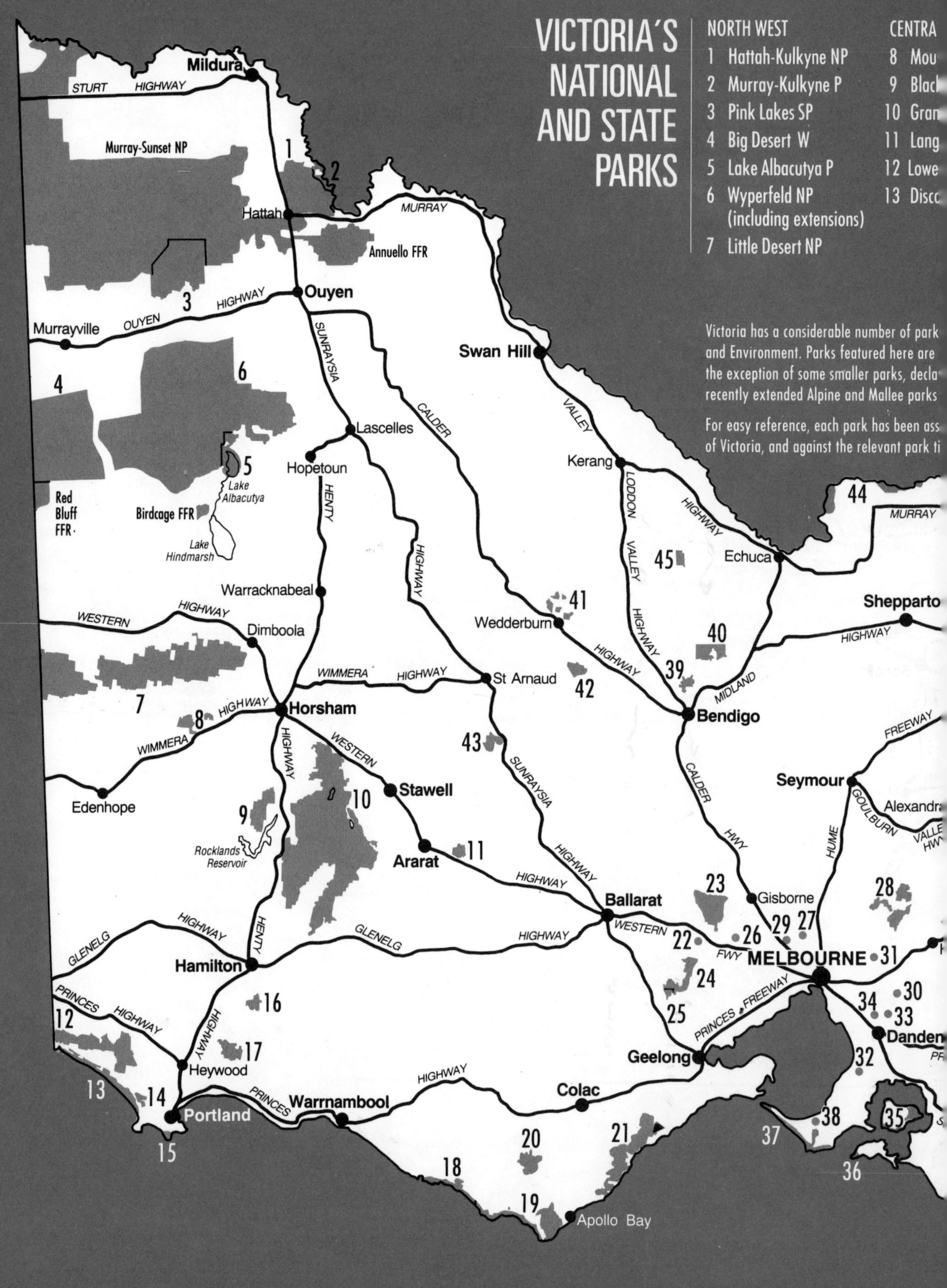
VICTORIA'S NATIONAL AND STATE PARKS
NORTH WEST
1 Hattah-Kulkyne NP
2 Murray-Kulkyne P
3 Pink Lakes SP
4 Big Desert W
5 Lake Albacutya P
6 Wyperfeld NP (including extensions)
7 Little Desert NP
CENTRA
8 Mou
9 Blac
10 Gran
11 Lang
12 Lowe
13 Disc
Victoria has a considerable number of park
and Environment. Parks featured here are
the exception of some smaller parks, decla
recently extended Alpine and Mallee parks
For easy reference, each park has been ass
of Victoria, and against the relevant park ti
Mildura
STURT HIGHWAY
Murray-Sunset NP
Hattah
MURRAY
Annuello FFR
Ouyen
OUYEN HIGHWAY
Murrayville
SUNRAYSIA
Swan Hill
CALDER
VALLEY
Lascelles
Hopetoun
Kerang
LODDON VALLEY HIGHWAY
Red Bluff FFR
Birdcage FFR
Lake Albacutya
Lake Hindmarsh
HENTY
HIGHWAY
Echuca
Warracknabeal
Wedderburn
Shepparton
WESTERN HIGHWAY
Dimboola
WIMMERA HIGHWAY
St Arnaud
MIDLAND HIGHWAY
Horsham
Bendigo
WESTERN
FREEWAY
SUNRAYSIA
Stawell
Seymour
Edenhope
Alexandra
GOULBURN VALLEY HWY
Rocklands Reservoir
Ararat
HUME
CALDER HWY
Ballarat
Gisborne
GLENELG HIGHWAY
WESTERN FWY
MELBOURNE
Hamilton
PRINCES HIGHWAY
PRINCES FREEWAY
Heywood
Geelong
Dandenong
Colac
Portland
Warrnambool
Apollo Bay